Language Conflict and Language Rights

As the colonial hegemony of empire fac̶ ̶.̶.̶ ̶ ̶ ̶ ̶.̶.̶ ̶ ̶ ̶ ̶.̶.̶ ̶o̶ɪ̶ language in ethnic conflict has become increasingly topical, as have issues concerning the right of speakers to choose and use their preferred language(s). Such rights are often asserted and defended in response to their being violated. The importance of understanding these events and issues, and their relationship to individual, ethnic, and national identity, is central to research and debate in a range of fields outside, as well as within, linguistics. This book provides a clearly written introduction for linguists and non-specialists alike, presenting basic facts about the role of language in the formation of identity and the preservation of culture. It articulates and explores categories of conflict and language rights abuses through detailed presentation of illustrative case studies, and distills from these key cross-linguistic and cross-cultural generalizations.

WILLIAM D. DAVIES was Professor and Chair of Linguistics at the University of Iowa. He has published four books, three edited volumes, and sixty-seven articles and book chapters, largely on the morphology and syntax of various languages, including Balinese, Basque, Choctaw, English, Fula, Javanese, Madurese, Sundanese, and Telugu. He was also an Associate Editor of *Oceanic Linguistics*.

STANLEY DUBINSKY is a Professor of Linguistics and former director of the Linguistics Program at the University of South Carolina. He has published three books, four edited volumes, and sixty-one articles and book chapters on the syntax and semantics of various languages, including English, Japanese, Korean, Hebrew, and two Bantu languages (Chichewa and Lingala).

Language Conflict and Language Rights

Ethnolinguistic Perspectives on Human Conflict

William D. Davies
University of Iowa

Stanley Dubinsky
University of South Carolina

CAMBRIDGE
UNIVERSITY PRESS

CAMBRIDGE
UNIVERSITY PRESS

University Printing House, Cambridge CB2 8BS, United Kingdom

One Liberty Plaza, 20th Floor, New York, NY 10006, USA

477 Williamstown Road, Port Melbourne, VIC 3207, Australia

314–321, 3rd Floor, Plot 3, Splendor Forum, Jasola District Centre, New Delhi – 110025, India

79 Anson Road, #06–04/06, Singapore 079906

Cambridge University Press is part of the University of Cambridge.

It furthers the University's mission by disseminating knowledge in the pursuit of education, learning, and research at the highest international levels of excellence.

www.cambridge.org
Information on this title: www.cambridge.org/9781107022096
DOI: 10.1017/9781139135382

First published 2018

Printed in the United Kingdom by TJ International Ltd, Padstow, Cornwall

A catalogue record for this publication is available from the British Library.

Library of Congress Cataloging-in-Publication Data
Names: Davies, William D., 1954– author. | Dubinsky, Stanley, 1952– author.
Title: Language conflict and language rights : ethnolinguistic perspectives on human conflict / William D. Davies, Stanley Dubinsky.
Description: New York : Cambridge University Press, [2018] | Includes bibliographical references and index.
Identifiers: LCCN 2017045853| ISBN 9781107022096 (hardcover) | ISBN 9781107606586 (softcover)
Subjects: LCSH: Linguistic change – Social aspects. | Group identity – Social aspects. | Ethnocentrism.
Classification: LCC P40.5.L54 D28 2018 | DDC 306.44–dc23
LC record available at https://lccn.loc.gov/2017045853

ISBN 978-1-107-02209-6 Hardback
ISBN 978-1-107-60658-6 Paperback

Additional resources for this publication at www.cambridge.org/languageconflict

This book is dedicated to all people past and present who have lost their language / their (original) voice or had it forcibly ripped from them and have suffered the countless attendant indignities.

In Memoriam

William D. Davies
(May 24, 1954 – August 18, 2017)

William D. Davies passed away on August 18, 2017, one day after the last page of this book was completed and the book was put into production. One can truthfully say that he worked as a linguist until the last day of his life.

Completing his PhD at UCSD in 1981 with a dissertation on Choctaw syntax under the direction of David M. Perlmutter, Bill went on to a thirty-year career at the University of Iowa, publishing widely on topics such as Choctaw, grammatical relations, raising and control, and the syntax of Indonesian languages, especially Madurese.

Starting his career as an empirically focused theoretician, Bill made it his business to venture into untouched areas of discovery – focusing in the main on languages (such as the Amerindian Choctaw and the Indonesian Madurese languages) that few others had bothered with. In this way, his research brought light to the languages of less recognized and (previously) less valued peoples. Even to the end, his work with the Baduy people of Indonesia sought (as always) to light up the places and peoples that were in the margins and in the shade. His theoretical work was, invariably, coupled with efforts to give back to the people who so graciously allowed him into their space to do his research – studying the grammar of the Madurese while, at the same time, preserving and rendering accessible the rapidly disappearing folk story traditions for their next generation. His inspired dedication of this book speaks volumes about his desire to make his scholarship relevant and to leave the world better than he found it, "This book is dedicated to all people past and present who have lost their language/their (original) voice or had it forcibly ripped from them and have suffered the countless attendant indignities."

Bill Davies was so much more than a linguist, although he was certainly that, too. He was a mentor, a guide, a model, and an inspiration to all those who he touched professionally. The several books and dozens of published articles and chapters he produced are but the visible surface of a rich record of deeply engaged scholarship, impressively insightful empirical discovery, innovative collaborations, and the mature and generous mentoring of junior colleagues. As one who benefitted from the sometimes undeserved joy of collaborating with him, for some thirty years, this writer can regret that we didn't have longer. But that regret cannot erase the gifts of those three decades – decades of discovery, comradery, and friendship.

At home, in his own university, he led his Linguistics Department (both officially and unofficially) for most of his thirty-plus years there, and held it together for the sake of his colleagues when many others might have walked away. It is because of him, and nearly only because of him, that the University of Iowa still has a Linguistics Department today. His sacrifice for his department, his colleagues, and the department's students stands as a monument to the goodness of his soul.

I will miss him for as long as I am lucky to live, and know that others who walked with him will miss him at least as much as I. Grateful I am for having been lucky enough to know him, and proud I am for having had the privilege to call him, truly, my best friend and colleague.

STANLEY DUBINSKY

Contents

Figures

Tables

Preface and Acknowledgements

The initial idea for this volume began with discussions in 2010 between the two authors about there being no dedicated text for a Language Rights course developed by its first author, Bill Davies. Having invited Stan Dubinsky to join him in the development and writing of such a book, the project was retitled *Language Conflict and Language Rights*, and the two authors set about teaching and refining the course, as a path to developing a coherent book proposal. On gaining the support of Helen Barton at Cambridge University Press and having our proposal approved, we committed ourselves in earnest to the book project, alternately using the draft chapters of the book to teach the course and using the outcomes from our classes to further revise and refine the book. This went on, for perhaps too many semesters, but it ultimately resulted in the book which you now hold in your hands (or see on your screen). Any large endeavor requires the goodwill and support of many people, and this book is no exception. It could truthfully be said that a virtual army of people helped to make this book what it is, including students who took the course, local colleagues who taught and helped develop it, university administrators and department chairs who saw fit to underwrite the project with funding, local and external readers of draft chapters, and all those at Cambridge University Press who inspired, encouraged, and helped us to complete it.

At Cambridge University Press, Helen Barton has been, and remains, the authors' chief navigator and inspiration, and it is to her credit that the present volume made it all the way through to publication. Adam Hooper, also at the Press, played a key role in shepherding the production process along, and making sure that we stayed on task. Kay McKechnie, as copy-editor, not only did an excellent job of poring through the typescript and making more corrections than she ought to have had to, but also was kind enough to tell us that she enjoyed the book. Thanks as well to my own graduate assistant, Drew Crosby, without whose help the book would have had no index at all.

We would like to thank the anonymous referees for Cambridge University Press, who read the initial book proposal, as well as all others who patiently listened to our developing ideas and enthusiastically encouraged us to complete it. Among them there are some who deserve special mention. Here, at the University of South Carolina, we are supremely grateful to Pia Bertucci, who read early versions of many of the book's chapters, and whose initial feedback and encouragement is deeply felt. At the University of Iowa, Jill Beckman extended herself more than once to step into the breach and help support Bill Davies on the "home front," and Mercedes Niño-Murcia helped in the development of some of the materials for the book. Also to be thanked for their input are Doug Cole, Ari Natarina, and Eri Kurniawan (and if Bill were with us today, he would undoubtedly have added several more to this list).

As mentioned above, this volume was developed out of several versions of a course that we and other colleagues have taught since 2010. The feedback from instructors who taught, or helped teach, the course, along with the questions, comments, puzzlements, and outrage of the students who took it, helped shape the book and gave us confidence along the way that the project was worth all the effort. First among those who contributed to the course is Elaine Chun, at the University of South Carolina, who helped to fashion it into a university-wide core course and who also provided additional material and topics that were folded into the book. Also key in helping trial runs of the course were graduate students at the University of South Carolina (Wei Cheng, Drew Crosby, Chris Farina, and Angelina Rubina) and at the University of Iowa (Karee Garvin).

We also thank those who contributed to our 2015 LSA Linguistic Summer Institute course "Language Conflict & Language Rights," at the University of Chicago, thereby giving us a unique opportunity to refine the content of this book. These include the Institute's directors, Karlos Arregi and Alan Yu, along with some thirty-five Institute participants, who enrolled in the course and contributed their reflections on the material and ideas on language conflict issues. Also critical to the successful organization of the course was our own graduate student, Kory Salajka, who was instrumental in helping us manage the logistics of teaching a course on another campus.

Financial assistance for various aspects of the work was variously provided by several units at our respective universities, including the Department of English, the College of Arts & Sciences, and the Provost's Office at the University of South Carolina, as well as the Department of Linguistics and the College of Arts & Sciences at the University of Iowa. Thanks go out, as well, to international colleagues who enabled us to visit and collect information needed for the book – principally, S. Ron Simango and Russell Kaschula at Rhodes University (South Africa), Joel Walters at Bar-Ilan University (Israel), and Surachman Dimyati at Universitas Terbuka (Indonesia).

As usual, our families provided more support and forbearance than we merit, through our many absences and unexpected presences, always providing the right balance of inspiration and exasperation. We continue to be grateful for their love and support through it all. So, our very special thanks to Melissa, Elijah, and Isaac, and to Patty, Billy, and Kate.

Finally, we would like to thank each other. We certainly had an awfully good time putting this all together, and we are supremely grateful for the opportunity that we had to complete yet another collaboration.

Cover Acknowledgements

Another, separate, set of acknowledgements is in order. The image on the cover of this book was inspired by a "word cloud" poster used for a 2016 conference titled "Respecting Linguistic Diversity? Language Discrimination in the European Union" organized by the European Free Alliance (EFA) Group in the European Parliament (https://efa.greens-efa.eu/en/article/event/respecting-linguistic-diversity/). Moved by the theme of this conference and its publicity poster, the authors identified nine key descriptive phrases for this book (*ethnolinguistic conflict, language rights, language laws, naming rights, minority language, immigrant minority, dialect awareness, indigenous language, writing systems*) and translated them into fourteen of the many languages that are featured in the book (Basque, Bulgarian, Chinese, Greek, Hindi, Indonesian, Italian, Japanese, Korean, Kurdish, Māori, Tamil, Xhosa, and Welsh). The design team at Cambridge University Press did a masterful job in creating a word cloud for the purpose, and in superimposing it over an image of the globe. In this regard, the authors wish to acknowledge the generosity of Michael Hammond (University of Arizona), Pritty Patel-Grosz (University of Oslo), and the following other language specialists and linguists, in helping to render accurate translations of the English language terms on the book's cover. Any remaining errors and inaccuracies are the fault of the authors.

Basque:	Jose Ignacio Hualde, *University of Illinois*
Bulgarian:	Mila Tasseva-Kurktchieva, *University of South Carolina*
Chinese:	Qiandi Liu, *University of South Carolina*
Greek:	Anastasia Giannakidou, *University of Chicago*
Hindi:	Rajesh Bhatt, *University of Massachusetts*
	Rajesh Kumar, *Indian Institute of Technology, Madras*
Indonesian:	Surachman Dimyati, *Universitas Terbuka*
Italian:	Pia Bertucci, *University of South Carolina*
Japanese:	Shinichi Shoji, *Mie University*
Korean:	Jiyeon Song, *University of South Carolina*

Kurdish: Salih Akin, *Université de Rouen*
Māori: Poia Rewi, *University of Otago*
               Arapera Bella Ngaha, *University of Auckland*
Tamil: Vasu Renganathan, *University of Pennsylvania*
Xhosa: Russell Kaschula, *Rhodes University*
Welsh: Tegau Andrews, *Bangor University*
               Peredur Webb-Davies, *Bangor University*

Introduction

Barring physical abnormalities, all human beings are born as linguistic equals. That is, at birth, any given human baby is endowed with the ability to learn the language of the community in which it is raised. However, the equality that exists at birth soon gives way to the politics of power, to linguistic conflicts, and to the political use of language, one of the tools of power. The importance of language rights to basic human rights such as freedom of identity and access to educational and economic opportunities cannot be overstated: more than 160 nations include specific provisions related to language in their constitutions.

Whether arising through conquest and colonization, immigration, enslavement, or the creation of a political state that ignores "natural" ethnic territories, linguistic minorities have existed at least since the dawn of history, and where there exist linguistic minorities, there also exist language conflicts and issues related to the rights of those minorities to use their languages freely and without prejudice. It is further the case that ethnolinguistic factors are becoming increasingly apparent in global conflicts in the twenty-first century, and must be taken into account alongside religious, ideological, economic, environmental, and resource bases of conflicts. Ethnolinguistic nationalism is resurgent in the face of globalism, and centuries'-old ethnolinguistic rivalries of Africa, the Middle East, and South Asia (temporarily papered over by European colonialism and UN-imposed post-colonial borders) have once again come bursting forth. This volume thus presents an ethnolinguistic view of human conflict.

With this background in mind, the present book is intended to provide a fundamental understanding of the issues surrounding language rights and how these are integral to human rights in general, as well as to an individual's definition of personal and cultural identity. It then explores language conflicts in a variety of nations, and shows how those conflicts have affected the rights of certain groups to use their own language, the groups' efforts to secure those rights, and efforts to deny those rights through legislation and other actions. Through careful and linguistically informed presentations of these matters, the book critically examines the significant intellectual issues underlying what can be an extremely emotionally charged subject.

The utilization of language data in understanding linguistic conflict and competition requires the competencies and analytical tools of the linguistic discipline (much as cultural data need the expertise of the cultural anthropologist). As any linguist is aware, languages are not holistic, unitary objects, which might be variously held out and compared with one another, as one might compare two gemstones. Rather, they consist of interlocking webs of modular structure: phonology (sound systems), morphology (word-building systems), lexica (inventories of words and word parts), sentence grammars, and conventions of use.

Accordingly, this book introduces the reader to the tools of language description (in a non-technical fashion), affords an understanding of the mechanics of linguistic conflict, and provides an overview of language rights issues and cases. In this way, the book attempts to provide a vehicle for making language issues relevant to non-linguists and show how tools of linguistics can be useful for understanding socio-political phenomena.

By juxtaposing successful and unsuccessful cases, it also gives the reader some idea of possible policy decisions in education, government, media, etc. – that is, it sheds light on applications of academic knowledge. In addition, its comparative approach not only highlights similarities across groups and situations that might be seen as different (how two languages thought of as different are in fact structurally similar; how language conflict situations share some basic similarities), but also showcases the disparate range of possibilities of language structure as well as language conflict situations and their solutions and trajectories.

Content of the Book

This volume is thus partitioned into four sets of chapters. The first three chapters of Part I succinctly introduce (in a minimally technical fashion) three major components of spoken language: phonetics and phonology (the sounds of spoken language and the manner in which they are perceived), lexicon and morphology (the words and affixes with which expressions are built), and grammar and semantics (the rules by which expressions are organized and interpreted). The fourth chapter explains how the gradual process of language change (e.g. the development of Old English to Middle English to Modern English) involves changes in each of these components, and illustrates how language variation (differences between related languages and dialects of the same language) can be understood through reference to them.

Part II, "Language in the World," introduces the reader to the major roles that language plays in human society, and the ways in which it plays these roles. The first three chapters in this part focus on the role of language in creating and articulating three sorts of identity: personal, cultural, and national. Chapter 5, on language and personal identity, uses the manner in which personal names are given, changed, and controlled, in order to illustrate both how important language is in creating personal identity and how naming practices reflect the structure of the language that is used to give names as well as the cultural traditions of the society in which naming is practiced. Chapter 6, on language and cultural identity, focuses on the relation between language and thought, showing not only how language and culture mutually influence each other, but also importantly the limitations of that influence. Chapter 7, on language and national identity, describes the contributions of language to national identity and the role of language in building national unity (or, sometimes, in preventing that unity from coming about). This chapter examines the history of national language formation in three post-colonial states: Indonesia, India, and South Africa.

Chapter 8 takes an excursion away from spoken language into the domain of written language and language orthography, discussing the (relatively recent) emergence of writing in human history, the types of writing systems that have emerged, and the role (independent of speech) that writing systems have in representing cultural and ethnic identity. The last chapter in this part presents language rights in the context of, and as a category of, human rights, and discusses the history of language rights in the United States (from English dominance in the American colonies to present-day efforts to make English the official language of the United States).

Part III, "A Typology of Language Conflicts," presents cases of language conflict and assaults on language rights drawn from around the world. The part is divided into five chapters, with each chapter focused on a particular category of language conflict. Chapters 10–13 each distinguish a different class of minority speakers, based largely on the way in which each group came to be a minority. The classes which form the bases of these chapters are: indigenous minorities (peoples who lived in a region for some substantial period of time before the currently dominant group moved into it) (Chapter 10); geopolitical minorities (minority groups who came to have that status as a consequence of border shifts, wars, and territorial acquisitions) (Chapter 11); dialectal minorities (minority groups who speak, or who are perceived to speak, a "wrong" – i.e. stigmatized – variety of the dominant language) (Chapter 12); and migrant minorities (typically immigrant groups that have moved into a host country and have retained or attempted to retain, to some extent, the language of their own culture and heritage) (Chapter 13). Chapter 14 depicts conflict situations in which there is a straightforward competition for linguistic dominance between two groups, each of whom has at one time or another held the upper hand in that conflict.

The five chapters devoted to a typology of linguistic conflicts each present conflict cases that are prototypical of the class.[1] The conflict cases presented variously depict the history behind the conflict, its linguistic characteristics, the impact of the conflict on the nations or peoples affected, and the conflict's resolutions (if any). For instance, the chapter on indigenous minorities (Chapter 10) describes the struggles of the Sámi in Norway, Ainu in Japan, and American Indians in the United States. In Chapter 11, we read about the following geopolitical minorities: Hungarians in Slovakia, Hispanics in the southwestern United States, and Kurds in Turkey. Chapter 12, covering minorities of migration, introduces Roma in Europe, Koreans in Japan, and Puerto Ricans in the United States. Chapter 13, on intra-linguistic (dialectal) minorities, discusses Okinawans in Japan and African Americans in the United States. Chapter 14, on competition for linguistic dominance, takes up the cases of Flemish versus Walloons in Belgium, Tamils versus Sinhalese in Sri Lanka, and French versus English in Canada. At the end of each of these five chapters, a small number of "additional cases for exploration" are provided to the reader. These are given in order to stimulate the reader to think further about the class of conflicts depicted and to imagine how and why a particular case fits into a certain class.

The final two chapters of the book, comprising Part IV, "Language Endangerment, Extinction, and Revival," explore the relevance of linguistic taxonomy, ecology, and ownership to the central matter of the book, and then turn to cases of language revitalization (e.g. Welsh) and revival (e.g. Hebrew). Chapter 15 discusses the problems inherent in trying to isolate or count individual languages, the potential negative effects of widespread language death globally, and the ownership of, and control over, linguistic capital and cultural heritage by those who speak a language and those who study it. Chapter 16 takes up the parallel issues: the revitalization of endangered or dying languages and the revival of dead or dormant ones. In both cases, the feasibility of doing so, the determination of its value to the group most affected and others, and the likelihood of success are central to the discussion.

---

[1] It should be noted that many, if not most, language conflicts are not purely of a single class. For example, the English language–Spanish language conflict in the United States has attributes of a geopolitical minority conflict, a migrant minority conflict, and (to a much lesser extent) a dialectal minority conflict.

Part I

Language and the Speaker

1   The Sounds and Sound Systems of Language

One of the first things that one discovers, surveying the many hundreds of languages used throughout the world, is that many of them (perhaps a third or more of the world's 7,000 living languages) have no written form. And if one were to travel back in time to an earlier age, the proportion of languages having a written form would be far less. What this means for us is that written language is both secondary to spoken language and derivative of it. So, one might accurately state that all languages are spoken languages, but only some languages (albeit many of them) are also written languages.[1] Thus, while this book will explore the nature of writing systems (in Chapter 8) and the significant role that these indeed do play in language conflicts, it is essential that we first examine the properties of spoken language.

Speech Sounds versus Written Representations

Having asserted a meaningful distinction between speech and writing, one of the first things that one notes is that the letters (or other symbols) used to represent speech ordinarily only approximate the sounds that they are intended to represent, and often do so rather badly. If we wished to have a system of writing for our speech sounds which accurately represented these, then we might reasonably want that system to observe the following two principles:[2]

---

[1] This statement overlooks the nature of signed languages (i.e. those used by the deaf, such as American Sign Language or ASL), for which gesture takes the place of sound. While such languages are not technically "spoken" languages, it is nevertheless the case that the gestural system used to express them is far more akin to speaking than to writing. We would therefore class signed languages in the category of spoken languages.

[2] There is in fact a symbol system, the International Phonetic Alphabet (IPA), designed to do this. Developed in 1888 by the Association Phonétique Internationale, IPA symbols are used precisely for the purpose of transcribing/representing speech sounds in a manner that is precise and language-independent. For this very reason, we will use IPA symbols in this book, when discussing sounds.

(i) Each symbol always represents the same sound and each sound is always represented by the same symbol.

(ii) Each symbol represents one sound and each sound is represented by one symbol.

To draw a parallel, we could not reliably and articulately talk about numbers, nor make accurate arithmetic calculations, if our numeral system did not follow the analog of the above principles. For instance, if the numerals were used ambiguously to represent either positive or negative integers, we would not know upon combining them which one each represented.

"2" plus "6" might, given such ambiguity, represent: $+2$ plus $+6$, or $+8$
$+2$ plus -6, or -4
-2 plus $+6$, or $+4$
-2 plus -6, or -8

However ambiguous our imagined system of numerals might be, the real world of letters representing sounds is far worse. Consider, for example, the letter "a" and the different sounds that it represents in the words *bat, bay*, and *bawl*. In each of these words, the letter "a" represents a distinct sound (violating the principle of "Each symbol always represents the same sound"). Consider, too, that the first vowel sound in the word *even* and the single vowel in the words *seem, steam*, and *priest* are all identical, but variously represented by "e," "ee," "ea," and "ie." This case violates both the principle that "each sound is always represented by the same symbol" as well as "each sound is represented by one symbol" (since the latter three each involve two symbols standing in for one sound). Finally, consider the case of the letter "x," which clearly violates the principle "each symbol represents one sound." One only need compare the words *books* and *tax*. In *books*, the final two consonants in the word are each represented by one symbol, "k" and "s" respectively. In *tax* the same two consonants are represented by the single symbol "x."

The imprecise and multiply ambiguous relationship between speech sounds and letters (especially in English) is perhaps best caricatured in this 1894 poem titled "O-U-G-H" by Charles Battell Loomis, which depicts a French speaker's frustration with the spelling conventions of the English language (read this poem with the best French accent you can muster):[3]

> I'm taught p-l-o-u-g-h
> S'all be pronouncé "plow."
> "Zat's easy w'en you know," I say,
> "Mon Anglais, I'll get through!"
> My teacher say zat in zat case,
> O-u-g-h is "oo."

---

[3] Loomis 1917.

And zen I laugh and say to him,
"Zees Anglais make me cough."
He say "Not 'coo' but in zat word,
O-u-g-h is 'off.'"
"Oh, Sacré bleu! Such varied sounds
Of words make me hiccough!"
He say, "Again mon frien' ees wrong;
O-u-g-h is 'up'
In hiccough." Zen I cry, "No more,
You make my t'roat feel rough."
"Non, non!" he cry, "You are not right;
O-u-g-h is 'uff.'"
I say, "I try to spik your words,
I cannot spik zem though."
"In time you'll learn, but now you're wrong!
O-u-g-h is 'owe.'"
"I'll try no more, I s'all go mad,
I'll drown me in ze lough!"
"But ere you drown yourself," said he,
"O-u-g-h is 'ock.'"
He taught no more, I held him fast
And killed him wiz a rough.

Phonetics: Describing Speech Sounds

In addressing ourselves to the matter of language sounds, we will first discuss how they can be described and then examine how they are organized. Apart from saying things like "the sound represented by the letter 'b' in the word *ball*" or "the last sound in the word *bass*," there are two major ways that one can describe the sounds of human language: we can describe how they are produced or we can describe the nature of the sounds themselves.

The former (description of production) involves focusing on the manner in which those sounds are **articulated**. We would, for example, note that the sound represented by the letter "b" in the word *ball* is produced through a closure of one's lips – the term for this being **bilabial**. In this respect, the sound is similar to the sound represented by the letter "m" in the word *mall*, and dissimilar to the sound represented by the letter "d" in the word *doll* (which is itself made by bringing the tip of one's tongue up against the gum ridge behind the front teeth).

The description of speech sounds themselves involves attention to the acoustic properties of the sounds. Accordingly, the last sound in the word *bass* might be deemed similar in some ways to the last sound in the word *bash*, as they both involve what sounds like white noise (e.g. similar to the hissing sound of steam escaping from a pressurized pipe). They are produced through the audible friction made by forcing air through a narrow opening, and using the technical term for this, the two sounds are called **fricatives**. Notice, as well, that the varieties of "white noise" represented by the "ss" in *bass* and the "sh" in *bash* are also different (a bit) from each other. The first has a higher pitch than the second, the first sounding like a smaller "leak" than the second (you can confirm this for yourself by saying both words several times in alternation).

In both of the above cases, we've been discussing the sounds themselves, based on objective measures of the manner in which they are produced (articulation) or their acoustic description. This perspective on speech sounds is referred to as phonetics, and can be studied without special attention to the language(s) which utilize these sounds, although phonetic description is often critical in understanding the differences between languages which might be thought, at first glance, to be drawing from the same inventory of speech sounds.

Take, for instance, the sounds represented by the letter "t". In English, the sound represented by the letter "t" in the word *toll* is, just like the sound represented by the letter "d" in the word *doll*, made by bringing the tip of one's tongue up against the gum ridge behind the front teeth. This fleshy part of the mouth is called the alveolar **ridge** (between numbers 4 and 5 in Figure 1.1)

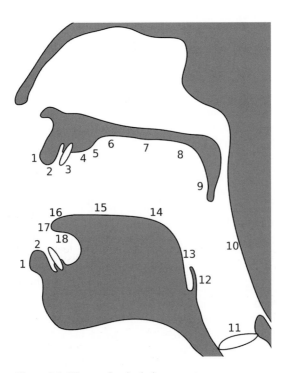

Figure 1.1 Places of articulation

Table 1.1 *IPA symbols for American English vowels*

	IPA		IPA		IPA
meet	iː			boot	uː
mitt	ɪ	bird	ɝ	book	ʊ
mate	eɪ	mutt	ʌ	boat	oʊ
met	ɛ	about	ə	bought	ɔː
mat	æ	might	aɪ	pot	ɑː
		boy	ɔɪ		
		bout	aʊ		

Table 1.2 *IPA symbols for American English consonants*

IPA		IPA	
p	pie	f	fie
t	tie	θ	thigh
k	kite	s	sigh
b	by	ʃ	shy
d	die	h	height
g	get	v	vie
m	my	ð	thy
n	night	z	zoo
ŋ	sang	ʒ	vision
l	lie	ʧ	chin
r	rye	ʤ	just
w	why		
j	yes		

and the sounds produced by bringing the tongue into contact with it are called
alveolar.

One may contrast the articulation of the first sound in the English word *toll*
with the articulatory description of the first sound in the French word *tête*
('head'). Although the same letter is used, a native French speaker will produce
the sound by bringing the tongue into contact with the teeth (number 3 in
Figure 1.1). While the difference between the two "t" sounds is a subtle one, it
is more than sufficient to allow a native French speaker to hear the difference
between their own pronunciation of the word and that of a native (and unprac-
ticed) English speaker.

From this point on, we will refer to sounds by using International Phonetic
Alphabet (IPA) symbols, enclosed in square brackets. Thus, the sound of the
letter "t" in the word *test* is [t]. Charts of the IPA symbols used for American
English sounds are provided in Tables 1.1 and 1.2.

Phonology: Perception of Speech Sounds and What Native Speakers Know

Another way of thinking about language sounds involves attention to how they are perceived by speakers and hearers of a particular language, and how the language sounds of a particular language, such as English, are organized. Here we are engaged in understanding what speakers "know" about the sounds of their own language, rather than merely (and objectively) observing, measuring, and categorizing the sounds themselves. For instance, speakers of a language (e.g. English) are aware of the inventories of sounds that are particular to their language, as well as which sounds are not. They are also aware of the ways in which the sounds of their language may combine, and the ways in which they may not. Finally, they perceive certain groups of phonetically distinct sounds as "counting" for the same sound in their own language, despite the articulatory and acoustic differences between them. When we speak of sounds vis-à-vis their role in the sound system of a language, we are no longer in the domain of phonetics (the objective domain of sound description) but in the domain of phonology (which deals with how sounds are perceived and organized in the mind of a speaker/hearer).

Consider first the inventory of sounds in one's own language. We readily identify certain sounds as "belonging" to English and other sounds as not. It should be clear enough that all the sounds discussed thus far, excepting the [t] sound of French, are in the inventory of English sounds. When we hear English spoken, we can often tell if the speaker is not a native speaker of our language, because such speakers sometime substitute non-English sounds for English ones.

For instance, anyone who has studied or paid much attention to Spanish knows that the sounds represented by the letter "r" in that language are rather different from our own, so that the single "r" in *pero* ('but') is a sound produced by a rapid flap of the tongue against the alveolar ridge and the double "r" in *perro* ('dog') is produced with a tongue trill in the same position. Accordingly, when a native speaker of Spanish asks me if I can *reach* the top shelf, he might pronounce the first sound in *reach* the same as the "r" in *pero*. Hearing this, one would immediately know that this person in not a native speaker of English – because they are using sounds that are not in the English inventory.

Turning to the matter of sound combinations, we observe that our knowledge of the sounds of our own language is not confined to knowing which sounds "belong" and which do not. We are also quite sensitive to the limitations on the ways in which sounds may be combined. We can demonstrate this by acknowledging that we know what is, and what is not, a "possible word" in our own language.

Take, for example, the English words *halt* (i.e. 'stop') and *pelt* (i.e. 'animal skin'). The first word has the sounds [h], [ɔː], [l], and [t], and the second consists of the sounds [p], [ɛ], [l], and [t]. If we were to swap the first sound of the first word with the first sound of the second word, we would produce two English non-words *palt* and *helt* (the first is a Swedish word meaning 'meat-filled dumpling' and the second is a Danish word meaning 'whitefish,' but that is of little concern to us here). While *palt* and *helt* are indeed non-words where English is concerned, they are certainly possible English words. That is to say, if someone were to borrow the Swedish word for meat-filled dumpling into English, we would have no difficulty accepting it as an English word from that point on.

Now consider what would happen if we tried to rearrange the sounds of the English non-word *palt*, [p], [ɔː], [l], and [t], reversing them to produce the word *tlap*. This, too, is a non-word in English, but unlike *palt* it is not a possible word in English. This is because the sounds [t] and [l], while in the English sound inventory, cannot appear in that order at the beginning of an English word. We have words that begin with [f] and [l] (*flop*), with [s] and [l] (*slop*), and with [p] and [l] (*plop*). We have words that begin with [t] and [r] (*trod*), with [p] and [r] (*prod*), and with [f] and [r] (*fraud*). We just don't permit words that begin with [t] and [l]. This is something that English speakers "know" intuitively, without necessarily having ever thought of it.

How native speakers group (or categorize) the sounds that they use presents one additional way of highlighting the distinction between the mental organization of language sounds (phonology) and the objective description of their physical properties (phonetics). It is a readily observable fact that speakers of a given language will group certain sounds together as variants of the same sound, despite articulatory and acoustic differences among them. This is to say that a recognizable (to us) single sound of our language might not be exactly the same sound in every instance of its use.

Take, for example, the English sound [l], which appears (broadly speaking) as the first sound of the word *leaf* and the last sound of the word *pull*. Now, if you (as an English speaker) pronounce each of these words very carefully, paying attention to the articulation of the [l] sound, you may notice that they are not exactly the same. The initial sound in *leaf*, like the [d], [t], and [n] sounds of English, is an alveolar sound, produced by bringing the tip of the tongue to the alveolar ridge (between numbers 4 and 5 in Figure 1.1). The final sound in *pull* is also produced this way, but in addition, the back of the tongue (number 14 in Figure 1.1) is raised toward the velum (which is the soft tissue constituting the back of the roof of the mouth, and number 8 in Figure 1.1). The IPA symbol for this "velarized l" is the letter "l" with a "tilde" or a bar drawn through it, [ɫ]. A fact about English speakers' use of these two similar, but not identical, sounds is that the [l] is always used at the beginning of words (i.e. before vowels) and the [ɫ] is always used at the end. English speakers rarely notice the difference between them, and consider both to be variants of the same sound. If we adopt the term phoneme to refer to the mental idea of a single language sound and use forward slash marks to indicate this, then we can say that [l] and [ɫ] are distinct realizations (i.e. variants) of the English phoneme /l/.

Note that the distribution of /l/ sounds in English is particular to the English language and not an inevitable fact about /l/ sounds in general. To illustrate, there are languages which only have one or the other of these variants, and which each use that one variant in all positions. Speakers of Russian, for example, produce their /l/ sound in a manner similar to the end-of-word English [ɫ] in all positions. So, when Russian speakers pronounce the English word *leaf*, they often pronounce it using the last sound in *pull* at the beginning of the word. Their production of the two words would have the same /l/ sound in both positions: [ɫif] and [pʌɫ]. Contrasting with the Russian pronunciation of English /l/ sounds, we find that speakers of Egyptian Arabic don't use the "velarized l" at all. Accordingly, an Egyptian Arabic speaker is likely to pronounce the English word *pull* using the first sound in *leaf* at the end of the word. Their production of the two words would also have the same /l/ sound in both positions, only a different one than that used by the Russian speaker: [lif] and [pʌl].

So, part of our knowledge regarding the sound system of our own language involves identifying (slightly) different sounds as belonging in the same category, using these different sounds in the right places, and being able to tell when someone else isn't doing so. It can take as little as one word for us to know that a speaker isn't a native speaker of our own language. A Russian pronouncing *leaf* as [ɫif] or an Egyptian pronouncing *pull* as [pʌl] will alert the native English speaker to the possible nationality of each of these speakers. Likewise, an American pronouncing the French word *tête* ('head') with an alveolar [t] can be sufficient for the native French speaker to identify them as American.

Identifying and singling out a foreigner by their pronunciation of a single word has a long tradition. The first recorded instance of this occurs in the Hebrew Bible Book of Judges (chapter 12), which records from over 3,000 years ago a dispute (that turns into a minor tribal war) between the Israelite tribe of Ephraim (living west of the Jordan River) and other tribes (living east of the Jordan) in a region called Gilead. In the story, the Ephraimites cross the Jordan River to engage the Gileadites in battle and are defeated by them. After their victory over the Ephraimites, the Gileadites try to block the remnants of the Ephraimites' fighting force from retreating back across the Jordan.

And the Gileadites took the fords of the Jordan against the Ephraimites; and it was so, that when any of the fugitives of Ephraim said: "Let me go over," the men of Gilead said unto him: "Art thou an Ephraimite?" If he said: "Nay," then said they unto him: "Say now Shibboleth"; and if he said "Sibboleth," for he could not frame to pronounce it right, then they laid hold on him, and slew him at the fords of the Jordan; and there fell at that time of Ephraim forty and two thousand.[4]

Apparently, members of the tribe of Ephraim spoke a dialect of Hebrew in which the [ʃ] sound in *shoe* was pronounced the same as the [s] sound in *sue*; an Ephraimite would have pronounced the two words *shoe* and *sue* identically: [su]. The Gileadites knew this, and used the word *shibboleth* as a test to identify the fugitive Ephraimites (and kill them).

At the time of the Book of Judges, the word *shibboleth* referred to the part of a plant that contained the edible seeds (such as "an ear [of corn]" or "a stalk [of wheat]"). As a consequence of the incident described above, *shibboleth* itself has come to mean any word whose pronunciation can distinguish members of a group from outsiders. And the use of shibboleths during "close quarters combat" has occurred many times (e.g. in World War II, American sentries would often use the word *lollapalooza* as a shibboleth, to expose Japanese spies posing as Americans or Filipinos, knowing that the Japanese were likely to mispronounce the word as *rorraparooza*).

Phonological Processes: Gaps between What We Do and What We Think We Do

Once we understand that there is a difference between the objective properties of sounds and our own mental perceptions and representations of them, it should be unsurprising that our perception of sounds does not always correlate with what is actually produced. Likewise, we often produce sounds that are objectively and measurably different from what we think we are producing.

As speaking typically involves rather rapid articulation (i.e. movements of the tongue, lips, jaw, etc.), we unconsciously utilize ways of pronouncing words which facilitate production without too seriously compromising our listeners' understanding of them. Consider the word *unbelievable*, which is formed by adding the prefix *un-* (meaning 'not') to the word *believable*. If you say the word slowly and carefully, you will invariably pronounce the prefix with the vowel [ʌ] (as in the word *bud*) and the consonant [n] (as at the end of the word *ran*). However, if you try to say the word as quickly as you can, you may catch yourself pronouncing that prefix with an [m], in place of the [n]. In pronouncing the word as if it were spelled *umbelievable*, we are led to ask why does this happen, as well as why doesn't it matter.

---

[4] Judges 12:5–6; translation by Mechon Mamre, Jerusalem, Israel.

The answer to the first question (why it happens) has to do with articulatory efficiency (that is, ease of production). The consonant [n] at the end of *un-* is an alveolar consonant (like [t], [d], and [s]). It is immediately followed in this word by the [b] at the beginning of *believable*, which is a bilabial consonant (like [p] and [m]). Simply put, if one is in a hurry, it is easier to pronounce an [m] and a [b] – two bilabial consonants in a row – than it is to pronounce an [n] followed by a [b]. The phenomenon of one sound changing to be like another neighboring sound is called **assimilation**, and it is one of the ways in which we subtly alter our articulation to make it easier to speak quickly. As to the issue of why it doesn't matter, it is simply the case that, as long as the articulatory shortcut does not impede our understanding, we accommodate the change without much noticing. Given that *umbelievable* is not an English word, hearers simply perceive it as the intended *unbelievable*, there being no alternative to doing so. So, a speaker "A" wishing to say the word *unbelieveable*, rapidly, produces an [m] in place of the [n] (without noticing it). And a hearer "B" interprets the word as having an [n], rather than an [m] (again without noticing it). As far as "A" and "B" are concerned, the sound produced and perceived in this word was [n], not [m].

Deletion and insertion are two other articulatory processes frequently utilized in rapid speech. The first involves, as its name suggests, dropping sounds that impede articulation and that are not essential for understanding. In English, unstressed vowels or syllables are often candidates for deletion (also sometimes referred to as **vowel elision**). Take, for example, the four-syllable word *comfortable*, which is stressed on the first syllable [kʌmfərtəbəl].[5] While it can certainly be pronounced with all four syllables [kʌm-fər-tə-bəl], it is often pronounced in rapid speech with only three syllables, [kʌmf-tə-bəl], with the [f] from the second syllable joining to the end of the first. As before, there is no danger here of confusion arising from the deletion, since English lacks a word *comftable* that would correspond to this reduced pronunciation. All the same, we find that deletion occasionally does creep into the language and result in different forms. This can often happen with names. The three-syllable name *Barbara* [bɑːr-bə-rə] is often pronounced with only two syllables, the [b] in the second syllable joining the last: [bɑːr-brə]. This has led, over time, to the rise of a differently spelled two-syllable name *Barbra*, which is derived in this fashion from the first.

The articulatory process of insertion is nearly as transparent as deletion, and involves the addition of sounds which make pronunciation easier. Take, for instance, the words *mince* and *prince*, which should be pronounced [mɪns]

---

[5] The upside-down "e" used here [ə] (called a "schwa") is used to represent the neutral unstressed vowel. It does not appear in the vowel chart above because it does not correspond to any full vowel.

and [prɪns], respectively. In fact though, we most often pronounce them the same as *mints* [mɪnts] and *prints* [prɪnts]. The reason for this is that both [n] and [s] are consonants that involve continuous sounds (that is, unlike [t], [b], [k], and [g], you can make [n] and [s] last until you run out of breath). It is difficult to transition from one continuous sound to another, and there is therefore a tendency to insert a stop consonant between them ([t] in this case) to make the transition easier. Since [n] is an alveolar consonant, it is natural for an alveolar stop [t] to be inserted after it. The same thing happens when the two consonants are [m] and [s], with the difference being that a bilabial stop [p] is inserted after the bilabial [m]. Thus, even though *hamster* [hæmstər] has no [p] in it, the word is quite often pronounced as though it does, with a [p] sound between the [m] and the [s], similar to *dumpster*: [hæmpstər]–[dʌmpstər]. A Google search for the misspelled word *hampster* actually yields about 400,000 hits, showing that some people are spelling the word as they are pronouncing it. As was shown in the case of deletion (e.g. *Barbara* → *Barbra*), insertion has changed the spelling of not a few names. Accordingly, many *Simsons* became *Simpsons*, and a few *Stansons* became *Stantsons*.[6]

Syllables and Word Stress

Another factor that distinguishes languages from one another, and plays a role in our perception of differences between our own and other languages, is how word stress or word accent is organized and produced. By word stress, we mean the cues by which we make one part of a word (usually a syllable) more prominent than other parts.

For example, the English word *politics* is stressed on the first syllable, **PO**-*li-tics*, while the word *political* is stressed on the second, *po-**LI**-ti-cal*. Notice that the stressed syllable for both words is the syllable preceding the second to last (i.e. the **antepenultimate** – ultimate=last, penultimate=next-to-last, antepenultimate=before next-to-last). English has a very strong tendency to place stress on the antepenultimate syllable in three-syllable (or longer) words.

While the placement of stress is normally regular and pretty standardized, it is also the case that it can vary with the speaker's dialect, much as pronunciation can do. For instance, while Mainstream American English (MAE) speakers pronounce *police* and *insurance* as *po-**LICE*** and *in-**SU**-rance*, Southern American English (SAE) speakers pronounce them with word-stress on the first

---

[6] It is not uncommon for the rapidly produced forms to become associated both with casual speech and with less-educated or lower-class speech. Thus, a person who regularly and intentionally produces *umbelievable*, in place of *unbelievable*, might be signaling their affinity with less-educated speakers. Other casual speech permutations, such as *irrevelant* in place of *irrelevant*, or *supposably* in place of *supposedly*, can also be used in this way.

syllable, **PO**-*lice* and **IN**-*su-rance*.[7] Such differences can play a role, along with other pronunciation differences, in our identifying a speaker's dialect.

One important way in which languages can differ is in how they realize (or mark) word stress. In English, stressed syllables tend to be longer, louder, and higher than unstressed ones. However, not all languages mark stress with length, amplitude, and pitch. Some, such as Japanese and Norwegian, only use relative pitch to mark stressed syllables. For example, the Norwegian word *bønder* (farmers) is pronounced with a lower pitch on the first syllable and a higher pitch on the second, while *bønner* (beans) has the reverse, a higher pitch on the first and a lower pitch on the second. In other respects, e.g. length and loudness, the syllables are equal. It is for this reason, in part, that English speakers can readily recognize a non-native Scandinavian speaker of English. Such a speaker will typically replace the standard word stress in a word such as *education, e-du-**CA**-tion*, with a pitch pattern typical of their own language: e_{LOW}-du_{HIGH}-ca_{LOW}-$tion_{HIGH}$.

Conclusion

In this chapter, we have discussed some of the ways in which language sounds can be examined and studied. In so doing, we have observed the need for distinguishing between language sounds themselves, and the written symbols used to represent them. We have also considered the differences inherent in regarding these sounds objectively, versus taking into account speaker and hearer perceptions of them. In this respect, our observations about the contrast between phonological and phonetic descriptions can be traced back to the work of Edward Sapir, a linguist who wrote on "the psychological reality of phonemes" over eighty years ago. Sapir ([1933] 1949: 46) distinguished between objectively definable "sounds" (i.e. "phonetic elements") and the functionally significant and subjectively classified units that he calls "phonemes."

In illustrating the difference between phonetic elements and phonemes, he compares the ways in which a researcher might (objectively) study and categorize various tools with the ways in which a user of tools might (functionally)

---

[7] The term Mainstream American English (MAE) has recently come into use among sociolinguists, as a preferred alternative to the more familiar Standard American English (SAE). Reasons for this are several, but one of them is that the term "standard" is inaccurate in this context, since the United States does not have any official "standard language" and since there is not a single variety of English which could carry this label. As Wolfram and Schilling (2015: 13) describe it, "MAE seems to be determined more by what it is not than by what it is. . . speech samples rated as standard by a cross-section of listeners exhibit a range of regional variation in pronunciation and vocabulary items, but they do not contain grammatical structures that are socially stigmatized." It is further the case that MAE is more readily usable as an acronym when contrasted with Southern American English (SAE), as we have reason to do in this book.

categorize them. While a physicist might measure the weight, dimensions, and composition of a number of long wooden objects, finding each one distinct from the other, a native user of these objects might readily classify them into "clubs" or "poles," according to their perceived function. And while the physicist might be able to find an object that is "halfway between club and pole," the native user is likely to classify it as either one or the other, and will "feel it to be such." Sapir recounts his attempts, during his fieldwork, to train a speaker of Southern Paiute, Tony Tillohash, to transcribe his own language phonetically. In this process, Tony would invariably write down the symbol for each sound as he perceived it, rather than as Sapir through his own observations knew the sounds to be pronounced. Sapir realized, in working with Tony, that he was unable to "override" the native-speaker perceptions that Tony brought with him to the task. The take-away lesson in this for Sapir was that establishing a "maximally correct" orthography of a language would depend on whether one were seeking to have the most phonetically accurate system or the system that most accurately reflects the sound patterns of the language and a native speaker's perception of them.

This difference between objectively demonstrable facts about a language and the sometimes distinct "psychological reality" of that language's native speakers is one that will arise repeatedly throughout this book. We will often find a misalignment between our objective descriptions of language properties and speakers'/hearers' own understanding and valuation of them. And the misalignment that we have observed regarding language sounds will also be found to exist in the domain of words, grammar, and discourse.

2   Words and Word Structure

When we think of language, the first thing that most people think of is words. That is, we tend to think of words as what are sometimes referred to as the "building blocks" of language. Looked at this way, language is a collection (or a store) of words, and we use language by putting those words together to form sentences (to express thoughts), which in turn are themselves chained together to form conversations, paragraphs, arguments, and so on.

As we have already seen, such a view ignores the importance that language sounds themselves have in this system. While the sounds of language don't themselves carry meaning, the sound system of a language is the substance out of which words are formed. This view also fails to take into account the grammatical structures needed to organize these selfsame words into understandable phrases, a topic which we will take up in the next chapter.

Morphemes: Words and Their Parts

When we look closely at words, though, we can immediately see that they themselves have structure, and that it is the units of word structure rather than the words themselves which carry the meaning. Just as chemical compounds consist of elements, which themselves can be combined in various ways and proportions to form other chemical compounds, so is it the case that many words can be broken down into smaller, meaningful elements.

Take, for example, the adjective *unbelievable*. The word consists of three parts: the verb *believe*, a prefix *un-*, and a suffix *-able*. The suffix *-able* combines with the verb *believe*, to form the adjective *believable*, which then combines with the prefix *un-*. If we were to look at this as a chemical process, it might look like this:

believe + -able   → believable
un-   + believable → unbelievable

Each of the three parts makes a definite contribution to the meaning of the entire word. The suffix *-able* (which can combine with a great number of verbs) means something on the order of 'able to be VERB-ed,' such that *believable* means 'able to be believed,' *decidable* means 'able to be decided,' and so on. The suffix -*able* also converts any verb that it attaches to into an adjective. For its part, the prefix *un*- attaches to adjectives (such as those produced by the addition of -*able*), and means 'not [whatever the adjective means].' So, *unbelievable* means 'not believable,' *unkind* means 'not kind,' and so on. What is important to take from this is that each part carries its own meaning, and the meaning of the entire word can be calculated from the meaning of its parts.

Seeing that words are not necessarily the smallest unit of meaning in a language, we shall have a separate term for that concept: **morpheme**. Some morphemes, such as the verb *believe*, can stand alone as words by themselves, and we would call these **free morphemes**. Some other morphemes, such as the prefix *un*-, need to be attached (or bound) to another word in order to be used, and we classify these as **bound morphemes**. Prefixes and suffixes, collectively referred to as affixes, are all bound morphemes.

Another way to classify morphemes is with reference to the kind of meaning that they have (or use they are put to). In this regard, we can identify a class of grammatical morphemes, such as verbal inflections, plural endings on nouns and suchlike, which don't really add meaning per se. The -*s* suffix that makes *dog* into the plural *dogs* and the -*ed* suffix that makes *carry* into the past tense *carried* are both of this sort. Morphemes that clearly carry lexical meanings, on the other hand, can be classed as content morphemes. Both the noun *dog* and the suffix -*able* belong to this class. Some elements might be grammatical morphemes when used one way and content morphemes in another instance. For example, the preposition *to* when used to indicate direction toward a place (e.g. *I'm going **to** school*) is clearly a content morpheme. But when it's used to signal a verbal infinitive (e.g. *I want **to** buy some*) it is merely a **grammatical free** morpheme.

It is important to keep in mind that it's not a morpheme just because it looks like a morpheme. For an element to be considered a morpheme, it must have both an identifiable "shape" and a clearly definable meaning or use. The bound

Table 2.1 *Morpheme types*

Morpheme classes	Free		Bound	
Content	dog		un-	(in *unkind*)
	believe		-able	(in *lovable*)
	to	(in *He went to school*)	-ment	(in *government*)
	of	(in *oldest brother of Sue*)	re-	(in *rewrite*)
Grammatical	to	(in *He wants to leave*)	-s	(plural noun suffix)
	of	(in *donation of money*)	-ed	(past tense verb suffix)

morpheme *un-*, for example, consists of the sounds [ʌn] and the meaning 'not' (applied to adjectives).

It is not hard, in this regard, to find pieces of words that look like morphemes (i.e. that consist of the sounds associated with a particular morpheme), but that are not morphemes themselves. For example, the words *dogs* and *lens* both end in [s], but only the [s] in *dogs* is a morpheme, since its addition to *dog* counts as adding plurality to the originally singular noun. One cannot count the [s] at the end of *lens* as a morpheme, since it is not a plural of anything (there being no singular noun *len* to attach it to). Similarly, the *er* in *nicer* (meaning 'more nice') is a morpheme, but the *er* in *feather* is not (there being no word *feath* that one might attach *er* to; *feather* therefore does not mean 'more feath').

It is further the case that a given morpheme may appear in a number of distinct, but related, "shapes." Consider the case of the past tense verbal suffix usually written as *-ed*, and consider at the same time how it is pronounced when attached to different words.[1] Sometimes, the past tense ending sounds like the simple consonant [d], as in:

    solve + [d] → solved
    try   + [d] → tried

Other times, the addition of *-ed* to a word is pronounced [t], as in:

    laugh + [t] → laughed
    pass   + [t] → passed

Finally, the addition of *-ed* to a verb that itself ends in [t] or [d] will result in its being pronounced as a full syllable, [əd].

    hate   + [əd] → hated
    hood   + [əd] → hooded

These several variants of the past tense suffix ([d], [t], and [əd]) are all considered as different realizations of the same morpheme, whose sound "shape" is determined by the environment it is inserted into. A group of related sound "shapes" such as these that are all used for the same meaning or function are called allomorphs. So, the three allomorphs [d], [t], and [əd] collectively represent the past tense verbal inflection *-ed*, and their appearance can be predicted on the basis of what verb they attach to. [əd] attaches to verbs ending in [t] or [d], [t] attaches to verbs ending in "voiceless" sounds [f], [p], [k], [s], and [d] attaches to any verbs that are left over.

---

[1] Remember that sound is primary, and spelling conventions secondary, when understanding and analyzing language.

Prefixes, Suffixes, and Making New Words

In the previous section, it has been shown that words may be made up of more than a single morpheme, and it would be informative to have a closer look at the ways in which this happens. In addition to the plentiful number of free content morphemes – single morphemes that can stand alone as words, such as *dog, believe, kind, around* – there are innumerable possibilities for augmenting the vocabulary of a language by combining morphemes.

We have already examined cases of affixation, where content affixes are added to free morphemes. This process, while not completely open-ended, can be rather complex, involving many such additions. Take a not overly compli-cated word such as *overgeneralizations*. Starting with the free adjectival morpheme *general*, we add the suffix *-ize* to form a verb *generalize*. Then, the prefix *over-* is added, to form another verb *overgeneralize*. The verb *over-generalize* is turned into a noun, by the addition of the suffix *-tion*, giving *overgeneralization*. Finally, the plural suffix *-s* is added, to give the plural noun *overgeneralizations*. If we were to represent all these several affixation opera-tions on one line, it might look like this:

$$[[[\text{over} + [[\text{general }_{\text{ADJECTIVE}}] + \text{ize }_{\text{VERB}}] \text{ VERB}] + \text{ation }_{\text{NOUN}}] + \text{s }_{\text{NOUN}}]$$
$$3 \qquad 1 \qquad\qquad 2 \qquad\qquad 4 \qquad\qquad 5$$

Each of the pieces of this word (that is, the adjective we started with and every affix) adds a fixed bit of meaning and/or changes the part of speech to which the word belongs.

When we examine these pieces closely, we find that they (unlike "beads on a string") actually combine in very specific and orderly ways. We can see that this is so, if we examine the right words. Take, for instance, the case of *untieable*. The "word" is ambiguous, and can mean 'not able to be tied' (as in, *I left the laces loose, because they were untieable*) or 'able to be untied' (as in, *I'm sure that knot is untieable. Try it again*).

The reason for the ambiguity can be attributed to three separate facts. First, there are two homophonous prefixes pronounced *un-*. One of these attaches to adjectives and means 'not' (as in, *unkind* 'not kind' and *unreal* 'not real'). The other attaches to verbs, and means 'reverse the action of the verb' (as in, *unbutton, unwrap,* and *unfold*). Secondly, the suffix *-able* attaches to verbs, turning them into adjectives (as in, *foldable* 'able to be folded' and *washable* 'able to be washed'). Finally, the verb *tie* represents a reversible action.

Taking all these facts together, we can see that *untieable* is not an "ambig-uous word," but is rather two words that happen to be pronounced the same (i.e. are homophonous). To form the word *untieable* meaning 'not able to be tied,' one first attaches *-able* to *tie* to form the adjective *tieable* 'able to be tied.' Then, the prefix *un-* 'not' is added to form the adjective *untieable* 'not able to be tied.'

Step 1:   [[tie $_{\text{VERB}}$] + able $_{\text{ADJECTIVE}}$]
Step 2:   [un + [tieable $_{\text{ADJECTIVE}}$] $_{\text{ADJECTIVE}}$]

To form the word *untieable* meaning 'able to be untied,' one first attaches prefix *un-* 'not' to *tie* to form the verb *untie*. Then, the suffix *-able* is added to *untie* to form the adjective *untieable* 'able to be untied.'

Step 1:   [un + [tie $_{\text{VERB}}$] $_{\text{VERB}}$]
Step 2:   [[untie $_{\text{VERB}}$] + able $_{\text{ADJECTIVE}}$]

More Ways of Making New Words

Besides the mechanism of affixation, there are numerous other ways in which new words come into a language. Some involve the creative manipulation of words already in the language. Some involve taking in (i.e. borrowing) words from other languages. And some involve reallocating or revising the meaning of words currently in use.

One of the most common means of creating new words in English (and many other languages) is **compounding**. Forming a new compound word involves nothing more complicated than taking two (or more) existing words and putting them together. Examples of well-established compound words in English are *highchair* (*high* + *chair*) and *blackbird* (*black* + *bird*).

Notice, though, that the meaning of a compound word is not the sum of its parts. While a *blackbird* might name a species of birds that are black, not every *black bird* is a *blackbird* (some being crows and magpies). Likewise, a *highchair* is not simply a chair that is high, but is a specialized piece of furniture used for feeding infants and toddlers.

Note, as well, that speakers are quite able to distinguish between compound words such as *blackbird* and multiword phrases such as *black bird* even when they are not written, and there is no typographic space between the parts. Compound words in English tend to have stress on the first element and not on the second, *blackbird*, while the elements in a multiword phrase are likely to be equally stressed, *black bird*.

Not only do compound words not represent the meaning of their parts, but their meanings can be quite unpredictable from their parts. While a *milkman*, a *garbage-man*, and a *fireman* are all workers whose jobs have, respectively, to do with milk, garbage, and fire, you want the first to bring milk, the second to take away the garbage, and the third to suppress or put out the fire. A *snowman*, in contrast to all these, is not someone who brings or takes away snow, but something made out of snow. And *snow-tires* are not made of snow, but devised for use in snow. So, compound word meanings are established by convention and context, which is what allows us to understand that *cheesecake* is made of cheese and that *Girl Scout cookies* are not made of Girl Scouts.

There are several other means of inventing words that are worth a mention here. They are clipping and blending, initialism and acronym formation, and genericization. The first of these, **clipping** and blending, involve taking parts of existing words and using them in place of the original word (clipping) or putting these parts together in a fashion akin to compounding (blending). Clipping will produce *math* from *mathematics, bio* from *biology, gator* from *alligator*, and *phone* from *telephone*. Typically the more distinctive end of the word is retained (e.g. *math* is more clearly a reduction from *mathematics* than is *matics*, which could be clipped from any of: *informatics, cinematics*, or *dramatics*). That said, it is not always possible to predict which end of a word gets sliced away. Americans clip the beginning of *telephone* to get *phone*, while British speakers use *telly* (pronounced [tɛli]) for *television*, clipping the end of that word.

It is also not possible to predict with complete certainty which words do or do not have clipped forms. So, while we have *bio* for *biology*, we don't have *geo* for either *geography* or *geology*.

Two clipped forms put together can form a **blend**. Examples of this abound in English, where the clippings of *motor* and *hotel* (*mo-* and *-tel*) are combined to form *motel*. Similarly, *br-* (from *breakfast*) plus *-unch* (from *lunch*) are combined to get *brunch*, and *emoti-* (from *emotion*) plus *-con* (from *icon*) for *emoticon*.

One very creative and productive use of clipping and blending involves taking a piece of a word to represent part or all of its meaning, and combining it with a succession of other clippings. The best-known examples of this are the *-aholic* words. On its own, *alcoholic* is a combination of *alcohol* plus the suffix *-ic*, which means 'characteristic of' or 'pertaining to.' Taking the word *alcoholic* in its meaning 'addicted to alcohol,' English speakers clipped off the piece *-aholic* and gave it the meaning 'addicted to something.' From this we get *chocoholic* 'addicted to chocolate,' *workaholic* 'addicted to work,' and *shopaholic* 'addicted to shopping,' among others.

Initialisms and acronyms are similar in the way that they are formed, but distinct in how they turn out. Both involve taking the first letter of a series of words, and putting them together to create a new form/word. Taking the first letters of the main words in *Federal Bureau of Investigation* gives *FBI*, and doing the same with *National Aeronautic and Space Administration* results in *NASA*. The difference between them is that when we say *FBI* we pronounce the names of the letters [ɛf biː aɪ], and when we say *NASA* we pronounce it as a word [næsə]. The first of these is called an initialism (because one pronounces the "initials" of the composite words), and the second an acronym (a "nym" or "name" formed from the "acro" or "extremities" of other words). Whether a phrase becomes an initialism or an acronym has quite a bit to do with what letters make it up, it being rather more difficult to pronounce *FBI* and *LSD* as words (e.g. [fˈbiː] and [ləsd]) than *NASA* and *AIDS* (e.g. [næsə] and [eɪdz]). All the same, there is some amount of arbitrariness. The internet/SMS form *LOL* (for *laugh out loud*) began its career as an initialism [ɛl oʊ ɛl], and has since taken the form of an acronym in its merger with *cats*, to form the name of the internet meme *lolcats* [lɔːlkæts].[2]

One fact that holds true for both initialisms and acronyms is that speakers tend to lose track of the phrases that they abbreviate, once they've been around for a while. Thus, quite a few speakers may still be able to tell you what *AIDS* stands for (acquired immune deficiency syndrome), it having first come into use in 1982. Very much fewer will be able to accurately parse the meaning of *LASER* (light amplification by stimulated emission of radiation), even though they may still know that it has something to do with "light." The literal meaning of *LASER*, having first appeared in 1960, is older and more remote. Likewise, hardly anyone remembers the phrase that gave rise to *RADAR*, a similar acronym from twenty more years earlier (1941). It is 'radio detecting and ranging.'

The last path to word invention that we will mention here (there are others) is called genericization. This is the process by which the commercial name for a product supplants the generic name for it. Take, for example, the fact that *Kleenex* is a brand of *facial tissue*, that *Q-tip* is a brand of *cotton swab*, and that a *Xerox machine* is a *photocopying machine* produced by a particular company. When we use the terms *Kleenex, Q-tip,* and *Xerox* to refer to things not made or sold, respectively, by Kimberly-Clark, Unilever, or the Xerox Corporation, we are genericizing their brand names. It should come as no surprise that corporations who own popular brand names will spend much effort and fortune to protect their trademarks and to fight the (sometimes losing) battle against genericization.

Borrowing Words from Other Languages

Another, and perhaps the most important, way in which a language adds to its stock of words is through the mechanism of borrowing. Languages borrow from each other copiously, whenever the opportunity arises, and lexical borrowings from one language to another present some of the best evidence for language contact (which may arise on account of conquest, migration, trade, and other forms of cultural contact, such as religious proselytizing). In this regard, as we shall see shortly, lexical borrowing and attitudes to it can be rather revealing indicators of language conflict and accommodation.

---

[2] www.lolcats.com

Borrowed words are often words for new things, introduced in the course of such cultural and commercial contact. They can be words for imported foods and tools, animals and plants, customs and clothing, or political and religious practices. What languages tend not to borrow are words for things that speakers already have and refer to often. So, one rarely finds that a language will borrow family kinship terms (e.g. *brother*, *cousin*, *grandfather*), number expressions, native species of plants and animals, words that express location such as prepositions and directional terms (e.g. *between*, *east*, *nearby*), or grammatical words such as articles and pronouns (e.g. *my*, *the*, *them*).

Among the world's languages, English (perhaps on account of the multitude of contact situations throughout its history) has an enormous percentage of borrowed vocabulary as well as an incredible number of source languages for its borrowings. English (or "Anglish") – from Anglo-Saxon, the language of the Angles and the Saxons – is fundamentally a Germanic language, being brought to the British Isles in the period between the fifth and seventh centuries by Germanic-speaking tribes out of the present-day areas of Holland, north-western Germany, and Denmark.

Conquered by Old French-speaking Norman invaders in the eleventh century and dominated denominationally by the Catholic Church, Anglo-Saxon borrowed massively from (Old) French and Latin. Significant, but less numerous, borrowings were had from Greek, by way of Latin. Later on, partly as a consequence of British exploration, commerce, and imperialism, English came to borrow from dozens upon dozens of other languages, with attested vocabulary from such disparate sources as Arabic, Chinese, Finnish, Hebrew, Hindi, Korean, Malay, Tamil, Ukrainian, Welsh, and Yiddish.

In present-day English, only about 25 percent of the lexicon can be traced back to the language's Germanic roots. This includes, unsurprisingly, words for numbers, family terms, and body parts. French and Latin loan words each account for nearly 30 percent, and Greek for an additional 6 percent or so. The remaining 10 percent of the lexicon comes from all the other sources (e.g. *karaoke* from Japanese, *shibboleth* from Hebrew as we encountered in Chapter 1, and *toboggan* from the Native American language Mikmaq).[3]

Stepping away from English, which is a "borrower par excellence," we might consider the case of other languages, and how they borrow words. First off, one must understand that a borrowed word must fit, or be fitted, into the sound system and word structure system of the borrowing language. This is, of course, just as true for borrowings into English. The borrowed English word *chipmunk* comes from the relatively unpronounceable word *tchitmoo* in the Native American Odawa language.

---

[3] Williams 1975.

Likewise, when a language borrows from English, the borrowed word has to be "fitted" into the receiving system. Japanese, since the end of World War II, has borrowed relentlessly from English. But Japanese does not have words that begin with multiple consonants, such as [str] in *strike*, and mostly doesn't have words that end with consonants either. So, borrowing a word like *strike* requires a few "renovations" to its pronunciation. In this case, a vowel is added after each potentially offending consonant, giving *sutoraiki*. In borrowing the word into Japanese, advantage is taken of this fact, in order to disambiguate between a labor strike which has [i] at the end, *sutoraiki*, and a strike in baseball which is pronounced with an [u] at the end, *sutoraiku*. Further complicating the picture is the fact that Japanese has its own very special method of clipping and blending words; it takes the first bits of each and joins them together. Thus, the phrase *personal computer* is borrowed and fitted into the Japanese sound system as *pasonaru konpyutaa*, and then each form is clipped, respectively, to *paso* and *kon*, and blended to *pasokon*. The resulting word, an attested borrowing from English, winds up completely unrecognizable to speakers of the language it was borrowed from.

With an understanding of lexical borrowing as it arises from language contact, we can briefly examine the ways in which lexical choices figure in language conflict situations. Suffice it to say that one's choice of words to express a given meaning on a particular occasion can often be a difficult and vexing task.

As we noted in Chapter 1, in the discussion of *shibboleth*, the way a person speaks will often mark them clearly as belonging (or not belonging) to a group, in much the same way that one's clothing or grooming habits do. Unlike exterior affectations such as clothing, hairstyle, and facial hair, language behavior is less easily manipulated and is seen as a surer mark of group membership. And just as we identify the stranger or "the other" based on their pronunciation of words, we also do this based on their choice of words.

For instance, if you are at a reception where television and newspaper journalists are present and if a stranger at your elbow asks whether someone standing nearby is a *press* person, you can be almost certain that the questioner is an English speaker from India. Likewise so, if someone suggests to you that certain grievances are in need of *redressal* (rather than *redress*). These, and many other word choices, may not stand out as marking a person as **belonging** to a particular group, so much as **not belonging** to your own.

Other lexical differences are more obvious and recognizable, such as the use of *trunk* and *boot*, by American and British speakers respectively, to refer to the closed space at the rear of a car which holds luggage (and everything you forgot to drop off at the recycling station last week). Lexical choices also mark members of other ethnic and racial groups, and often the words used by such groups are less familiar to outsiders. For instance, the term *skrilla* (used by African American English speakers) means 'money' and emerged out of hip-hop song lyrics in the 1990s. Someone unfamiliar with hip-hop music or culture would be unlikely to understand the sentence *I'd buy a car, but I don't have any skrilla!* (although they might work it out from context).

Sometimes, lexical choices reflect subtle regional differences that speakers are barely aware of. For example, the Lampyridae beetle that flies about on summer nights emitting yellow or pale green light from its abdomen is variously called a lightning bug or a firefly. *Firefly* predominates in the western states, *lightning bug* is used in the Appalachian region and the lower Midwest, and the two terms are used interchangeably elsewhere (e.g. Texas, Michigan, Florida, and New England). Interestingly, the areas where *lightning bug* is the preferred term correspond, roughly, to the range of the 'common eastern firefly' (*Photinus pyralis*), which happens to be the most common species of firefly in North America. In other cases, speakers are quite aware of, and sometimes very self-conscious about, their lexical choices.

In American English, for example, the generic term for carbonated soft drink is distinct in different regions of the country. The Harvard Dialect Survey included among its 122 survey questions: "What is your generic term for a sweetened carbonated beverage?"[4]

Figure 2.1 indicates the top three answers (by zip code) to the question: "What is your generic term for a sweetened carbonated beverage?" Nine answers predominated (i.e. constituted >97% of the 10,669 responses). Ranked in order of popularity, they were: soda (52.97%), pop (25.08%), coke (12.38%), soft drink (5.89%), tonic (0.67%), cocola (0.29%), fizzy drink (0.14%), dope (0.03%), lemonade (0.01%). The three most popular terms *soda*, *pop*, and *coke* together accounted for around 90 percent of the responses. Furthermore, preference for each of the three was clearly regionalized, with *soda* dominant in the Northeast and West Coast, *pop* being preferred in the Midwest, and *coke* winning out in the South. The three maps display the distribution of these three terms, superimposed on an outline map of the continental United States.

The prevalence of the term *coke* in the American South is not surprising, considering the dominance of the Atlanta-based Coca-Cola Company in the region's soft drink industry. The two other terms *soda* and *pop* (sometimes combined into *soda pop*) derive, respectively, from the **sod**ium salts that were traditionally added to carbonated waters and from the **pop**ping sound made when a bottle of the stuff was opened. Speakers of American English will sometimes quiz each other about the terms that each uses, and poke fun at those who use what they consider to be the "wrong" word.

---

[4] Vaux and Golder 2003.

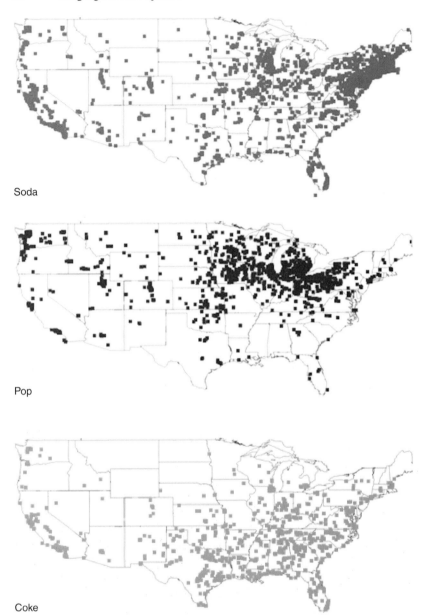

Soda

Pop

Coke

Figure 2.1 Regional use of the terms *soda*, *pop*, and *coke* (Vaux and Golder 2003)[a]

[a] The original questions and maps can be found at http://dialect.redlog.net/

Lexical borrowing and lexical choice becomes a charged matter when one considers language contact situations. As we already noted, different languages (on account of their particular phonological and morphological differences) borrow words in different ways.

We saw how English words borrowed into Japanese are transformed phonologically, sometimes into forms that are hardly recognizable when compared with their sources. In Semitic languages, such as Hebrew and Arabic, verbs borrowed from other languages (such as English) wind up keeping only their consonants, due to the simple fact that vowel sounds form the framework for verbal conjugations. Thus, for instance, the verb *telephone* [tɛlɛfoʊn] (e.g. *Jack telephoned Jill*) retains only the consonants [t], [l], [f], and [n] in the Hebrew expressions *l'talfen* 'to telephone,' *tilfanti* 'I telephoned,' *yitalfenu* 'they will telephone.' Again, we see the special properties of a language work to absorb the word and make it its own. In yet other languages, such as Chinese, the character-based writing system precludes borrowing words as they are pronounced, and instead tends to create new native words based on the concepts contained therein. Thus, the meaning of *telephone* is reformed in Chinese as the word *dian hua*, with *dian* meaning 'electricity' and *hua* meaning 'talk.' And *computer* is realized as *dian nau* 'electric brain.'

Borrowed words and concepts, regardless of whether they reappear in their adopted language in a recognizable form, are not meaning-neutral. Newly imported words, **minimally**, often have extra connotations and stand out as being somewhat different, sophisticated, or alien. In the worst case, they can trigger negative associations or official derision.

Consider, for instance, the English word *croissant* (borrowed from French). The word, in French, means 'crescent' and is used as a noun to refer to a crescent shape, a new moon, and a buttery, flaky pastry that has a crescent shape. Used as an adjective, it means 'growing,' 'swelling,' or 'increasing.' Borrowed into English, it is only used as a noun, and only carries the 'baked-goods' meaning of the French word. Now, one might wonder, why do we need this word? The pastries referred to are also called *crescent rolls*, which is a perfectly adequate term for them. The Pillsbury division of General Mills, which used the Pillsbury Doughboy to introduce its crescent rolls to the television marketplace in 1965, now simply calls them *crescents*. The difference between the borrowed word *croissant* (with its vaguely French-sounding pronunciation) and the non-borrowed word *crescent* is that the former sounds (to the average American) more "cosmopolitan" and the latter more "homespun." Accordingly, you find *crescent (rolls)* in the refrigerator case in the supermarket, and *croissant* as a sandwich-bread choice at an upscale downtown café (which also has loads of other borrowings on its menu, e.g. *espresso*, *latte*, etc.).

Lest anyone think that this phenomenon is somehow an American one, we only need take another look at Japanese, which has borrowed the English word *milk* (as *miruku*), despite already having the perfectly sufficient native word *gyuunyuu* (lit: 'cow milk'). Once again, the native word winds up as the "homespun" term, and the word that your mom would use if she were sending you to the store to pick up some. And the borrowed word takes on the cosmopolitan or cultured usage, and is found on café menus.

The Politics of Borrowing Words

Having discussed some of the linguistic complexities of lexical borrowing, we close with a look at how borrowing figures into linguistic conflicts (anticipating, in this way, some of the issues to be dealt with in later chapters).

In some cultures and in some countries, lexical borrowing is deemed a threat to the integrity of the indigenous or national language, and is heartily and officially resisted. Nowhere does this seem to be truer than in the Francophone (French-speaking) polities of France and Quebec (official and societal attitudes toward lexical borrowing are somewhat distinct in Francophone Africa, where the French language was imposed through colonialism).

The resistance in these two places to lexical borrowing is understandably focused on borrowings from English. No matter that many of the words which creep from English into French were originally borrowed in English itself from Old French some 700–900 years ago, it is modern English which has displaced French as the world's lingua "franca." And it is English, more than any other global language, which threatens to make French internationally unimportant.

In France itself, the Académie Française (the official learned authority on the French language, established in 1635) has, for centuries, promulgated decisions regarding proper usage, vocabulary, and grammar. It has, in the past several decades, gone on the offensive "to protect the [French] language from English." In past decades, we've seen the Académie rail against the use of expressions such as *le weekend* in place of the "proper" French *la fin de la semaine*. Now, given the widespread and innovative use of English throughout the world, and especially over the internet, the task has become quite formidable. On its website, the Académie now features specific and current recommendations; suggesting that *impacter* (from the English *impact*) be replaced with *affecter*, and that the English–French mélange *le best of* be eschewed in favor of *le meilleur de*.[5]

While the civilized, but strident, recommendations of the Académie Française might amuse, borrowing from English into French in the province of Quebec is not so much a matter of linguistic propriety as it is part of

---

[5] Samuel 2011.

a language war, and a fight for Francophone cultural survival in North America. There, the Office Québécois de la Langue Française (OQLF, 'Quebec Office of the French Language') wields enforcement powers over public usage of language, prohibiting English invasions of French with the force of law (rather than the weight of academic judgment, as with the Académie Française).

As recently as 2013, the OQLF forced a couple of high-end Montreal restaurants to change to French, signage and notices that were in English, or to do away with them entirely. A grocery list written on a chalkboard, "*salade, oeuf, sucre, steak*" ('salad, egg, sugar, steak'), was deemed to have an offensive borrowing from English, *steak*, which had to be replaced with the French *bifteck*. Another offense, the words *on* and *off* on a hot water switch, was resolved by covering them with opaque tape.[6] These incidents are the tip of a long and deep iceberg of language conflict and rights issues which have plagued the Canadian province for more than forty years. We will return to these issues in later chapters.

---

[6] CBC News 2013.

3   Grammar and the Organization of Words into Expressions

Having looked at the properties of language sounds and words, we now turn our attention to the nature of phrases and sentences, to the mechanics of putting words together to form utterances (which differs greatly from language to language). We will first survey the roles of word order, grammatical case and gender, and other types of grammatical inflection in conveying the meaning of phrases. We will also look at how the meanings of phrases are sometimes directly calculable from the meanings of the words that they contain, and sometimes not. Finally, we will consider how the sentences and phrases are often made up of parts which are themselves sentences and phrases, and how combining the same string of words in different ways can give rise to robust ambiguities.

The Organization of Sentences and Phrases: Word Order

We begin with the most familiar (to English speakers) component of sentence organization, word order. For English and many other languages (such as Chinese), which don't have other ways to signal this, the grammatical role (e.g. subject or object) is indicated by the order of elements relative to the verb. It is in this way, and this way pretty much alone, that we understand *dog bites man* to be an unremarkable occasion and *man bites dog* to be worth at least a couple of column-inches in the local paper. It is also the reason we know that the manager supervises Joan in the first phrase, below, and not in the second:

(1)   a. The manager that promoted Joan
       b. The manager that Joan promoted

The general rule at work here, in its simplest form, is that the verb is preceded by its subject and that the verb precedes its object.

In some word-order-dependent languages, the verb precedes or follows both subject and object. But this doesn't prevent word order from playing a critical role in the organization of the sentence. One such language, Ainu – an aboriginal language of Japan – situates the verb at the end of the sentence. Nevertheless, the ordering of the two nouns is crucial, as the pair of sentences below shows. In the first sentence the *kamuy* 'bear' is the killer and the *aynu* 'person' is dead. In the second, the order of these elements and their roles are reversed:

(2)　　　a. Kamuy　aynu　　rayke.
　　　　　　bear　　person　kill
　　　　　　'The bear killed the man.'
　　　　　b. Aynu　　kamuy　rayke.
　　　　　　person　bear　　kill
　　　　　　'The man killed the bear.'

Word order also affects how we interpret words preceding nouns in English. For example, both *Spanish teacher* and *English teacher* have the potential to be ambiguous. They might mean 'a teacher **of** Spanish' and 'a teacher **of** English,' or they might mean 'a teacher **from** Spain' or 'a teacher **from** England.'[1] However, if one places both *Spanish* and *English* before the noun, then the phrase can have only one meaning. *A Spanish English teacher* can only mean 'a teacher of English from Spain,' and *an English Spanish teacher* can only mean 'a teacher of Spanish from England.'

In addition to affecting meaning, word order (in languages which use it) can determine whether a sentence is or is not grammatical. So, for English, the verb normally comes between the subject and the object, as we observed above, and neither before nor after both of them. Accordingly, neither *bites dog man* nor *dog man bites* are possible sentences in English (though the last word order is quite fine for Ainu). Similarly, *English math teacher* means 'a teacher of math from England,' while *math English teacher* means nothing and is just a badly arranged sequence of English words.

In other languages, such as Spanish and Italian, variations in word order can affect meaning. The Italian adjective *cara*, for example, means 'expensive' when it follows a noun (*la macchina **cara*** = 'the expensive car') and 'dear' or 'cherished' when it precedes the noun (*la **cara** amica* = 'the dear friend'). Similarly, the Spanish adjective *pobre* 'poor' has different connotations depending on whether it precedes or follows the noun: *hombre pobre* 'poor [impoverished] man' and *pobre hombre* 'poor [misfortunate] man.'

The Organization of Sentences and Phrases: Case

Another means of determining sentence organization is the use of grammatical case on the noun phrases. English still has a little of this (it used to have more),

---

[1] If one wanted *Spanish teacher* to mean 'a teacher from Spain,' then, in speaking, one would place approximately equal stress on both words. If one wanted it to mean 'a teacher of Spanish,' then one would place greater stress on the word *Spanish*. It is for this reason that the two-word phrase, in its latter meaning, might be considered a compound word.

Table 3.1 *Nominative and accusative pronouns for English[a]*

	Nominative (subject) form	Accusative (object) form
first-person singular pronoun	I	me
third-person masculine singular pronoun	he	him
third-person feminine singular pronoun	she	her
first-person plural pronoun	we	us
third-person plural pronoun	they	them
question word for persons	who	whom

[a] Note that the second-person pronoun *you* and the third-person neuter pronoun *it* do not have differently case-marked forms.

enough to serve for illustration. English pronouns and some question words still appear in what we call **nominative** and **accusative** forms.

As Table 3.1 shows, nominative forms are used as subjects and accusative forms are used as objects. There are additional pronoun forms, namely those used to express possession (sometimes referred to as genitive case): e.g. *my*, *your*, *his*, *her*, *its*, *our*, *their*, and *whose*. Focusing on the nominative and accusative forms, we see that case reinforces word order in signaling which element of a sentence is the subject and which is the object:

(3)   a. She loves him.
         b. They hit us.

Using the wrong form of a pronoun (i.e. putting subject pronouns in the place of object pronouns, and vice versa) results in an ungrammatical sentence,[2] even though the word order is correct:

(4)   a. *Her loves he.
         b. *Them hit we.

In the two sentences immediately above, one could reasonably say either that the pronouns have the wrong form or that they are in the wrong positions.

Outside this small group of pronoun forms, English doesn't utilize case much. So, while grammatical case can occasionally reinforce what we know about a sentence (i.e. which is its subject and which is its object), most often it doesn't play any role. Regular common nouns don't have different forms according to whether they are subjects or objects, and it is for this reason (among others) that word order plays such an important role in English.

[2] The notation "*" is used to indicate that a sentence is ungrammatical or unacceptable, and will be used throughout this book, when appropriate.

It wasn't always this way. Old English (the ancestor of Modern English, spoken in the British Isles from the fifth century until the eleventh century) had a very robust system of cases, which were used for both nouns and adjectives. Subjects were marked with nominative case, such that if "a good man laughed," "good man" would be rendered *gōd wer*. As an object, as in the case of "someone hurt a good man," the adjective "good" had the accusative suffix *-ne*, as in *gōdne wer*. If we were discussing possession, as in "a good man's hat," then both the adjective and the noun would have the genitive *-es* suffix, *gōdes weres*. If "good man" were an indirect object or recipient, as in "we gave it to a good man," then dative case would be used, *gōdum were*. Finally, in the instrumental case, as in "we got it done with a good man," the form used would be *gōde were*. As one might expect, given what we've said about the interaction of word order and grammatical case, Old English (having a well-developed case system) had freer word order than does Modern English.

Other modern languages, such as Japanese, use grammatical case *instead of* word order to specify the grammatical (e.g. subject and object) roles in a sentence. The subject of a sentence is marked by a suffix *-ga*. The object is normally marked by *-o*. And a sentential "topic" is marked by *-wa*. To illustrate how this works, we can observe a simple sentence such as *Taroo hugged Mariko*. In Japanese, this sentence could be rendered as:

(5)   Taro-ga   Mariko-o   dakishimeta.
       Taro-nominative Mariko-accusative hugged
       'Taro hugged Mariko.'

If one wanted to make Taro the topic of the conversation, we might have:

(6)   Taro-wa   Mariko-o   dakishimeta.
       Taro-topic   Mariko-accusative hugged
       'As for Taro, [he] hugged Mariko.'

If Mariko were to be the topic, then we would have:

(7)   Mariko-wa   Taro-ga   dakishimeta.
       Mariko-topic   Taro-nominative   hugged
       'As for Mariko, Taro hugged [her].'

And if the word order in the first sentence were changed, the basic meaning of the sentence would not:

(8)   Mariko-o   Taro-ga   dakishimeta.
       Mariko-accusative Taro-nominative   hugged
       'Taro hugged Mariko.'

This, relatively, free word order that Japanese displays is a direct consequence of the fact that the grammatical roles of the participants are directly marked on the nouns themselves, leaving the meaning of the sentences understandable in spite of permutations in word order.

The Organization of Sentences and Phrases: Verb Conjugation

The last means of indicating sentence organization that we will discuss here is grammatical agreement **expressed on the verb** (sometimes referred to as verbal conjugation, as opposed to **nominal declension**). Verb agreement can make clear, just like case, which noun is the subject of a sentence (and also, in some languages, which one is the object). Just as grammatical case is a way of marking the noun to make clear its relation to the verb, grammatical agreement is a means of marking on the verb which nouns have certain relations to it.

As we discussed in regard to grammatical case, Modern English does not have a very robust system of verbal inflection that one can point to (another reason that English word order is so important). However, it once did have. We needn't go all the way back to Old English to illustrate this either. Middle English had a fairly well-articulated system of subject agreement, one that is not all that strange to us.

Although verbal endings differed somewhat by verb class, and different English dialects had slightly different sets of endings, the general pattern (as exhibited in the Middle English spoken north of London) was for the verb to agree in person and number with the subject. Regular verbs, such as *tell* or *bid*, would have *-e* added for first person singular, *-est* added for second person singular, *-eth* added for third person singular, and *-en* added for plurals. Examples of this are:

(9)   a. I bidd-e yow go forth   [I bid you go forth]
       b. thow bidd-est me go forth   [you bid me go forth]
       c. he bidd-eth yow go forth   [he bids you go forth]
       d. they bidd-en us go forth   [they bid us go forth]

In Modern English, there are remnants of this system found with the verb *be* (e.g. *I am*, *you are*, *he is*), but not much more than that.

In addition to person and number agreement, some phrases (in other languages) exhibit grammatical gender **agreement**. In Spanish (and other Romance languages, such as Italian and Portuguese), adjectives are inflected so as to agree with the nouns that they modify. In these cases, however, rather than agree in person and number they agree in **gender** and number. Typically, masculine singular takes no suffix or *-o*, masculine plurals commonly have *-os*, feminine singular takes *-a*, and feminine plural has *-as*. The following examples present the pattern, where *libro* 'book' is a masculine noun and *mesa* 'table' is feminine. *Pequeñ-* is the adjectival base for the word 'small.'

libro pequeño   'small book'
libros pequeños   'small books'
mesa pequeña   'small table'
mesas pequeñas   'small tables'

When speakers of languages that do not have grammatical gender, such as English, encounter it in a language such as Spanish, they often mistakenly think that the "gender" is somehow real. That is, they imagine that Spanish speakers think of books as "male things" and tables as "female things." Such conclusions, though, are unwarranted, since grammatical gender is better thought of as an arbitrary way of dividing nouns into classes (i.e. one might as easily consider *-o* and *-a* to be "type 1" and "type 2" endings, as "masculine" and feminine").

Calculating the Meaning of the Whole from Its Parts

Since the point of combining words via grammatical structures is to produce phrases and sentences that have meanings, it is appropriate here to examine the manner in which this happens. One way of understanding how meanings are calculated is to consider that, by and large, "the meaning of the whole (phrase or sentence) is a function of the meaning of its (word or phrase) parts." This is, as we will shortly see, an overstatement, but it's a good place to start.

Take, for example, a noun modified by an adjective such as *green balloon*. Presumably, we know what *green* means, and we might imagine it to refer to all things that are (some shade of) green. Likewise, *balloon* can refer to all those things which count as balloons, assuming we have agreement about what a balloon is. From this starting point, we can understand *green balloon* as referring to something that is in the intersection of the set of balloons and the set of green things, as shown in Figure 3.1.

Now, having a maximally simple example of calculating phrasal meaning from word meanings, we acknowledge that things are never as simple as the first

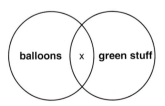

Figure 3.1 Compositional meaning through intersection

illustration. For instance, not all adjectives describe properties (like "being green") which can be assessed in isolation. The meaning of some adjectives, such as *large, tall*, and *lush*, can only be calculated relative to the nouns they modify. For example, one would *not* say that *large mosquito* refers to something in the intersection of mosquitos and the set of large things. A *short tree* is likely to be quite a bit taller than a *tall man*. Likewise, Tucson (AZ) is a *lush desert* (annual precipitation > 11 inches) in comparison with Las Vegas (annual precipitation about 4 inches). But, in the larger scheme of things, Tucson isn't lush (just lush "for a desert").

Other adjective–noun combinations require even more complicated calculations. Take, for instance, phrases such as *faux diamond* and *counterfeit banknote*. One might, somewhat rashly, say that a faux diamond refers to something that is not a diamond, but that can't be all of it. A peanut is not a diamond, but is also not a faux diamond. So, how does one calculate a combination such as this one? Well, a *faux diamond* and a *counterfeit banknote* both need to be nearly real, or at least real enough to fool anyone but an expert. So, a *faux diamond* can't be a red gem, and a *counterfeit banknote* can't be hand-drawn. On this basis, we might say that *faux* refers to things that are "almost authentic" and *faux diamond* refers to something which comes as close to being in the set of diamonds as possible, without actually being in the set. We might observe from all this that the meaning of a phrase is indeed calculable from the meaning of its parts, but that the calculations are sometimes rather intricate.

Meaning Puzzles: Idiomatic Expressions

Set against the examples that we've just considered are a class of multiword phrases that are not calculable at all from their "word parts." Some examples of these are:

kick the bucket	[die]
rain cats and dogs	[rain torrentially]
let the cat out of the bag	[reveal a secret]
bite the dust	[die]

These phrases, termed idioms, are more like compound words in that they are fixed both in meaning and in form, and in that their meaning is, at best, only dimly connected to the words that make them up. While there may be a story behind some of these idioms, their etymology is at once usually uncertain and also quite irrelevant to their use, in that most speakers don't reflect on the connection (if there is one).

One way in which idioms, such as those above, differ from compound words is that they also have literal meanings, and can be readily used to express these.

In the following pair of sentences, the first uses *let the cat out of the bag* as an idiom and the second one uses it literally:

(10)   a. John was supposed to keep Virginia's resignation secret, but he let the cat out of the bag.
        b. John, after calming it by swaddling it in a burlap sack, let the cat out of the bag.

However, as mentioned above, the form of an idiom cannot normally be altered and still retain its idiomatic meaning. If you have "let **a** cat out of the bag," you have done so literally and there's a cat, not a secret, that's been let out. If you "kick the **large five-gallon** bucket," you have not died.

Just about every language has idiomatic expressions such as those above, and in learning or coming into contact with another language, it is often these expressions which are the hardest to learn (since one cannot readily calculate their meaning, and since one has to be exceedingly careful to use exactly the right form). Spanish, for instance, has an idiomatic phrase *tirar la casa por la ventana* (literally, 'to throw the house through the window'). In its idiomatic use, it means something like 'to spare no expense,' and could be used as follows:

(11)   Tiré la casa por la ventana cuando compré mi nuevo coche.
        Literally: I threw the house through the window when I bought my new car.
        Idiomatically: I spared no expense when I bought my new car.

Much in the same way that "shibboleths" function to identify speakers as belonging to an insider group, so too the correct use of idiomatic expressions lets others know whether a speaker is a genuine member of the group. In this regard, inauthentic appropriation of ethnically identifiable idioms can subject the person using them to ridicule. For example, a white person using the African American colloquialism *shorty* or *shawty* to mean 'girlfriend' will often be derided as being affected and insincere.

Deriving Different Meanings from Order of Combination

Understanding how grammar works, beyond noting the overt indicators such as word order, case, and agreement, involves examining phrase and sentence construction as a process – one in which the process of combining words with one another is repeated to yield more and more complex expressions.

Earlier in this chapter, we looked at the effects of word order in determining the meaning of expressions such as *Spanish English teacher* and *English Spanish teacher*. In those two phrases, it was explained, the first modifier indicates the teacher's country of origin and the second modifier indicates which subject (i.e. language) the person teaches. This is seen more clearly by observing that one can refer to an individual as *an English biology teacher*, but not as **a biology English teacher*. The second phrase is ungrammatical because (1) the word referring to the subject that is taught must immediately precede the noun (so one can say *a tall biology teacher*, but not **a biology tall teacher*) and (2) there can be only one word that refers to the subject of instruction (one can refer to a teacher of biology and chemistry as *a biology **and** chemistry teacher*, but not as **a biology chemistry teacher*).

Although these facts can be, superficially and truthfully, described as word order effects, these word order effects actually arise from the **order** in which the elements are **combined** with one another. So, what we're actually seeing in these three-word phrases is the effect of first combining the subject taught, e.g. *chemistry*, with the noun *teacher*:

[chemistry teacher]

and then combining other modifiers, e.g. *capable*, with that:

[capable [chemistry teacher]]

This is no different from the fact that one has to combine the verb *teach* with its object, before adding an adverb:

[teach chemistry]
[[teach chemistry] capably]

If *capable* or *capably* is positioned closer to the noun or verb than *chemistry*, both phrases are unacceptable:

*chemistry capable teacher
*teach capably chemistry

In addition to the restrictions that are due to the order in which elements may be combined, there can be restrictions on the number of times a given type of element may appear. While nouns may have, in principle, any number of adjectival modifiers:

hungry child
playful hungry child
kind playful hungry child

there are other elements of which there can only be one, such as articles (e.g. *the*), demonstrative adjectives (e.g. *this*), and possessive pronouns (e.g. *my*). Thus, we can have *the child, this child*, or *my child*, but not:

*the my child
*my this child
*the this child

Not only is it the case that only one of these may combine with a noun phrase, but they must (in English) be added last. It is for this reason that we can have:

[my [playful child]]
[the [hungry child]]

but not:

*[playful [my child]]
*[hungry [the child]]

Languages can differ quite a bit from one another in this regard. Japanese has a very productive suffix -no which is added to nearly any element that modifies a noun. Thus, for example, kono is 'this,' watashino is 'my,' and kuufukuno is 'hungry.' These may be combined with kodomo 'child' to give:

(12)   watashi**no** ko**no** kūfuku**no** kodomo
         my   this   hungry   child

Notice that both 'my' and 'this' can simultaneously modify 'child,' in Japanese, unlike English where it is not possible (e.g. *this my child or *my this child). Furthermore, the order of elements is relatively unconstrained, and one can also get:

(13)   ko**no** watashi**no** kūfuku**no** kodomo
         this   my   hungry   child

Order of Combination Ambiguities

Having discussed restrictions on the ways in which elements may combine to form phrases, we must also point out that it is sometimes the case that elements may optionally combine in different orders, and when this happens, the meaning of the phrase can be affected. Take, for example, the phrase watch the man with binoculars. It is obvious that the object of the verb, the man, must combine with it before the prepositional phrase with binoculars:

(14)   [watch the man]
         [[watch the man] with binoculars]

The reverse order is not possible, as we can see here:

(15)   [watch with binoculars]
         *[[watch with binoculars] the man]

However, it is indeed possible to combine with binoculars with the man, before combining with the verb watch:

(15)   [the man with binoculars]
        [watch [the man with binoculars]]

Notice that both of these possible operations results in a phrase having the same surface word order:

(16)   watch the man with the binoculars

However, if *the man* is first combined with the verb, then the phrase *with binoculars* is understood to describe the means by which the man was watched. In the second case, *with binoculars* describes *the man*, meaning that the man has the binoculars. Thus, the ambiguity of the phrase *watch the man with the binoculars* can be attributed to the fact that the elements in the phrase are amenable to two distinct orders of combination.

It is from this sort of "combinatory" ambiguity that many jokes are fashioned, with some comic strips (such as Jeff MacNelly's *Shoe*) relying on this device quite often. In one worthy strip, the character named Marge tells her friend Roz:

I tried on that red dress in the window of Dingle's department store today!

And Roz replies:

Yeah, I heard . . . You know, Marge. They do have dressing rooms.

The joke plays on the fact that *in the window of Dingle's department store* might first combine with *that red dress* (for Marge's intended meaning) or might instead combine with *tried on that red dress* (for Roz's humorous interpretation).

Grammatical Differences between Languages

Having laid out some of the major organizing principles of sentence and phrasal grammar, it is worth applying these here, briefly, to illustrate how they might be used to illustrate differences among languages. Further on in the text, we will have occasion to examine how linguistic differences play out in actual language conflict, but for the moment we shall simply provide some illustrative examples.

In this chapter we have looked at the roles of word order, case marking, and agreement in mediating grammatical relationships among phrasal elements. In doing so, we have noted that these grammatical devices are used to different degrees in different languages, and even in different varieties of the same language. For instance, we saw that English is highly dependent on word order to keep subject and object relations sorted out (even though grammatical case and grammatical agreement play minor roles – when pronouns and the copula verb *be* are involved, respectively). This is in contrast with older varieties of English (Old English and Middle English), wherein case and agreement are more widely utilized and word order is thereby not as critical.

There are some languages, Chinese being a good example, in which case and agreement are entirely absent, and word order is the only organizing principle. Unlike English, Chinese pronouns don't even have nominative or accusative forms. Nor are they even inflected for gender. There are merely first-, second-, and third-person forms (*wo* 'I,' *ni* 'you,' and *ta* 'he, she, or it') plus a plural suffix *-men* (*women* 'we,' *nimen* 'you plural,' and *tamen* 'they'). Accordingly, there is no Chinese ungrammatical equivalent for the English *Them love she* or *Her love they*. The two sentences would be rendered in Chinese as:

(17)   a. Tamen ai ta. 'They love him, her, or it.'
        b. Ta ai tamen. 'He, she, or it loves them.'

It might be unsurprising, given this difference, that Chinese learning English often have difficulty choosing the correct pronouns in a sentence.

With respect to case marking, we saw (above) that Japanese is quite dependent upon it and, by virtue of this, exhibits a much freer word order. Once the language has a device to mark and keep track of subjects and objects (among other grammatical elements), the maintenance of strict word order becomes less important. That said, Japanese word order does play a critical role in keeping track of embedded sentences, and the fact that Japanese sentences have verbs at the end, rather than the middle, makes learning Japanese that much more difficult for English speakers.

To illustrate this, it is first necessary to illustrate sentence embedding in English. This involves the insertion of a perfectly good sentence inside a larger sentence, as in:

(18)   [Marge thought that [Sheila ate lunch]]

This can be done repeatedly:

(19)   [Tony said that [Marge thought that [Sheila ate lunch]]]

Notice that the outer sentence has a subject and a verb, and takes the embedded sentence as its object. We might schematically represent the above sentence as follows:

(20)   [subject verb [subject verb [subject verb object]]]

In Japanese, because the verb of each sentence comes at the end, embedding looks rather different:

(21)   [Tony-ga [Marge-ga [Sheila-ga ronchi-o tabeta]-to omotta]-to itta]
         Tony$_{\text{SUBJECT}}$ Marge$_{\text{SUBJECT}}$ Sheila$_{\text{SUBJECT}}$ lunch$_{\text{OBJECT}}$ ate-that thought-that
         said

Schematically, the embedding looks like this:

(22)   [subject [subject [subject object verb] verb] verb]

In other words, where the English speaker gets a verb to go with each subject
as he goes along, the Japanese speaker hears a subject, and then another
subject, and then a third subject, without ever knowing what the verbs will
be. He then gets the verbs to go with the subject, all at once, but in the reverse
order.

Just as we find languages heavily reliant on word order and case, there are
also many languages which exhibit a high degree of dependence on agreement (i.e. verbal inflection). Bantu languages, including Swahili, are among
these. Swahili verbal inflection includes not only affixes which agree with
the subject (like Spanish and Italian), but also inflections that agree with the
object. A Swahili verb typically has four parts: a morpheme that marks
the subject, a tense morpheme, a morpheme that marks the object, and
a verb root:

(23)   Subject Marker(SM)–Tense(T)–Object Marker(OM)–Verb

Having a verb complex that carries so much information pretty much elim-
inates the need for pronouns, and leads to the possibility of having sentences
which are comprised of a single word. In the following example, *ni-* is a first-
person singular subject marker ('I'), *li-* indicates past tense, *mu-* is a third-
person singular object marker ('him'), and *ona* is the verb 'see':

(24)   Nilimuona.   'I saw him.'
         ni- li-   mu- ona
         I   PAST him see

Obviously, languages like Swahili present a very different picture of what
"sentence grammar" might be about, when contrasted with languages that
rely on the combining of words to form phrases, as English does.

One take-away lesson from our examination of all these different grammatical systems is that grammatical differences between languages can present
obstacles no less formidable than lexical and phonological differences, when
attempting to bridge the divide between languages. To the extent that the
grammar of one language is vastly different from another, it will be difficult
for speakers of the first to master the second (and vice versa). This, unsurprisingly, can make it more difficult to implement solutions to linguistic conflicts
than would be the case if they were less different. We might imagine, for
example, that asking French speakers to accommodate themselves to using

English, or English speakers to using French, is (from a purely practical standpoint) less overwhelming than asking South African Zulu speakers to use English or asking English speakers to use Chinese. French and English have similar grammars (relatively), share a vast lexicon, and have an overlapping history.

Of course, speaker attitudes to other languages (such as in the case of French and English speakers in Canada) can lead to obstacles in mutual accommodation that are not connected with grammar, lexicon, and phonology. In the following chapters, we will explore the separate issue of how speakers subjectively perceive their own language and their own dialect, in contrast with others. We will examine the objective and subjective bases upon which speakers decide whether two linguistic systems are different languages or different varieties of the same language.

4   Language Change and Variation: Languages versus Dialects

As language can change (in quite similar ways) across time and space, this chapter addresses both phenomena together. We will first examine variation through time, also called "language change." We will then observe ways in which language differs across space, inclusive of physical space, social space, ethnic and cultural space, and gender space. This study is, generally, referred to as the study of "language variation."

Language Change: Variation through Time

While most people imagine the language they speak to be fixed, something that is relatively stable in their lives, it is actually the case that language is changing, incrementally, all the time, with some domains changing more rapidly than others.

The most rapid and noticeable kind of language change is lexical, and involves both the coinage of new words as well as shifts in meaning among existing ones. It doesn't take much searching to find words that have recently come into existence, usually on the back of new technologies, contact with other cultures, and new fashions. For instance, in each generation, changing technology (among other things) brings new words into existence. Consider the following lists of technology-related words coming into use since the 1940s:

> 1940s: *ack-ack* (anti-aircraft artillery), *atom bomb, bazooka*
> 1950s: *aerospace, alphanumeric, digitize, meter maid*
> 1960s: *area code, ASCII, biohazard, microwave oven*
> 1970s: *biofeedback, diskette, electronic mail*
> 1980s: *boom box, caller ID, channel surf, voice mail*
> 1990s: *digerati, netnanny, World Wide Web*
> 2000s: *blog, cybersquatting, defriend, emoticon, tweet, wi-fi*

Examining this small sample of technical terms, it is easy to see how quickly changes in our environment are reflected in our vocabulary, as regards both the introduction of new words and the abandonment of those that have outlived their use. In 1940, no one could have told you what diskette might refer to (personal computers then being thirty years down the road), and by 2000 many

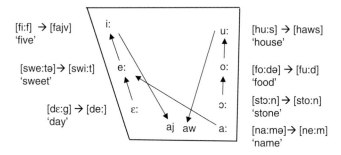

Figure 4.1 Trajectory of vowel shifts in fourteenth–sixteenth-century English

would no longer know what it means (with these memory devices long having been replaced with other forms of digital storage).

It is also the case that the meanings of existing (and especially vernacular) words can change over time, such that their present-day use may no longer be understood by those who are somewhat older. Take, for example, the word *wicked*, which is a pejorative adjective and a synonym for *sinful* in its older usage. Today, the word's meaning has been inverted, such that it has come to mean *fantastic* or *great*. In even more recent usage, it has shifted from being a positive adjective to also being used as a positive adverbial intensifier, such that *wicked cool* means really cool.

Meaning shifts such as this have been going on for a long time, for as long as anyone has been able to track them. The word *gyrle* ('girl') is borrowed into Early Middle English (around 1300 CE) from Low German, with the meaning 'a small child.' The plural *gyrles* meant 'children,' and a young male child was referred to as a *knave gyrle* and a young female as a *gay girl*. By the end of the century, the meaning of *gyrle* had narrowed to refer only to females.[1]

Other aspects of language, sound and grammar in particular, change and shift at a relatively slower pace than does the lexicon. Sound change, when it does occur, takes place over the course of centuries rather than decades. Additionally, unlike lexical changes which can affect single words, sound change is regular and system-wide. That is to say, sound changes affect all and any words that contain the changed sounds.

The most well-known, and important, sound change in the history of English is called the Great Vowel Shift. This began sometime in the mid fourteenth century, continued until the end of the seventeenth century, and involved to a greater or lesser extent every vowel sound in the language.

As the chart in Figure 4.1 shows, the tongue height normally used to pronounce a given vowel shifted upwards, and the vowels having the highest

[1] Liberman 2008: 97.

tongue height already (being unable to raise at all) shifted into the lowest possible position.

Let us examine a few examples to see how this worked. The word *name* was pronounced in Middle English as a two-syllable word in which the first vowel was the same as the Modern English word *cod*: [nɑːmə]. After the vowel shift, it was pronounced as one syllable, using a higher vowel [eɪ] as found in *play*: [neɪm]. The word *eke* (preserved in the modern phrase *to eke out a living*) was pronounced in Middle English as a two-syllable word whose first vowel was the same as the Modern English *aid*: [ekə]. After the shift, it became a one-syllable word using the high vowel [iː]: [iːk]. The Middle English two-syllable word *rite* was pronounced using the same high vowel as Modern English *eat*: [riːtə]. After the shift, it was a one-syllable word with the low vowel [aj]: [rajt].

The first thing one notes is that the rate of phonological change is a fraction of that of lexical change. Where lexical changes are recorded over decades, sound changes take centuries to complete. Notice, as well, that spelling tends not to change in conjunction with sound changes. Thus, the spelling of the words we examined still reflects, over 600 years on, the pronunciations of Middle, rather than Modern, English. The "silent e" of Modern English is nothing less than a letter that was fully pronounced six centuries ago, but which has been retained despite the fact that we no longer use it.

Grammatical change tends to be more like phonological change, with respect to its rapidity (or lack thereof). However, when one looks over a long enough stretch of time, the changes one observes are rather impressive. Take, for instance, the way in which Modern English forms yes–no questions. If your answer to a question was:

Yes, I am hungry.

... the question you were asked might have been:

Are you hungry?

Forming this question involves placing the verb in front of the subject. Such is the case with sentences containing any form of the verb *be*, the perfective verb *have*, and modals such as *would*, as the following examples show:

Is he here?
Have they left yet?
Would you like some?

These (*be*, *have*, and modals) fall into a category called auxiliary verbs, which have a special status in English with respect to several kinds of grammatical behavior. When a sentence does not contain an auxiliary verb, then forming a yes–no question is slightly different. Instead of placing the verb in front of the subject, the verb *do* is placed there. We see this in the following question–answer pairs:

Does she write well?	Yes, she writes well.
Did they leave already?	Yes, they left already.

Notice that the *do*-verb carries the tense information (e.g. present, past).

It was not always this way. In Shakespeare's time, there was no separate category of auxiliary verbs. All verbs performed the same way that Modern English auxiliary verbs do now. On account of this, in Early Modern English, the previous two question–answer pairs would have looked more like this:

Writes she well?	Yes, she writes well.
Left they already?	Yes, they left already.

What we can take away from these (lexical, phonological, and grammatical) changes is that language changes, whether we notice it or not and whether we approve of it or not.

Attitudes toward Language Change: Lexical Change

It is interesting to examine, in this context, what people think about language change. Mostly, they don't – think about it, that is. This is to say, people are largely unaware of changes – especially those that take place over a long stretch of time. By the time that most phonological and grammatical changes have occurred, those who would notice are long gone and buried. Lexical changes, though, are rather more rapid, as we have seen. With respect to these, people do often notice, and they do have attitudes about them.

To the extent that anyone takes note of language change, the general consensus (regardless of what century it is) is that "language is going to hell." A Google search of "decline of the English language" yields 48 million hits. This is telling, and, as a brief examination of the sites reveals, the general consensus is that change is bad, innovations are terrible, and the only thing that ever happens to language is that it degrades, declines, and is corrupted. The interesting thing about this attitude is that it has been with us for as long as language has been changing. An insightful webpage, compiled by Princeton linguist Margaret Browning (www.princeton.edu/~browning/decl ine.html), cites six memorable quotes about the decline of the English language from Harvey Daniels' 1983 book[2] and, as she points out, only three of them are less than 100 years old. An example of these, reproduced here, is typical:

---

[2] Daniels 1983.

Unless the present progress of change [is] arrested ... there can be no doubt that, in another century, the dialect of the Americans will become utterly unintelligible to an Englishman ... (Captain Thomas Hamilton, 1833)

Apparently, English has been in decline for as long as it's been spoken (but hasn't hit bottom quite yet).

To the extent that generational differences in language use make themselves known, they often function to anchor speakers' generational identity. Younger speakers innovate, with new words, spellings, grammar, and idiomatic expressions, while older speakers resist such innovation. With the rise of social media and instant messaging, some of this change has become more obvious if not more prolific. Examples of current innovations (some from a 2009 honors thesis by Hannah Peace) are illustrative:[3]

Spellings/abbreviations

ur	(you're)
thx	(thanks)
jk/jaykay	(joking)
rofl/roffle	(rolling on the floor laughing)

New words

noob	(from newbie, someone inexperienced)
noobtard	(a stupid newbie)
pwn	(pronounced [pown], from own, to defeat)
leet	(from elite, really good at something)

The pace of lexical innovation is such that each generation gets to have its own lexicon and expressions, with which they can identify and with which they can express solidarity with others of their own generation. Young people in the 1920s and 1930s used slang words such as *swell* and *keen* to describe things they liked. By the 1940s and 1950s, these were supplanted by *hip* and *cool*. In the 1970s and 1980s, the word *wicked* was often used to describe something great, and in the 1990s it would be *dope*. In the last decade, people would describe something as *hella good* (from *hell of a*, meaning 'very'). Some words, such as *cool*, will fall out of fashion for a generation and then come back (like fluctuating hemlines), while others, such as *swell*, seem to disappear forever.

Not only do people tend to use words appropriate to their own generation, but they are expected to do so. If you're under 30, people would find it odd were you to describe a movie that you enjoyed as being *swell*, but if your 80-year-old grandfather used the word, they likely would not. At the same time, you wouldn't expect your grandparents to describe the novel that they just finished as *dope*. It wouldn't sound right. It would appear as though they were trying to

---

[3] Peace 2009.

be something they're not (i.e. very young) or attempting to mock you. In this way, language varieties generated through language change become a tool for expressing and maintaining one's identity.

Language Change: Phonological and Syntactic

What about changes (phonological and syntactic, in particular) that take place over a much longer time? While we don't typically perceive such changes in our own lifetime, they do tend to pile up over the course of several centuries, until the language has changed beyond recognition. Take, for instance, a text that has been around for millennia, *The Lord's Prayer.* The first few lines of it in Modern English are as follows:

> Our Father in heaven, hallowed be your name.
> Your kingdom come, your will be done, on earth, as it is in heaven.

Some 400–500 years ago, in Shakespeare's time, the same lines (in sixteenth-century Early Modern English) read:

> O oure father which arte in heaven, hallowed be thy name.
> Let thy kyngdom come. Thy wyll be fulfilled, as well in erth, as it ys in heven.

It is more than noticeably different from the Modern English, but still recognizable. Two centuries earlier than this, during the time of Chaucer, the fourteenth-century Middle English prayer began:

> Oure fadir that art in heuenes, halewid be thi name.
> Thi kyngdoom come to, be thi wile don in erthe es in heuene.

While 700-year-old English still has a strong resemblance to English, even if the grammar, spellings, and words are unfamiliar, the same text from the eleventh-century (Old English) is utterly unrecognizable.

> Fæder ure þu þe eart on heofonum; Si þin nama gehalgod
> to becume þin rice gewurþe ðin willa on eorðan swa swa on heofonum.

It is manifestly clear from the changes undergone by this brief passage over the course of 1,000 years, that the accumulation of several centuries of change results not in a language "gone to hell" but in a different language.

While English changed greatly over the course of centuries, the language maintained its integrity in that it continued to be called English. Thus, the tenth-century epic poem *Beowulf,* Chaucer's fourteenth-century *Canterbury Tales,* and Shakespeare's sixteenth-century plays are all deemed to be important works of English literature. The same cannot be said of Latin, following the decline and breakup of the Roman Empire.

At the height of the Roman Empire, (Classical) Latin was the language of commerce, law, education, and government. The beginning of *The Lord's Prayer*, discussed above, is as follows:

Latin

Pater	noster	qui	es	in	caelis	sanctificetur	Nomen	Tuum
father	our	who	is	in	heaven	sanctified	name	your
adveniat	Regnum	Tuum	fiat	voluntas	Tua	sicut	in	caelo	in	terra.
come	kingdom	your	done	will	your	as	in	heaven	in	earth

This text approximates the Latin language as it was used between 100 BCE through the second century CE. As we have seen, language changes. In the case of Latin, there were many common vernaculars in use across the territories of the Empire, stretching at its greatest extent from the Iberian Peninsula in the west all the way to past Anatolia (Turkey) in the east. The vernaculars (called Vulgar Latin) were used by illiterate commoners, soldiers, and slaves. In each region, the vernacular varieties of Latin changed, and they did so independently of one another. By the tenth century, they were all distinct enough from Latin so as not to be recognizably Latin any longer (in the same way that Old English is so different from Modern English). They were also distinct enough from each other that they were perceived to be autonomous languages. These Romance languages, as they are called, developed into a family of related, but separate, languages – the most widely spoken of these being Spanish, French, Portuguese, Italian, and Romanian. The beginning of *The Lord's Prayer* is shown here below for each of them:

Spanish
Padre nuestro que estás en los cielos, santificado sea tu nombre.
Venga tu reino. Hágase tu voluntad, así en la tierra como en el cielo.

French
Notre Père, qui es aux cieux, Que ton nom soit sanctifié,
Que ton règne vienne, Que ta volonté soit faite sur la terre comme au ciel.

Portuguese
Pai nosso que estás nos céus, santificado seja o teu nome;
venha o teu reino, seja feita a tua vontade, assim na terra como no céu;

Italian
Padre nostro che sei nei cieli, sia santificato il tuo Nome,
venga il tuo Regno, sia fatta la tua Volontà come in cielo così in terra.

Romanian
Tatăl nostru Care ești în ceruri, Sfințească-se numele Tău.
Vie împărăția Ta, Fie voia Ta, precum în cer așa și pe Pământ.

Comparing them to each other, it is easy to see that they are related, as well as that they are descended from Latin.

Languages and Dialects: Variation through Space and among Communities

The story of the Romance languages and their development from regional varieties of Latin into full-fledged languages brings us to a discussion of dialects (i.e. regional varieties), what regional variation consists of, how these varieties serve the formation of identity, and how they can become (or not become) separate languages. In the same way that language changes along several trajectories (phonological, lexical, and grammatical), so too do regional varieties of a language vary (typically as a result of independent changes they have undergone). Some of our discussion in the previous chapters has high-lighted such differences.

In Chapter 1, we noted that regional linguistic varieties can exhibit distinct ways of pronouncing the same words. In Southern American English (but not in other American dialects), the words *pin* and *pen* are pronounced the same – such that speakers often refer to the first as a *stick pin* and the second as an *ink pen* in order to disambiguate between them. In New York and New Jersey, people with a strong regional accent will often pronounce the words *sauce* and *source* as homophones – something you are unlikely to hear anywhere else. And in the Midwest, speakers do not distinguish between the words *caught* and *cot*. Each of these homophonic pairings is the result of a general pattern of vowel pronunciation that is particular to that region and not exhibited elsewhere.

Regionally particular patterns of pronunciation are not limited to vowels. As we saw in Chapter 1, regional differences can extend to stress patterns. While Mainstream American English (MAE) speakers pronounce *police* and *insurance* with stress on the second syllable (e.g. po-**LICE** and in-**SU**-rance), Southern American English (SAE) speakers pronounce the same words with stress on the first syllable (e.g. **PO**-lice and **IN**-su-rance). All these differences (and more) play a role in identifying a speaker's dialect.

In the matter of lexical differences, regional variety also plays a prominent role. Sometimes the lexical differences are minor and somewhat quaint, and rarely result in confusion. Such is the case, as we noted in Chapter 2, with regard to the Lampyridae beetle, which is called a firefly in the western states, and a lightning bug in the Appalachian region and the lower Midwest. At other times, lexical differences between dialects can be rather confusing, or simply incomprehensible. British English uses the term *lorry* for what Americans call a *truck* – that is, a motorized goods-carrying vehicle that travels on roadways. The word *truck*, in turn, is used by the British to refer to the goods-carrying containers pulled by a railway engine along a track – that which Americans call a *car*, or more specifically a *box car*. If the thing pulled by the railway engine carries passengers, then the British call it a *carriage* and the Americans refer to it as a *passenger car*. Of course, Americans also use the word *car* to refer to a vehicle that one drives down the highway, which the British also use, except that the former fuel theirs with *gas* and the latter fill up with *petrol*.

Grammatical differences between dialects are also worthy of mention. In Early Modern English, as one might recall from looking at *The Lord's Prayer* excerpt above, the second-person singular pronoun was *thou* (which had the possessive form *thy*). The second person plural was *you*. Gradually, *thou* came to be used as a more intimate expression of second person, while the use of *you* came to include both singular and plural. This created a situation in which *you* is ambiguous (e.g. I don't know whether the *you* in *Would you like to come with us?* refers to one person or a group). Speakers of different regional dialects have solved this problem by creating a plural form of *you*. But they go about it in different ways. Speakers from Ohio use the pronoun *yuns* (derived from *you ones* and then from *you'uns*). Speakers from the Northeast will use *youse* or *youse guys*, and speakers from the South will say *y'all* (derived from *you all*). Each form is particular to a region, and marks the speaker that uses it as coming from, or having an affinity with, that region.

Alongside, and just as important as, regional varieties (dialects) are varieties used by ethnic groups. African Americans, Hispanics living in the US, American Jews, and many others have developed their own distinct patterns of pronunciation, lexicons, and grammar. These ethnic varieties, as we will see, are just as important for group identity and cohesion as are regional varieties.

Attitudes toward Language Variation

Having established that language varies regionally in multiple ways, we might ask:

- What do people think of these dialects, and why?
- Why do dialects endure, in American English for example, in spite of people's regular exposure to the mainstream (or standard) variety?
- How does one particular variety get to be the "standard" (i.e. the one everyone is expected to use)?
- When and how does it come to be that dialects can be considered different languages?

People who use their regional or ethnic variety in a salient fashion (and not everyone does) are self-identifying with their own region or ethnic group. Not every Southerner says *Bye, y'all* in place of *Good-bye*, and even those who use the expression don't say it on every occasion where *Good-bye* might be used. But those who do use Southern American English, when they use it, are signaling their membership in a group that is identifiable through its dialect expressions and features. And one need not have been born in a region or into an ethnic group in order to identify and use the associated dialect. An immigrant to a Southern state might use dialect features as a means of expressing affinity for the culture and people of their adopted home – and it needs to be said that some are better at doing this than others. Of course, one takes a risk in doing so, since using an adopted dialect badly or inappropriately is likely to earn the user a healthy amount of derision.

What do people think of the dialects used by other regional and ethnic groups? The answer to this depends almost entirely on what they think of the people associated with the dialect, rather than with any specific and measurable property of the dialect itself. A clear example of this can be found in a phonological phenomenon called "r"-lessness, which occurs in many English dialects. "R"-lessness involves not pronouncing the sound [r] when it appears at the end of a syllable. Some examples of "r"-less pronunciation include: a New Jersey speaker pronouncing *source* in a manner that sounds like *sauce*; a Boston speaker's production of the classic "r"-less sentence *He pahked the cah in Hahvahd Yahd*; and a Charleston, South Carolina, resident leaving the [r] sound out of the name of her home town.[4] It is also the case that Standard British English speech abounds in "r"-less pronunciations. While "r"-less pronunciations in Boston and New York were once indicators of higher status, they are now mostly associated with lower, working-class speech. In Charleston and England, however, "r"-less speech is esteemed. Clearly, there is nothing inherently good or bad about leaving the [r] sounds out of words. Rather, it is simply a matter of what one thinks of those who do it.

People in different regions of the United States have definite opinions regarding the dialect that they themselves speak as well as the varieties spoken in other regions. One researcher who has published a good deal on this matter is Dennis Preston.[5] In his interviews and surveys of American English speakers, he found that residents of Michigan considered their own variety of American English to be the most "correct" and considered English spoken in their own state plus that of Illinois, Minnesota, Colorado, and Washington to be the most "pleasant". Correspondingly, they assessed the speech patterns of the South to be the least "correct" and least "pleasant", with Alabama rated as the worst of the worst in both categories. Alabamans'

---

[4] Some dialects of English have the reverse of this, where [r] sounds are inserted at the ends of syllables in which they would not normally occur. The pronunciation of *Washington* as if it were spelled *Warshington* and *idea* as if it were spelled *idear* are examples of this.
[5] Preston 1989.

responses to the survey were quite different. On the one hand they gave their own speech (along with that of Louisiana and Texas) the lowest marks for "correctness" (and gave Maryland residents the highest ratings in this). However, they ranked their own speech (along with that of Georgia, Virginia, and the Carolinas) as most "pleasant", with New Jersey and New York in the "least pleasant" categories. All this shows that our evaluation of whose speech we consider correct or proper and of whose speech we like or dislike are separable.

It might be thought that we like the speech of ethnic and regional groups of people who we like, and the converse. But how do we determine whose language variety is "correct"? As our discussion of "r"-lessness implies, it has less to do with any particular property of the variety at hand, and everything to do with who is using it. Thus, African American English or Tejano English (a dialect spoken by Mexican Americans in southern Texas) is unlikely to be esteemed as a standard variety for reasons having to do with the lack of economic and political power held by its speakers.

A very revealing example of the political and social power behind standardization is to be found in the history of Japan. From the Nara period in the eighth century until the beginning of the seventeenth century, the imperial capital of Japan was in the western part of the **main island, Honshu** (i.e. the Kansai region) – first in Nara and then in Kyoto (which are less than 30 miles from each other). During this 900-year period, western Japan was the primary seat of political and economic power, and unsurprisingly the regional dialect Kansai was the standard/mainstream dialect of Japanese. This situation changed rather quickly and dramatically in the year 1600, when the forces of the Tokugawa clan won a decisive battle (Battle of Sekigahara) to end a civil war and consolidate their rule over the whole of Japan. In 1603, the Tokugawas set up a capital at Edo in eastern Japan (which is the modern city of Tokyo). From that point onward, the Kantoo (eastern Japanese) dialect gained stature and eventually became the Standard Japanese that all Japanese speak today, while the Kansai (western Japanese) dialect was relegated to a low-status variety. Nothing about the language and its varieties changed here, only the locus of political power and social prestige. It would be fair to say that, had the Confederacy won the American Civil War, Southern American English might very well be a dialect with much higher prestige than it currently has.

From Dialect Differences to Independent Languages

One last question remains to be considered, and that is how it is that some regional varieties (dialects) become independent languages, while others don't. Related to this, we might also ask, how do we know whether two related varieties (descended from a common ancestor) are two distinct languages (e.g. French and Spanish) or are simply different dialects of the same language (e.g. American and British English)?

First, in our discussion of language change, we noted that English underwent enormous changes over the 1,000 years beginning in the tenth century, developing as it went a fair number of English dialects. Yet, English did not fragment into a family of languages, as did Latin. Latin, as we saw, evolved into regional varieties (of Vulgar Latin) and then into regional languages (e.g. Spanish, Portuguese, French, etc.). However, the regional varieties did not all develop into full-fledged languages. There are many varieties of Romance (i.e. Latin-based languages) which do not have full recognition as languages. These include the Galician dialect of northwestern Spain, Catalan and Occitan (spoken in northeastern Spain and southern France, respectively), Venetian and Corsican varieties of Italian, and lesser-known dialects of Romanian (among many others).

So, why is (Castilian) Spanish an official and autonomous language, while Venetian is not? It was Max Weinreich, a sociolinguist and scholar of Yiddish, who famously remarked in 1945,

אַ שפּראַך איז אַ דיאַלעקט מיט אַן אַרמיי און פֿלאָט
a shprakh iz a dialekt mit an armey un flot
'A language is a dialect with an army and navy.'[6]

While this statement might not be strictly true in every instance, it is a true enough generalization that it is worth noting and remembering. It was the Kingdom of Castile (among all the rest) that led the reconquest of Iberia from the Moors, and established its own dialect as the standard for Spanish. It was the fact that the throne of France was consolidated in the northern part of the country, rather than the south, that guaranteed that Occitan and other southern varieties would not be privileged.

So, are there objective measures to determine whether one is dealing with separate languages or with distinct dialects? Linguists often base their assessment of whether two varieties are different languages or different dialects of the same language upon "mutual intelligibility." For example, the fact that speakers of American English and British English can converse with each other, each using their own variety, and can mostly understand each other, would lead us to say that British and American English are dialects of the same language; they are mutually intelligible. Similarly, because a speaker of French and a speaker of Romanian cannot converse with each other, each using their own variety (without one or both of them having studied the other's language), leads us to say that French and

---

[6] Weinreich 1945.

Romanian are separate languages (even though they once were, over 1,000 years ago, dialects of Latin).

While this might appear to be a fairly simple, straightforward, and reliable way to tell pairs of languages and pairs of dialects apart, it isn't. There are cases in which speakers of "A" can understand speakers of "B," but not the reverse. This is famously known about the relationship between Portuguese and Spanish; speakers of Portuguese typically can understand Spanish without having studied it, but speakers of Spanish cannot understand Portuguese. We nevertheless consider Spanish and Portuguese to be distinct languages.

Political and social factors can contribute to a determination of "language" versus "dialect" status in a way that obscures objective linguistic measures. For instance, before the 1992 breakup of Yugoslavia into what are now seven independent states (Bosnia and Herzegovina, Croatia, Kosovo, Macedonia, Montenegro, Serbia, and Slovenia), Serbo-Croatian was one of its three official languages (for the republics of Bosnia and Herzegovina, Croatia, Montenegro and Serbia). After the dissolution and independence of Bosnia, Serbia, and Croatia, the official languages of each of these new states were Bosnian, Serbian, and Croatian, respectively.[7] These "new" national languages are mutually intelligible, more so even than the standard dialects of English, and differ primarily in that Serbian is typically written using a Cyrillic alphabet (a writing system most recognizable from Russian use of it, but also used for other Slavic languages such as Bulgarian and Ukrainian), Croatian is written using a Latin script, and Bosnian uses both. Nevertheless, nationalism trumped linguistics during the 1995 negotiations to end the war in Bosnia. During these negotiations, the Serbian, Croatian, and Bosnian negotiators each insisted on having the choice of simultaneous translation into their own "languages": Serbian, Croatian, or Bosnian. However, "while there were three separate channels from which to select, there was only one translator [and one identical feed] for all three." The farcical fact that the identical language was heard by all three groups was less important to them than the principle of being able to each call what they were hearing by a different language name.[8]

Finally, just as political and social factors can cause people to refer to mutually intelligible "dialects" as distinct languages, the reverse of this can also occur. That is, languages that are quite distinct and not mutually intelligible can sometimes be considered "dialects" of a hegemonic language. One notable historical case of this is that of Latin. The decline of the (Western)

---

[7] In fact, a fourth language arose after Montenegro broke with Serbia and declared Montenegrin its official language in the constitution adopted in 2007.
[8] Macdonald 2013.

Roman Empire in the fifth and sixth centuries created a situation in which the local varieties of Latin began to diverge from one another, and while speakers of these local varieties were decreasingly able to communicate with each other, the language they spoke was still considered Latin. It wasn't until some 400–500 years later that these mutually unintelligible "dialects of Latin" began to be officially considered new "languages," and the linguistic remnants of the Roman Empire finally dissolved into the Romance family of languages (i.e. Spanish, Portuguese, French, Romanian, Catalan, Occitan, etc.).

Had the Roman Empire not come apart, there is a chance that the local varieties of Latin would have continued to be called Latin, that there would have continued to be an imperial standard, and that the local varieties would simply have remained stigmatized regional "dialects," even though they were so distinct from each other. In this case, Latin would have developed into what might be called a macrolanguage, which is a set of related languages that share a common identity even though they are not mutually intelligible.

The rise of macrolanguages is usually dependent upon some sort of political or social hegemony that ties the languages together under a higher authority. Modern Arabic and what we commonly refer to as Chinese are two such macrolanguages, the first being held together by the textual authority of the Quran and the second by the territorial and political hegemony of the People's Republic of China.

In the case of Arabic, even though many modern dialects of Arabic (Moroccan, Egyptian, Bedouin, etc.) are not mutually intelligible, Modern Standard Arabic is still the prevailing standard and functions as the language of education, law, government, and media through most of the Arabic-speaking world. The reason for this is primarily the centrality of the Muslim scriptures (i.e. the Quran) upon which Modern Standard Arabic is based. Similarly, Chinese has maintained its unity, despite having over a billion speakers and some nine separate language **groups** (each with its millions of speakers). In the case of China, both imperial hegemony and the Chinese writing system played a role (the latter which we will examine more closely in Chapter 8).

Glossary for Part I

accusative case: Grammatical case assigned to a noun or noun phrase, signaling that it is the object of a verb or the object of a preposition. E.g. *saw him*, *with her*.

acoustic: Properties of (speech) sounds that depict the characteristics of the sound itself.

acronym: A word formed out of the initial letters of a multiword phrase, and pronounced as it is spelled. E.g. LASER from Light Amplification by Stimulated Emission of Radiation.

affix: A morpheme that attaches to a word, changing its meaning, part of speech, or function. Prefixes, suffixes, and infixes are all affixes. E.g. *un-* meaning "not" attaches to adjectives.

allomorph: A set of forms, whose pronunciation differs depending on context, which stand for the same morpheme. E.g. [d], [t], and [əd] are allomorphs of the past tense suffix *-ed*.

allophone: A realization of a particular phoneme. A phoneme in a particular language may have one or more distinctly pronounced variants, and each of these is considered to be an allophone of the phoneme in question.

alveolar: Sound produced by bringing the tip of the tongue close to or into contact with the alveolar ridge (gum ridge behind the upper teeth).

articulatory: Properties of (speech) sounds that depict the manner in which they are produced.

assimilation: The process by which a speech sound comes to assimilate to (be more like) an adjacent sound.

bilabial: A sound produced by bringing the upper and lower lips into contact, or proximity.

blending: The process of creating a word by taking pieces (clippings) of two or more other words and attaching them together. E.g. *smog* from **smoke** and *fog*.

borrowing: The adoption of a word into a language from a foreign source. E.g. the English word *spaghetti* from Italian.

bound morpheme: A morpheme that cannot appear independently as a word. Affixes are all bound morphemes.

clipping: The process of creating a word by cutting off part of it and using what is left to stand for the whole. E.g. *stats* from **statistics**.

compounding: The process of creating a word by joining together two, or more, independent words. E.g. *pickpocket* from *pick* and *pocket*.

content morpheme: A morpheme that carries meaning or part of speech information. Some affixes and some free morphemes are content morphemes.

deletion: The process by which a speech sound is dropped from the pronunciation of a word.

free morpheme: A morpheme that can appear independently as a word.

fricative: A speech sound that involves the audible friction made by forcing air through a narrow opening.

gender agreement: The marking of grammatical gender, often with affixes. In this way, the connection between the noun and the word that it is connected with is reinforced.

genericization: The process of creating a word through the use of a brand name to refer to the generic name for the item. E.g. *band-aid* to refer to adhesive bandages generally.

genitive case: Grammatical case assigned to a noun or noun phrase that (in English) appears before another noun, indicating, among other things, possession (as in *the carpenter's hammer*) or agentivity (as in *John's prediction*).

grammatical agreement: Any morphological means whereby one element in a phrase or sentence is marked with some property of another element, in order to establish a connection between them. Includes both gender and person agreement.

grammatical case: A morphological marker (usually on a noun or noun phrase) which signals the role of the element in the phrase. E.g. sentential subjects are usually marked with nominative case.

grammatical gender:	A system of dividing nouns into classes. The most common categories are masculine, feminine, and (sometimes) neuter.
grammatical morpheme:	A morpheme that functions as a grammatical marker, and does not carry meaning. E.g. the suffix *-ing* and the infinitival marker *to*.
grammatical role:	The role that a particular phrase (usually a noun phrase) plays in a sentence. The grammatical roles most frequently used in sentences are subject, object, and indirect object.
idioms:	Phrases that have idiosyncratic meanings, whereby their meanings are not directly calculable from the words that they contain (e.g. *spill the beans* taken to mean "tell a secret"). These phrases are rather rigid in their form, and rarely allow their components to be changed (e.g. neither *spill ten beans* nor *spill the peas* can mean "tell a secret").
initialism:	A word formed out of the initial letters of a multiword phrase, and pronounced by reciting the names of its letters. E.g. USA [yu-ɛs-ey] from United States of America.
insertion:	The process by which a speech sound is added to the pronunciation of a word.
morpheme:	A **phonological** form that is a minimal unit of meaning or function (i.e. cannot be broken into constituent parts). E.g. *un-*, *red*, *-ing*, and *boy* are all morphemes in English.
nominative case:	Grammatical case assigned to a noun or noun phrase, signaling that it is the subject of a sentence. E.g. *he swam*, *we left*.
object:	The grammatical role carried by, among other things, the complement of a verb. E.g. in the sentence *I saw Jim earlier*, *Jim* is the object of the verb.
person:	The grammatical property that tracks the role that a participant has in discourse. First person (e.g. *I*, *we*) denotes the speaker. Second person (e.g. *you*) denotes the addressee.
person agreement:	The marking of person, often with affixes. In this way, the connection between the noun and the word that it is connected with is reinforced.
phoneme:	A basic unit of sound in a given language, which is psychologically distinct from other sounds in that

	language. A given phoneme may have distinct realizations (i.e. allophones), each with its own distribution.
phonetics:	The study of speech sounds through an examination of their acoustic and articulatory properties.
phonology:	The study of speech sounds through an examination of how they are organized in the mind of the speaker.
prefix:	An affix which is attached to the beginning of a word.
sentence embedding:	The inclusion of a sentence within another sentence. Embedded sentences may be, among other things, the objects of a verb (e.g. *he said that [she left]*), or adverbial clauses (e.g. *They left, so that [she could sleep]*).
subject:	The grammatical role carried by the most prominent noun in a sentence (e.g. *John* in *John fainted*). Every sentence has a subject, and subjects need not be referential (e.g. *it* in *It might be hard to leave*).
suffix:	An affix which is attached to the end of a word.
verbal conjugation:	The morphological marking on verbs of certain properties of the verb's grammatical dependents (e.g. its subject, object, etc.). By marking the person, gender, number, or animacy of a sentence subject, for example, it is possible to single out that noun phrase, often without recourse to word order.
vowel elision:	The compression of an unstressed vowel to the point where it is not perceived as a vowel sound, but is instead eclipsed by its surrounding consonants. Elided vowels can still be present to the extent that they and their surrounding consonants are perceived as a syllable.
word order:	The linear positioning of words in a phrase or sentence, relative to one another. This factor is most important in languages that don't mark grammatical roles in any other way.
word stress:	The prominence given to one or more syllables in a word.

Further Reading and Resources for Part I

Dubinsky, Stanley, and Christopher Holcomb. 2011. *Understanding language through humor*. Cambridge University Press.

Language Files, 11th edn. 2011. The Ohio State University.

Liberman, Anatoly. 2008. *An analytic dictionary of English etymology*. Minneapolis: University of Minnesota Press.

Radford, Andrew, et al. 2009. *Linguistics: An introduction*. Cambridge University Press.

Preston, Dennis. 1989. *Perceptual dialectology*. Dordrecht: Foris.

Sapir, Edward. 1949. The psychological reality of phonemes. In David. G. Mandelbaum (ed.), *Selected writings of Edward Sapir in language, culture and personality*, 46–60. Berkeley: University of California Press (originally published in French as "La réalité psychologique des phonèmes," *Journal de Psychologie Normale et Pathologique* 30 (1933): 247–265).

Trudgill, Peter. 2016. *Dialect matters: Respecting vernacular language*. Cambridge University Press.

Williams, Joseph M. 1975. *Origins of the English language: A social and linguistic history*. New York: Free Press.

Wolfram, Walt, and Natalie Schilling. 2015. *American English: Dialects and variation*, 3rd edn. Malden, MA, and Oxford: Wiley-Blackwell.

Part II

Language in the World

5   Language and Personal Identity: Personal Names in the World

Language is frequently cited as the principal characteristic distinguishing humans from other animals: language identifies people as members of the species *homo sapiens sapiens*. Additionally, it distinguishes members of the species from one another and is arguably one of the key factors in the development of one's identity – both personal identity and social (i.e. group membership) identity. As was briefly illustrated in the previous three chapters in the discussion of language sounds, words, and grammar, we often evaluate and categorize others on the basis of the language or dialect that they speak and the manner in which they speak it.

The Role of Language in Personal and Social Identity Formation

Language figures prominently in social-psychological theories of personality development (e.g. Erikson, Vygotsky), as language is one of the principal means by which individuals undertake the social interactions hypothesized to be necessary for identity formation. Erik Erikson refers to identity as "a subjective sense of an invigorating sameness and continuity,"[1] which develops through eight psychosocial stages, each of which is accompanied by an identity crisis (by which he means a conflict to be resolved). Regarding the role of language in identity formation, Erikson notes that "linguistically, as well as psychologically, identity and identification have common roots."[2] Lev Vygotsky, the Russian developmental psychologist, posited a close relationship between language and identity formation, most famously in his work *Thought and Language*, hypothesizing that personal identity develops through social interaction and arguing that language is a crucial tool in social interaction and means of persuading others about who we are and what we value. Sapir considered language not only to be an important personality trait but also to be "the most potent single known factor for the growth of individuality":[3]

---

[1] Erikson 1968: 19; emphasis in original.   [2] Erikson 1968: 158.   [3] Sapir 1927.

The fundamental quality of one's voice, the phonetic patterns of speech, the speed and relative smoothness of articulation, the length and build of the sentences, the character and range of the vocabulary, the stylistic consistency of the words used, the readiness with which words respond to the requirements of the social environment, in particular the suitability of one's language to the language habits of the person addressed – all these are so many complex indicators of the personality.[4]

But at the same time, in addition to its role as a formative of individual identity, Sapir recognized the role of language in determining social identity – i.e. in establishing and maintaining the social bond that one has with other speakers in one's linguistic community. In Sapir's view "it is not too much to say that one of the really important *functions of* language is to be *constantly declaring* to society the psychological place held by all of its members."[5] It comes as no surprise then that some consider language and identity to be "ultimately inseparable."[6]

There are several ways in which language, in addition to being a vehicle of communication, is one of the primary means by which individuals identify and situate themselves in their world and among their peers. Chief among these are the vehicle of naming and the use of dialect (i.e. regional, generational, ethnic, and social varieties of a language which are particular to the community of use). In this chapter, we will discuss the various ways in which individuals acquire and maintain names, the manner in which language undergoes change (leading to generational variation), and the structure and identification of dialects (including how they are distinguished from autonomous languages).

Names and Identity

One of the most personal bits of language for any given individual is their name. People often see their own name as their own special label, something that represents them and their personality, something that distinguishes them from others around them in the same manner as their facial features and their voice. It is for this reason, perhaps, that people with overly common names sometimes change them, augment them with middle names, or adopt nick-names or pet names.

It is further the case that we often use different variations of our name in different contexts. Both of the authors have first names that can be shortened or changed for use in informal situations. Accordingly, we use *William D.* and *Stanley*, respectively, in situations where formality is appropriate, but *Bill* and *Stan* among friends and acquaintances. It is further the case that William (or Bill) has a nickname, *BD*, which is used by those in his immediate family and some of his in-laws.

---

[4] Sapir 1933: 160.   [5] Sapir 1933: 161.   [6] Joseph 2004: 13.

In addition to being a distinctive label, or set of labels, an individual's names also serve to mark a person's cultural identity. For example, the names *Agostina* (Italian), *Bao Li* (Chinese), *Helga* (German), *Ramesh* (Indian), and *Ali* (any Islamic background) can at times provide clues regarding part of an individual's social identity. Sometimes, of course, they don't – e.g. names such as *Destiny*, *Hope*, and *Apple* (the last being the name that Gwyneth Paltrow gave her daughter in 2004).

It is useful to examine naming practices by dividing the topic into a discussion of first or given names and a discussion of family names. Given names typically perform the function of identifying an individual within their immediate community (and as we've seen, these can vary for a single individual depending on how that community is circumscribed). Family names, on the other hand, are typically used to group related individuals together, and as well to describe the family's provenance.

Given Names

How first names are assigned varies widely from culture to culture. Often (and especially in modern Western societies), choosing a name is the prerogative of a child's parents. However, even when this is so, they are frequently constrained by their particular familial and ethnic traditions. Children can be named after living relatives or deceased ancestors. They can be given names that reflect desirable qualities (e.g. *Charity*) or a hoped-for future (e.g. *Fortune*). Their names might reflect the order of their birth or which generation they belong to (e.g. *Carl Jr.* or *Junior*, and *Carl III* or *Trey*). They might also bear a name that reflects the circumstance of their birth. Different cultures have different traditions in this regard, and some naming practices involve more than one.

Among American Christians, for example, children are often named after living relatives – firstly after their parents (e.g. the son of James Jones might be *James Jones Jr.*), and secondarily after grandparents or other important family members. In other traditions (e.g. among American Jews of European origin), children may not be named after living relatives, but are rather named to honor those who are deceased. In the American South, it is not uncommon for a child to carry a given name that is their mother's family name (e.g. the daughter of James Jones and Elizabeth Tilman might be named *Tilman Anne Jones*). Most American children are also given two names, partly in order to afford their parents the opportunity to honor two family members with the birth of a single child (e.g. their mother and their grandmother, or both grandmothers). In Jewish families, children are also given a Hebrew name, which is used in religious rituals. Sometimes their English and Hebrew given names are versions of the same name, as in the case of *Samuel* and *Shmuel*; sometimes they are translations of each other, as in the case of *Rose* and *Shoshanna* (which means *rose*); and sometimes they might only share an initial consonant, as with *Barry* and *Baruch* (President Obama's given name follows the same tradition in Islam, having the English name *Barry* and the Arabic name *Barak*). These traditions are often connected, either underlyingly or explicitly, with some system of beliefs. Among Inuit Eskimos, for example, the required practice of naming a child after a beloved ancestor is explicitly connected with the belief that the child will receive the ancestor's reincarnated spirit along with the name. In Jewish tradition, the same practice is not explicitly connected with such a belief, although naming a child after a deceased relative in this way is taken to be a way to "honor" that person's memory (and thought by some to bring "comfort" to their soul).

In some cultures, some names are given which express the parents' hopes for their child or particular virtues. This is reflected in some common names in Indonesia, including *Agung* 'great,' *Ayu* 'beautiful,' *Harta* 'treasure,' *Lestari* 'eternal,' *Setiawan* 'faithful man,' and *Utari* 'patient.' We frequently see this tradition carried out in American families, mostly with female children, giving out names such as *Grace, Charity, Faith, Felicity, Hope, Joy, Patience,* and *Prudence* (the first of these among the top twenty most popular girls' names in the US). In other cultures names may be given that signify circumstances of the child's birth. Among the Yoruba of Nigeria the name *Idowu* may be given to the next child born after a set of twins and *Ige* to a child born feet first.

Birth order is reflected in the naming practices of many cultures, including those of Japan, Java, and Bali. In Japan, common given names (for boys only) that reflect their order of birth are: *Taro* (first), *Jiro* (second), *Saburo* (third), *Shiro* (fourth), and *Goro* (fifth). Similarly, Javanese parents might name their first-born child *Ekawati* or their second-born *Dwita*. However, no culture adheres to this naming principle as strictly as the Balinese of Indonesia, who will name their first-born son *Wayan* (or sometimes *Putu* or *Gede*), the second-born *Made*, the third *Nyoman*, and the fourth *Ketut*. While other cultures have birth order reflected in some names, it is only mandatory with the Balinese.

It is further the case that given names are sometimes changed or a person acquires a secret name, according to some cultural practice or the requirements of tradition. Among the Navaho, for example, people are given a secret name, which is actually considered to be their real name, but which is never spoken and remains a secret from almost everyone. Such names are used only during ceremonies. In Jewish tradition, as well, children are often given Hebrew names in addition to their Romanized or public legal names. Here, the Hebrew name (while not the person's legal name) is considered to be their "real" name for ritual purposes (being the name by which they are referred to when they participate in religious ceremonies, when they are married, when they are ill, and when they die). In European Jewish tradition, up until several decades ago, it was a custom to change the given (Hebrew) name of a seriously ill person (or to give them an additional name), so as to fool the "Angel of Death" who was thought to come for people according to their names. Names chosen in such instances represented healing or long life, e.g. *Chaim* ('life'), *Rafael* (the angel of healing), *Alter* ('elder') – and for girls, *Chaya* ('life') or *Alta* ('elder'). In the tradition of the Baduy people of western Java (Indonesia), a parent ceases to use their own given name as soon as they have children. From the birth of their first child, they are styled "father of [name of child]" or "mother of [name of child]." The parents of a girl named *Dainah* would be named *Ayah-Dainah* ('father of Dainah') and *Ambu-Dainah* ('mother of Dainah'), respectively. The parents of a boy named *Karmain* would be called *Ayah-Karmain* ('father of Karmain') and *Ambu-Karmain* ('mother of Karmain').

Family Names

Family names, as we suggested, are often markers of one's provenance, in terms of ancestry, location, or occupation, and arose first and most prominently in medieval Europe.[7] Accordingly, the Johnson or Stevenson families are most likely descended (at one time) from someone named John or Steven, respectively. Likewise, the ancestors of the Fields and Woods families may have dwelled in the middle of some fields or adjacent to a forest. The forebears of the Cooper, Brewer, and Miller families, for their parts, were most likely people who made barrels, brewed beer, and milled grain into flour.

   Of the family-naming traditions mentioned here above, it is the ancestral convention that is most widely used across cultures. These morphemes, called **patronymics** (pater = father, and nym = name), are found in numerous languages, the most readily recognizable such suffix (to an English speaker) being the rather ubiquitous Germanic and Scandinavian suffix, *-son* or *-sen*. A look through any reasonably long list of American names (especially in regions of German or Scandinavian settlement) will find numerous individuals who are descendants (i.e. sons) of Johan (*Johansen*), Steven (*Stevenson*), and Peter (*Peterson*).

   Although mostly opaque to speakers of English, many other languages have patronymic prefixes and suffixes. In areas inhabited by Gaelic peoples (e.g. Scottish and Irish), the patronymic *Mac* and *Mc* (both meaning "son") are found. The descendants of Donald would carry the name *MacDonald*, while the descendants of someone named Iver might be *McIvers*. Slavic

---

[7] Scott and Mittleman 1999.

languages (e.g. Polish, Russian, and Czech) use a range of patronymic suffixes, including -*owicz* and -*ski* in Polish. Thus, a son (descendant) of someone named Jan (the Polish equivalent of *John*) might carry the name *Janowicz* or *Janowski*. What distinguishes Slavic naming from those we've seen so far is that some suffixes have a feminine-gendered version (e.g. -*ska*) that means 'daughter' rather than 'son.' Thus, if Petr (Peter) and Marta (Martha) are siblings in the "descended from Jan" family, they would be, respectively, *Petr Janow**ski*** and *Marta Janow**ska***.

As might be expected, patronymic forms of family names derive from an older and deeper tradition of using the patronymics literally. In the English-speaking world, for the most part, people named *Peterson* and *MacDonald* are not the children of fathers named *Peter* or *Donald*. Accordingly, Harry MacDonald's two children might very well be named *Roger MacDonald* and *Sheila MacDonald*. Patronymic suffixes used in this fashion reference a "founding father" (i.e. the progenitor of an entire tribe). This is reflected in both Arabic and Hebrew. Osama bin Laden (where *bin* means 'son') was not the child of a man named *Laden*. His full name was *Osama bin Mohammed bin Awad bin Laden* (literally, Osama son of Mohammed son of Awad son of Laden). The lineage of the bin Laden clan itself can be traced back to "Sheik Mohammed bin Laden, a native of the Chafeite (Sunni) Hadramout who emigrated [from South Yemen] to Saudi Arabia at the beginning of the century."[8] Likewise, people of the Jewish faith refer to themselves as *Bnai Israel* (literally, the children of Israel), where *Israel* is the new name given to Jacob in Genesis 35:10 ("And God said unto him: 'Thy name is Jacob: thy name shall not be called any more Jacob, but Israel shall be thy name'; and He called his name Israel.")

Cultural Variation in Surname Practices

While the family names we are most familiar with are of the "founding patriarch" variety, there are still cultures that use patronymics quite literally (Osama bin Laden's full name being an expression of this). The best example of this is Iceland, where surnames are almost exclusively patronymic. The popular singer Björk Guðmundsdóttir is 'Björk, Guðmun's daughter,' and independence leader Jón Sigurðsson is 'Jón, Sigurð's son.' Although far less common, **matronymic** naming conventions also exist in some cultures. The Minangkabau of Indonesia have the largest matrilineal society in the world, and children take the name of their mother's clan, as did one of the leaders of the Indonesian independence movement, Mohammad Hatta. In Iceland, too, some children are named after their mothers for various

[8] WGBH Educational Foundation 1995–2014.

reasons; for example, Heiðer Helguson, a famous football player, is Heiðer, son of Helga.

In these cultures, surnames are not family names at all, but are simply a means to identify an individual through reference to their parents. This is clear when one considers naming across more than two generations. If Jón has a child named Sigurð, Sigurð has a son named Guðmun, and Guðmun has a daughter named Björk, Jón's three descendants would be named:

Sigurð Jónsson	[Jón's son]
Guðmun Sigurðsson	[Jón's grandson]
Björk Guðmunsdóttir	[Jón's great-granddaughter]

Obviously, there's no way to calculate their relatedness beyond one generation through their names, and practical matters in Icelandic society reflect this. The telephone directory is, unsurprisingly, organized alphabetically by first name; and now, with the advantage of digital mapping tools, one can locate every one named *Björk* on a map of the island (which would presumably help one to figure out which of the eight *Björk Guðmunsdóttir*s one wanted to phone).

The Muslim Uyghur minority of northwest China also follows the same naming practice as the Icelanders, except that their names do not incorporate any patronymic or matronymic morphology. In their practice, a son or daughter is given a "first" name and their "second" name is their father's "first" name. So, if Mahmud's father's name is Salam, then Mahmud is called *Mahmud Salam*. Table 5.1 shows how three generations of Uyghur children might be named.

As is clear from the Icelandic naming convention, family names are not a cultural universal. There are other societies (e.g. Indonesia, Turkey before World War I, and Japan until the mid nineteenth century) where there is no tradition of using family names. In some of these societies, people go (or went) by a single given name, while in others people may have (had) more than a single given name. It was the spread of Western influence (and religion) that changed this in some cultures (although other circumstances led to the adoption of family names in other societies). In many instances the adoption of family

Table 5.1 *Example of Uyghur naming practice*

Generation	Father	Given name	Full name
1	Mahmud	Salam (boy)	Salam Mahmud
2	Salam	Tursun (boy)	Tursun Salam
3	Tursun	Gul (girl)	Gul Tursun
3	Tursun	Salam (boy)	Salam Tursun

names was a "voluntary" and gradual process, but in others government laws mandated the use/adoption of a family name.

For instance, the Act to Regulate Names, promulgated in 1860 by the Hawaiian King Kamehameha IV (and not repealed until 1967), required all Hawaiians to adopt family surnames and to also have a "Christian" first name. This legal action was most certainly a consequence of Western Christian influence in Hawaii and of the fact that King Kamehameha was educated by Calvinist missionaries. Traditional discomfort with the use of family names was still evident a century after the law was passed, with historian Mary Kawena Pukui saying, "My name isn't supposed to be given away. My name is for me. But people are always naming babies after me, so I have many namesakes. I don't want any of them hurt if there's any *kapu* (taboo) that goes with my name. So I pray, 'Since so-and-so named this child for me, then please do me the favor to *'oki* (cut away) the *kapu* (taboo) and bless the name.'"[9] In other words, 'please don't let anything bad happen to this child on account of any bad "karma" associated with my name.'

A similar law was passed in Turkey in 1934, the Surname Law, and while the law was most likely a result of Western European (modernizing and secularizing) influence, the law itself was part of the nationalistic Turkification movement led by Mustafa Kemal Atatürk.[10] Turkish Muslims, who normally did not have family names, were required to adopt them, and non-ethnic Turks who already did have family names were required to change them to Turkish ones (e.g. an ethnic Greek whose name ended with the Greek patronymic suffix *-ides*, such as *Pastides* or *Amarides*, would have been required to replace the suffix with the Turkish equivalent *-oğlu*, yielding *Pastoğlu* or *Amaroğlu*.

The history of Japan's surnames is an interesting one, in that Japan in 1587 forbade "all non-samurai (90 percent of the population) from bearing either swords or, that other mark of distinction, surnames."[11] And then in 1875, under its modernizing efforts, the Meiji government passed a law requiring all Japanese to acquire and register surnames. If the sixteenth-century law was intended to reinforce class distinctions, it could not exactly be said that the nineteenth-century law was designed to remove them. Rather, it is assumed that the government was primarily interested in "conscripting, taxing, and educating [the citizenry] with maximum efficiency – for universal conscription and compulsory education were central to the Meiji reforms."[12] To meet the sudden, and urgent, need for surnames, villagers enlisted the help of their local temple priests. The priests, for their part, would create names for each family, often based on where the family lived. If a family's abode was in the

---

[9] Pukui, Haertig, and Lee 1972: 100.   [10] Türköz 2007.   [11] Hoffman 2009.
[12] Hoffman 2009.

middle (*naka*) of a rice field/paddy (*ta*), they could be *Tanaka*. If the family lived next to a small (*o*) stream (*sawa*), they might become *Ozawa*, and if their residence was between the temple (*tera*) and the rice fields (*ta*), their name could be *Terada*. Thus were created some 100,000 different surnames (or one for every 1000 Japanese), which eclipses just about any other society (e.g. China makes do with about 200 official surnames). Of course, unlike the lineage-based names of the West, a Japanese surname is unlikely to indicate any relatedness among its different bearers (especially if they originate from different locations).

Language Rights and Personal Naming Rights

Having discussed different aspects of naming, and how names function as markers of identity, we turn now to the ways in which naming figures into language rights and, specifically, naming rights issues. An explicit rights-based connection between human language rights and naming is recognized by the United Nations in its *Declaration of the Rights of the Child*. Principle 3 of this document states, "The child shall be entitled from his birth to a name and a nationality."[13] It is telling that the *Declaration* refers to names and nationality in the same principle as fundamental rights of children (and, by extension, of persons of all ages).

Due to the importance attached to names, it is not surprising that governments will try to interfere with these rights, in the process of trying to control identity and ethnicity within their borders. Many states (including but not limited to: New Zealand, Germany, Spain, Portugal, Denmark, Norway, Sweden, Morocco, Japan and Malaysia) have specific regulations regarding what names parents may give their children as an attempt to ensure social, cultural, and linguistic homogeneity (and, at times, protect children's interests). In Sweden, tax authorities must give their blessing to both first and surnames before they can be used. In China, it is the police who control the names given to children as they issue identity cards. In Germany, there is an entire government department (the Standesamt) that decides upon suitability of names.

In keeping with this level of government control, many countries maintain official lists of acceptable names, usually forcing people to adopt them and sometimes restricting who can use them. For example, the Personal Name Act of 1996 gives the Icelandic Naming Commission jurisdiction over the first names of its citizens. There is a list of 1,712 approved names for males and 1,853 names for females. Portugal publishes an eighty-page annotated list of acceptable and unacceptable names (*Vocábulos admitidos e não admitidos*

---

[13] United Nations 1959.

como nomes próprios). And in Japan, children's names must be selected from a list of 2,232 official Japanese names, although non-citizens (i.e. until 1985, children whose father is not a Japanese citizen) are not allowed to use these names.

Which names are and are not permissible can sometimes be reflective of cultural values and sometimes be about maintaining some sort of "linguistic purity." For instance, New Zealand passed legislation in 1995, titled the Births, Deaths, and Marriages Registration Act, which states among other things that "it is undesirable in the public interest for a person to bear a name or combination of names if, and only if, (a) it might cause offence to a reasonable person; or (b) it is unreasonably long . . . " On this basis, the government has banned a number of names, including *Lucifer*, *Christ*, and *Messiah*. For their part, Malaysian authorities in 2006 published a list of undesirable names which were deemed as not in keeping with the religious traditions of the country. Notorious among the banned names was *Chow Tow*, a Cantonese name meaning 'Smelly Head,' and one wonders whether the name was truly offensive to the country's official Muslim religion, or whether officials simply didn't like it because it was (a) Cantonese and (b) embarrassing. In Sweden as well, the law stipulates that "First names shall not be approved if they can cause offense or can be supposed to cause discomfort for the one using it, or names which for some obvious reason are not suitable as a first name."[14] On these grounds, Swedish officials disallowed the use of *Ikea* as a given name, although for some inexplicable reason they did approve both *Lego* and *Metallica*. In the case of *Metallica*, though, permission for a couple to use this name for their daughter only came as a result of a six-year legal battle with the government authorities.

Linguistic restrictions also play a role in determining which names are acceptable. In many countries, where nouns in the national language exhibit grammatical gender (e.g. are "masculine" or "feminine"), names that are grammatically or typically of one gender are not allowed as names for children of the opposite gender (along, sometimes, with names that are indeterminate in this regard). In Italy, for instance, the courts can step in "when the child's name is likely to limit social interaction and create insecurity." In one instance, the (typically) boy's name *Andrea* was rejected for a girl, and the child's name was ordered to be changed to *Emma*. Similarly, in Germany, all approved names must be clearly gendered. Thus, the name *Miatt* was rejected for a child, because it isn't clearly masculine or feminine. In a 2009 case in Sweden, a couple who wished to honor Michael Jackson's legacy by giving their daughter the middle name *Michael* appealed to the Tax Authority for permission to do so. Since

---

[14] Namnlag 1982: 670. www.notisum.se/rnp/sls/lag/19820670.htm#P34

Michael is considered an established male name and inappropriate for a female, their request was denied.[15]

Iceland has, perhaps, the most highly articulated policy in this regard, with restrictions on the orthographical and morphological form of names. Laws specify that names must fulfill requirements that include "Icelandic grammatical endings," display the "linguistic structure of Icelandic," and have "Icelandic orthography." In accordance with these rules, the name *Harriet* is disallowed because it cannot be declined as a regular nominal, *Carolina* because the letter "c" is not part of Iceland's alphabet, and *Blaer* (meaning 'light breeze') because the noun has masculine gender and is thus inappropriate for a girl. Many of the examples cited here are real. In 2014 a 10-year-old girl was denied a new passport because her given name, *Harriet*, which her mother used on the application form, is not an approved name for girls. Her previous passport had identified her only as *Stulka*, which means 'girl.'[16] In the case of *Blaer*, which was highly publicized in the media, it took fifteen years to overcome official disapproval. Finally, in January 2013, a Reykjavik court overturned a naming committee's judgment, ruling that a 15-year-old girl could after all use the name *Blaer*, that her mother had given her at birth. The committee had prevented the girl from using the name on the grounds that *Blaer* should be a male name because it takes masculine grammatical markings, such as the masculine suffix *-urinn*. For those fifteen years, in all official documents, the girl had been referred to simply as *Stulka*.[17]

The marital or national status of a child's parents also figures into naming regulations and restrictions. In the case of Japan, for example, until 1985, the status of the child's father (but not the mother) determined what a child may be named. Japan requires all ethnically Japanese residents to take Japanese personal names (e.g. *Yoko*, *Masuo*, and *Shinichi*). At the same time, it also forbids non-ethnic Japanese from registering their children with such names (also forbidding them from ever having citizenship). Until 1985, Japanese ethnicity was legally deemed to be inherited from the father only; children of mixed marriages would be required to give their children Japanese names if the father was Japanese, but would not be allowed to give their children Japanese names if only their mother was Japanese. The rights to citizenship (and to a Japanese name) were thus passed along from generation to generation. Thus, at that time, a child whose mother, grandmother, and great-grandmother were native-born ethnic Japanese, but whose father, grandfather, and great-grandfather were not, were not permitted to have a Japanese given name (nor have citizenship). This situation changed in 1985, when Japan was preparing to ratify the UN Convention on the

---

[15] Landes 2009.   [16] Velez 2014.   [17] BBC 2013.

Elimination of All Forms of Discrimination Against Women. The amendment to the citizenship law, intended to eliminate unequal treatment of men and women, "provided that a child born to either a Japanese father or a Japanese mother was a Japanese citizen, whereas previously only children born to Japanese fathers were considered Japanese citizens."[18] Japan, nevertheless, still maintains a *jus sanguinis* rule, whereby the nationality of the parent is passed on to the child.

In Sweden, marital status also plays a role in naming. Sweden's naming laws, as recently as 2007, do not allow the child of a married couple to be given both the mother's maiden surname and the father's surname as a family name, even though it was perfectly legal at that time for unmarried couples to do so. In one high-profile case, a couple (Lars Jensen and Lina Wernström Jensen) actually considered getting a divorce when the Swedish Tax Authority prevented them from naming their son *Aksel Wernström Jensen*. They wanted their son to have the same surname as their daughter, who was born before they were married, and whose surname was *Wernström Jensen*. They did not prevail.[19]

Minority Language Rights Violations in Personal Naming Practices

In some countries with strict naming regulations, the goal is to "manufacture" cultural homogeneity by denying the expression of minority cultures through their traditional names. Examples taken up in later chapters include Hungarians in Slovakia, the Ainu in Japan, Kurds in Turkey, and Native Americans in Indian boarding schools in the US. Here we briefly illustrate how such restrictions have applied to Turks in Bulgaria, the ethnic Chinese in Indonesia, and Uyghurs in China.

The Turkish minority in Bulgaria has often been the target of oppression; in part this has been a reaction of ethnic Bulgarians to the history of advantage granted to the Muslim (largely Turkish) population during the rule of the Ottoman Empire (roughly from the late fourteenth century until the late nineteenth century). For years the Bulgarian government recognized the Turkish minority as a distinct minority in the country. However, beginning in the 1970s, the government adopted an aggressive policy of assimilation, which reached a peak during the "Process of Rebirth" from 1984 to 1989, in an attempt to create the myth of an ethnically homogeneous population. As part of this campaign Turks were forced to adopt Bulgarian names (along with eschewing all outward signs of "otherness," such as non-Western dress) and Turkish place names were replaced with Bulgarian names. During this period government

---

[18] Murazumi 2000: 421–422.   [19] Dacey-Fondelius 2007.

troops surrounded many predominantly Turkish towns and issued residents new identity papers. People who did not use the new identity cards were denied salary and pension payments as well as banking services. Additionally, marriage licenses were only issued to those people with Bulgarian names. Some resisting assimilation were sent to labor camps or resettled, and between 500 and 1,500 lost their lives.[20] This resulted in an exodus of over 300,000 Turks to Turkey in what came to be known as "The Big Excursion." After the collapse of the Soviet Union, rights were reinstated and many regained their Turkish names.

In Indonesia, ethnic Chinese have always faced some resentment from the Javanese and other ethnic groups. Despite this, under Sukarno's leadership from Independence in 1945 until 1965, Chinese-language newspapers and schools were permitted, and ethnic Chinese were free to carry out ancestral cultural practices. However, after the rebellion of 1965 (the so-called "Year of Living Dangerously"), under Suharto's New Order, things changed radically. In 1966, the government issued a policy strongly recommending that Chinese Indonesians permanently adopt 'Indonesian' names in order to prove their loyalty to the country, as they were widely assumed to be associated with the Communist Party, which was believed by many to have been behind the attempt to overthrow the government. This was followed by a 1967 decree signed by Suharto which banned the public use of Chinese customs, language, and religion. Although this decree was rescinded in 2000 by President Abdurrahman Wahid following Suharto's 1998 ouster, it is still the case that ethnic Chinese Indonesians predominantly use the "Indonesian" names they or their parents and grandparents adopted.

In the case of Uyghurs in China, authorities wreak havoc with their naming traditions by forcing them to adopt names that can be fitted into Chinese naming conventions and the Chinese writing system, and habitually insult members of this group in the process. First, recall from earlier in the chapter that Uyghur children are given a first name and that their last (i.e. second) name is that of their father. So, a child named *Tursun Salam* is the son of a man named *Salam*, and a child named *Gul Tursun* is the daughter of a man named *Tursun*. However, traditional Chinese names involve a family name first, followed by a given name. This is standard practice for Japanese and Korean names as well. In the Chinese paradigm, a man named *Zhang Wei Bo* is a member of the *Zhang* family whose given name is *Wei Bo*.

For the Uyghurs, having Chinese authorities registering and deciding their children's names usually does not turn out well. For one thing, the Chinese typically use a Uyghur child's first name as a family name and their second as a given name. This means that *Salam Tursun* and *Gul Tursun* (a brother and

[20] Curtis 1992.

Table 5.2 *Sample Chinese-character name for a Uyghur*

Gul ('rose/flower')	Tursun ('should stay')
gu-li	tu-er-xun
古 里	吐 尔 逊
old-village	spit-you-inferior

sister whose father's name is *Tursun*) will be given different "Chinese-like" surnames *Sa-lang* and *Gu-li*, and will bear the same "given name" *Tu-er-xun*. This will be especially difficult for *Gul*, since the "given name" that the Chinese give her is a boy's name.

In addition to the confusion imposed by the naming practices themselves, Chinese authorities often take the additional step of choosing for Uyghurs names that have derogatory meanings in Chinese. For any given syllable, there are many different Chinese characters that have the same pronunciation. So, if one wishes to find a character to use for the pronunciation *gu* and *li*, there are dozens of choices (forty-four characters in the dictionary, some archaic and not often used, are pronounced *gu*). Since the characters have a wide range of meanings, one can easily choose characters with positive and complimentary meanings or characters with negative or insulting meanings. For Uyghurs, Chinese authorities often choose the latter. Table 5.2 illustrates. Take our fictional Ms. Gul Tursun, for example. Her name *Gul* means 'rose' or 'flower' and her father's name *Tursun* is a common male name meaning something like 'should stay' (or 'a child we will keep'). As the meanings associated with a likely official choice of Chinese characters indicate, the Chinese authorities appear to go out of their way to insult these people when they apply for official Chinese-character names.

As is apparent from the example given in Table 5.2, the Chinese authorities are not satisfied with merely forcing Uyghurs to use Chinese orthography for their names, but also engage in insulting them when they do so.

6   Language and Cultural Identity: Language and Thought

We have seen that language and names play a role in forming our personal identities, an important part of which is our social or cultural identity. As described in Chapter 5, different cultures have different naming conventions. From the Balinese practice of naming children according to the order of their birth to the Jewish tradition of naming a child to honor a deceased relative to the Icelandic convention of assigning a surname by adding either *dóttir* or *son* to the name of their father (or in some rare cases mother), the name one is given can be an important reflection of one's culture. This is simply one aspect of the relationship of language and culture.

Not only did Sapir note the role of language in the identity of individuals (Chapter 5), he also recognized the role of language in determining social and cultural identity. Sapir asserted that "common speech serves as a peculiarly potent symbol of the social identity of those who speak the language."[1] It is well established that language is a factor in social solidarity – traditionally one identifies closely with those who speak the same language and even more so with those who speak the same variety of that language. The idea that language and culture go hand-in-hand is thus intuitively appealing. In fact, so appealing is this idea, that many people take language as a proxy for culture, and what are presented as language conflicts are often in fact socio-cultural conflicts, as we will see in later chapters.

But what precisely is the nature of the relationship between language and culture? Is language simply emblematic of culture or is there a deeper, causal relationship? Does language guide how we perceive the world, as some have proposed? People have debated these issues throughout history. While we do not intend to give a full-blown exposition of the subject (there are plenty of those already), given the intertwined nature of language and culture and the reference that many make to it in instances of language conflicts and language rights, a few words are in order.

---

[1] Sapir 1933: 159.

Language, Thought, and Culture

Greek philosophers such as Plato and Aristotle mused over the origin of language, particularly about whether language came from the gods or was the work of man. In arguing that it was indeed humans and not gods that were responsible for the genesis of language, Epicurus (341–270 BCE) pondered the question of why so many different languages existed. He concluded that there were so many different languages in the world because different peoples perceived the world differently, saying, "Men's natures according to their different nationalities had their own peculiar feelings and received their particular impressions."[2] In other words, each "nation" (i.e. each ethno-linguistic or cultural group) had its own characteristic psychological make-up and perceived the world differently according to it. It was hypothesized, then, that there arose distinct languages, each based on a distinct worldview or culture. Epicurus explicitly linked the form that a language takes to the characteristics of its speakers, both mental and environmental. Each distinct group was associated with a language that embodied their own patterns of thought and culture. This idea, and the nature of the relationship between language and thought (and whether thought is even possible without language), has occupied philosophers and other thinkers for thousands of years, and still does so today.

In more modern times, one particularly influential group of scholars that addressed this question were the German philosophers and linguists of the seventeenth through nineteenth centuries. The German philosophers promoted the idea that a language reveals the inherent characteristics of a people, of their culture, and therefore of their nation. From this they reasoned that it was the natural order that nations should be separate political entities (according to their separate languages). Their position was instrumental in the development of the nation states of Western Europe (and elsewhere) in the nineteenth century (see Chapter 7). So strongly was this view held that the German philosopher Wilhelm von Humboldt asserted that without a common language as a driving force a nation cannot exist. Underpinning this assertion was von Humboldt's view that a language's structure reflects the worldview and knowledge of its speakers, that language is the outward manifestation of the essence of a people. From this it follows naturally that languages will necessarily be as different from one another as are the speakers that use them.[3]

Epicurus' and Humboldt's ideas are captured in two modern linguistic concepts: *linguistic determinism* and *linguistic relativity*. *Linguistic determinism*, naming the stronger of these two claims, asserts that the structure

---

[2] Joseph 2000: 98.   [3] *Encyclopaedia Britannica* 1894.

and nature of our language causes us to perceive the world as we do. The grammatical categories and the vocabulary of our language thus determine the way we think. *Linguistic relativity* is the label given to a more circumscribed claim. It asserts that the grammatical categories and vocabulary of our language *may* influence our thought to some extent but that our language's grip on our perceptual faculties is looser. The language that a people speaks may underlie and affect various perceptions of the speakers who use it, the perceptions that their culture is based on. In both cases one can see that there is claimed to be a causal link between language on the one hand and thought and culture on the other.

These ideas about language and thought are often now referred to together as the Sapir–Whorf Hypothesis, after the linguist Edward Sapir and his student Benjamin Lee Whorf. The idea is often referred to this way not because Sapir and Whorf ever collaborated on any particular formulation of the hypothesis, but because the two men were the chief proponents in the United States of the notion that language shapes thought and culture. Sapir portrayed thought as being shaped in part (though not wholly) by language, remarking, "the 'real world' is to a large extent unconsciously built up on the language habits of the group"[4]), and he wrote of "thought grooves" (i.e. our customary way of thinking) as being bound up with language.[5] Whorf, who did propose a specific principle, one that he called the "Linguistic Relativity Principle," considered the grammar of a language to be "the shaper of ideas," playing a role in guiding perceptions, and that the "formulation of ideas ... is part of a particular grammar."[6] In laying out his view of linguistic relativity, Whorf states:

[W]hat I have called the "linguistic relativity principle" ... means, in informal terms, that users of markedly different grammars are pointed by their grammars toward different types of observations and different evaluations of externally similar acts of observation, and hence are not equivalent as observers but must arrive at somewhat different views of the world.[7]

Explanatory Limitations of the Sapir–Whorf Hypothesis

The Sapir–Whorf Hypothesis is directly relevant to considerations of language and culture inasmuch as culture is to a large extent the product of the collective thinking of a group of people. While many modern linguists are skeptical of the idea that grammar determines how we perceive the world around us, it is an attractive idea to many non-

---

[4] Sapir 1929: 209.   [5] Sapir 1929: 217–218.   [6] Whorf 1940b; Carroll 1956: 212.
[7] Whorf 1940a; Carroll 1956: 221.

linguists, especially as the links among language and culture and thought seem so intuitively correct. But is the relationship causal?[8]

A popular example often given in support of the Whorfian view is the apparently large number of words for 'snow' in languages of the Inuit (i.e. Eskimos)[9]. The fact is that there are several different peoples included in the category *Inuit* (or *Eskimo*), each with a distinct language, a fact often overlooked by many non-linguists (and some linguists) in discussing this case. For the sake of this discussion we will sometimes lay aside this important distinction. Whorf himself uses the snow example in his discussion of his relativity principle:

We have the same word for falling snow, snow on the ground, snow packed hard like ice, slushy snow, wind-driven flying snow – whatever the situation may be. To an Eskimo, this all-inclusive word would be almost unthinkable; he would say that falling snow, slushy snow, and so on, are sensuously and operationally different, different things to contend with; he uses different words for them and for other kinds of snow.[10]

As chronicled by anthropologist Laura Martin (and famously cited in Pullum's 1991 collection *The Great Eskimo Vocabulary Hoax and Other Irreverent Essays on the Study of Language*), many claims about there being 50 or 100 or even 200 words for snow in languages of the Inuit are not based on data uncovered by linguists but are simply fabrications of particular individuals, from science writers in the *New York Times* to a TV weatherman in Cleveland. The fact is, however, that some linguists who study Inuit languages have indeed identified multiple 'words' for snow in these languages.[11] Anthony Woodbury identifies 15 distinct roots in Yupik (an "Eskimoan" language of Alaska).[12]

---

[8] Sapir (1921: 218) explicitly lays out the notion that there is no causal relationship between language and culture: "Nor can I believe that culture and language are in any true sense causally related."

[9] The term *Eskimo* is deemed a pejorative label by many, mostly due to the (mistaken) assumption that it is an Algonquian word meaning 'eater of raw meat'. Goddard (1984) writes that the word is, more reliably, a Montagnais word meaning 'one who nets a snowshoe' (which would not be pejorative). Nevertheless, the currently accepted term for Eskimo people (in Canada and Greenland) is *Inuit*.

[10] Carroll 1956: 216.

[11] Words are difficult to identify in polysynthetic languages like those spoken by natives of the Arctic area because there are multiple suffixes that are combined with noun and verb roots to form utterances, much as speakers of English combine words to form sentences. For instance, the following is a single 'word' in Inuit, if by word we mean a root and its affixes.

(i)   Angya- liur-   vig-   pa-   li-   ciq- uq
        boat-   work.on- place- big- build- he.will
        'He will build a big place for working on boats.'

Clearly this is not a word as we know it in English and many other languages. Thus, Eskimologists refer to distinct roots rather than words.

[12] Woodbury 1991.

Further, Lawrence Kaplan, while not attempting to provide any particular number, states that the Inuit language Inupiaq "at least has an extensive vocabulary for snow and ice."[13]

Such facts clearly demonstrate the importance of snow to Inuit and Yupik peoples. But does this mean that the perceptions of Yupik and Inupiaq speakers are determined by the language they speak? Or does it simply mean that different peoples have reasons to focus on different concepts and thus devise a way to talk about them, such as Arctic dwellers whose lives may depend on being able to identify environmental conditions?

The impact of culture on lexical distinctions that a language makes can be quite apparent when one considers particular professions or specific domains (which we might consider subcultures). For example, English includes the general, non-specific word *horse* for the equine animal that we are all familiar with. However, there is a large set of English words that identify these animals, including *bronco, brumby, charger, cob, colt, foal, gelding, hack, mare, pony, stallion, steed, thoroughbred, trotter,* and quite a few others. The typical native speaker of English will know only some (and perhaps very few) of these words. So, when we meet someone who is familiar with the majority of these words, it tells us something about that person's subculture: horses must be very important to this person, either as a job or an avocation.

Another, more contemporary, example of this phenomenon comes from the world of computers, which offers a panoply of lexical distinctions, many of them being unfamiliar to most speakers of English. The word *computer* itself is a generic term that applies to a large number of specific types of devices, just as *horse* is a generic term for equine animals. When this book was written, the terms *desktop, laptop, tablet,* and (perhaps) *mainframe* were familiar to most people, except possibly to the most hard-core of *luddites* (a term that itself may be unfamiliar to many, even some younger tech-savvy types who may have a hard time believing that such folks still exist). Of course, many more terms for types of computers exist, among them: *PC, notebook, subnotebook, netbook, ultrabook, 2-in-1, laplet, phablet, handheld, PDA, smartbook, home console, palmtop, ultra-mobile, mobile internet device,* and others. And this does not even include specific, commonly used, commercial names, such as *Mac, Dell,* and *iPad.* Naturally, with technology changing at such as rapid pace, some of these terms are as out-of-date as the devices they describe, and new terms must continually be coined to keep pace with the technological innovations (and there are liable to have been new innovations between the time this book was written and when it went to press). Nowhere is the need for innovative

---

[13] Kaplan 2003.

terminology more apparent than in the terms that have described memory storage throughout the years:

    magnetic core
    magnetic tape/tape drive
    magnetic disk drive
    floppy drive/disk
    diskette
    CD-ROM memory
    zip disk
    CD-RW
    (external) hard drive/disk
    USB Flash drive/USB key/memory stick/thumb drive/jump drive
    cloud/Dropbox/Google docs/OneDrive

Each set of terms applies to a particular innovation. Again, knowledge of the majority of these terms would help us to identify individuals who belong to the technology subculture, be it through vocation or hobby, or because they are just plain geeky.

But as with the words-for-snow example, it is not the case that distinctions made in one language cannot be perceived in others. In English we have the basic word *carry* referring to transporting a physical object.[14] One can find a number of synonyms in a thesaurus: *bear, bring, lug, tote,* and others. Most of these synonyms mean something slightly different than *carry*, identifying that the carrier is moving toward a location, *bring*, that the load is heavy for the carrier, *lug*, and so on. Likewise in Indonesian there is a general word *bawa* best translated as 'carry' or 'bring', but a host of other words specify the manner in which the transported object is held. They include:[15]

angkat	'lift up and carry out'
apit	'carry something under one's armpit'
bopong	'carry something cradled in one's arms'
dukung	'carry something in a sling'
embah	'carry something in a cloth on one's front'
gendong	'carry something resting on the hip or the small of the back'
gotong	'carry something with the help of a lot of people'
jinjing	'carry something hanging from the hand while walking' (e.g. briefcase)
junjung	'carry something on one's head'
muat	'carry people or cargo in a vehicle'

---

[14] *Carry* can also be used with regard to media, e.g. *That stations carries the news at 5:00*, and success, e.g. *The veteran player carried the team to victory.* These senses of *carry* are not relevant here.

[15] Quinn 2001.

panggul	'carry something resting on the shoulder'
papah	'carry someone by supporting them under the armpits or with their arm around one's shoulders/neck'
pikul	'carry two things suspended from a bamboo pole'
sandang	'carry something on a strap, string or cloth hanging from the shoulder'
sunggi	'carry something on top of the head'
tanggung	'carry something heavy on the shoulder'
tatang	'carry something on a tray out in front of you'
usung	'carry someone in a sedan chair or stretcher'

In English we can convey these meanings (and just have), so speakers can obviously perceive these actions. English just does not have distinct words for them, and thus requires multiple words to describe them. At the same time knowing these are words in Indonesian tells us something about how important it is (or was) in Indonesian life to get an item from one place to another without a vehicle. People dissect the world in different ways, and vocabulary reflects this.

The Expressive Potential of Languages beyond Cultural Restrictions

However, not all lexical distinctions among languages seem to be so culturally relevant. One example of this may be the phenomenon of number as it is expressed in pronouns. In English there are separate pronouns for singular and plural: *I* vs. *we* and *he/she/it* vs. *they* (*you* is an interesting exception). Singular pronouns are used when referring to only one object and plural when there is more than one. Some other languages make an additional distinction though. They include specific pronouns (and/or affixes on verbs) to indicate that precisely two people or things are involved. This type of pronoun is referred to as "dual" (in contrast with both "singular" and "plural"). Diverse, unrelated languages that include a dual in addition to singular and plural include Modern Standard Arabic, Chinook, and Fijian.

	Singular	Dual	Plural
Arabic	heyya 'she'	humaa 'they (2)'	hunna 'they (> 2)'
Chinook	naika 'I'	ntaika 'we (2)'	ntshaika 'we (> 2)'
Fijian	i'o 'you'	'emudou 'you (2)'	'emunuu 'you (> 2)'

In Modern Standard Arabic we find *heyya* 'she' vs. *humaa* 'they (2 females)' vs. *hunna* 'they (more than 2 females),' in the Native American language

Chinook there are *naika* 'I' vs. *ntaika* 'we (2)' vs. *ntshaika* 'we (more than 2),' and Fijian has *i'o* 'you (1)' vs. *'emudou* 'you (2)' vs. *'emunuu* 'you (more than 2).' Perhaps unexpectedly, English actually once included dual pronouns: in Old English *ic* meant 'I,' *wit* 'we (2),' and *wē* 'we (more than 2).' This was true of second-person pronouns as well: *þū* 'you (only 1)' vs. *git* 'you (2)' vs. *gē* 'you (more than 2).' At some point in the development of Middle English, though, this distinction disappeared and only singular and plural pronouns remained. This is a grammatical fact, which most likely reflects nothing in particular about these cultures that have the dual form (and undoubtedly not the same thing in such diverse cultures), and the same concept is readily expressible in Modern English 'we two,' 'you two,' and 'they two (those two).'

Motion verbs provide another example of different distinctions being made in languages, in this case a difference between English and Spanish (as well as other Romance languages such as French and Italian). Both languages have words to convey the general idea of motion – verbs such as *go, move, come* and others in English and *ir, mover,* and *venir* in Spanish. But English also includes more specialized verbs that combine the idea of motion with the manner of motion, describing the way in which a person or thing moves. So, alongside *She came into the room*, it is possible to substitute more descriptive verbs for *come*, verbs such as *dash, march, dance, slip, sidle, sashay*, along with a host of others:

(1)   a. She dashed into the room.
       b. She marched into the room.
       c. She danced into the room.
       d. She slipped into the room.
       e. She sidled into the room.

If we say *She marched into the room* or *She slipped into the room*, we include much more information than simply the fact that some female entered the room. Using a more descriptive manner-of-motion verb conveys not only the way she entered the room but something about her attitude or intention. One *marches* into a room if one wishes to be noticed and express one's determination, while one *slips* into a room if one wishes not to be noticed upon entering the room. This is not only true when the movement is by a person. Alongside *The ball went into the room*, we can say:

(2)   a. The ball rolled into the room
       b. The ball bounced into the room

or any of a number of ways in which the ball moved. In Spanish, it is not possible to use the verb *rodar* 'to roll' to describe a similar situation. As intuitively plausible as it might sound to an English speaker, one cannot say in Spanish:

(3)   *La pelota rodó en la sala.
         'The ball rolled into the room.'

Rather one conveys the same meaning by using the generalized motion verb *entrar* 'enter' and then adding a description of the manner of motion, using a participial verb form, as in:

(4)   La pelota entró en la sala, rodando.
         'The ball entered the room, rolling.'

Clearly, it is possible to convey the same idea in Spanish as in English. It is simply necessary to use a different grammatical construction to do so.

However, while manner-of-motion verbs are not available in Spanish, the language does have direction-of-motion verbs (combining the notion of movement with the direction (or path) of such movement), as in the following:

(5)   a. El globo bajó por la chimenea.
            'The balloon moved down (or descended) through the chimney.'
         b. El globo subió por la chimenea.
            'The balloon moved up (ascended) through the chimney.'
         c. La botella cruzió el canal.
            'The bottle moved across (crossed) the canal.'

As we can see in the above examples, English has direction-of-motion verbs (similar to those of Spanish) as well as verb-plus-preposition constructions which involve the simplex verb *move* plus a directional preposition.

Language as a Reflection of Culture

While not all differences one observes between languages are a reflection of cultural differences, oftentimes they are, especially with respect to vocabulary. Thus, in many ways the language we speak can contribute to our cultural identities. This reinforces the widely and strongly held belief that language and culture are so inextricably connected that it is essentially impossible to ignore culture when there are language conflicts, as we will see played out in much of what follows.

The form and use of pronouns is but one grammatical phenomenon that can reflect the culture of the speakers of a language. Quite a few languages of East and Southeast Asia have very complex pronominal systems, especially for first and second persons – that is, for the speaker and the addressee in a conversation. First- and second-person pronoun use in these languages reflects a number of socio-cultural variables such as the gender, age, background and social status of the speaker and addressee, as well as the degree of formality or politeness in a speech situation, among other considerations.

Perhaps nowhere is this clearer than in Japanese. Japanese contains at least 23 first-person singular pronouns, i.e. expressions meaning 'I,' referring to the speaker, and at least 19 forms for second-person 'you,' referring to the addressee.[16] The first-person pronouns are: *watasi, atasi, watakusi, atakusi, watai, atai, wate, ate, boku, ore, ora, oira, wai, wasi, assi, oidon, uchi, zibun, ware, soregasi, sessha, temae, onore* and *shosei*. The forms *boku, ore, ora, oira, wai, wasi, assi* and *shosei* are used exclusively by males and *atasi, atakusi, atai* and *ate* are used only by females. A boy or young man is liable to use *boku*, while a man of retirement age would most likely refer to himself as *wasi*. *Boku* and *ore* are used in informal speech situations, such as a conversation between friends, but are inappropriate in formal situations such as in a public speech, a business meeting or a job interview. In these settings only *watasi* and *watakusi* are acceptable.

The relative social status of speaker and hearer also determines which pronoun should be used. When addressing a person of higher social status or an older person, a speaker would refer to himself as *boku*, whereas a speaker may use *watasi* if speaking to a younger person or a person of lower social status. Speakers of equal status may use *boku* or *ore* if they are close associates but the more polite formal *watasi* if they do not know each other very well. Complex pronominal systems of this kind, and the principles that guide pronoun selection, reflect the cultural values of the speakers who use them. Japanese society is well known for social politeness and the respect accorded to elders because of their greater experience and wisdom, and to persons of higher status (which implies great experience and wisdom).[17]

English provides another instance of pronoun usage reflecting culture (or at least subculture). In recent years, there has been a growing trend in speakers of American English using the plural pronoun *they* to refer to a singular third person of unspecified (or unknown or mixed) gender, as in *Each student was told that they must read their own book by themselves.* If it were the case that the speaker knew that all of the students in question were female, the speaker could have used the third-person feminine pronouns, as in *Each student was told that she must read her own book by herself.*

Traditionally, however, third-person masculine has been used prescriptively to refer to a singular third person of unspecified gender, in which case the preferred sentence would be *Each student was told that he must read his own book by himself.* For years most English grammar guides and textbooks have instructed users that the masculine pronoun is to be used in this kind of

---

[16] The Madurese language of Indonesia is a bit impoverished by comparison to Japanese, there being 'only' 12 first-person pronouns and 13 forms for second person.

[17] See Shoji 2016.

environment. As Geoffrey Pullum points out, "Nearly all published grammars" are wrong on this point.[18]

The rise of the women's movement in the 1970s (eventually) brought with it increased sensitivity regarding gender equality and a feeling that the use of the masculine pronoun to refer to someone of unspecified gender was sexist or at least inappropriate. A means that some speakers have employed to avoid this situation is to use both masculine and feminine pronouns, that is, *he or she*, *him or her*, and so on. At times, this can result in sentences that are quite cumbersome or inelegant such as *Each student was told that he or she must read his or her own book by him or herself* (in writing, people would sometimes use two pronouns separated by a slash character "/" to indicate the alternatives – *he/she*, *his/her*, and *him/herself* – producing written forms that are equally cumbersome). As a way of avoiding such unwieldy locutions and written forms, many speakers simply use the third-person plural form, which in Modern English is undifferentiated for gender. (Note that such a solution could not work for a language such as French, which distinguishes third person plural masculine and feminine, as in the masculine *ils* 'they' and the feminine *elles* 'they').

This use of third-person plural in place of indefinite third-person singular has become so prevalent that in 2015 the American Dialect Society voted singular *they* as the "Word of the Year."[19] However, the Society was quick to note that this use of third-person plural is not a new innovation, having previously appeared in the works of Chaucer, Shakespeare, and Jane Austen among others. Nevertheless, its reemergence in current usage reflects a change that has taken place in American cultural dispositions toward gender in language in recent years.

Japanese provides yet another example of language reflecting the culture of its speakers. There are two verbs meaning 'give' in Japanese, *ageru* and *kureru*, which differ in a significant way. *Ageru* includes in its meaning the notion of giving 'upward,' indicating that the giver is the social inferior of the recipient. This verb must be used when the speaker is the giver; the sentence with *ageta* 'gave' is acceptable, whereas the version with *kureta* is not:

(6) Watasi-ga   Taro-ni   hon-o   ageta/*kureta.
     I-NOMINATIVE Taro-DATIVE book-ACCUSATIVE gave
     'I gave Taro a book.'

Conversely, *kureru* includes the notion of giving 'downward' on the social scale; the recipient assumes a humbler social position compared to the giver. This verb is used when the speaker is the recipient:

[18] Pullum 2011.   [19] www.americandialect.org/2015-word-of-the-year-is-singular-they

(7)   Taro-ga   watasi-ni hon-o   kureta/*ageta.
       Taro-NOMINATIVE I-DATIVE   book-ACCUSATIVE gave
       'Taro gave me a book.'

Here again we see how the language reflects the culture of its speakers. The choice of verbs in these cases plays a role in maintaining the ideal of a civil society. As we saw in the case of first and second pronoun choices, the Japanese have traditionally undertaken to pay careful attention to individuals' position in the social hierarchy and to the power structure of their social relationships. The use of *ageru* and *kureru* here goes beyond the simple directionality expressed in 'give upward' or 'giving downward' and instead identifies a social distinction, creating a formal grammatical difference between reference to oneself and reference to others via the speaker's humbling him or herself.

   This specialized function of the *ageru–kureru* distinction extends to situations in which the speaker is neither giver nor recipient, but is describing a situation involving third persons. The speaker's use of *ageru* or *kureru* in these cases requires adopting the perspective of either the giver or the receiver (this is technically referred to as *empathy*), whichever person they most closely identify with socially. If the person closest to the speaker is the giver, then *ageru* is selected, just as it is when the speaker is the giver. When the person socially closest to the speaker is the receiver, then *kureru* must be used. In the following sentence, for example, the speaker takes the point of view of Taro, the giver:

(8)   Taro-ga   Ziro-ni   hon-o   ageta.
       Taro- NOMINATIVE Ziro- DATIVE book-ACCUSATIVE gave
       'Taro gave Ziro a book.'

By using *ageta* here, the speaker signals to the addressee that Taro is closer to the speaker's social circle than is Ziro (perhaps they are classmates or friends). In describing the same giving event, if the speaker most closely identifies with Ziro, the recipient of the book, then *kureta* is used:

(9)   Taro-ga   Ziro-ni   hon-o   kureta.
       Taro- NOMINATIVE Ziro-DATIVE book-ACCUSATIVE gave
       'Taro gave Ziro a book.'

In this case, Ziro might be a friend, relative, or co-worker of the speaker's. In both cases, the social relationships of the speaker to the individuals referred to in the sentence must be calculated and are reflected in the language used.

   One syntactic structure that sometimes reflects the culture of the speakers of a language is what is referred to as a Serial Verb Construction (SVC). In an SVC, two (or more) verbs are used together to form a single idea. This is a rare construction in English, though some have claimed that the *go get* and *come get* constructions of colloquial English are examples of (quasi-) SVCs, as in:

(10)   a. They should **go get** some money for the gift.
         b. Chris will **come see** what you've made.

This is very limited in English. Only *come* and *go* are possible first verbs. However, in other languages (primarily spoken in Africa and Asia), SVCs are not rare. For example, in Lao (the national language of Laos), the construction is fairly productive:[20]

(11)   a. Còòj   khaa   muu   khaaj.
            Joy   kill   pig   sell
            'Joy killed the pig and sold it.'

         b. Nòòj   sak   khùang   taak
            Noy   wash   thing   hang.up
            'Noy washed the clothes and hung them up.'

         c. Candii   puuk   ùan   khaaj
            Jandi   build   house   sell
            'Jandi built the house and sold it.'

In these examples, there are two verbs that share the same object, for example *muu* 'pig' is the object both of *khaa* 'kill' and *khaaj* 'sell.' The English translation requires the conjunction *and* in order to convey these meanings, and speakers of English interpret these as two separate events, for example a killing event and a selling event. Lao speakers, however, consider the killing and selling in this case to all be part of the same activity. In order to interpret these as separate activities, the conjunction *lèka* 'and then' is required, just as in English:

(12)   Còòj khaa muu lèka   khaaj man
         Joy   kill Pig and.then sell   It
         'Joy killed the pig and then sold it.'

The Lao SVC is not simply a different grammatical construction though. There are restrictions on its use. It is not possible for just any two verbs to be combined in this way. The combining verbs must be such that Lao speakers view them as actually comprising a unitary action. The verb pairs must denote actions which are typically done together: actions such as washing clothes and hanging them up, or killing a pig and selling it. So, for instance, although carrying and saving a child could be conceived of as related activities, it is impossible to combine them to form an SVC. They just are not activities that occur together with sufficient frequency for Lao speakers to conceive of them as comprising a single event. The following sentence is unacceptable to a Lao speaker for this reason:

---

[20] Lao data from Cole 2016.

(13)   *laaw   um   dêl-nòòj   suaj
        he   carry   child   help
        'He carried the child and saved him.'

Acceptable SVCs reflect Lao culture inasmuch as they illustrate activities so common to everyday Lao experience that they are conceived of as comprising a single event.

The restriction on verbs that can combine in an SVC is not peculiar to Lao but is found in other languages as well. Again, the actions denoted by the verbs in question must be viewed by speakers in that culture as making up a single event. This thus reflects an aspect of the speakers' culture, as illustrated by the following pair of sentences from Alamblak, a language of Papua New Guinea:[21]

(14)   a. miyt ritm   muh-hambray-an-m
           tree insects   climb-search.for-I-them
           'I climbed the tree looking for insects.'
        b. *miyt guiim   muh-heti -an-m
            tree stars   climb-see-I-them
            'I climbed the tree and saw the stars.'

The relevant fact is that Alamblak people regularly climb trees in search of insects for food but rarely in an effort to scan the sky for stars. The former can be conceived of as a single event and can thus be expressed in an SVC whereas the latter cannot. Lao works differently. Although the eggs of a certain variety of ants are prized as a delicacy and the nests of these ants are found up in trees, climbing trees in search of these nests is not a common enough activity for Lao speakers to consider the climbing and searching to make up a unitary event. Therefore, these actions cannot be expressed in an SVC, and the following sentence is ungrammatical for a speaker of Lao:

(15)   *laaw   khùn   ton-maj   sòòk   mèèng
        he   ascend   tree   search   insect
        Intended: 'He climbed the tree to look for insects.'

It is not that this notion cannot be expressed in Lao. It can, but only in a complex sentence including a subordinating conjunction:

(16)   laaw khùn   ton-maj phùa   sòòk   mèèng
        he   ascend tree   in.order.to search insect
        'He climbed the tree to look for insects.'

The different possibilities for well-formed SVCs in Lao and Alamblak hence reflect aspects of the culture of the speakers of these languages.

---

[21] Bruce 1988: 29.

Language and Culture: The Limits of Mutual Influence

As we have seen, languages sometimes reflect the culture of their speakers, most noticeably (but not exclusively) in their vocabulary. However, this usually reflects the simple fact that the domain associated with that vocabulary is of particular importance to speakers, e.g. names of different breeds of horses for those who spend a lot of time around horses or the various words for different kinds of computers and peripherals for techies. As we have also seen, lexical (and grammatical) distinctions made in one language can almost always be translated or borrowed into any other. If humans can think it, they'll find a way to express it. Thus, it is important to avoid the temptation to "exoticize" linguistic facts, and in so doing treat the speakers of the language exhibiting those facts as a curiosity or in some way abnormal, something which is done not only by writers in the popular press but also by otherwise conscientious scholars. As Pullum cautions in connection with what he refers to as the "great Eskimo vocabulary hoax," we must guard against "popular eagerness to embrace exotic facts about other people's languages without seeing the evidence." If we don't, it will lead us straight into a fabricated and imaginary "lexicographical winter wonderland," a place in which we are deluded by the fallacy that "primitive minds categorize the world so differently from us."[22]

It does not take much effort to unearth similar cases in which naïve researchers and writers construct for themselves and their audiences romanticized (and fictitiously depicted) "other peoples." For example, one author notes of the Dena'ina people of Alaska that they identify directions not by points on a compass but according to the flow of rivers and streams, which are a source of food and a striking feature of the landscape, in contrast to Inuits, who live by the sea and orient themselves according to the coast. The thoroughly smitten author remarks, "The logic of this – even for me, who came to this Alaska shore from afar and only as an adult – is obvious, and truly lovely."[23] Of course, this is no more remarkable (or precious) than people living along the Mississippi River speaking of "upriver," "downriver," "across the river," and "this side of the river." She comments further:

Along my trail in Dena'ina country, I try to imagine how differently – or more clearly – I might see my world if I had the Dena'ina language precision with which to know my surroundings and my place in them. I look at a fern and think "fern." But if instead I thought of *uh t'una*, I would know that I was seeing and thinking about the leafy part of the plant, in contrast to *uh*, its underground parts used for food. And if I thought of another part of the plant, *elnen tselts'egha* (literally "ground's coiled rectum"), I would find humor in the fiddlehead fern.[24]

---

[22] Pullum 1991: 162.   [23] Lord 1998: 20.   [24] Lord 1998: 23.

Clearly the facts about ferns strike the author as quite noteworthy. But we should ask, is this any more noteworthy than the fact that in English we refer to the orange root of a particular plant as a *carrot* and refer to the visible part above the ground as "carrot greens," "carrot leaves," a "carrot plant" or some other thing? To her credit, the author does not fully embrace Whorf's Linguistic Relativity Hypothesis, noting that: "Whorf's somewhat circular theory turned out not to be provable by scientific methods, and has since been largely discredited."[25] Most linguists agree that language does not determine how we perceive the world, though it may at times influence it.

It is a fairly straightforward and unremarkable fact that a language at times is going to reflect the location in which it is spoken and certain aspects of the culture of its speakers. However, such facts should not be overly romanticized. They simply reflect the things that speakers most need to refer to in their daily lives. Still, the reflection of the culture of peoples in the language that they speak comes as little surprise to most.

[25] Lord 1998: 22.

7   Language and National Identity

Chapters 5 and 6 describe the ways in which language acts as a symbol of personal and social identities. With respect to the latter, Sapir asserted that "common speech serves as a peculiarly potent symbol of the social identity of those who speak the language."[1] The potency of this symbol manifests itself writ large in the concept of national languages. Governments use language as a unifying force of the population. Independence movements use language as a rallying point. Politically minded social movements use language as a means of identifying who to include or exclude. But what precisely are national languages, how do they arise, and how (effectively) do they function?

National, State, and Official Languages

Despite seeming to identify the same concept, national languages, state languages, and official languages can serve different functions. As we see below, it is important to distinguish among them, though at times the same language can serve all three functions. To get at the distinction among national, state, and official languages, it is first necessary to understand the difference between a nation and a state. Although often used interchangeably, the terms nation and state "technically" identify different entities.

While dictionary definitions vary and some academics consider the notion problematic to define precisely,[2] a 'nation' is generally taken to identify a population with a shared identity based on culture, ethnicity, history, religion, language, or some other characteristic. A "state," on the other hand, is a political entity, in which a government has sovereignty over a particular territory. A nation does not always constitute a state: the Kurds, who number some 30 million and who inhabit contiguous portions of the present-day states of Turkey, Iraq, Iran, and Syria, are often characterized as the largest nation in the world without a state. By the same token, a state is rarely comprised of people from a single nation. The Turkish state, for instance, includes Turks,

---

[1] Sapir 1933: 159.   [2] Seton-Watson 1977; Anderson 1983.

Kurds, Greeks, Armenians, Circassians, and others, and these Turkish minorities comprise some 25 to 30 percent of the population.

The distinction between nation and state also manifests itself in popular culture. The internet company NationBuilder illustrates the distinction. In advertising its "community building" service, it asserts that "A nation is a group of people united behind a common purpose. Everyone who cares about what you are doing – your fans, followers, constituents, members, donors, volunteers, customers, shareholders, and partners – all are part of your nation."[3] Obviously nation here has nothing to do with territory or government. The same usage of the term "nation" is also evident in comedian Steven Colbert's characterization of his fans as the *Colbert Nation*. Again, territory and government are irrelevant. In neither instance would the use of "state" be appropriate.

The fact that "nation" and "state" are distinct notions is made clear by the term "nation-state," which arose to identify geographical areas in which political and national identity coincide.[4] While language has always been one of a number of markers of a nation – a people – it has not always been associated with political entities. Vast empires such as the Roman Empire, the Persian Empire, the Ottoman Empire, the Habsburg Empire, and the British Empire included many ethnolinguistic groups – many nations – and were never thought of as nation-states, in contrast with some of their present-day constituent parts, such as Italy, France, and Hungary. In multi-ethnic empire states, such as Rome, a particular language (e.g. Latin) might have been used for administrative and legal purposes, but the state itself was not characterized by a common language being used by the general population. There are, of course, many present-day countries (i.e. states) whose citizens come from diverse linguistic stock, as in the previous example of Turkey, despite their official claims to be nation-states. In fact, as we will see in later chapters, some states have gone to great lengths to create a myth of ethnic purity, and the suppression of minority languages is one of the tools used.

The close association of language with national identity and geopolitical divisions arose in Western tradition in part through the influence of German philosophers. In the late seventeenth century, Gottfried Leibniz observed that "usually nation and language flourished together."[5] In an attempt to revitalize the German nation following the Thirty Years War (1618–1648), he advocated the use of German in public discourse to promote unity across social strata (at that time the German aristocracy largely spoke French) and to educate the general population, which he believed would improve society as a whole. Leibniz promoted the creation of a German standard by enriching vocabulary and codifying the rules of grammar, work to be overseen by a German language

---

[3] http://nationbuilder.com/business_faq   [4] May 2012.   [5] Cited in Coulmas 1988.

academy. While Leibniz himself did not seek to promote German as being superior to other European languages, many who followed him did just that, e.g. Johann Christoph Gottsched, Johann Gottlieb Fichte, and others. Philosophically, they championed the notion that language and thought were inextricably intertwined. Thus, out of a desire to refine German culture, they sought to purify the German language, in part by purging the language of foreign words. In this regard, Friedrich Gottlieb Klopstock declared that "every language is ... a repository of the most characteristic notions of a nation."[6] Wilhelm von Humboldt – a diplomat, philosopher, and linguist – asserted that nations could not exist without a common language and that language is an outward manifestation of the people. These arguments were pressed by German nationalists who wanted to create a unified German homeland where none had existed previously. In 1871, Germany finally coalesced into a nation-state. Based on the sort of arguments made by the German philosophers and nationalists and in the aftermath of the French Revolution, language use became politicized throughout Europe, and linguistic nationalism became a cornerstone of nationalist movements in Greece, Finland, Estonia, Albania, France, and elsewhere.[7]

A key ingredient in this type of linguistic nationalism is the establishment of a standard language around which the people can rally. The desired standard to promote this cause needs to be more delimited and ethnically homogeneous than that of the empire-state, but more widely used and far-reaching than local dialects. But how is such a standard developed and decided upon? There are several components to the process. One is the *selection* of a norm. The variety chosen is generally one which is perceived as a prestige dialect, that is, a dialect associated with social and economic power. As such, it is often the variety spoken in the capital city, such as Parisian French, Tehrani Persian, or (educated) London English. Of course, this choice immediately disadvantages speakers of varieties that are not selected as the standard, which can create conflicts among speakers.[8] Another component in the formation of a national vernacular is the process of *elaboration*, which is the process by which the locally prestigious dialect is made into a full-fledged language of culture, education, commerce, and law. This is accomplished largely by the infusion of additional vocabulary needed to express modern concepts of science, commerce, and so on, as well as the development or refinement of a writing system. *Codification* of the language through the creation of dictionaries and grammars is also necessary, since the presumptive national language will need to be taught to those who are not native speakers. And the final component is *restriction*, which involves the elimination of some linguistic options, such as non-native lexical items, the pronunciation of some sounds or application of

[6] Coulmas 1988.   [7] Coulmas 1988.   [8] Wee 2011.

some phonological rule (e.g. /r/-less pronunciation in the eastern United States, as described in Chapter 4), and so on.

In some instances, the process of establishing a national language may involve the deliberate efforts of a language academy, a group of "academicians," or even influential individual national leaders. In other cases, these processes happen without an organized effort to create a standard, as was the case with British English for the most part. With or without official or governmental involvement, standardization may occur due to the economic and intellectual forces that demand it. The case of British English is instructive in this regard. There was, to be sure, some discussion about standardization of English among those most interested in language, but no English language academy or other body was charged with the task of standardization as was instrumental in other cases (e.g. Germany, France, and Spain). A major force in the standardization of English was the introduction of printing in England in 1476 by William Caxton, which truly set the process in motion. Caxton for all intents and purposes selected the standard when (largely for economic reasons) he chose to publish books in the East Midlands dialect.[9] He also began regularizing spelling, as did printers who followed. Interest in literature and language toward the end of the Renaissance and in the Age of Enlightenment ensued, and through literature and science the English vocabulary was elaborated. It is estimated that from 1500 to 1700, 30,000–50,000 new words were added to the English lexicon.[10] Codification came through the publication of grammars, such as John Wallis' *Grammatica Linguae Anglicanae* (1653) (written in Latin!), and dictionaries, such as Robert Cawdrey's modest *Table Alphabeticall* (1604) and Samuel Johnson's 1755 *A Dictionary of the English Language*, which served as the gold standard for well over a century.

With the notions *nation*, *state*, and *nation-state* in place, we can more precisely identify a *national language* as a language that is associated with a *nation*, that is, with a group of people who have a particular, shared culture and/or ethnicity. A national language need not be a state or official language. Linguist Ralph Fasold proposes three functions that a language can serve in a nation-state: (1) as a national symbol, (2) as a vehicle for government operations, and (3) as a common means of communication among people.[11] A *state language* – in opposition to a national language – is one that fulfills only the second function, i.e. the administration of government, official commerce, and law.

An *official language* is a state language that is mandated by law or is written into the constitution of a state. Consider the status of English in the United States. It is, as a symbol of the American populace, the national

---

[9] Harris and Taylor 1989.   [10] Leith et al. 2007.   [11] Fasold 1988.

language of the United States, and it is also the state language, as it is the language in which government business and commerce are normally conducted. That is, all laws of the United States are recorded in English and the business of governmental bodies and offices is conducted in English. However, English is not the *official language* of the United States because there is no law mandating that government business be conducted in English nor is there any mention of English in the US constitution. (The movement to make English the official language of the United States will be taken up in Chapter 9.)

The situation of official languages differs widely and somewhat arbitrarily from country to country. Many countries are like the United States in having no specific constitutional or legal provisions regarding an official language. Countries such as these include China, Germany, Iceland, Italy, Mexico, the Netherlands, and the United Kingdom, among others. In all of these named countries, government business and commercial affairs are conducted in a particular national language (e.g. Chinese in China, Italian in Italy) and that language is recognized as a national symbol; thus, both the state language and the national language are the same, although neither is recognized as such by law.

French, on the other hand, is designated in the French constitution as the official language of France, and although it is not officially and legally designated as such, it is the language of the French nation. The situation is the same in Bulgaria with respect to Bulgarian, as it is in many other countries. In some instances, a country may have more than one official language. This is the case in Ireland, where two official languages fill distinct roles. The Irish constitution declares Irish to be a national language (alongside English), despite the fact that a very small percentage of the population can speak it. Irish, then, as symbol of the Irish people (including the many Irish people who cannot speak it), is an official national language, and English, as the default language of trade, government, and law, is an official state language.

National, State, and Official Languages in the Aftermath of Colonialism

Many formerly colonized African, Asian, and Latin American countries faced a rather different situation after they achieved their independence (some in the nineteenth century and most in the twentieth century). In the majority of cases, Western colonial powers paid little attention to national or linguistic boundaries when establishing colonies, preferring instead administrative boundaries which were geometrically easier to map or natural borders (e.g. rivers, mountain ranges) which were easier to defend. This practice very often resulted in disparate peoples and languages being aggregated within the borders of a single colonial governmental unit.

Many times, due in part to the desire to avoid interethnic conflict and civil wars, these political divisions and boundaries went unchanged after independence, and the new countries created under this regime retained the artificial boundaries and oftentimes incoherent ethnic composition of their colonial antecedents. The creation of states in this manner frequently resulted in newly independent counties that were multilingual from the outset (e.g. Kenya and Sudan), and which then had the sometimes difficult task of determining which language or languages would be used to administer the government.

In many cases, these newly independent states had no alternative to using the pre-existing colonial administrative and educational structures that had been established by their former European colonial rulers, and which functioned in the language of the colonists. These former colonies, therefore, retained the language of their former rulers as state or official state languages in order to maintain these institutions. Another reason for their officially adopting colonial languages was because doing so served to facilitate communication among citizens of different linguistic groups and because using the colonial languages did not usually outwardly privilege one ethnic group over any other. It also helped to preserve the economic and political power of the indigenous elites, because it was typically members of those local upper classes that were most proficient and best schooled in the colonial language. At the same time, partly in order to avoid interethnic discord, indigenous languages were also accorded official status.

For instance, Niger and Senegal both adopted French as the official state language, yet officially recognized the languages of many of their several indigenous ethnic groups as national languages.[12] In other cases, the colonial language was adopted as one of two official languages, as in Rwanda, where French and Kinyarwanda are official languages and Kinyarwanda the national language, and the Philippines, where Filipino is both the national language and an official language and English is an official language. Naturally, not all newly formed countries exercised this option. For example, Algeria did not adopt French as a state language but declared Arabic to be both the national language and the official language. At the same time, Algeria did not recognize the Berber language (spoken by about a quarter of its population), thus sowing the seeds for several decades of conflict.[13]

---

[12] The constitution of the Republic of Senegal declares "The national languages shall be Diolo, Malinke, Poular, Serer, Soninke and Wolof and any other national language which has been codified." http://landwise.landesa.org/record/892

[13] Berber remained unrecognized from independence (1962) until 2002, when a constitutional amendment declared Berber to be a "national" (but not "official") language.

Because language is so closely tied to personal, social, and national identity, the decision in a multilingual state of whether to designate the former colonial language, the majority indigenous language, minority languages, or some combination of these as national and/or official languages is an emotionally charged issue. The choices made can have profound impacts on the development and the identity of a nascent country. In this regard, it is instructive to examine the outcomes of two countries that used very different strategies regarding the establishment of national/official languages and achieved very different results.

The Establishment of National Languages in India and Indonesia

Two newly independent countries with similar profiles, which were facing their language issues at the same moment in history, are India and Indonesia. A Dutch colony since the seventeenth century, Indonesia declared independence on August 17, 1945, and India, a British colony from the eighteenth century, did so on August 15, 1947. Currently India and Indonesia are the second and the fourth most populous countries in the world, respectively, and both had large, ethnically diverse populations at the time of independence, with India counting 350 million inhabitants in 1947 and Indonesia counting 72 million in 1945.[14] It is estimated that there are currently approximately 450 different languages (plus dialects) from five different language families spoken in India, and that over 700 different languages (plus dialects) from two different language families are currently spoken in Indonesia.[15] In neither country is there a true majority ethnolinguistic group. However, at the time of independence, Hindi speakers made up 42 percent of the population of India,[16] and in Indonesia 45 percent of the population was Javanese. India selected Hindi as an official language, while Indonesia made a form of Malay, not Javanese, the state language. The two strategies had dramatically different results.

Indonesia

Europeans first arrived in Indonesia in the early sixteenth century. Historically, the 17,000+ islands making up the current territory were not all politically united. Stretched across the vast archipelago were over 300 ethnic groups speaking some 700 languages (as shown in Figure 7.1). Various large kingdoms

---

[14] In 2013, the population of India was approximately 1.25 billion and that of Indonesia approximately 250 million.

[15] *Ethnologue* 2016.

[16] This figure includes not only speakers of Hindi proper but also of varieties that some identify as dialects and others as distinct languages, e.g. Punjabi (the majority Indic language of the inhabitants of the Punjab region of northwestern India).

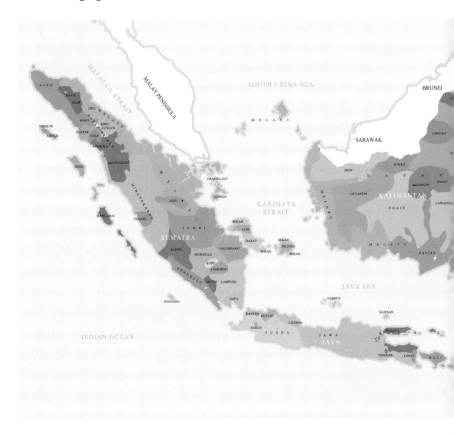

Figure 7.1 Map depicting some of Indonesia's over 300 ethnic groups

controlled much of the territory at different points, but people's loyalties remained with smaller kingdoms and regencies. By the early eighteenth century, the Dutch controlled European trade in Indonesia, first through the Dutch East India Company and later as a colony under the rule of the Dutch government.

Bahasa Indonesia ('Indonesian language'), as it came to be known, was based on a particular dialect of the Malay language that was used as a contact language among indigenous groups that did not speak a common language. It was referred to as Riau Malay, the dialect spoken in an area including parts of the Indonesian island of Sumatra and the coast of the Malay Peninsula. First brought eastward by seafaring traders from the Johor Kingdom, as well as traders passing through the area, it was spread widely from the seventh century on, in part because of its grammatical properties. The Indonesian linguist S. T. Alisbjahbana cites the "simplicity" of the grammatical structure of Malay as enhancing its use as a contact language, referring to the fact that there is neither case marking nor verb agreement in the

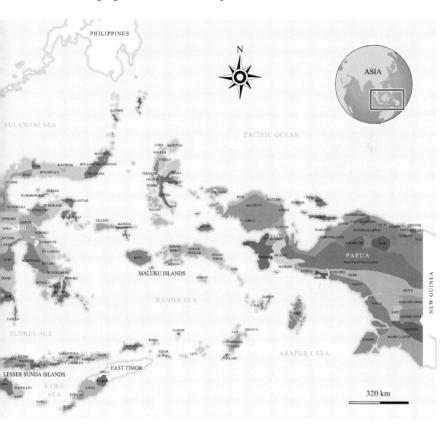

grammar.[17] Recall (from Chapter 3) that "case marking" refers to inflection on nouns that indicates whether they are the subject, object, or some other relation in the sentence, and verb agreement refers to inflection on verbs that identifies subjects and/or objects in a sentence. Malay uses word order, the other means of identifying subjects, objects, and other relations in a sentence. Like English, the subject of a Malay sentence precedes the verb, which in turn precedes the object, so in the following sentence *Bambang* is the subject and *you* the object:

(1)   Bambang melihat kamu.
        Bambang saw   you
        'Bambang saw you.'

There is no case marking or verb agreement in the sentence. This is clear if we compare the previous sentence to the following:

(2)   Kamu melihat Bambang.
        you   saw   Bambang
        'You saw Bambang.'

---

[17] Alisbjahbana 1974.

There is no change in the form of the nouns or the verb *melihat*; this indicates that there is no case marked on nouns or agreement on verbs.

The Dutch colonists were also instrumental in the spread of Malay. From early on, Malay was used as an auxiliary language of the Dutch colonial government. And in 1850, the Dutch governor suggested that the Malay spoken in Riau be the medium of education in Dutch-run schools for the indigenous population.[18] In 1865, Malay was adopted as the second official language of administration. This "lingua franca" Malay had no single agreed-upon form, and the Dutch felt a need to promote its standardization, especially as it was the language of most of the sanctioned schools. To aid in this process, the Dutch created a Bureau of Popular Literature in 1908, to translate popular texts in science and literature into Malay and thereby to aid in the education and development of a "literate" populace.

The decision to adopt Malay as the national language was actually made informally quite early on by the Indonesian independence movement. Young Indonesian intellectuals, educated as they were in Western-type schools, were the first to start using the term "Indonesia" to refer to their country and its people, and began at that time to advocate the use of the Malay language as a symbol of national unity.[19] Groups formed to promote local cultures began conducting their meetings in Malay even though "most of these young nationalists spoke Dutch better than Malay."[20] During this time, their actions provoked dissent from some of the established social and political elite, who felt that Javanese, as the language of the most powerful and largest ethnic group, should be used instead. But the decision settling this matter was all but finalized at the All-Indonesian Youth Congress held in Jakarta in 1928. There, Congress participants took the *Sumpah Pemuda* 'the Youth Pledge' in which they declared that they "belong to one fatherland, Indonesia … to one nation, Indonesia … " and that they would "uphold as the language of unity, the Indonesian language."[21] From that point on, the language was called Indonesian by all those who affiliated with the nationalist movement.

As the purpose of a trade language such as Malay/Indonesian is to enable people to conduct business, it generally lacks vocabulary for many concepts, especially those associated with science, philosophy, government, and so on, as well as the vocabulary associated with much of modern material culture. This trade language, unsurprisingly, also lacked a literary tradition. Realizing this, the leaders of the nationalist movement set about the task of developing and standardizing their nascent national language, holding the First Indonesian Language Congress in 1938. These national language building efforts were continued throughout the Japanese occupation of World War II, a time when the Dutch language was outlawed and Indonesian used by the Japanese to govern. (The Japanese attempted to impose Japanese on

---

[18] Abas 1987: 31.   [19] Anwar 1980.   [20] Dardjowidjojo 1998: 37.   [21] Abbas 1987.

the Indonesian people, but found that doing so was a stumbling block to controlling the population and to efficiently governing the territory and extracting maximum labor for the war effort.) And so, by the time independence was declared in 1945, the advantages of choosing Indonesian as the constitutionally sanctioned official national language were already quite well established. Chief among the considerations favoring its adoption was that, when the constitution was written, native speakers of this variety of Malay/Indonesian comprised a mere 5 percent of the population. Thus, by adopting it, none of the competing dominant groups (such as the Javanese) were advantaged. It then fell to the new government to make Indonesian truly the state language.

Recognizing the need to establish and propagate a standard language, the government re-inaugurated the language development process that had begun in the 1920s and 1930s, and which had continued to some degree under the Japanese occupation. The Research Institute for Language and Culture was established for this purpose in 1947, followed in 1948 by the *Balai Bahasa* 'Language Office' within the national Department of Education and Culture. Working groups within these agencies were charged with different standardization tasks: enriching the vocabulary through the coining of new words for daily activities and the creation of terminology for science, technology, and government, and the writing of standard grammars and dictionaries (i.e. the codification and restriction of usage). In addition to and in support of these efforts, academics, language planners, writers, and others gathered periodically at national conferences to discuss standardization efforts and the dissemination of the national language.

The Indonesian government's continued active role in sponsoring print and broadcast media, both nationally and locally, has been instrumental in spreading Indonesian to all parts of the country. Perhaps more important, however, has been the role played by the educational system. Indonesian is firmly established as the language of instruction in all public schools, although children may be taught in a local language concurrent with their instruction in Indonesian for the first three years of schooling, where necessary. These efforts are abetted by the fact that school attendance is compulsory (during the year 2002–2003, 94.4 percent of primary-school-aged children attended school).[22] In addition to the language instruction offered in the public schools, the government sponsors supplemental literacy programs. All of these efforts combined have resulted in an adult literacy rate of 93 percent, as reported by the United Nations in 2012.[23]

The successful establishment of Indonesian as the official national language (all within a period of some sixty to eighty years) is the result of choosing a language that advantaged no ethnic group, and which was accepted thereby as a new national symbol, and of the careful development and vigorous promotion

[22] UNESCO 2005.   [23] UN Data 2012.

of it from 1928 onward. The outcome of this process was, by any standard, rather "miraculous," in that an entire nation was created by convincing the population that "a particular outside language should become their own integrative, inter-ethnic, unifying tongue."[24]

India

A traditional home to many hundreds of ethnic groups and roughly 450 languages plus dialects, the Indian subcontinent has a complex and diverse

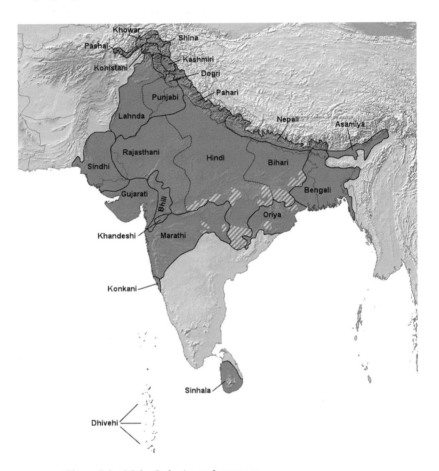

Figure 7.2a Major Indo-Aryan languages

[24] Fishman 1978: 333.

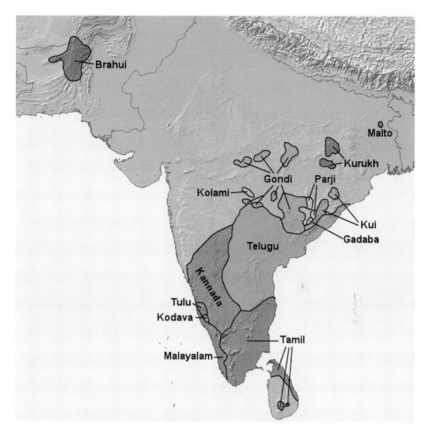

Figure 7.2b Dravidian language family

history during which greater or lesser areas of it have been governed both byindigenous kingdoms and by foreign empires. It is hypothesized that India was first inhabited by Dravidian peoples, who developed into the Kannada, Malayalam, Tamil, Telugu and other peoples. As Aryan peoples arrived from the north and settled in the northern regions of the subcontinent, the Dravidians moved south-ward, where they are the dominant population today (see Figure 7.2b). The Vedic kingdoms, whose cultural legacy of Hinduism dominates our conception of India, flourished between 1750 and 500 BCE. The period of the Vedic kingdoms pro-duced the *Vedas*, the sacred texts of Hinduism, which were composed in the literary language Sanskrit, the spoken form of which evolved into the modern Indo-Aryan languages of Hindi, Urdu, Marathi, Panjabi, and Sindhi, among others (see Figure 7.2a). As Hinduism spread over the subcontinent as the dominant religion during this period, Sanskrit (the liturgical language of Hinduism) spread throughout India as a literary and scientific language.[25] Although Sanskrit never rose to become a unifying language of the people (i.e. a national language), Dravidian and other non-Aryan languages came to incorporate many words of Sanskrit origin. However, perhaps on account of the religious importance of Sanskrit, it was the related vernacular languages of Hindi and Urdu, among all of the indigenous languages, which came to dominate India's official language debate.

Hindi and Urdu emerged from the same stock but were born of different traditions. Urdu developed under the influence of the Muslim Mughal (also spelled Mogul) Empire, which controlled increasingly large portions of India from the mid sixteenth century and into the eighteenth century. Through the Mughals, Persian and Arabic vocabulary was infused into the local Hindi dialects spoken by north Indian Muslims. During this period, Urdu became the language of the court, elevating the status of its speakers, and bringing economic advantage, as knowledge of Urdu and Perso-Arabic culture helped secure government positions and education.

Beginning in the early eighteenth century, the British began to establish themselves in the Indian subcontinent, gradually expanding into the areas of Mughal rule. The British East India Company first gained a foothold in Bengal in eastern India in the early 1600s. As the Mughal Empire began to decline in the early eighteenth century, British influence grew and the East India Company controlled more and more territory. The British inaugurated educational initiatives in the early nineteenth century.[26] The Hindus embraced Western education and modernization, whereas the Muslims distrusted them. This, combined with the British interest in Hindu culture and antagonism toward the Mughals, led the British to favor Hindus over Muslims in terms of government positions and education.[27]

The British government took control of the territory after the 1857 Sepoy Rebellion against the East India Company. Among the outcomes of the rebellion were an official end of the Mughal Empire and the consolidation of British rule, with Queen Victoria taking the title Empress of India in 1877. In the early years of British rule, Hindi writers purged the language of Persian and Arabic words to the extent possible and Urdu writers retained the vocabulary while purging Sanskrit vocabulary, so the two became more distinct as literary languages.[28] Language came to be used as a proxy in competition between Hindus and Muslims for social and economic benefit, and in the latter portion of the nineteenth century, language associations were formed to promote the language and linguistic identity of its members. As the associations turned more political, they became an important vehicle for the growing independence movement. The need to communicate with the populace led to the development of publications in regional languages, many

---

[25] K. L. Gandhi 1984.   [26] Groff 2007.   [27] Das Gupta 1970.   [28] Das Gupta 1970.

of which had a rich literary tradition. The necessity of communicating modern concepts enriched and modernized the regional languages. However, leaders of the movement also recognized the importance of communication across ethnolinguistic groups. For this, Hindi was selected and embraced by diverse populations.[29]

Seeing English as a symbol of colonial oppression, in the early 1900s Mahatma Gandhi began advocating the use of Indian languages in the social, political, and educational lives of the general populace. Following World War I, Gandhi began to promote Hindustani (the nearly identical vernacular form of Hindi and Urdu) as the language for "All-India" communication after independence. At the time, many groups were conducting their meetings in English, including the Indian Congress Party, a lead organization in the independence movement. However, in 1925 the Congress Party amended its constitution, resolving that "the proceedings of the Congress shall be conducted as far as possible in Hindustani, allowing that English or a regional language could be used as necessary but also declaring that local meetings of the Congress should be conducted in the local language or Hindustani."[30] Pro-Hindustani advocates such as Gandhi and Jawaharlal Nehru, the first prime minister of India, endorsed the notion that Hindustani would unite both Hindus and Muslims and the virtue that both the Hindi Devanagari syllabary and the Urdu Perso-Arabic alphabet could be used to write Hindustani. In addition, they advocated the use of regional languages for government and education at the state level.

However, as independence grew nearer, pro-Hindi activists in the Congress Party pushed for a purer, "Sanskritized" form of Hindi as the official language of independent India. Thus the stage was set for the rancorous debate that ensued both prior to and at the 1949 Constituent Assembly, during which the Indian constitution was crafted.

In non-Hindi/Urdu-speaking areas, particularly south India, the initial agreement regarding Hindustani as a language for inter-ethnic communication and symbol for the independence movement started to erode. Congress Party governments in modern-day Tamil Nadu declared Hindi the state language for government and attempted to make it a compulsory course in government-supported schools. This led to widespread protests in 1937 as Tamils saw their culture and identity under attack. There was frequent agitation and unrest of the local populace against the state government leading up to independence.

In the 1940s, wishing to develop a Muslim communal society and not to be subsumed by a Hindu majority, the Muslim League appealed to Britain to create a separate Muslim state. This resulted in the partition of India into the Union of India and the Dominion of Pakistan in 1947, with the majority of Urdu speakers now belonging to the latter polity. In India, though, as the Constituent

[29] Das Gupta 1970.   [30] Kumaramangalam 1965: 11.

Assembly met in 1949 to draft India's constitution, the language question still loomed large. While Urdu had essentially been taken out of the equation with the formation of Pakistan, the matter of language was one of the longest, most contentious debates of the Assembly. Various motions were made to declare English, Hindi, Hindustani, Sanskrit, and Bengali as the official language of the Union. English and Hindi had the most vocal and numerous advocates, with the other three possibilities being raised largely in response to the rancorous nature of the debate.[31] Hindi supporters argued that a pure form of Hindi with its Sanskrit roots written in the Devanagari script best reflected Indian culture, that Hindi and closely related languages were spoken by the largest percentage of the population, and that 99 per cent of the population had no fluency in English. Further, given the influence of Sanskrit over all languages of India, Hindi could be easily learned, they claimed, by all those Indians who did not speak it.[32] Fearing northern cultural hegemony and great disadvantage for non-Hindi speakers, representatives from the south argued that English should be the official language, that it was the language of government institutions, and that it was an international language which would provide India with economic and diplomatic benefits. Further, they rejected the claim that learning Hindi would be as easy as had been claimed. The majority of the Congress Party, which constituted the Assembly, came from the north, and so the English advocates had to content themselves with maintaining English as an option for government activity for as long as possible.

The constitution of 1949 declared "The official language of the Union shall be Hindi in the Devanagari script" and charged the government to develop and promote Hindi and to phase out English by 1965. At the same time, English was declared the language of the Supreme Court and high courts and could be used in Union government business. The constitution further provided that individual states could "adopt any one or more of the languages in use in the State or Hindi as the language or languages to be used for all or any of the official purposes of that State,"[33] with a schedule of fifteen indigenous languages (including Hindi and Urdu) to choose from. (That number has since increased to twenty-three languages including English.)

The implementation of Hindi as the official language of government and the vehicle of all-India communication has been as contentious as the debate

[31] K. L. Gandhi 1984.
[32] Gandhi asserted in a 1921 issue of *Young India*, "An average Bengali can learn Hindustani in two months if he gave it three hours per day and a Dravidian in six months at the same rate. Neither a Bengali nor a Dravidian can hope to achieve the same result with English in the same amount of time" (M. K. Gandhi 1956: 19).
[33] Constitution of India 1949, part XVII, chapter II. 345 Official language or languages of a State. www.advocatekhoj.com/library/bareacts/constitutionofindia/345.php

leading up to its adoption. By constitutional mandate, a language commission was convened in 1955 charged with the task of evaluating the progress of, and recommendations for, facilitating the transition to Hindi as the sole language of government. Protests and conventions held in non-Hindi-speaking areas decried the Commission's recommendations and the phasing out of English by 1965. Those protests and continued agitation resulted in the passage of the Language Act of 1963, which extended the use of English as a language of government beyond the 1965 deadline. Further protests, largely by students in Tamil Nadu, led to anti-Hindi agitations (sometimes referred to as language riots because of their violent nature) in 1965, 1968, and 1986 in reaction to government deadlines and decrees. The Indian legislature has repeatedly passed resolutions continuing English as a language of government to the present time, and the language issue remains controversial.

Indonesia and India

Indonesia and India took very different tacks in approaching the designation of an official language of state. In both cases, a language was chosen early that served as a symbol of the independence movement. However, in the case of Indonesia a choice was possible that gave no particular group privileged access to economic, educational, or political advantage, thus ensuring continued support of all ethnolinguistic groups after independence. In the case of India, the native language of a large ethnolinguistic group was chosen and was perceived by some others as a threat to their cultural identity and economic and social opportunity. It is estimated that 85 percent of Indonesians can speak Indonesian, but most speak it as a second or third language. Only 15 percent speak it as their first language. In India, on the other hand, 54 percent of the population can speak Hindi, but 41 percent speak it as their first language. While certainly not a predictor of national economic success, the different choices produced quite distinct levels of national linguistic unity.

At least some of the differences in the national language experiences of Indonesia and India may be attributed to the distinctly different goals of their colonizers. The British, in much the same manner as the French, Portuguese, and Spanish, brought their language and culture with them to their colonies, and consciously imposed it upon their colonial subjects. It is for this reason, in part (with another part being Christian evangelism), that the former colonial properties of Britain, France, Spain, and Portugal are nations where English, French, Spanish, and Portuguese are maintained as state languages, at the very least. As mentioned above, one of the complicating legacies of British rule, which became a factor in the Indian national language debate, was the fact that institutions of British colonial government, law, and education all conducted their affairs in English.

The Dutch, through their United East India Company (Verenigde Oost-Indische Compagnie or VOC), did not necessarily seek to impose their language and culture upon their colonial subjects. The primary object of the company being trade, they were content to operate in other languages, as long as there was money to be made. This was certainly the case when the VOC established a "trading post" in 1641 on the small Japanese island of Deshima. Granted this concession only because the Japanese trusted the Dutch not to be "cultural imperialists," the VOC maintained a complete monopoly over trade with Japan for 200 years (until 1853). Perhaps it was their own struggles against the Spanish crown and the Catholic Church which inclined them to operate in this fashion. Whatever the reason, the Dutch in Indonesia conducted themselves in a similar fashion, choosing (as we noted above) to run their colonial affairs in Indonesia using Malay as an official language. As a consequence of this, the Indonesians (unlike the Indians) were not saddled with the institutions that operated using the language of the colonizers.

South Africa

Moving the clock forward some fifty years, we turn to a more modern case of national language negotiation and development, that of South Africa. It was in 1994 that South African apartheid ended and the country began to institute democratic reforms, including a constitution (1996), which addressed the matter of official languages. The case of South Africa is relevant for several reasons. First, South African solutions to their national language situation were addressed in a context in which linguistic human rights as a subset of human rights were already internationally recognized, or coming to be recognized (see Chapter 9). Second, the South African language situation is uniquely African – i.e. it arises in an environment of a patchwork of African tribal languages, multiple waves of European colonization, and inter-colony migration within the British Empire. Finally, it presents an opportunity to observe the resolution of language conflict in progress, with the 1996 constitution promulgating goals and the nation still striving toward those goals some twenty years later.

Historical Background   To fully understand the language situation in South Africa, one must go back some 2,000 years to a time before nearly all of the constituent peoples of South Africa lived there. At that time, contemporaneous with the height of the Roman Empire, the region of present-day South Africa (and its immediate neighbors of Botswana, Namibia, Angola, Zambia, Zimbabwe, and Lesotho) was inhabited by genetically similar groups of aboriginal peoples who have been variously known as San, Khoi, Khoikhoi, Hottentots (a derogatory Dutch term for the Khoikhoi), or Bushmen (a term for the San derived from the Dutch *Bossiesman* [*bossies* = small bushes + *man*

= person]), and Khoisan. The terms San and Khoi are meaningfully distinct, with San referring to groups that were primarily hunter-gatherers and Khoi referring to groups that engaged in pastoral life, herding goats, cattle and sheep. *Khoikhoi* is a name that the pastoralists of the Cape used to refer to themselves, and can be translated to mean 'the real people' or 'people with domestic animals.' The term *San* (San = Sanqua = Soaqua) was a name given to hunters by the Khoikhoi and means 'people different from ourselves.'[34] These two aboriginal populations, collectively pre-dating any other people in southern African by tens of thousands of years, ranged over a large portion of the southern parts of the continent, as in Figure 7.3, and may once have been the most numerous group of humans on the African continent, if not the planet.[35] Today, they (and other ethnically related groups) number fewer than half a million speakers, with only a few thousand living in (northwestern) South Africa.

The fate of the Khoisan, and specifically the reasons for their decline, is a matter of dispute. However, it is clear that most of the areas once peopled by the Khoisan are now inhabited by speakers of various Bantu languages. This dispossession began with the arrival of Bantu-speaking groups in the eastern parts of South Africa around 300 CE (these having gradually spread eastward and southward from their original homelands in present-day Nigeria and Cameroon over the course of 2,000 years). While some might envision a Bantu invasion and conquest of southern Africa, it is more likely that the Bantu incursions were at first gradual and involved some level of co-existence, including trade and intermarriage. Author Jared Diamond speculates that the Bantus' ultimately overwhelming the indigenous Khoisan was due to several factors common to other cases of more technologically advanced farming cultures coming into contact with stone-tool-using hunter-gatherer cultures. The Bantu brought iron tools and weapons with them, along with immunity to diseases (e.g. malaria) that they often carried. Thus, the agrarian Bantus most likely carved out more and more farming territory, reducing Khoisan's range, while the Khoisan succumbed to raids on their villages, and epidemics of diseases that they were not equipped to fight.[36] By 500 CE the Bantu had established themselves in the central inland parts of southern Africa, and until the arrival of the first European colonists continued to expand their dominance over the area (most notably through a succession of kingdoms – Mapungubwe, Zimbabwe, and Mutapa) from the ninth through the sixteenth centuries.

The end of the fifteenth century saw the first European contact with southern Africa, as the Portuguese explored the coast on their way to establishing trade outposts and trade routes in other parts of Africa and in India. While

---

[34] Frankental and Sichone 2005.   [35] Gibbons 2014.   [36] Diamond 1997.

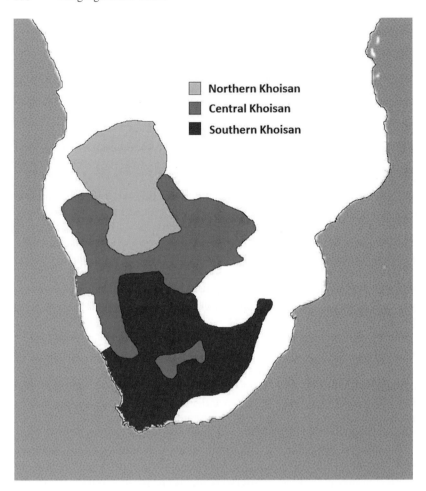

Figure 7.3 Distribution of Khoisan language families in Southern Africa

the Portuguese did not themselves establish a territorial presence in South Africa, their later occupation of Mozambique and regional pursuit of the slave trade negatively impacted peoples in South Africa who lived close to the Mozambique coast. By the end of the seventeenth century, the Dutch had established a permanent presence on the western coast in Cape Town, from which they gradually expanded their settlements in the interior. For well over 100 years, until the arrival of the British at the end of the eighteenth century, the Dutch were the only significant European linguistic and cultural presence in the area. Other European immigrants to the Cape (such as the French-speaking

Huguenots) were required by the ruling Dutch East India Company (also known by their Dutch name, Verenigde Oost-Indische Compagnie or VOC) to adopt the Dutch language, and these settlers, much like the Bantu in centuries before them, traded and intermarried with the local Khoisan inhabitants (and the local slave and ex-slave population), resulting in a colony in which as many as one-quarter of all marriages were mixed-race unions.[37] Many settlers, who called themselves Boers (the Dutch word for 'farmer') and who spoke a language that diverged from Standard Dutch, Afrikaans-Hollands or Afrikaans, were motivated by the oppressive rule of the colony on the part of the VOC to migrate inland. In this way, European settler presence in South Africa expanded to areas that were removed from the coast.

The nineteenth century saw a tremendous amount of upheaval and conflict, as the British moved into the picture and began to assert themselves in southern Africa. After initially seizing the Cape Colony in 1795, they sealed their sovereignty over it at the Congress of Vienna in 1815. The British quickly outlawed the use of Dutch in the colony, with the aim of installing British language and culture.[38] This led many Dutch settlers to move further inland, far away from the area controlled by the British. The United Kingdom also persuaded several thousand British subjects in 1820 to leave their homeland and settle in the new British colony, largely in the eastern reaches of the territory (in the area around Port Elizabeth). The colonial expansion of the British Empire into the eastern parts of South Africa was contemporaneous with the rise of a militant Zulu empire in the east. The simultaneous rise of both powers, one an imperialist Bantu kingdom and the other a European colonial enterprise, destabilized the region for the next 100 years.

The Zulu Kingdom began its expansion in earnest in 1818, when King Shaka Zulu assumed control of the tribal territory and organized it as a centralized ethnically Zulu state (see Figure 7.4). The militaristic expansion of this kingdom had the intended effect of driving several other Bantu peoples from their territory, and engendered further conflicts between the expelled tribes and the inhabitants of the lands that they were driven to. On the British side, the imposition of the English language and British culture, coupled with the 1832 abolition of slavery by the British, had the effect of driving the Afrikaans-speaking Boers into regions not controlled by the British Empire (Natal, Transvaal, and the Orange Free State). This exodus had the effect of bringing the Cape Colony exiles into conflict with the tribes living in those areas (including the tribes who had been expelled by the Zulu Kingdom).

---

[37] Heese [1985] 2011.   [38] Kamwangamalu 2009.

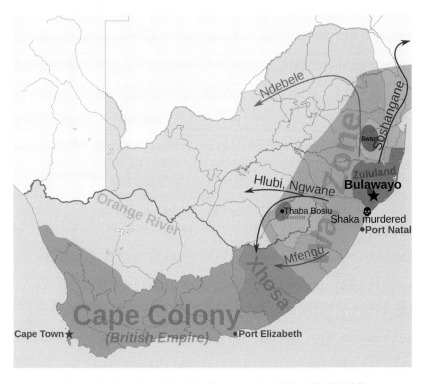

Figure 7.4 The rise of the Zulu Empire under Shaka (1816–1828)

The period, from 1815 until the creation by the British of the Union of South Africa in 1909, saw seemingly endless conflicts and wars. The Boers and the British each fought various wars with the Xhosa, Zulu, Basotho, and Bapedi. The Boers for their own part fought with the Ndbele, ultimately driving them into what is present-day Zimbabwe. The most serious wars, however, were fought between the British and the Boers, the British with the aim of consolidating imperial control over the whole of southern Africa and the Boers with the aim of regaining and preserving independence from British rule. The two Anglo-Boer wars (in 1880 and 1899) were also triggered by the desire to control the substantial gold deposits near Johannesburg. In the second Anglo-Boer War, British troops and reinforcements from across the British Empire (e.g. Southern Rhodesia, Canada, India, Australia, and New Zealand) outnumbered the Boers' forces by a factor of 10–1 (nearly 400,000 British fighting some 40,000 Boers). In fact, the number of British troops outnumbered the entire

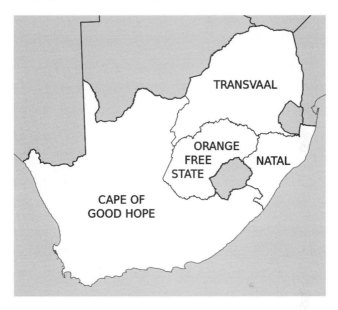

Figure 7.5 Union of South Africa (1914)

Boer population by some 150,000.[39] Needless to say, the British won that one (unlike the one 120 years earlier in North America), and by the South Africa Act of 1909 created the Union of South Africa from the colonies of Cape of Good Hope, Natal, Orange Free State, and Transvaal (leaving the undefeated tribal kingdoms of Basutoland – now Lesotho – and Swaziland as protectorates), as shown in Figure 7.5.

Language Background   The Bantu groups of note populating South Africa, then and today, include two major linguistic groups: (i) Nguni, who include Zulu, Xhosa, Swazi (Swati), and Ndebele and who largely live close to the eastern coast of South Africa, and (ii) Sotho–Tswana, who include Tswana, Pedi, and Basotho and who are mostly settled in the interior plateau. Other, smaller Bantu groups are Venda, Lemba, and Shangaan-Tsonga, who are concentrated in the northeast. Bantu-language speakers comprise some 75 percent of the current population of South Africa. The two major European (i.e. Indo-European) languages are both members of the Germanic language family, Afrikaans and English. Speakers of these two languages currently constitute a little less than one quarter of the population, with native Afrikaans speakers

[39] Davitt 1902.

Table 7.1 *South African population by first language spoken*

Language	Language group	Population	% of population
Zulu	Nguni	11,587,374	22.7
Xhosa	Nguni	8,154,258	16.0
Afrikaans	Germanic	6,855,082	13.5
English	Germanic	4,892,623	9.6
Northern Sotho	Sotho–Tswana	4,618,576	9.1
Tswana	Sotho–Tswana	4,067,248	8.0
Sesotho	Sotho–Tswana	3,849,563	7.6
Tsonga	Shangaan-Tsonga	2,277,148	4.5
Swazi	Nguni	1,297,046	2.5
Venda	Venda	1,209,388	2.4
Ndebele	Nguni	1,090,223	2.1
Other languages		828,258	1.6
Sign language		234,655	0.5
	Total	**50,961,443**	**100.0**

Source: www.statssa.gov.za/census/census_2011/census_products/Census_2011_Census_in_brief.pdf

outnumbering native English speakers by some 2 million. Table 7.1 lists the major languages of South Africa, according to the 2011 census of first-language speakers.

Considering Table 7.1 and the discussion before it, one of the most obvious omissions involves the indigenous Khoisan languages. As discussed earlier, these languages and the people who speak them have largely been displaced from, or diminished in, South Africa, such that the only Khoisan languages still spoken in the country are: !Xû[40] (2,000–3,000 speakers), Khoekhoegowap or Nama (5,000–7,000 speakers), and Khwedam (1,600 speakers), all in the Northern Cape Province. These remaining 10,000–15,000 Khoisan speakers in South Africa are a tiny portion of the (also diminished) number of Khoisan language speakers across the rest of southern Africa (principally in southern Angola, Botswana, Namibia, and Zimbabwe). Accounting for no more than 0.03 percent of the present-day population of South Africa, the Khoisan people are lumped together with the 800,000 speakers of "other languages" in the 2011 census.

Going from the most aboriginal languages of South Africa to the least, we find nearly 12 million speakers of Afrikaans and English (about 23 percent of

---

[40] The "!" symbol represents the (post-alveolar) click consonant preceding "X." Clicks are consonantal sounds occurring in (mainly) South African languages, which involve a sucking (ingressive) sound familiar to English speakers as the "tsk! tsk!" (American spelling) sound used to express disapproval or pity, or the "clip-clop" sound used to imitate a trotting horse.

the population). These two languages, coming to southern Africa over 350 and 250 years ago, respectively, are related languages belonging to the Western Germanic group of the Germanic language family. The Western Germanic language group includes English, Dutch, German, Frisian, and Scots (with Danish, Swedish, Norwegian, Faroese, and Icelandic making up the Northern Germanic group). English and the Afrikaans variety of Dutch are thus quite close to one another, lexically, grammatically, and phonologically.

As noted above, speakers of Bantu languages are the most numerous in South Africa, accounting for 75 percent of the current population. These Bantu languages are a large family within the Niger–Congo phylum (superfamily of languages). The Bantu language family accounts for 25–50 percent of the Niger-Congo languages spoken. And speakers of Bantu languages comprise a little over half of the Niger–Congo language-speaking population of Africa (330 out of 600 million speakers).

The nine official Bantu languages of South Africa themselves belong to the Southern Bantu group of languages, and these are further divided into smaller subgroups. Four of these ((isi)Zulu, (isi)Xhosa, (si)Swazi (Swati), and (isi)Ndebele) belong to the Nguni subgroup, and their speakers account for 43 percent of South Africa's population (with half of the Nguni language speakers being Zulu). Speakers of the three Sotho–Tswana languages (Northern Sotho (Sesotho sa Leboa), (Se)Tswana, and Sesotho) number 12.5 million and account for 25 percent of the population. Speakers of the two other Bantu languages, (Xi)Tsonga and (Tshi)Venda, number 2.3 million and 1.2 million, respectively.

Notice that the Nguni languages are spoken mostly in the eastern regions of South Africa, nearer to the coast. Sotho–Tswana language speakers live mostly in the inland eastern regions, with Venda and Tsonga speakers living close to Botswana and Mozambique, respectively. Afrikaans is most widely used in the western parts of the country, and English speakers are mainly found in urban areas. It is also worth pointing out that the speakers of the Nguni group of languages and the Sotho group of languages collectively amount to nearly 70 percent of the population. This, combined with the fact that the four Nguni languages are to some extent mutually intelligible, as are the three Sotho languages, has led some to propose that South Africa might be better off having one standardized Nguni and one standardized Sotho official language, rather than the current seven official languages/dialects from those groups.[41] This will be discussed again, below, as we examine the issue of South African national language(s).

[41] Louw 1992.

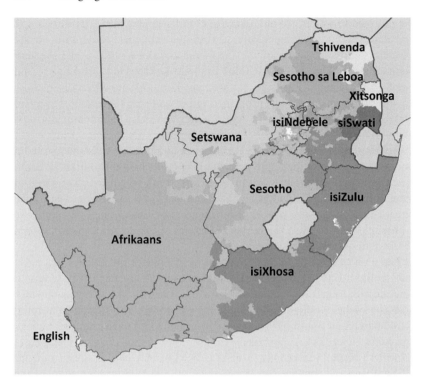

Figure 7.6 Languages of South Africa

Language in South Africa, 1910–1948   The assertion of British control over the whole of South Africa was accomplished with the British defeat of the Boers in 1902 following the Second Anglo-Boer War, and with the creation of the Union of South Africa as an independent dominion of the British crown in 1909. Just as in the takeover of the Cape Colony in 1815, political consolidation was accompanied by efforts at Anglicization, including efforts to impose the English language throughout the newly conquered territories. But just as the Boers had resisted Anglicization in the nineteenth century, so they did once more at the beginning of the twentieth. The depredations of the British campaigns against the Boers did not endear them to the English language. Efforts to impose English were thus necessarily short-lived, and English and Dutch remained official languages. By 1914, World War I led the British to focus their attention on other, more pressing needs, such as the 1915 campaign to dislodge the Germans from German Southwest Africa (present-day Namibia).

From 1910 until 1924, South Africa was ruled by the Afrikaans-dominated and centrist South African Party (Suid-Afrikaanse Party). In 1924, the more conservative and nationalist Afrikaans-dominated National Party came into power, and one of its early initiatives, linguistically, was to promote the Afrikaans language (previously regarded as an uneducated form of Standard Dutch) to co-equal status with English, replacing Dutch. During this period, the Bantu languages spoken by the black African majority were not suppressed, but were merely subject to neglect, and offered as a medium of instruction for the few blacks privileged enough to attend mission schools. The white government, for its part, was mostly preoccupied with the wholesale elimination of black Africans' property rights, their freedom of movement, and the suppression of their political participation. There was, at the time, little attention paid to the status and use of Bantu languages, per se, perhaps because the Bantu-speaking population had never had any language rights to begin with.

Language in South Africa, 1948–1994 While segregation and racist laws were instituted and expanded both before the 1909 Union and afterward, 1948 represented a watershed year for South Africa. The years leading up to World War II had been a divisive time in South Africa, during which the neutral (or German-sympathizing) National Party, under the leadership of Prime Minister Herzog, had formed a unity party and government with the pro-British South African Party, under the leadership of Jan Smuts. Smuts became prime minister in 1939, and led South Africa until the first post-war elections of 1948.

While Smuts had been in favor of segregation all along, his positions were not sufficiently radical for the most conservative Afrikaans-speaking voters. His support for the idea that black Africans be given permanent residency in white South Africa (rather than continue to be temporary workers with permanent residency on tribal reservations) was enough to tip the electoral scales in 1948 to a unity government of the right-wing National Party and the righter-wing Afrikaner Party. Upon the formation of a government free from the somewhat moderating influences of the pro-British parties, South Africa commenced to further codify and extend the racism of previous governments in a system labeled "apartheid."

From 1949 until the mid 1950s, a dazzling array of laws was passed to institutionalize the apartheid system. These laws, variously, (i) categorized and registered everyone in South Africa as White, Coloured, or Native; (ii) prohibited marriage or sexual relations between whites and blacks; (iii) restricted, according to their race, people's right to reside in certain areas and their access to amenities (e.g. parks and beaches) and services (e.g. train stations and postal offices); (iv) required blacks to carry documents that registered their race, restricting their movement in areas populated by whites; and (v) removed the right of blacks to vote.

Not to be outdone in the domain of language and education, the apartheid legislation also included the 1953 Bantu Education Act, which was devised to remove control over the education of black African children from the mission schools. Rather than forcing education in languages of government and power (i.e. English or Afrikaans) on the native population, as was done in American Indian boarding schools run by the United States Bureau of Indian Affairs, this legislation was aimed at preventing it. As William Beinart (2001: 160) states, "Education at the 5,000 or so mission schools had produced, in Nationalist eyes, an academic training with too much emphasis on English and dangerous liberal ideas." The Act also required more extensive use of African (i.e. Bantu) vernacular languages up through the eighth year of schooling, so as to "cement ethnic awareness in African children." Thus, the Act was designed, at once, to be a linguistic brake on the acquisition of knowledge and as a vehicle to promote tribal (rather than African) identity among African schoolchildren.

The path to a fully institutionalized apartheid state culminated in 1960 with a referendum on whether South Africa should remain a dominion of the British crown or become independent of it. By a margin of 4.5 percent (52.3 percent in favor of independence and 47.7 percent opposed), the referendum passed, converting the Union of South Africa into the Republic of South Africa and leading to its exit from the British Commonwealth. Along this path, too, was established the legal apparatus for effecting an ethnolinguistic separation of Bantu people from South Africa's "white" (and "coloured") citizens, as well as a separation of the various Bantu tribes from one another. Before 1948, black Africans were associated with various tribal reservations, but the 1951 Bantu Authorities Act gave power in each "homeland" to the traditional tribal leader(s) of each group. This had the effect of reinforcing the separateness of each tribe, according to their language, and all but eliminating any mechanism for cooperation among them. This arrangement was strengthened in 1970 through the Bantu Homelands Citizenship Act, which forced black Africans to have citizenship in the homeland belonging to their own ethnolinguistic group, regardless of whether they lived in it. These consisted of four nominally independent states (Transkei, Bophuthatswana, Venda, and Ciskei) and six self-governing entities (Gazankulu, KaNgwane, KwaNdebele, KwaZulu, Lebowa, and QwaQwa). These ten homelands represented the nine Bantu languages spoken in South Africa, and were established in the regions where the languages are dominant (see Figure 7.6). The speakers of the four Nguni languages were assigned to five homelands: Zulu to KwaZulu, Xhosa to Transkei and Ciskei, Swazi (Swati) to KaNgwane, and Ndebele to KwaNdebele. Speakers of the three Sotho-Tswana languages were assigned to three homelands: Northern Sotho to Lebowa, Tswana to Bophuthatswana, and Sesotho to QwaQwa. The Tsonga speakers' homeland was Gazankulu, and the Venda homeland was Venda.

By means of these laws, coupled with the forced relocation of 3–4 million black Africans into these homelands, the Republic of South Africa was able to achieve a situation in which over half of the black Africans (14 million), representing 42 percent of the total population, were confined to areas representing about 13 percent of the country's territory. With black Africans constituting 75 percent of South Africa's population and 14 million out of 25 million of them confined to homelands, the proportion of blacks among the remaining 19.5 million people was a more manageable 56 percent. This proportionality was even more manageable when one takes into account that most of the remaining black Africans had no rights outside their assigned homelands, and were condemned to live as "guest workers" in shanty towns and other slums ringing the metropolitan areas.

Ultimately, despite the most careful concoction of laws and regulations designed to maintain minority white rule, the situation was unsustainable in the face of internal unrest, economic sanctions, and international condemnation. By 1989, the wheels were beginning to come off the apartheid vehicle, and (though accompanied by a fair amount of resistance from white Afrikaans-speaking South Africans and from the ruling cliques within the Bantustans) apartheid ended in 1994.

Language in South Africa, 1996 to the Present   Soon after the end of apartheid and the extension of suffrage to all South Africans in the 1994 elections, the Republic of South African adopted a new constitution, reflective of the major changes that had been brought about. Significant and somewhat surprising in the 1996 constitution of the Republic of South Africa is the prominence given to matters of language. The first section of the constitution sets out the Founding Provisions of the newly constituted state, addressing familiar matters such as the name of the state, citizenship, the flag, and the national anthem. The sixth of the six Founding Provisions is titled "Language," and if the amount of space given over to it is any indication of the importance and complexity of the matter, we note that over half of the 450 words in the section are in this sixth part:

- Section 6.1 names the eleven official languages "Sepedi, Sesotho, Setswana, siSwati, Tshivenda, Xitsonga, Afrikaans, English, isiNdebele, isiXhosa and isiZulu," changing South Africa in one sentence from a bilingual (English and Afrikaans) state to a many-lingual one.
- Section 6.2 stipulates that the state "must take practical and positive measures to elevate the status and advance the use" the newly enfranchised Bantu languages.

- Section 6.3 enjoins the national, regional, and local governments to take the needs and preferences of the population into account when deciding on the implementation of official languages in government.
- Section 6.4 provides that "all official languages must enjoy parity of esteem and must be treated equitably."
- Section 6.5 mandates promoting "the development and use of (i) all official languages; (ii) the Khoi, Nama and San languages; and (iii) sign language" and "respect for (i) all languages commonly used by communities in South Africa, including German, Greek, Gujarati, Hindi, Portuguese, Tamil, Telugu and Urdu; and (ii) Arabic, Hebrew, Sanskrit and other languages used for religious purposes in South Africa."

Language is further referenced in the constitution's Bill of Rights, wherein language rights form part of the rights that are spelled out in the topics of Education, Language and Culture, Cultural, Religious, and Linguistic Communities, and Arrested, Detained and Accused Persons. Therein it states that:

- Everyone has the right to receive education in the official language or languages of their choice in public educational institutions where that education is reasonably practicable.
- Everyone has the right to use the language and to participate in the cultural life of their choice.
- Persons belonging to a cultural, religious or linguistic community may not be denied the right, with other members of that community ... to enjoy their culture, practise their religion and use their language.
- Every accused person has the right ... to be tried in a language that the accused person understands or, if that is not practicable, to have the proceedings interpreted in that language.

The primacy given over to matters of language in the 1996 constitution merits some comment. First of all, where South Africa prior to 1994 had been primarily focused on race-based identity, the 1996 constitution shows a remarkable shift toward the recognition of other forms of identity (i.e. ethnic, cultural, religious) and the explicit marker of these is asserted to be language. Second, it is noteworthy that the 1996 additions to the list of official languages include not only Bantu languages generally, but add each one of the nine tribal languages formerly represented as Bantustans under the apartheid regime. As Eric Louw states:

The Afrikaner Nationalism [was] built on and systematized the colonial British divide-and-rule policy. Since whites constituted a minority of South Africa's population, the most effective way to rule was to prevent the 75% black-African population from cohering into a unified group. A key means of achieving this was an active state-sponsored encouragement of African tribalism in South Africa.[42]

---

[42] Louw 1992: 52.

It would thus appear, on the face of it, that the 1996 constitution neither confronted nor cured the divide-and-rule policies established in prior generations.

Recall from the language background commentary, above, that seven of the nine Bantu languages belong to two groups – Nguni (Zulu, Xhosa, Swazi (Swati), and Ndebele) and Sotho (North Sotho, South Sotho (Sesotho), and Tswana) – and that the languages in each cluster are, for the most part, mutually intelligible and might be considered dialects, as opposed to distinct languages. This fact has been long recognized, and some fifty years before the end of apartheid, in 1944:

Jacob Nhlapo, a well-known educator and member of the African National Congress, proposed the harmonisation [i.e. standardization and merger] of the mutually intelligible varieties of the Nguni cluster of Bantu languages (mainly isiZulu and isiXhosa) on the one hand, and of the mutually intelligible varieties in the Sotho cluster (mainly Sepedi, Setswana and Sesotho) with a view to creating two standard written languages out of the many different spoken varieties.[43]

Following on Nhlapo's observations, Neville Alexander proposed in the 1990s that English be South Africa's national language and that a standardized Nguni and Sotho be adopted as the two regional languages. Louw (1992: 53) suggests adding Afrikaans as a regional language, noting that "85% of South Africans fall into one of ... three linguistic categories (i.e. 46% Nguni; 23% Sotho; and 16% Afrikaans). Louw's map, Figure 7.7, illustrates how the regional languages might be assigned territorially.

The reasons for there being eleven, rather than four or six, official languages, are complex and not completely certain, but one can certainly see how the history of South Africa before and during the apartheid era led to the current situation. For example, the creation of a Nguni language (unifying Zulu, Xhosa, Swazi (Swati), and Ndebele) would require choosing standards from among the various Nguni dialects and, given that Zulu speakers comprise more than half of the Nguni speakers, was likely to favor Zulu over the other dialects.

This raises immediate issues, both historical and linguistic. Recall that it was the Zulu who drove out or subjugated many other tribes in the region during the nineteenth century, and the other Nguni groups might be resistant to Zulu linguistic hegemony due to historical resentment of Zulu political hegemony. The Xhosa people, in particular, have a long history of asserting themselves politically and culturally in opposition to both the Zulu and the British, having periodically fought with each. Consider the fact that Xhosa is a Bantu "click language," having long ago borrowed the click consonants of the Khoisan

[43] Alexander 2001: 12.

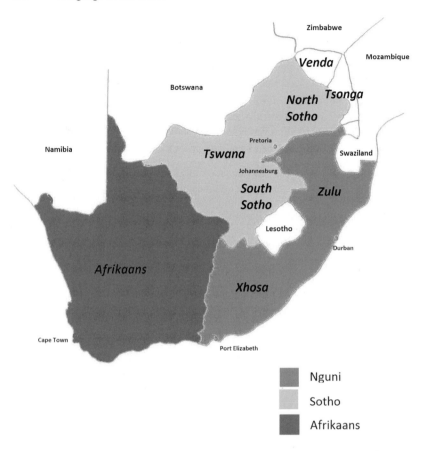

Figure 7.7 Proposal for standardization and regional language areas in South Africa

languages,[44] probably through extended contact with those indigenous peoples. Zulu, in contrast, uses clicks far less frequently, and, unlike Xhosa, is not a tonal language. Would "Standard Nguni" be non-tonal and not make much use of click consonants, both of which are important to Xhosa speakers? Or would it include them, rendering Nguni a language that Zulu speakers would have more difficulty learning? The phonological problems are only one small part of the matter, there also being lexical and other differences that would need to be bridged.

[44] See note 42.

Beyond the intertribal resistance that might preclude an agreement on the formulation of regional Nguni and Sotho languages, it is further the case that it serves the white minority to continue a situation in which each tribal language (i.e. dialect) alongside Afrikaans and English enjoys "parity of esteem and must be treated equitably." If each of the former Bantustans is represented in the constitution as an official language (with Xhosa representing two of them), then Afrikaans and English are the third and fourth most important official languages out of eleven, rather than out of four or six.

Whatever the reasons, the choice to affirm seven Nguni and Sotho languages, rather than have one uniform standard variety of each, was made constitutionally in 1996, and is a choice that South Africa has had to live with since. It is fair to say that compliance with the language provisions of the 1996 constitution has not been either easy or greatly successful. Evidence for this comes in the passage of the Official Languages Act 12 of 2012, designed to address the myriad problems that have arisen from the somewhat draconian stipulations set forth in Article 6 of the constitution. It is one thing to declare that each one of eleven official languages must be treated equitably and with parity of esteem. It is another thing to determine precisely what it means to do so, and further to ascertain how to go about it. This is an unavoidable problem arising from the simple fact that not all languages are used in the same contexts, with the same frequency, or for the same purposes. The use of English in a university lecture on biology and the use of Xhosa at a social gathering on that same university campus cannot be felicitously interchanged. Thus, one of South Africa's major goals, especially in the domain of higher education (were linguistic parity is least easily effected) is to work toward the ideals of the 1996 constitution by providing speakers with the resources necessary for them to become proficient in more than one or two languages, and by providing the languages (especially to their lexicons) with the resources needed for them to be useful in all contexts. The success of these arduous tasks will be known in the coming decade.

8   The Role of Writing Systems

One of the properties that distinguishes human language from animal communication systems is the property of displacement, which is the ability to communicate things that are displaced in time and/or location from the time of the communication.[1] As Bertrand Russell famously said, "No matter how eloquently a dog may bark, he cannot tell you that his parents were poor but honest." Nowhere is the property of displacement more salient than in written language. The development of writing allowed humans to communicate with others who were not present and also allowed communication with larger numbers of people (pre-dating, of course, audio recording and broadcasting).

It is the timelessness of written language which makes it so different from spoken language and which has imbued it (and those who had control over it) with power and even a degree of mysticism not associated with common spoken language. While all normal humans acquire language without much conscious effort, learning to write (and read) requires great effort and explicit instruction. Before the era of "universal" education and literacy, writing was the province of the elite: even half a millennium in the past, if a book such as the one you are holding had been written, an exceedingly small percentage of the population would have been able to read it. Sacred texts are considered sacred in part simply because they are texts, and the physical texts are often revered. In many religions, for example, the tradition of reading passages aloud to worshippers traces back to an age when none but the clergy could read. In many cultures, written words were thought to hold magical power. In Yiddish folklore, for example, the legend of the Golem involves the creation of a living being out of clay, who is brought to life by inserting into its mouth the name of God written on paper.

It is the relative permanence of written language and its link with the past that helps explain why written languages – and actually the standard languages on which they are based (see Chapter 4 regarding "standard languages") – are often held up as the "standard" by which people's spoken language is judged.

[1] Hockett 1960.

Given the centrality of written language to human communication, and given the elevated status accorded to it, it is important to examine the origin and role of orthography (that is, writing systems) in the world's languages. Before embarking on a discussion of the origins of writing and a description of the major types of writing systems, it is important to emphasize the distinction between written and spoken forms. In Chapter 1, we took great pains to distinguish between sounds and letters, demonstrating that letters were simply graphic representations of sounds, rather than sounds themselves, and that they often (especially in English) bear inconsistent relations with the sounds that they are supposed to represent.

So it is with writing systems (to a degree). To the extent that selected orthographic systems have the symbols to represent the sounds appropriately, a language could be written using any of them. Take, for instance, the English word *many* (as in "not a few"). While translating the word into other languages would require knowledge of the target lexicon, transcribing the word *many* (or rather, the sounds that make it up) into other writing systems is much more straightforward:

many	Latin	(used for English, French, etc.)
мени	Cyrillic	(used for Russian, Bulgarian, etc.)
メ二	Japanese Katakana	(used for Japanese)
μενι	Greek	(used for Greek)
מאני	Hebrew	(used for Hebrew)

Each of these forms is pronounced [mɛni] in the named writing system (note the name of each writing system may or may not correspond to the language which uses it). This will be an important fact to remember when we consider, later in the chapter, that languages may change their writing systems without necessarily changing anything else and that the choice of writing system is often a political or sectarian, rather than linguistic, decision.

Broadly speaking, writing systems are based on one of two aspects of human language, either the lexical semantics of the language (the conceptual meaning of the morphemes and words) or its phonology (the sounds). The first type is generally referred to as a logographic or ideographic system, and is best exemplified by some of the Egyptian hieroglyphic and Chinese characters. The second type includes alphabetical writing, such as the Latin alphabet used for English and Spanish, and syllabaries, such as the "kana" of Japanese. Systems involving each of these two aspects played a role in the development of Western writing.

Given the time depth and distribution of writing systems and what is known about migration patterns, it seems clear that some writing systems were developed independently of one another, some were spread through migration and trade, and some evolved out of earlier systems (and underwent radical change in doing so).

Here, in what follows, we will first describe the major types of writing systems humans have developed over the past 5,000–8,000 years, as well as some theories regarding the genesis of Western alphabetic writing.

The Mesopotamian Genesis of Early Writing

The most plausible theory of the origins of one of the earliest writing systems is that it developed out of a system of accounting. It is argued that in Mesopotamia as early as 8000 BCE small clay tokens were used for keeping track of quantities of grain, livestock, and other goods. These tokens were plain and smooth and came in various circular and conical shapes. Scholars hypothesize that the different shapes and types of tokens each represented a particular quantity.

Over the next few thousand years, this system of accounting tokens evolved substantially. Some tokens were no longer smooth, but had markings on the surface. They also occurred in many more plentiful and more intricate shapes. At this stage, the tokens no longer were mere counting devices, since some had come to represent specific items. For example, in Figure 8.1, the circular token with crossed lines in the first row means 'sheep'; the arced striped token in the fourth row means 'metal'; the striped round token in the sixth row represents 'garment'; and the double-sided conical token in the seventh row means 'bracelet.'

Eventually, in order to dispense with the trouble of carrying clay tokens, people started to use them as a means of imprinting the image of a token into a wet clay tablet. In this way, the record of a single accounting could be preserved on one tablet (which avoided, among other things, the possible loss of tokens). In this way, the tokens themselves were transformed into 'writing' tools.

One of the difficulties encountered in the transition from using the tokens themselves to utilizing their impressions into clay was the fact that more complex and detailed tokens often did not leave a readable impression. This led to the use of a stylus to mark the form of the token into the tablet. In this way Sumerian writing came into being, a system in which the stylus-created symbols were more-or-less faithful representations of the tokens.

The Transition from Idea-Based to Sound-Based Writing

Many ancient writing systems, including the Sumerian system discussed above as well as the early Chinese symbolic writing system (approx. 3,000–3,500

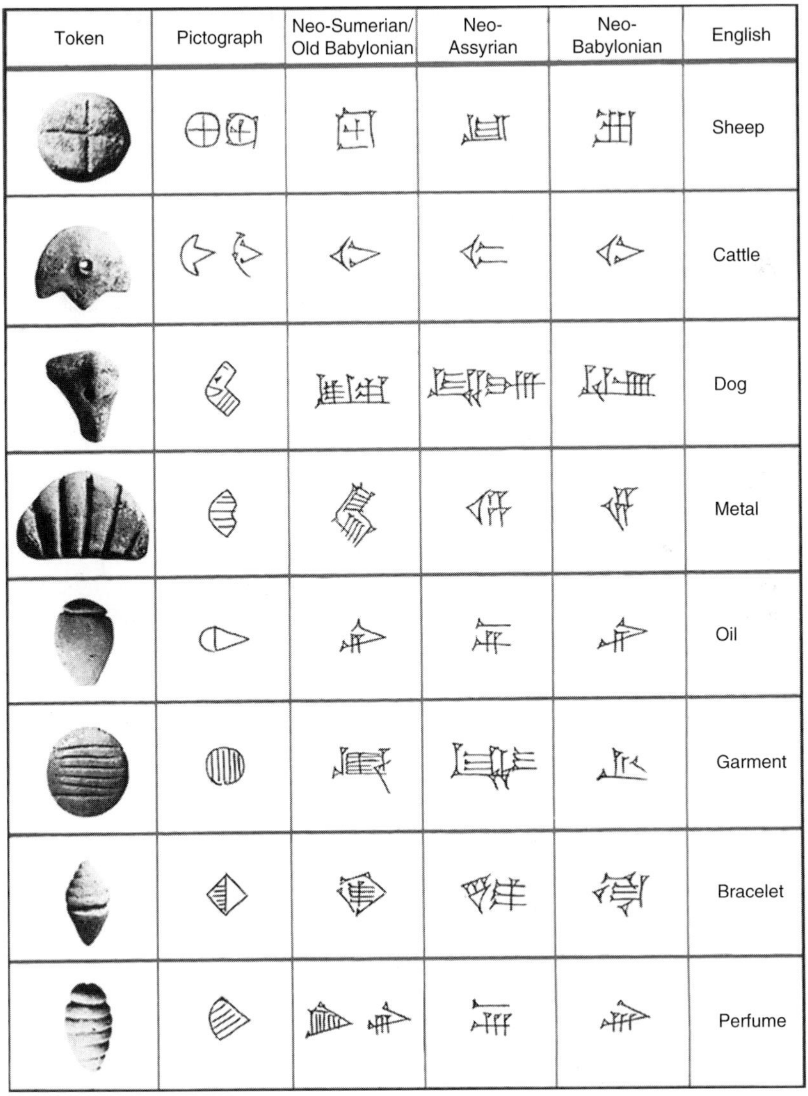

Token	Pictograph	Neo-Sumerian/ Old Babylonian	Neo- Assyrian	Neo- Babylonian	English
					Sheep
					Cattle
					Dog
					Metal
					Oil
					Garment
					Bracelet
					Perfume

Figure 8.1 Evolution from tokens to pictographs

years ago), used single symbols to represent either the image or idea of a word or morpheme. Writing systems that are made up of characters that represent entire words or morphemes are called **logographic** and a symbol in the system is called a **logograph**.

Oracle bone script						Shang or Yin Dynasty 1400–1200 BCE
Bronze script						Zhou Dynasty 1100–256 BCE
Large seal script						Zhou Dynasty 1100–256 BCE
Small seal script						Qin Dynasty 221–207 BCE
Clerical script						First appeared during Han Dynasty 207 BCE–220 CE
Standard script						
Running script						Handwritten script since Han Dynasty
Draft script						Used since Han Dynasty
Simplified script						Used in PRC since 1956/1964
	horse	cart	fish	dust	see	

Figure 8.2 Evolution of Chinese pictograms

As we have seen, the most common Sumerian symbols were pictorial representations of what they referred to, or **pictographs**. As we see in several columns of Figure 8.1, Sumerian writing evolved from using pictographic clay tokens, to using the tokens as writing tools to impress their image into clay, to using a stylus with a triangular tip to draw the image into clay. In this process, the images became increasingly "stylized" and abstract. This method of writing with a stylus came to be known as **cuneiform** (from the Latin word *cuneus*, meaning 'wedge') on account of the wedge-shaped appearance of the stylus marks in the clay.

Chinese pictographs underwent similar transitions, as we see in Figure 8.2.[2] The earliest Chinese pictographic characters were intended to be pictures of

---

[2] Many of the examples of writing systems provided in this chapter are taken from Omniglot.com, an online encyclopedia of writing systems and languages, created and maintained by Simon Ager. Omniglot presents (among other things) the most comprehensive and accessible encyclopedia of writing systems available.

what they represented, and were scratched (i.e. incised) into bones and tortoise shells. As writing tools, materials, and surfaces were developed (e.g. writing with a brush onto bamboo, pottery, or shells) the symbols evolved to become increasingly abstract.

Similar to, and alongside, pictographs were logographs that were used to express ideas that are not readily pictured. These **ideographs** can develop out of metaphorical extensions of pictograph. The Chinese character for the word for 'bright,' for example, is a combination of the pictographs for sun and moon:

[ming]
'bright'

The same process was observed with Sumerian cuneiform logographs, where a single symbol could be used to represent more than one word. So, for example, a pictograph of a starry night . . .

was variously used to mean 'black,' 'night,' and 'dark.' Similarly, a pictograph of a foot . . .

was used to represent the concepts 'go,' 'move,' and 'stand.'

With both Sumerian cuneiform and Chinese characters, the frequent ambiguity of symbols, the need to have symbols for words that were difficult or impossible to represent pictographically, and the sheer number of symbols needed for a comprehensive writing system all led to innovations in which the logographs were made to incorporate phonological information alongside the semantic information that they already presented.

In Sumeria, scribes began to take advantage of phonetic similarities between words and began to use the **rebus principle**, which is the term used to describe the reuse of a pictograph to represent a word that is pronounced with the same (or nearly the same) sound. Accordingly, a symbol for a word that is readily represented pictorially is used for a **homophonous** word that does not lend itself as easily to a visual presentation. An example of the rebus principle is offered here below, where the picture of a can is used to symbolize the modal verb *can* and the picture of a well stands in for the adverb *well*:

CAN   YOU SEE   WELL?

To understand how this worked in Sumerian cuneiform, we can use as an example the word for 'arrow,' pronounced [ti:], and reproduced here:

[ti:]
'arrow'

Now, it happened that the word for 'life' was also pronounced [ti:], and not having a pictograph for 'life' (it's hard to imagine what such a pictograph would be) the scribes used the homophonous symbol for 'arrow' when they wished to write the word 'life.'

[ti:]
'life'

Given that the context would normally signal when the symbol meant 'arrow' and when it meant 'life,' this did not present a major problem for understanding text (when used in moderation). It would be no different if we were to write the following sentence, using homophones for the intended words:

Eye Sea Ewe Knead Sum Gnu Close

Anyone reading the sentence carefully will instantly understand it to mean 'I see you need some new clothes.' The Sumerian scribes similarly utilized pictographs for other concrete things that were homophonous with abstract concepts; e.g. the pictograph for 'water,' pronounced [a], was used for the preposition 'in,' also pronounced [a], and so on.

Their efforts to avail themselves of the phonological properties of symbols was developed further by application of the **acrophonic principle**, in which a symbol that represents a word that begins with a certain sound or syllable comes to represent that single sound or syllable. In this way, for example, the pictograph for 'arrow' came to be used to represent the syllable [ti:] whenever it occurred in a word. The symbol, thus stripped of any meaning, changed in this use from a **logograph** into a **syllabograph** (i.e. a symbol for the syllable [ti:]).[3]

---

[3] http://en.wikipedia.org/wiki/TI_(cuneiform)

[ti:]

In this fashion, Sumerian script became a mixed system with both semantically based and phonically based elements.

Much like Sumerian, Chinese underwent an evolution which involved rebus-like innovations. In the beginning, the approaches were analogous. Chinese scribes, too, used the rebus principle to insert pictographs into places in which a homophonous abstract word might be wanted. For example, the pictograph for 'wheat' was the following character, pronounced [lai]:

來

[lai]
'wheat'

Using the same homophonic principle, the character was used for the verb 'come':[4]

來

[lai]
'come'

As with Sumerian, the rebus principle of using homophones could be carried only so far. The Chinese answer to this, however, was different. Chinese is a tone language in which a single monosyllabic sequence can mean a variety of things depending on the pitch with which it is uttered. Because of this there are a great many near-homophones in the language, and this was reflected in the early writing. Rather than apply the **acrophonic principle** and move in the direction of using the characters phonically, Chinese scholars during the Qin and Han dynasties (approx. 200 BCE – 200 CE) moved to standardize the writing system, which had previously varied across the many pre-dynastic kingdoms. The main principle of organization was the addition of a semantic element to the homophone – these *semantic radicals* would indicate whether you were dealing with a place name, a plant-type organism, or any of a couple of hundred other classes.

Take, for example, the pictograph for 'horse,' pronounced [ma]:[5]

---

[4] DeFrancis 1984.
[5] The words represented in this discussion have a tone (high, rising, low, or falling) in addition to a consonant and vowel, and this renders some of them slightly less homophonic than they would otherwise be. This distinction is ignored here, for the purpose of keeping the explanation clearer.

馬
[ma]
'horse'

The word for 'mother' is also pronounced [ma] (with a slightly different tone) and written with the following character. The right side of the character has the familiar rebus homophone, while the left side has a character that means 'woman.' Thus the character can be described as "the word which sounds like *horse* and is related to *woman*."

媽
[ma]
'mother'

A similar example is given here, where the meaning element on the left refers to 'insect' and the meaning of the logograph is 'ant':

螞
[ma]
'ant'

Approximately 90 percent of the several thousand Chinese characters contain a semantic "radical" and a phonetic element.

Although the Chinese did not do so, the Japanese did apply the acrophonic principle to create a phonic writing system based on the (Japanese) pronunciations of certain Chinese characters. The table below illustrates three (of several dozen) Chinese characters that came to be used acrophonically to represent Japanese syllables.

The earliest recorded phonetic use of Chinese characters in Japanese was found on a burial mound sword, the Inariyama sword, dated around the end of the fifth century CE.[6] This iron sword, recovered from a warrior's burial mound in 1968, had on it a 115-character inscription that was accidentally discovered in cleaning it for display in 1978. The inscription uses Chinese characters to record the names of the warrior, Wowake, and his many children.

It wasn't until much later, though, that Japanese developed a full-fledged and regular phonetic writing system based on Chinese. In fact, Japanese has two such sets of symbols: the **hiragana** which evolved out of abbreviated cursive forms of selected Chinese characters as used in the tenth and eleventh centuries by women of the imperial court, and the **katakana** which was devised by Buddhist priests by using specific parts of certain characters.[7] Figure 8.3 shows

[6] Seeley 1991.   [7] Bowring and Uryu Laurie 2004.

Table 8.1 *Chinese character: Japanese kana correspondences*

	Chinese character	Japanese phonetic syllable
Form	毛	も
Pronunciation	[mao]	[mo]
Meaning	'hair'	————
Form	太	た
Pronunciation	[tai]	[ta]
Meaning	"great"	————
Form	安	あ
Pronunciation	[an]	[a]
Meaning	'peace'	————

A	ア 阿	I	イ 伊	U	ウ 宇	E	エ 江	O	オ 於
KA	カ 加	KI	キ 機	KU	ク 久	KE	ケ 介	KO	コ 己
SA	サ 散	SI	シ 之	SU	ス 須	SE	セ 世	SO	ソ 曽
TA	タ 多	TI	チ 千	TU	ツ 川	TE	テ 天	TO	ト 止
NA	ナ 奈	NI	ニ 仁	NU	ヌ 奴	NE	ネ 祢	NO	ノ 乃
HA	ハ 八	HI	ヒ 比	HU	フ 不	HE	ヘ 部	HO	ホ 保
MA	マ 末	MI	ミ 三	MU	ム 牟	ME	メ 女	MO	モ 毛
YA	ヤ 也			YU	ユ 由			YO	ヨ 與
RA	ラ 良	RI	リ 利	RU	ル 流	RE	レ 礼	RO	ロ 呂
WA	ワ 和		ヰ 井					WO	ヲ 乎

Figure 8.3 Japanese katakana syllabary and its associated Chinese characters

the second of these systems. Each box in the table contains the katakana symbol on the left and the printed Chinese character, on which the symbol is based, to its right. The hiragana (not pictured) and parallel katakana symbol sets are **syllabaries** – that is, symbols that stand for syllables (either a vowel alone or a consonant–vowel combination). Reading the topmost row beginning with:

the five symbols stand for: [a], [i], [u], [ɛ], [o]. The second row, beginning with:

reads: [ka], [ki], [ku], [kɛ], [ko]. The symbols in each subsequent row stand for a different consonant, followed by the same five vowels. There are no symbols to represent a consonant independently of the syllable that it occurs in.[8]

The Birth of Western Alphabetic Writing

We turn now to the lineage of the Western writing systems, which, as we shall see, all share a common heritage. It is historically well documented that both Western and Middle Eastern alphabetic orthographies have their origin in an alphabet used by the Phoenicians, who lived in present-day Lebanon and coastal Syria but who traded throughout the Mediterranean from its eastern Levantine shores to the Straits of Gibraltar. Although the Phoenicians, like so many Middle Eastern societies from Persia to the Mediterranean, first used a cuneiform orthography that evolved from the Sumerian system of accounting, the alphabetic writing system that they ultimately developed had a far different genesis, one which can be traced back to Egyptian hieroglyphics.[9]

Egyptian Hieroglyphics

Egyptian hieroglyphics (from the Greek *hiero* 'sacred' and *glyph* 'writing') were developed some 5,000 years ago, and are well known from the many Egyptian inscriptions found in the ancient tombs and monuments and as popularized in fiction and film. It bears pointing out that there are many popular misconceptions about the system. People often think of hieroglyphics merely as pictograms, with each symbol being a direct graphical representation of some concrete concept – a vulture being interpreted as a vulture, a crocodile as a crocodile, a queen as a queen, and so on. It is true that many symbols were originally pictograms, with the concept of the bird 'swallow' represented by a picture of a swallow, and 'cat' represented by a picture of a cat. However, the system as fully evolved was far more complex and sophisticated – at least as

---

[8] Japanese actually uses a mixed system for writing. There are 2,136 "regular-use Chinese characters" (*jōyō kanji* 常用漢字) established by the Japanese Ministry of Education. These are used in combination with the syllabaries. Hiragana is used for native Japanese words and katakana for non-Chinese loan words, onomatopoeic words, foreign names, in telegrams, and for emphasis (the equivalent of bold, italic or upper case text in English).

[9] There are those who hold that all writing systems, including Western orthographies (and Chinese characters), can ultimately be traced back to the Sumerian system (e.g. Gelb 1952 and Powell 1981). This is a minority position disputed by many (e.g. Sampson 1985).

'Aset'

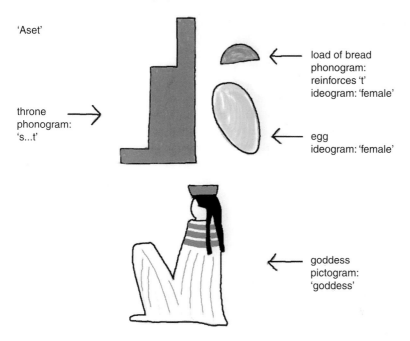

throne
phonogram:
's...t'

load of bread
phonogram:
reinforces 't'
ideogram: 'female'

egg
ideogram: 'female'

goddess
pictogram:
'goddess'

Figure 8.4 An example of hieroglyphic inscription with interpretation

much so as Sumerian, using elements according to the rebus principle, the acrophonic principle, and even adding semantic elements in the manner of Chinese.[10]

Figure 8.4 provides an example of a hieroglyphic word. The four elements combine to represent the name of the Egyptian goddess Aset (also known as Isis). The top left element is a pictograph of a throne, which is used here as a phonetic element to represent the consonants [s] and [t], indicating the word contains those two consonants. The top right element is a pictograph of a loaf of bread, but is also used here as a phonetic element to reinforce the fact the word contains (ends with?) [t] and also invokes the meaning 'female.' The oval element on the left below that is a pictograph of an egg, and is used as an ideograph indicating the referent of the word is 'female.' Below these is a pictograph of a goddess, also used here as a semantic element. The four

---

[10] The hieroglyphic system was sufficiently complex that it remained undeciphered for many centuries after the end of the Egyptian civilization in which it was used. It was not until 1799 that the discovery of the Rosetta Stone provided the key to understanding it. Dating from 198 BCE, the Rosetta Stone contained a decree from King Ptolemy V in three scripts: hieroglyphics, Demotic script (another ancient Egyptian script) and Ancient Greek. The eventual interpretation of the Ancient Greek provided the key to unlock the meaning of the hieroglyphs.

elements of the first word combine to tell us that the word represents 'the female goddess whose name contains the consonants [s] and [t], and ends with [t],' i.e. Aset.

The Proto-Sinaitic Alphabet

Although the Phoenician alphabet can be traced back to the Egyptian system, it was actually the Canaanites in the Sinai from whom they borrowed and developed a phonetic alphabet based on some of the Egyptian glyphs. In 1905, in the mountains of the southwestern Sinai Peninsula (not far from the Gulf of Suez) in an area known as Serabit el-Khadem, a set of inscriptions dating from the mid nineteenth century BCE were discovered. These inscriptions were written in what is referred to as the Proto-Sinaitic alphabet (or the Proto-Canaanite alphabet), which is hypothesized to have been invented by Canaanites involved in the mining and transport of turquoise.[11] The Canaanites living in this area borrowed some of the pictographic symbols found in Egyptian inscriptions, and adapted them to their purposes without reference to their Egyptian meanings. Rather, using the acrophonic principle, they utilized each of the symbols to represent the first sound of the Canaanite word represented by the pictograph.

For example, the Canaanite word for house was *bêt* and the Egyptian pictograph for 'house' was the following symbol, which the Canaanites appropriated for writing the sound [b]:

'house' [bɛt]
[b]

In the same way, their word for 'ox' being pronounced [ʔalp], with an initial glottal stop [ʔ], they used the Egyptian pictograph for 'ox' to represent the glottal stop consonant:

'ox' [aʔalp]
[ʔ]

In this manner, the Canaanites of Serabit el-Khadem created graphemes for each of the consonants in the phonemic inventory of their language. This first alphabet was technically referred to as an **abjad**, a system that

---

[11] Goldwasser 2010.

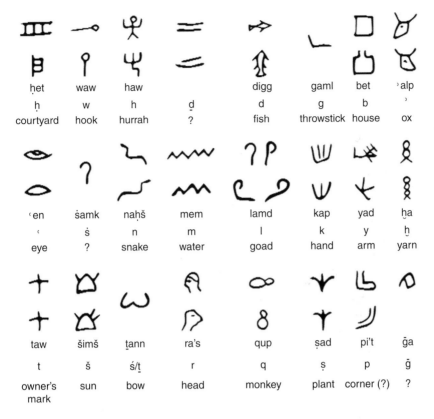

Figure 8.5 Canaanite Proto-Sinaitic symbols

has symbols for each of the consonants in a language but does not represent the vowels. Figure 8.5 gives a list of these symbols and their correspondences.

The Phoenician Alphabet

The Phoenicians, most likely descendants of the earlier Canaanites who inhabited the area around present-day Lebanon and coastal Syria, provided the link between the Proto-Sinaitic alphabet and the modern Middle Eastern and Western alphabets in use today. While Phoenicians initially used a cuneiform script, it is estimated that they began adapting the Proto-Sinaitic writing system for their own use in the fifteenth century BCE, with the first known inscriptions dating from around 1000 BCE. The Phoenician alphabet consists of 22 consonantal graphemes, most of

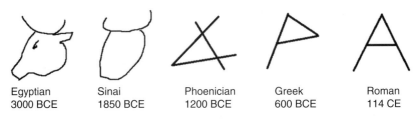

Egyptian	Sinai	Phoenician	Greek	Roman
3000 BCE	1850 BCE	1200 BCE	600 BCE	114 CE

Figure 8.6 The development of "alpha" from Egyptian through Roman

which are cognate with their Proto-Sinaitic antecedents, but much more abstract in form. As evidence for the cognate relationship between the Phoenician and Proto-Sinaitic symbols, it is observed that the Phoenician symbol set has the same mnemonics (wherein the symbols correspond to the Egyptian pictographic meanings upon which they are based). So, just as in Proto-Sinaitic, the first consonant symbol in the Phoenician alphabet is

and is called *'āleph*, which means 'ox.' The second symbol is

and is called *bēth*, meaning 'house,' and so on. Partly on account of this, it has been suggested that 'Phoenician' may actually just be part of a regional dialect continuum, which also includes Proto-Sinaitic Canaanite. Figure 8.6 illustrates some of the gradual stylization of the one of the characters, *aleph* or *alpha* or *a*, from its Egyptian origin through successive stages of Sinaitic, Phoenician, Greek, and Roman.

As successful seafaring traders, the Phoenicians navigated throughout the Mediterranean for some thousand years beginning in the mid fifteenth century BCE. Their most enduring legacy was the spread of alphabetic writing in the Middle East, southern Europe and northern Africa. It is believed that most, if not all, alphabetic systems can be traced back to the Phoenicians. The Paleo-Hebrew script and the Aramaic script, both dating from around the tenth century BCE, were derived from and bore a strong resemblance to the Phoenician alphabet.

Modern Consonantal Writing Systems (Abjads)

As we saw above, the parts of Egyptian hieroglyphs used to represent sounds (i.e. phonograms) only represented the consonants. Recall in Figure 8.4, the hieroglyph used to represent the goddess Aset. The oval shape is an ideograph denoting 'female,' and the seated figure at the bottom is another semantic element meaning 'goddess.' The other two symbols are phonetic elements. The one on the top left is a pictograph of a throne, and used to indicate that the word contains the consonants [s] and [t], and the top right symbol is a pictograph of a loaf of bread used phonetically to indicate that the word ends in [t].

In taking their inspiration from Egyptian hieroglyphics, those writing systems directly descended from them shared the property of only having symbols for consonants. Such writing systems are termed, following Daniels, **abjads**.[12] The term is an acronym for the first four letters of the Arabic alphabet, which represent the sounds: [ʔ], [b], [g], and [d].

As it happens, the Semitic languages of the Canaanites, Phoenicians, Israelites, and other peoples of that region were quite amenable to a consonantal writing system. These languages, typified by modern Arabic and Hebrew, are characterized by a lexicon in which major word meanings are represented by consonantal roots. In this system, a series of consonants (usually three) forms the basis for groups of semantically related words. In Arabic, for example, the consonant group *k-t-b* means something like 'write.' By adding vowels and certain other consonants to these roots to form syllables, the language derives the specific lexical items in a very systematic way. The following illustrate:

C_1 a C_2 a C_3 a	kataba	'he wrote'
C_1 i C_2 aa C_3	kitaab	'book'
ma C_1 C_2 a C_3	maktab	'office'

Each vowel pattern can be used with a number of different roots, for a particular part of speech and inflection. Thus, the pattern C_1-a-C_2-a-C_3-a is for a third-person past tense verb, and can be used with *k-t-b* 'write,' with *w-j-d* 'find,' or with *k-s-b* 'earn, gain':

C_1 a C_2 a C_3 a	kataba	'he wrote'
C_1 a C_2 a C_3 a	wajada	'he found'
C_1 a C_2 a C_3 a	kasaba	'he earned'

There are four abjads still in use today: Arabic, Hebrew, Samaritan, and Syriac. The first two are used rather widely in religious texts, and as modern languages. Samaritan is spoken in a small Israeli

[12] Daniels and Bright 1996: 4.

يولد جميع الناس أحراراً متساوين في الكرامة والحقوق. وقد وهبوا

عقلاً وضميراً وعليهم ان يعامل بعضهم بعضاً بروح الإخاء.

يُولَدُ جَمِيعُ النَّاسِ أحْرَاراً مُتَسَاوِينَ فِي الْكَرَامَةِ وَالْحُقُوقِ. وَقَدْ وُهِبُوا

عَقْلاً وَ ضَمِيراً وَ عَلَيهِمْ أنْ يُعَامِلَ بَعْضُهُمْ بَعْضاً بِرُوحِ الإخَاءِ.

Figure 8.7 Arabic writing

community of about 700, and Syriac is used only by the Syrian Orthodox Church.

The Arabic script evolved from the Nabataean Aramaic script. It has been used since the fourth century CE, but the earliest document, an inscription in Arabic, Syriac and Greek, dates from 512 CE. The Aramaic language has fewer consonants than Arabic, and during the seventh century CE new letters were created by adding diacritic dots to existing letters in order to avoid ambiguities. The system of writing that developed has consonants as individual letters – vowels go unrepresented much of the time, but diacritics placed above or below the consonant can be included, especially in teaching circumstances and to ensure the correct reading of the Quran (see Figure 8.7).

As it is closely associated with Islam, the Arabic script has been adapted for use with a great many non-Semitic languages with significant Islamic populations, including Bosnian, Farsi (Persian), Hausa, Kashmiri, Kurdish, Punjabi, and Urdu, to mention a few. To accommodate consonant sounds not found in Arabic and in some instances to represent vowels, new symbols have been added to the orthographies used for some of these non-Semitic languages.

The other major abjad in use today is that of Hebrew. Modern Hebrew script was developed in the fifth century BCE from the Imperial Aramaic script used in the Achaemenid Persian Empire, and was based on what was known as the Assyrian alphabet. It contains twenty-two basic consonant letters, plus diacritics and special forms of some final-position consonants (see Figure 8.8).

כל בני האדם נולדו בני חורין ושווים בערכם
ובזכויותיהם. כולם חוננו בתבונה ובמצפון, לפיכך
חובה עליהם לנהוג איש ברעהו ברוח של אחווה.

כֹּל בְּנֵי הָאָדָם נוֹלְדוּ בְּנֵי חוֹרִין וְשָׁוִים בְּעֶרְכָּם
וּבִזְכֻיּוֹתֵיהֶם. כֻּלָּם חוֹנְנוּ בַּתְּבוּנָה וּבְמַצְפּוּן, לְפִיכָךְ
חוֹבָה עֲלֵיהֶם לִנְהוֹג אִישׁ בְּרֵעֵהוּ בְּרוּחַ שֶׁל אַחֲוָה.

Figure 8.8 Hebrew writing

Alphabetic Writing

Modern European (and many other) languages are written in one of the major alphabetic writing systems, which are Greek, Latin, and Cyrillic. The first of these was Greek.

Long ago, Greek was written in a syllabic orthography that looked nothing like the Greek alphabet we are familiar with (from Ancient Greek writings and Modern Greek). But roughly 3,000 years ago, the Greeks started using an adaptation of the Phoenician alphabet. As Greek has only seventeen consonantal sounds, there were a number of unused symbols. The innovation of the Greeks was to use some of the unused symbols to represent vowels. Since Greek has no phonemic [ʔ] (glottal stop), it was easy to reassign the Phoenician letter ✕ 'ālp from [ʔ] to the vowel [a]. The name 'ālp ('ox') was retained and became *alpha* in Greek. Other Phoenician letters for consonants reassigned as vowels were:

⋏ *he*	'window'	[h]	→	E	*epsilon*	[e]
O *ayn*	'eye'	[ʕ]	→	O	*omicron*	[o]
⅂ *yodh*	'arm'	[j]	→	I	*iota*	[i]

Recall that the first two letters of the Phoenician writing system were the letters for [ʔ] and [b] 'ālp 'ox' and *bēth* 'house,' and the Greeks employed the same order of symbols. Thus, the term *alphabet* is derived from the names of the first two letters of the Greek writing system α and β, and ultimately comes from the Proto-Sinaitic/Phoenician writing systems.

Originally, Greek alphabetic writing was written as the Phoenician writing, right to left on the page. It then went through a stage of **boustrophedan** writing, in which the first line was written right-to-left, the next line from left-to-right, and so on. *Boustrophedan* means 'as the ox turns,' and the lines of script are reminiscent of the pattern made when plowing a field. Eventually, the left-to-right format was adopted. This evolution in the direction in which

А	Б	В	Г	Ѓ	Д	Ђ	Ѓ	Е	Ё
A	Be	Ve	Ge	Ge upturn	De	Dje	Gje	Ye	Yo

Є	Ж	З	Ѕ́	S	И	I	Ї	Й	J
Yest	Zhe	Ze	Zje	Dze	I	Dotted I	Yi	Short I	Je

К	Л	Љ	М	Н	Њ	О	П	Р	С
Ka	El	Lje	Em	En	Nje	O	Pe	Er	Es

Ć	Т	Ћ	Ќ	У	Ў	Ф	Х	Ц	Ч
[ɕ]	Te	Tshe	Kje	U	Short U	Ef	Kha	Tse	Che

Џ	Ш	Щ	Ъ	Ы	Ь	Э	Ю	Я
Dzhe	Sha	Shcha	Hard sign (Yer)	Yery	Soft sign (Yeri)	E	Yu	Ya

Figure 8.9 The Cyrillic alphabet

lines were read helps explain why some Greek letters (e.g. beta, gamma, and kappa) are reverse in orientation from the Phoenician originals.

The Latin (or Roman) alphabet evolved sometime in the sixth century BCE from a form of the Greek alphabet adopted by the Etruscans, who were trading partners of the Greeks living in modern-day Tuscany. The early Romans adopted the Etruscan writing system shortly thereafter and developed from this the Latin alphabet, which was spread throughout the Roman Empire with lasting effect in the western territories. Over time the Classical Latin alphabet was adapted for use with a wide variety of languages, which involved the addition of various diacritics and letters to accommodate sound systems that differed significantly from Latin.

The other major European alphabet is the Cyrillic alphabet. Named after St. Cyril, a Greek Byzantine missionary, it was invented in the First Bulgarian Empire (681–1018) sometime during the ninth or tenth century CE to write Old Church Slavonic, which had been adopted by St. Cyril and Greek missionaries as a liturgical language to convert the Slavs. The Cyrillic alphabet was derived from Greek capital letters along with another local alphabet (Glagolitic), and evolved into its current form by 1708 during the reign of Peter the Great. It is presently used in Russia, Central Asia, and Eastern Europe (see Figure 8.9).

Other Syllabaries

Earlier in the chapter, we examined the origin and form of the Japanese syllabary, a writing system that has separate symbols for each V (vowel-only) and CV (consonant-vowel) syllable. Japanese is perfectly suited to such a system, since its syllables are all comprised this way (excepting for those ending in [n], for which there is a separate symbol). As might be imagined, syllabaries are most suited for languages that have a limited range of possible syllables. English, for instance, would not be among them. English, and other languages like it, have a vast array of multiple consonant combinations that can begin a syllable, and having a separate symbol for each of these in combination with a vowel would rapidly become unwieldy. Taking just those combinations involving the sound [p], we know that English allows (in addition to *p* alone) [p] followed by [l] or [r], [p] preceded by [s], and [sp] followed by [l] or [r]. Allowing one symbol for each of these, followed by any one of five vowels (and English has many more than that), would require thirty symbols, one for each of the following:

pa	pi	pe	po	pu
pra	pri	pre	pro	pru
pla	pli	ple	plo	plu
spa	spi	spe	spo	spu
spra	spri	spre	spro	spru
spla	spli	sple	splo	splu

So, English is not (to put it mildly) a good candidate for using a syllabary.

There are, however, numbers of other languages that can get along quite well using a syllabary. In North America, two well-known syllabaries were developed for writing Native American languages, Cherokee and Cree. The latter is still in use, having been adapted for a number of other indigenous languages.

The Cherokee syllabary (see Figure 8.10), was reputedly invented by George Guess, a.k.a. "Chief Sequoyah of the Cherokee," and was introduced in 1819. Sequoyah's descendants claim that he was the last surviving member of his tribe's scribe clan and that the Cherokee syllabary was invented by persons unknown at a much earlier date. By 1820, thousands of Cherokees had learned the syllabary, and by 1830, 90 percent were literate in their own language. Books, religious texts, almanacs and newspapers were all published using the syllabary, which was widely used for over 100 years.

Abugidas

Some syllabaries are somewhat more alphabetic in nature, having a single set of syllabic symbols, e.g. all of the consonants + a, rather than completely different symbols for each consonant–vowel combination. Although sometimes called a "syllabic alphabet," technically speaking, this kind of writing system is referred to as an *abugida*. An abugida is a writing system in which consonant symbols

D a	R e	T i	ꭳ o	Oꞌ u	i v
S ga ꭺ ka	Ᏻ ge	ꭹ gi	A go	J gu	E gv
ꭿ ha	Ᏸ he	Ꭿ hi	Ᏺ ho	Γ hu	ꭽ hv
W la	ꭁ le	ꮅ li	Ꮏ lo	M lu	ꮑ lv
ꮚ ma	Ᏽ me	H mi	ꮋ mo	ꭹ mu	
Ꮎ na ꮏ hna Ꮐ nah ꮑ ne	h ni	Z no	ꮄ nu	Oꞌ nv	
Ꮖ qua	ꮗ que	ꮙ qui	Ꮖꞌ quo ꮙ quu	Ɛ quv	
Ꮀ sa ꮝ s	4 se	ꮟ si	ꮺ so	ꮪ su	R sv
Ꮣ da W ta	Ꮥ de Ꮦ te	Ꮧ di Ꮨ ti	V do	S du	ꮲ dv
ꮵ dla Ꮅ tla	L tle	C tli	ꮣ tlo	ꮤ tlu	P tlv
Ꮳ tsa	Ꮴ tse	Ꮵ tsi	K tso	ꮷ tsu	Cꞌ tsv
Ꮹ wa	ꮻ we	Ꮻ wi	Ꮼ wo	Ꮽ wu	6 wv
ꮿ ya	Ᏸ ye	Ꭿ yi	ꮀ yo	G yu	B yv

Figure 8.10 Cherokee syllabary

are associated with one particular following vowel, usually *a* or *ə*. Diacritics are then employed to signal a different vowel quality, say *i, e,* or *u*. This makes it different from a syllabary in which the different symbols are completely independent of one another. Most known abugidas arose as what is generally taken to be an independent invention of writing in South Asia. Not surprisingly then, one system that works this way is the Devanagari writing system developed for Sanskrit and used today to write Hindi and a number of other languages of India. Figure 8.11 illustrates the Sanskrit consonants as they are written when followed by the vowel [a]. An interesting aspect of the system is that it is set up to aid learning as the consonantal signs are grouped into six groups (rows) of five (columns). The first five rows progress as velar, palatal, retroflex, dental, and labial, corresponding to utilizing or touching the tongue to progressively outer parts of the mouth when making the sound. Figure 8.12 illustrates the symbols for vowels in isolation (first row) along with those same vowels following the sound [p] (second row).

Orthographies used for a number of languages spoken in Southeast Asia are demonstrably adaptations of the original Brahmi writing system developed in ancient India (from which Devanagari is also derived). Languages which currently use or traditionally used an abugida writing system include: Thai,

Figure 8.11 Sanskrit consonants (combined with [a])

Figure 8.12 Sanskrit vowels (alone and in combination with [p])

Tibetan, Cambodian, Lao, and various writing systems of the languages of Indonesia, such as the Kawi system for writing Old Javanese, Batak, Buginese, Sundanese, and others.

Hangul (Korean)

Thus far, we have seen **logographic** writing systems in which a single symbol represents a word or morpheme, **syllabaries** in which a single symbol represents a syllable, **abugida** syllabaries with phonemic enhancements, and **abjads** and **alphabets** in which a symbol represents a single sound.

It is appropriate to close out this discussion with an examination of the writing system of Korea, Hangul, which incorporates some elements from

ㄱ	ㄴ	ㄷ	ㄹ	ㅁ	ㅂ	ㅅ
기역	니은	디귿	리을	미음	비읍	시옷
giyeok	nieun	digeut	rieul	mieum	bieup	shiot
g/k	n	d/t	r/l	m	b/p	s
[k/g]	[n]	[t/d]	[l/r]	[m]	[p/b]	[s]
ㅇ	ㅈ	ㅊ	ㅋ	ㅌ	ㅍ	ㅎ
이응	지읒	치읓	키읔	티읕	피읖	히읗
ieung	jieut	chieut	kiuek	tieut	pieup	hieut
ng	j/ch	ch/ch'	k	t	p	h
[Ø/-ŋ]	[ʧ/ʥ]	[ʧʰ]	[kʰ]	[tʰ]	[pʰ]	[h]

Figure 8.13 Hangul writing system: consonants

each of these other types. In one sense, Hangul is alphabetic in that there are distinct symbols for each consonant and vowel. The way in which these symbols are arranged on a page, though, is syllabic; the initial consonant, vowel, and final consonant (if there is one) are arranged into a block to represent a syllable. Finally, there is a representational (semi-logographic) element to the writing system, in that the form of symbols has a direct (iconic) relationship to how they are pronounced, and similarly articulated sounds share graphic features. On account of its coherent logic and phonological transparency, linguists have deemed Hangul to be the best phonetic system of writing ever devised.

Created around 1444 by scholars at the order of King Sejong (the fourth king of the Joseon dynasty), the writing system was designed to replace the Chinese character-based writing system that had been in use for over 2,000 years. King Sejong's central purpose in having the writing system created was for the education of his people. It was recognized then that the time and effort required to learn Chinese character-based writing ensured that all but the small aristocratic class would remain illiterate. The result of these efforts paid off in promoting literacy throughout the Korean kingdom.

Figures 8.13 and 8.14 illustrate the phonological organization of the symbols.

ㅏ	ㅐ	ㅑ	ㅒ	ㅓ	ㅔ	ㅕ
a	ae	ya	yae	eo/ŏ	e	yeo/yŏ
[a]	[æ]	[ja]	[jæ]	[ʌ]	[e]	[jʌ]

ㅖ	ㅗ	ㅘ	ㅙ	ㅚ	ㅛ	ㅜ
ye	o	wa	wae	oe	yo	u
[je]	[o]	[wa]	[wæ]	[we]	[jo]	[u]

ㅝ	ㅞ	ㅟ	ㅠ	ㅡ	ㅢ	ㅣ
wo/wŏ	we	wi	yu	eu/ŭ	ui/ŭi	i
[wʌ]	[we]	[wi]	[ju]	[ɨ]	[ɨj]	[i]

Figure 8.14 Hangul writing system: vowels

Notice, for instance, that alveolar consonants (those pronounced with the tip of the tongue touching behind the teeth: [n], [t], [d], [r], [l]) are formed with the same shape, which is the lower left corner of a box. The basic shape (the corner alone) is [n]. The symbol for [t] and [d] adds a horizontal stroke above it, and the symbol for [r] and [l] adds a top right box corner on top of that. What is more, that basic shape mimics the articulation in the mouth: the tip of the tongue touching behind the teeth. Similarly, the bilabial sounds share a shape. The basic shape for [m] is a box, and the symbol for [p] and [b] has vertical side strokes extended above the top horizontal. Again, the basic box shape is meant to mimic the shape of the lips in making a labial sound. Vowel symbols are also logically arranged. Unrounded front vowels [a] and [eo] share a basic vertical stroke, while rounded back vowels share a basic horizontal stroke. Each member of the pair is distinguished by a short stroke, to the left, to the right, upwards, or downwards. Vowel sounds that begin with [y] (i.e. [ya], [yeo], [yo], and [yu]) each have a second minor stroke in the same direction as the short distinguishing stroke. There are additional secondary strokes that consistently distinguish other pairs of sounds – e.g. [d] from [t], [p] from [b], and [j] from [ch]. All in all, the system is logical, easy to learn, and easy to use.

Hangul has been taken as a symbol of Korean nationalism and pride and may be the only alphabet to have its own holiday. Hangul Day was declared a legal holiday in 1945, removed from the holiday calendar in 1991, and restored to the Korean calendar once again in 2013.

The Role of Orthography in Language Conflict and Rights

Writing systems, as we noted at the outset, are vehicles for representing languages, and not the language themselves. We also saw that words and sentences of a given language can be represented by any number of writing systems (with the proviso that some adjustments may be necessary in order to accommodate the sounds of that language). It is for this reason that writing systems may be borrowed and adapted from a society that speaks a wholly unrelated language. Case in point, Canaanite tribes adapted and borrowed their writing system from the Egyptians, the Phoenicians borrowed and adapted from them, the Greeks took from the Phoenicians, and the Etruscans adjusted the Greek system for their own use.

All this leads to the inevitable conclusion that writing systems have a role in human society and language use that is parallel to, but independent of, language itself. Because of this, writing systems are an important vehicle for the assertion of national or religious identity, and can be used as such even when the citizens of the nation or adherents of the religion speak fundamentally different languages. It also goes without saying that writing is a primary means of transmitting linguistic information, whenever speech-dependent means are inconvenient or impossible (e.g. when the speakers are too distant or are dead). Given this, control over a writing system entails control over information and its transmission.

Religion and Writing Systems

Historically, the selection of a writing system for a given language has been most often determined by religious or sectarian considerations. In continental Europe, the Latin and Cyrillic alphabets (adapted for use by individual languages) are the two major writing systems in current use (Greek is also used, but only in Greece). The Latin alphabet is predominantly used in countries that are (or were) Roman Catholic, and Cyrillic is used in countries associated with the Eastern Orthodox Church. And while Cyrillic is commonly associated with Slavic languages (i.e. Russian, Bulgarian, Serbian, etc.), there are several Slavic-language-speaking countries which use the Latin alphabet on account of their being (or having been) Roman Catholic: e.g. the Czech Republic, Slovakia, Poland, and Croatia. The importance of these writing system-based distinctions can be seen from the fact that Serbian and Croatian are principally (some might say only) distinguished by their written forms, being otherwise virtually the same language (despite native speakers' insistence otherwise).

Similarly, the Arabic writing system spread along with the Muslim faith, and was adapted and adopted for many languages that are quite unrelated to Arabic. The Persian language of Iran, for example, is more closely related to Hindi and other South Asian languages than it is to Arabic. However, since the ability to read the Quran was of primary importance, Arabic writing was given priority over any other system, and Persian came to be written in a modified Arabic script. Similar circumstances prevailed in the Turkic-language-speaking lands of Central Asia, from Turkestan (the modern Xinjiang Uyghur region of China) in the east to the Republic of Turkey in the West, leading to the use of Arabic script in these countries up until about 100 years ago.

Historically, Jews also adapted and applied the writing system they were most familiar with to the vernacular languages they learned to speak. Since literacy in Hebrew was of prime importance in Jewish communities, they tended to use the Hebrew alphabet to write the languages of the lands in which they settled. Often, their variety of the local language was infused with Hebrew words as well, but what typically made "Judeo-" languages stand out was their being written using Hebrew letters. This was the case for Yiddish (Judeo-German) and Ladino (Judeo-Spanish), as well as the lesser-known Judeo-Arabic, Judeo-Persian, and Judeo-Berber. It is for this reason that many people mistake Yiddish texts for Hebrew, even though (as does the Max Weinreich quote repeated from Chapter 4) it may not have any Hebrew words at all:

אַ שפּראַך איז אַ דיאַלעקט מיט אַן אַרמיי און פֿלאָט
a shprakh iz a dialekt mit an armey un flot
'A language is a dialect with an army and navy.'

The same sentence rendered into German shows clearly that Yiddish is indeed German and not Hebrew: 'Eine Sprache ist ein Dialekt mit einer Armee und Marine.'

Cultural, Political, and Economic Influences on Writing Systems

Cultural, economic, and political hegemony has played as important a role as religion in the spread of writing systems. We have already noted that the Phoenician alphabet was carried by them all across the Mediterranean Sea along their trading routes, and eventually adopted by Etruscan tribes in Italy. Likewise the Chinese writing system was spread to Vietnam, Korea, and Japan. Vietnam was introduced to Chinese writing quite early, when the nation was subjugated by the Chinese Han Empire in the second century CE. In the case of Korea and Japan, Chinese texts were carried by proselytizing Buddhist monks in the fourth and fifth centuries CE, respectively. The perseverance of Chinese (and Chinese-like) characters in these countries' writing systems is quite remarkable. The Koreans, as we've discussed, invented their own Hangul system about 1,000 years after adopting Chinese writing, but continued to use some Chinese characters in their texts until rather recently. The Japanese, despite having their own syllabaries, continue to use some 2,000 Chinese characters in their written texts today. The Vietnamese, for their part, continued to use Chinese characters and Chinese-based characters long after they became independent from China in 939 CE, until they were colonized by the French in the nineteenth century and had a Latin alphabet imposed upon them.

The recent history of writing in Vietnam points to how the determination of a writing system for a language is often, and repeatedly, used as a political tool. French rule of Indochina (including the modern nations of Vietnam, Laos, and Cambodia) began in 1862 and reached its territorial zenith at the end of the nineteenth century. For the French, as for any colonizer, controlling information, literacy, and education was paramount. The forced adoption of a Latin alphabet for the writing of Vietnamese had several intended consequences: it made Vietnamese texts readable for the colonial authorities; it made it easier for Vietnamese to learn French and promoted Western-style literacy; it facilitated the spread of Christianity; and it weakened the links between Vietnamese culture and the Chinese cultural hegemon to the north.

This tale of authorities' intentionally overturning an existing writing system can be retold in one country after another. The Ottoman Empire, the Islamic state that ruled the eastern Mediterranean from Constantinople/ Istanbul from 1453 CE and the Arab Middle East and north Africa from the mid sixteenth century, adopted an Arabic script for official purposes, replacing any other writing systems used previously. This situation lasted for about 500 years, until the defeat and dissolution of the Ottoman Empire in World War I. Following this, with the establishment of the Republic of Turkey in 1923, things took a distinctively nationalist turn, with Mustafa Kemal Atatürk and his followers promoting an ethnically Turkish polity (in place of the old Islamic one). This was accompanied by the abandonment of the Arabic script in favor of a specifically Turkish version of the Latin alphabet. And by 1929, it was illegal to use Arabic script to write Turkish.

An interesting, and somewhat parallel, story of writing system changes can be had from the Turkic republics of the former Soviet Union (Kazakhstan, Kyrgyzstan, Tajikistan, Turkmenistan, and Uzbekistan).

These, like Turkey, were Islamic states and used a Perso-Arabic script for their languages. In the case of Uzbekistan (i.e. the Khanate of Bukhara from 1500), Perso-Arabic script was used continuously for Persian and Uzbek until 1928 (after the creation of the Uzbek Soviet Socialist Republic in 1924). At that time, in an effort by the Soviets to promote ethnic nationalism and to separate the Turkic peoples from their Muslim influences, a Latinate alphabet, Yanalif, was adopted. This lasted only until 1940, when the Soviets under Stalin imposed Cyrillic, in order to bring the Turkic peoples more closely into the Russian sphere and away from Turkey (which was now an enemy of the USSR). In 1992, the break-up of the Soviet Union resulted in a return to a Latin script.

Just as writing systems can be imposed by religious authorities, secular rulers, or colonial powers, so too can writing systems play a role in the assertion of ethnic and linguistic identity. Hangul, for example, has long been a symbol of national pride and is associated almost exclusively with the Korean language (the exception being Cia-Cia, an indigenous language of Indonesia whose speakers recently adopted Hangul as the official orthography[13]). Other writing systems associated with individual languages include the Greek alphabet and the Cherokee syllabary. These orthographies themselves become symbols of cultural and sometimes national identities, and are a way for speakers to signal their identity with the language and their cultural group.

And, as might be expected, a writing system (just like a language) can be suppressed as a means of restricting the rights of a linguistic and ethnic group. A recent instance of this comes from northern Africa, where the linguistic rights of Berber (a.k.a. Tamazigh/Amazigh) peoples have been suppressed for centuries, since the Arab conquest of the Saharan regions. Berber tribes of southern Morocco, Algeria, and Libya and of northern Mali and Niger speak languages that are quite distinct from (though distantly related to) Arabic. It was only in 2001 and 2011, respectively, that Berber was given the status of an official language in Algeria and Morocco. In Morocco, today, one can find road signs in three languages, Arabic, French, and Tifinagh (the written form of Moroccan Berber). In Libya, by contrast, the situation until very recently was significantly worse. For forty years under the rule of Muammar al-Gaddafi (until 2011), it was forbidden to use Amazigh or even to acknowledge its existence.[14] Included in this prohibition was any use of their alphabet. It was thus notable that Tamazigh graffiti

[13] Park 2009.
[14] http://muftah.org/denied-existence-libyan-berbers-under-gaddafi-and-hope-for-the-current-rev olution/#.U_JMasVdVyI

was prominent in Amazigh villages during the anti-Gaddafi uprising of 2011. During the revolution (and since), Amazigh rebels have been coordinating a major drive to revive Amazigh culture and the Tamazigh language following decades of official repression by the Arab regime of Muammar al-Gaddafi.

9   Framing Language Rights in the Context of Human Rights

We have touched on some issues of language rights in previous chapters but have not yet addressed how the issue of language rights relates to the larger issue of human rights. Here we will set out some of the basic concepts and attempt to situate language rights in the context of international and national documents and the dialogue surrounding them, and the domains in which language rights have been restricted. This chapter will also include a discussion of language rights issues in the United States, with particular attention to "English Only" and "English First" movements.

Human Rights and Language

The potential for conflict arises any time groups of people from different cultures attempt to inhabit the same space: this can be due to ethnic, religious, economic, or other reasons real or imagined, and frequently it is a combination of factors. More often than not, one group is dominant and seeks to ensure its dominance through restrictions on the other group – whether these restrictions are explicit or unstated, codified in law or unofficial – restrictions on movement, access, participation in the economy and social life, and so on. Language, as a strong symbol of group identity, is sometimes cited as a reason for intergroup conflict. And throughout history up to the present day, restrictions on language use have played an important role in these conflicts.

These types of restrictions are frequently couched in terms of civil and human rights. While the notion of natural or human rights has a long history and there has been much debate regarding precisely what is properly regarded as a right of humans, the adoption of the Universal Declaration of Human Rights by the United Nations in 1948 ushered in an era in which human rights have taken on increased importance internationally.

The Declaration outlines a core set of fundamental rights that all human beings are deemed to be entitled to at birth. These include the right to "life, liberty and security of person," the right not to be held in slavery or servitude, and the right not to be tortured, rights which the UN Office for the High

Commissioner for Human Rights describes as "universal and inalienable." Among the rights contained in the Declaration are civil and political rights, such as equal protection under the law (set out in Article 7) and freedom of thought and expression (Article 19); social, cultural, and economic rights, such as the right to education (Article 26); the right to social security (Article 22);[1] the right of equal access to social services (Article 21); the right to work and the right to equal pay (Article 23). The Declaration also sets out collective rights, such as the right of assembly and association (Article 20). Throughout history, through the restriction of such rights, governments have sought to maintain control over and limit the power of internal minorities (as well as all citizens) and colonial powers have worked to subdue indigenous peoples. And while these conflicts are never really truly about language, to the extent that a nation's dominant group or the state wants to suppress, assimilate, or deny the existence of particular ethnic groups, or desires to create cohesion and a national identity, language has been and continues to be a powerful tool (or weapon) in the arsenal of control.

Language restrictions take a variety of forms in different domains of society. At times, all aspects of the justice system – from law enforcement to courts to penal institutions – are conducted in the dominant or state language, which shuts out or puts at a disadvantage non-speakers (and non-proficient speakers) of that language. This was true until recently in Turkey, where all court documents and proceedings were by law in Turkish. At one point Kurdish prisoners were not even allowed to speak to visitors in Kurdish. In New Zealand, the Māori won the right to have trial proceedings conducted in the Māori language only in the 1980s. Before that, English was the sole language used in the courts. At other times, services provided by governments are available only in the dominant language, which may be because the government workers are able to speak only the dominant language or because law dictates it. The 1995 Slovak State Language Law decreed that all state and local organizations had to conduct business in Slovak. As a result some native Hungarians could not take full advantage of government services. Tamil citizens in Sri Lanka faced a similar problem after the passage of the 1956 Official Language Act, which mandated that all government business be conducted in the Sinhala language.

Frequently government jobs and other employment are available only to competent speakers of the dominant language. As a result of the 1956 law, Sri Lankan civil service jobs required fluency in Sinhala, greatly reducing the number of Tamils in government service (which actually was a desired effect

---

[1] Article 22 of the Universal Declaration of Humans Rights reads, "Social security is understood to encompass the following nine branches: adequate health service, disability benefits, old age benefits, unemployment benefits, employment injury insurance, family and child support, maternity benefits, disability protections, and provisions for survivors and orphans."

of the law). In the 1960s, the Phillips Corporation forbade workers to speak any language other than Danish at a factory in Denmark, although it was indicated at the time that English would be acceptable. This edict was directed primarily at Turkish guest workers. A 1902 Norwegian Act allowed only those who could read and write Norwegian to buy land, greatly disadvantaging the indigenous Sámi.

Frequently, education is only provided in the state language. This has been true at times in New Zealand, Norway, Turkey, and countless other countries where indigenous populations have often been denied education in their native language. For example, from the mid 1800s to the mid 1900s, many Native American children were removed from their homes and forced to attend boarding schools where only English was permitted.

There may be restrictions on the language used to name towns, streets and other public areas, as has been the case in Slovakia and Turkey, where Slovak and Turkish names replaced traditional Hungarian and Kurdish names. As described in Chapter 7, many governments have restricted and continue to restrict the names that parents can give to their children. This sometimes targets specific groups, such as the Ainu in Japan and Hungarians in Slovakia, among others.

In the most extreme cases, people may be required by law to speak only an official language in public, or sometimes even in private. The Ainu were at one point prohibited from speaking their native language in public, as were the Kurds in Turkey. In Iowa, toward the end of World War I, the use of German was severely restricted. German-language churches were forced to close and several citizens were fined when they were overheard speaking German on the telephone. These restrictions are amply illustrated in chapters that follow. But what is the relationship between human rights and language? Is it a straightforward relationship? Or is it something less direct?

The Emergence of Language as a Right in International Declarations

The types of language restrictions just enumerated are clearly reminiscent of many of the rights spelled out in the UN Declaration. However, language itself was not included as a specific and separate right in the Declaration, nor in other early documents, such as the American Declaration of the Rights and Duties of Man, adopted by the Organization of American States in 1948 – a document which in fact was adopted a few months prior to the UN Declaration. Both documents explicitly include language only as one of a number of characteristics that should not form the basis of discrimination. Article 2 of the UN Declaration states:

Everyone is entitled to all the rights and freedoms set forth in this Declaration, without distinction of any kind, such as race, colour, sex, **language**, religion, political or other opinion, national or social origin, property, birth or other status.

Freedom of expression (including freedom of speech) figures prominently as a designated right (Article 19). Strongly implicated in the right to freedom of expression is the freedom to use the language of one's choice. However, a right to one's own language is not explicitly identified as a human right.

Because culture and identity are so closely bound up with language (see Chapter 4), as concern with human rights, especially the condition and rights of indigenous populations, gained momentum, language gradually became more of a focus in international documents. Article 27 of the UN International Covenant on Civil and Political Rights (1966)[2] includes the provision that,

minorities shall not be denied the right, in community with other member of their group, to enjoy their own culture, to profess and practise their own religion, or **to use their own language**.

The Covenant also specifies that a person charged with a crime should be informed of the charges "in a language he understands" and be provided with an interpreter when necessary for judicial proceedings. The right of accused persons to be apprised of charges in their language is also included in the OAS's American Convention on Human Rights (drafted in 1969 and ratified in 1978). Additionally, Article 18 of the OAS Convention also establishes that "Every person has the right to a name." Implied in this is that people may be named in the language of their choice according to any naming conventions of their culture.

Perhaps the earliest explicit attempt at recognizing the role of language in human rights was embedded in two articles of a 1957 convention of the International Labour Organization (ILO), a UN agency. Although largely focused on labor issues, the ILO Convention (No. 107) on Indigenous and Tribal Populations addressed the UN Declaration's concern for both cultural and educational rights in a way which put language front and center. Article 23 includes the provision that "Children belonging to the peoples concerned shall be taught to read and write **in their mother tongue** or, where this is not practicable, **in the language most commonly used by the group** to which they belong." Additionally, "Appropriate measures shall, as far as possible, be taken to **preserve the mother tongue or the vernacular language**."[3] The

---

[2] The Covenant was adopted by the General Assembly in 1966 but did not enter into force until 1976.
[3] Convention No. 107 also includes a provision that foreshadows a provision found in some later language rights documents, e.g. the Universal Declaration on Linguistic Rights discussed below, regarding the right to "know" a national language: "Provision shall be made for a progressive transition from the mother tongue or the vernacular language to the national language or to one of the official languages of the country."

convention addresses another important language rights issue: the government must inform indigenous populations of their rights and duties, stating explicitly that

If necessary this shall be done by means of written translations and through the use of media of mass communication in the languages of these populations.

The 1957 Convention did not gain much traction, being ratified by only twenty-seven countries in about a thirty-year span. However, as human rights gained additional mainstream momentum, Convention No. 107 was revisited. While the earlier Convention encouraged integration of "temporary" indigenous populations, the 1989 Convention Concerning Indigenous and Tribal Peoples in Independent Countries recognized the peoples as permanent societies. In addition to the provision for education of children, the Convention asserts that "Measures shall be taken **to preserve and promote the development and practice of the indigenous languages** of the peoples concerned." Similar, and frequently stronger, guarantees about language are contained in international documents that followed, including the European Charter for Regional or Minority Languages (Council of Europe, 1992), the UN Declaration on the Rights of Persons Belonging to National or Ethnic, Religious or Linguistic Minorities (1992), the OAS Draft American Declaration on the Rights of Indigenous Peoples (1997),[4] and others.

In addition to such international documents, countries may adopt constitutions and enact specific laws addressing language that sometimes protect (and sometimes restrict) its citizens' rights. As discussed in Chapter 7, the Indian, Indonesian, and South African constitutions all explicitly declare one or more official or national languages. However, the Indian constitution does not establish only official and national languages. There is also a provision that ensures the right of every citizen "having a distinct language, script, or culture . . . to conserve the same." The constitution of South Africa proclaims eleven official languages, but also asserts that "the state must take practical and positive measures to elevate the status and advance the use of these languages." Although Sweden's constitution does not designate a national or official language, it does provide for the protection of the rights of linguistic, as well as ethnic and religious, minorities. Like Sweden, Italy designates no national or official language, but explicitly safeguards "linguistic minorities." Other constitutions are either silent on language declarations (as is true of the United States, Australia, Chile, Israel, Japan,

[4] The American Declaration on the Rights of Indigenous Peoples was finally adopted on June 15, 2016.

the Netherlands, and others) or more muted.[5] Examples of laws specifically protecting or restricting language use that have been enacted in several countries are detailed in later chapters.

Tolerance- and Promotion-Oriented Rights

An important distinction that emerges in comparing the earlier and later international documents, as well as provisions in various constitutions, is the distinction between *tolerance-oriented* and *promotion-oriented* rights.[6] Tolerance-oriented provisions merely guarantee the right of individuals (or groups) to use any language they choose. For example, the 1976 UN Covenant states only that minorities cannot be **denied** the right to use their language if they wish. That is, while any language is tolerated, it is not incumbent on governments to take measures to support minority languages. The constitution of Sudan also falls into this category as it declares Arabic the official language but simply "**permits** the development of local languages." Several later documents contain conditions that seem to obligate signatories to take active measures to facilitate or promote the use of minority languages. The ILO Convention quoted above mandates preservation and promotion of minority languages. And like the ILO Convention, the 1992 European Charter, the 1992 UN Declaration, and the OAS Draft Declaration provide for the indigenous peoples' right to education in their minority language, with the implication that this entails state support. These types of promotion-oriented obligations are also present in the constitutions of South Africa (cited above), and a number of other countries. However, as pointed out by many scholars, in many of the international declarations these provisions are formulated in very general terms and states are given a great deal of discretion in their implementation.[7] This is apparent in the inclusion of provisos such as "wherever practicable," "where appropriate," and "whose number is considered sufficient." (The other documents as well as the 2007 UN Declaration on the Rights of Indigenous Peoples contain similar language.)[8]

Language as a Human Right

But what does it mean for language to be a human right? We have seen that human rights documents set out the rights of people in the society that they live

---

[5] Faingold (2004) proposes a typology of language provisions found in the constitutions of 187 countries.

[6] Kloss 1977.

[7] Tove Skutnabb-Kangas (2000) and Stephen May (2011), among others, have noted these "escape clauses" in various documents.

[8] May 2011 provides an extensive discussion of tolerance- versus promotion-oriented rights, specifically through the lens of political theory and international law.

in and the rights that a state (or government) must ensure for those living in its dominion. If a person is treated unequally by the criminal justice system, that person is being denied a basic human right. If a person is prevented from participating in the cultural life of the community or freely expressing religious beliefs, that person is being denied basic human rights. If a child is not afforded an education by the state, that child is being denied a basic human right. These cases are clear. However, oftentimes some citizens are unable to fully participate in society or fully enjoy the rights set out in rights declarations that the state has adopted not because the state actively denies these rights but solely because of the language that that person speaks. De facto, that person is being denied basic human rights. Thus, it is argued, language is a fundamental human right, or at least a human right whose forfeiture or denial can impact negatively upon the realization of other rights.

While the connection between language and human rights may seem obvious on the surface, the notion is nonetheless controversial and has fueled a lively academic and public policy debate. People have taken various positions on the entire issue of language rights. And so the implementation of language rights is far from straightforward.

The most extreme language rights position that can be adopted is that **any** persons under **any** circumstances should be able to use **any** language they choose, a view adopted by few. However, a stance approaching this position is adopted by some of the most ardent advocates of linguistic human rights, who take these to be inalienable rights, rights of both groups and individuals (by virtue of the individual belonging to a particular community).[9] The fundamental principles regarding personal identification with a mother tongue, education in that language, the use of that language in "**most** official situations" and others[10] were adopted in the Universal Declaration on Linguistic Rights (UDLR), which was finalized in 1996 at the World Conference on Linguistics Rights held in Barcelona, Spain. The UDLR was drafted by some sixty language rights activists and academicians from around the world, organized by the International PEN (now PEN International), a worldwide society of writers.[11] Despite the fact that the UDLR has not gained approval and has no legal status, it is perhaps the most comprehensive document addressing linguistic human rights and is worth some consideration. The Declaration delineates a set of "inalienable personal rights" and a

---

[9] Andrássy 2012 formulates an explicit argument for taking language to be a fundamental human right based on the premise that recognized rights such as freedom of expression, freedom of religion, and so on must be expressed in language and can only be true freedoms if people are free to use the language in which these rights are exercised.

[10] Phillipson and Skutnabb-Kangas 1995: 500.

[11] Established in England in 1921, PEN is an acronym for poets, essayists and novelists.

set of collective rights. The notion of personal and collective rights is set out in the preamble.

Individual rights which may be "exercised in any situation" include:
- the right to be recognized as a member of a language community;
- the right to the use of one's own language both in private and in public;
- the right to the use of one's own name;
- the right to interrelate and associate with other members of one's language community of origin;
- the right to maintain and develop one's own culture; . . .

The collective rights include:
- the right for their own language and culture to be taught;
- the right of access to cultural services;
- the right to an equitable presence of their language and culture in the communications media;
- the right to receive attention in their own language from government bodies and in socio-economic relations.

The fifty-two articles of the UDLR specify more explicitly and precisely these rights, rights that the drafters of the document believe should be guaranteed in all public and private domains.

Cultural rights have figured prominently in most human rights documents since the 1948 UN declaration, and the UDLR refers in many instances specifically to "language and culture." This is based on the familiar conviction that language is a significant component of cultural identity. A culture represents a collection (or community) of people, and the UDLR takes as its point of departure a *language community* (and its members), which is defined as "any human society established historically in a particular territorial space, whether this space be recognized or not, which identifies itself as a people and has developed a common language as a natural means of communication and cultural cohesion among its members." The English, the French, and the Japanese are majority language communities in their historical territories of England, France and Japan. The First Nations of Canada, the Welsh in Great Britain, and the Ainu in Japan are minority language communities in their homelands. The rights in the Declaration are guaranteed in both types of communities but are clearly more directed at protecting the interests of minority communities. For proponents of the linguistic human rights position, governments are responsible for providing the means to assure linguistic rights to all citizens. These then are conceived of as promotion-oriented rights.

A clear impetus for the linguistic human rights view comes from the pressure on the vitality and viability of minority languages in the societies in which their speaker communities live. (In fact, while maintaining a language rights as human rights stance, some have at times employed the term *minority language rights*, e.g. Stephen May.[12] Others, such as Sándor N. Szilágyi, while recognizing the issue facing minorities, speak of *rights for both majorities and minorities*.[13]) Various factors create this pressure on minority languages, including governments adopting official languages as a means of establishing a national identity and administering a state. As discussed in Chapter 7, in a multilingual society the establishment of a state language automatically advantages those who speak the language natively. Those who do not speak the state language fluently may be unable to enjoy all the rights and privileges of citizens of the state as laid out in the UN Universal Declaration of Human Rights. The Universal Declaration of Language Rights is intended to address this. Additionally, the rise in the global economy has brought with it an ascension of majority languages in which international business is transacted and scientific and technological advances are made. People who do not speak a majority language run the risk of being marginalized and thus often opt to operate in one of the global languages, in addition or instead of their own disadvantaged minority language. This marginalization and the potential loss of languages are frequently invoked by language rights proponents as a situation needing remedy, and in this regard it is sometimes the languages themselves (rather than the people who speak them) that appear to be deserving of rights, according to some linguistic human rights advocates. Proponents of this view sometimes compare language loss to the extinction of species in the environment. By ensuring language rights, they believe, the languages themselves will be preserved.

Language as a Human Right?

In opposition to this view, some who are genuinely concerned about discrimination and minority rights nonetheless assert that language should not be considered a human right and that the idea of language rights itself is misguided. They cite both philosophical and practical reasons for this. One issue to consider is the tension between individual and collective rights. The Universal Declaration of Language Rights states explicitly that the individual gains language rights on the basis of belonging to a language community or a language group.[14,15] Human rights are afforded to individuals from birth, regardless of membership in a "recognized community." Therefore, if language rights accrue to individuals only as members of some larger identified

---

[12] May 2005.   [13] Kontra 2009; Skutnabb-Kangas 2012: 239.   [14] Wee 2005.
[15] The Declaration distinguishes indigenous *language communities* from *language groups*, which may be comprised of immigrants, refugees, and others, defining a language group as "any group of persons sharing the same language which is established in the territorial space of another language community but which does not possess historical antecedents equivalent to those of that community."

community, they are fundamentally different from human rights and cannot be accorded the same status as individual human rights. (Of course, some arguing from the linguistic human rights position counter that these rights should be afforded to an individual without regard to group membership.[16]) Collective rights are also based on the existence of an established group. However, recognizing both individual and collective language rights creates a situation in which these different classes of rights may conflict with one another. One's individual right to use whatever language that person chooses includes the right not to use the language of the group one belongs to. Exercising this individual right may compromise the collective rights of the language community by jeopardizing the integrity of the group. If a language community is endangered by the exit of its members, it is argued, then any particular member may not truly feel free to exercise that individual right. This may effectively deny the individual a fundamental human right if language is taken in this way to be a human right. This differs subtly from an individual being pressured by a community (whether identified by ethnicity, religion, or some other non-linguistic criterion) not to renounce membership in that group. The right of freedom of assembly and association identified in the UN Declaration (Article 20) as a collective right is not jeopardized when someone chooses to exercise that right and *not* associate with a particular group. Since language communities require a sufficient number of members to remain viable (as discussed below in Chapter 10) in a way that other cultural expressions (such as religion) do not, language rights that are linked to recognized language communities (including individual rights) are thus open to being compromised in a way that other human rights are not.

Additionally, some argue that linguistic human rights advocates may be overlooking the fundamentally nuanced nature of language.[17] Identifying a particular language that is the object of a group's right ignores the fact that dialects are real and that languages are dynamic and change over time (as discussed in Chapter 4). Treating a language as a right creates a static entity, establishing an object that is identified as a particular form of that language, and one that may be representative only of a past, idealized instantiation of the language. Thus, individuals that are identified as being part of a group are in essence guaranteed the right to a language that may not really be their own. Therefore, the argument goes, language cannot be an important human right. Of course, as discussed in Chapter 7, the creation of a standard language (which is essential to identifying and establishing a state language) creates precisely this situation, in which non-standard varieties are compromised and their speaker communities are disadvantaged.

[16] Skutnabb-Kangas et al. 2006.   [17] Wee 2011: 130.

An argument frequently given by language rights advocates relates to language and identity – something which has fueled some nationalist movements and which to some degree motivates the Universal Declaration of Language Rights. Since language and cultural/ethnic identity are so tightly interwoven, speaking the language of the culture is important to one's identity. Thus, for example, in order to be a Native American Choctaw, one should not be denied the right to speak Choctaw, and for many linguistic human rights advocates this entails early education in Choctaw. Those who question language rights counter that language is actually only a secondary or surface marker of identity; one's cultural or ethnic identity is not determined by the language one speaks.[18] The only thing lost when a language is relinquished is the language itself; the rest of the ethnic identity remains intact and is "translated" into the adopted language. No one disputes the Irishness of a native of Dublin who does not speak Irish; in fact, according to 2011 census figures, only 4.4 percent of the population speak Irish at least weekly outside school settings. If language is not essential to one's ethnic identity, ethnic identity is not a cogent argument for linguistic human rights.

Further, many language rights opponents point out that speaking a minority language may be disadvantageous. This disadvantage has been an important motivation for language rights in the first place. Advocating or in some cases insisting that individuals of a particular group be allowed to speak their language may actually hinder social and economic mobility. As pointed out previously, some linguistic human rights advocates cite the rapid disappearance of the world's languages as one rationale for language rights. It is widely reported that perhaps half (or up to 90 percent) of the 6,000–7,000 languages currently spoken will no long be spoken by the end of the century.[19,20] For that reason, minority languages must be preserved and promoted, and speakers should insist on education for their young children in the mother tongue. Thus, language rights must be recognized as a basic human right. Opponents note that "forcing" minority language speakers to use their native language or their young children to be educated in the minority language does them a disservice as their fluency in the dominant language, an important "key to success" in the greater society, may be compromised.[21] Of course, many language rights supporters insist that one of these rights must be the right "to learn an official language of the country they live in."[22]

In some sense, one's view regarding language as a human right is irrelevant to the potential effects of linguistic discrimination. The inability to partake of all of

---

[18] Eastman 1984; Edwards 1985, 2003.   [19] Austin and Sallabank 2011.

[20] Figures vary, but *Ethnologue* reports that of the 7,100 living languages they document over 1,500 are "in trouble," that is, endangered or threatened. We examine the issue of language vitality in Chapter 16.

[21] Mufwene 2002.   [22] Phillipson and Skutnabb-Kangas 1995: 500.

the benefits of a society and be assured of safeguards set out in human rights documents due to an insufficient level of proficiency in the dominant language becomes a rights issue if no accommodation is made. Given the fact that it is a rights issue helps to explain why language has been used to deny access in some cases and to empower in others. As we have seen, efforts have been made to address this in international declarations and states' constitutions.

However, the international declarations and states' constitutions appealed to here are clearly not the only documents that tackle the issue of language rights. We have, in a few instances, referenced "language laws." Throughout history, there has been language legislation. Prior to the era of heightened concern for human rights, a great many laws (though certainly not all) restricted rather than protected language rights. Some of these pertained to particular domains, such as education, and some were quite broad. The Native School Act (1867) in New Zealand promoted English and restricted the Māori language. In 1898, a law went into effect in Norway, restricting the use of the Sámi language in state-run schools. The Hokkaido Former Aborigines Act (1899), among other things, mandated the use of Japanese and prohibited the use of Ainu.

However, in the past forty to fifty years, the language rights movement has met with some success, especially with regard to indigenous languages. Laws concerning minority rights specifically involving language have been enacted in many countries. The Treaty of Watangi Act (1987) in New Zealand, the Sámi Act (1987) in Norway, and the Ainu Cultural Promotion Act (1997) in Japan all contain provisions that address some of the previous laws, and redress the inequities. We will encounter these and other examples in the chapters that follow.

English (Only or First) in the United States

To understand current appeals to make English the "official," "national," or "only" language of the United States, one has to go back to colonial times. The competition for North America on the part of European powers in the sixteenth to eighteenth centuries was primarily an English, French, and Spanish affair (with minor supporting roles played by Germany, the Netherlands, Portugal, and Sweden).

Spanish (and Portuguese) exploration and conquest were largely focused on South America, Mexico, and the Caribbean, but extended into the present-day southeastern United States. The first extensive exploration of this area by the Spanish, some twenty-five years after Ponce de León "discovered" (the island of) Florida, was conducted by Hernando de Soto (1539–1541), and passed through Florida, Georgia, South Carolina, North Carolina, Tennessee, Alabama, Mississippi, Arkansas, Louisiana, and Texas (see Figure 9.1).

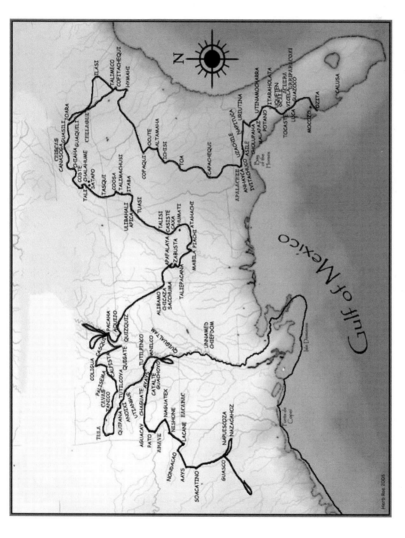

Figure 9.1 Hernando de Soto's probable route, 1539–1541

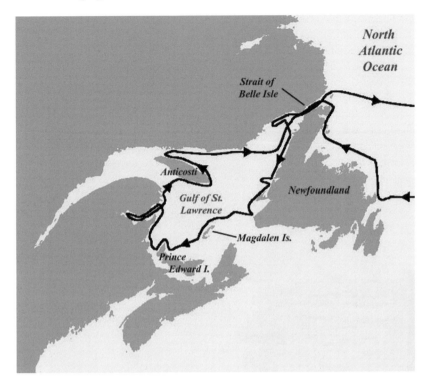

Figure 9.2 Jacques Cartier's 1534 expedition to North America

In the sixteenth century, the Spanish established (or attempted to establish) settlements in the American southeast: San Miguel de Gualdape (1527, Georgia), Pensacola (1559, Florida), Saint Augustine (1565, Florida), and Santa Elena/Fort San Marcos (1566/1577, South Carolina). Of these, only Saint Augustine on the northern Florida coast was ultimately successful, the rest succumbing to hardships or attacks.

French exploration of North America was mainly focused in the northern (present-day Canadian) parts of the continent, commencing in 1534 with the expeditions of Jacques Cartier, shown in Figure 9.2, to what are today the Canadian provinces of New Brunswick, Newfoundland, Nova Scotia, Prince Edward Island, and Quebec. The only attempt by the French to establish a presence along the southeastern Atlantic coast involved colonization of the coast at present-day Parris Island (Hilton Head, South Carolina) and St. Johns River (Jacksonville, Florida) by a group of French Huguenots (Protestants). These two settlements, named Charlesfort and Fort Caroline respectively, were established in 1562–1564 and abandoned or destroyed a couple of years later.

The Swedish and Dutch also had short-lived colonial enterprises in what became the Thirteen Colonies. The former established Nya Sverige (New Sweden), with settlements in western New Jersey, southeastern Pennsylvania, and northern Delaware, along the Delaware River valley, and the latter created Nieuw-Nederland (New Netherland) primarily around the Hudson River valley, building settlements and forts in present-day New York, New Jersey, and Connecticut. The Swedish venture lasted less than twenty years (1638–1655), before being incorporated into New Netherlands, and the Dutch colonial effort lasted longer, from 1613 until 1674, before capitulation to the English.

Thus, by the end of the seventeenth century, the entire Atlantic coast of British North America was an English-speaking colonial affair, from the St. Croix River in the north (separating Maine and Canada) to the St. Marys River in the south (separating Georgia and Florida). From this point onward, English-speaking societies in North America came into conflict with French speakers in Canada (see Chapter 14) and (mostly) with Spanish speakers and other non-English-speaking immigrants in the United States (as seen in Figure 9.3).

As stated, most of the English versus other-language conflict, through the present day, has been with Spanish-speaking groups. However, America's first language conflicts did not begin with Spanish speakers, those conflicts emerging after the Mexican–American War (see Chapter 11). Rather, the first publicly recorded animosity toward non-English speakers came from Benjamin Franklin, while America was yet still a British colony, and was directed at German-speaking inhabitants of Philadelphia. Franklin incongruously had tried unsuccessfully in 1732 to publish a German-language newspaper *Philadelphische Zeitung* (which failed in part because he did not have German type and couldn't spell the German words appropriately). Whether because they wouldn't buy his newspapers, or due to the more likely fact that German speakers comprised one-third of Pennsylvania's population, Franklin had come to resent and fear the German-speaking settlers in the colony, believing that they and others were polluting the English colonies linguistically and racially. He wrote in 1751:

Those who come hither are generally of the most ignorant Stupid Sort of their Own Nation … Why should Pennsylvania, founded by the English, become a Colony of Aliens, who will shortly be so numerous as to Germanize us instead of Our Anglifying them, and will never adopt our Language or Customs, any more than they can acquire our Complexion.[23]

[23] Franklin 1751.

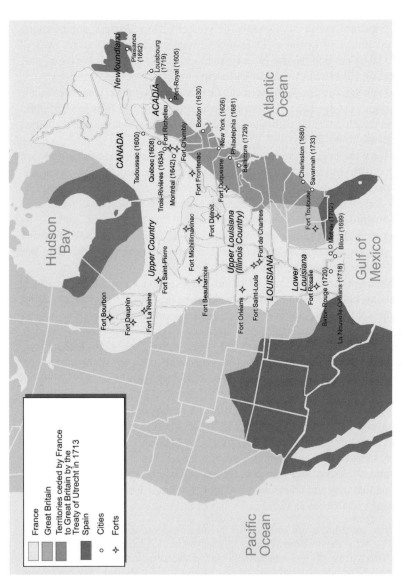

Figure 9.3 Map of North America, 1750

Note that, for Franklin, ethnicity/race, culture, and language were of a piece, and inseparable, and already, some twenty years before the Colonies declared their independence, he and others considered the English language to be a foundational part of the Colonies' character.

It should not come as a surprise that, from its independence, fear and loathing of other languages and their speakers has arisen in the United States either as a consequence of paranoia during times of war or as a result of large-scale immigration. Tracing the history of war- and immigration-related linguo-phobias, we encounter, in the historical record, the following:

- conflict with French speakers in Louisiana at the time of the Louisiana Purchase (from 1803);
- conflict with Spanish speakers in the American southwest following the 1846–1848 Mexican–American War (see Chapter 14);
- prejudice against Italian speakers (Catholics) and Yiddish speakers (Jews) who immigrated to the United States in great numbers at the end of the nineteenth century and beginning of the twentieth century;
- suspicion and repression of German speakers during World War I and Japanese speakers during World War II;
- suspicion of Russian speakers from the Bolshevik Russian revolution in 1917 through the Cold War period of the 1950s and 1960s;
- anti-Spanish sentiment in New York during the post-World War II influx of Puerto Ricans (see Chapter 12) and again in many large cities in recent decades in reaction to immigration from Mexico;
- suspicion of Arabic speakers since 9/11 and through the ongoing Middle East wars.

These circumstances have often manifested themselves as English-Only legislation (usually at the local or state level) or as local rules and discrimination against the targeted language(s).

The first such conflict arose in 1803, with President Thomas Jefferson's purchase of the Louisiana Territory from France. At the time of this purchase, it was Jefferson's intention to have Louisiana governed as a territory, rather than admitted as a state, since it was felt that the French-speaking inhabitants would not be able to integrate linguistically or politically into the United States, being speakers of only French in the first instance, and being used to monarchical rule in the second. This led, in 1805, to a petition (i.e. "remonstrance") being submitted to Congress, by two thousand heads of households in New Orleans, demanding that Louisiana residents have parity with other citizens of the United States, and that they be admitted as a state and allowed to govern themselves. Incorporated in this petition was the demand to conduct legal affairs in both French and English, insisting thereby that Louisiana be admitted to the

Union as a bilingual state.[24] As a result of this, the state of Louisiana did enter the Union as a bilingual state, and this bilingual status was enshrined in the 1845 constitution. Subsequently, after the Civil War, the US federal government abolished French language rights in the state (partly as punishment for Louisiana's support of, and membership in, the Confederacy). These rights were regained in 1879, after Reconstruction, when white "Radicals" came to power in the state.

Even though it took the United States until 1917 to enter World War I on the side of Britain and France in their World War I battles against the Germans (three years after the start of hostilities), this did not stop the Americans from getting quickly up to speed in targeting German immigrants as a potential enemy "fifth column" (as illustrated in Figure 9.4). Anti-German sentiment was directed at German imports, German culture, German-immigrant-owned businesses, German names, and, of course, the German language. In his Declaration of War to Congress in April of 1917, President Woodrow Wilson set the tone regarding the treatment of Americans of German extraction, stating, of the "millions of men and women of German birth and native sympathy [that] live amongst us" that "if there should be disloyalty, it will be dealt with with a firm hand of stern repression."[25] So encouraged, the American public readily took up the cudgel, both in cities with large German immigrant populations such as New York and Chicago, as well as in the Midwestern states (e.g. Michigan, Illinois, Iowa, Wisconsin, and Nebraska) where Germans were a significant minority.

The reaction to Germans in Iowa, where Germans were the largest immigrant group in the state, is instructive. In November 1917, the state proceeded to ban German-language instruction, first in the public schools and then in private parochial schools. To emphasize the point that they were making, German instructors were fired, and German-language textbooks were burned. To avoid hostility and discrimination, many German families changed their names and many places (towns and roads) were renamed, and German-language newspapers went out of circulation. Berlin Township in Clinton County became Hughes Township; Bismark Street in Muscatine became Bond Street; and sauerkraut was renamed liberty cabbage.

The public anti-German hysteria, leading in some instances to people being attacked in the street for speaking German, was certainly not discouraged by the words and actions of Iowa's Governor William L. Harding, who served to legitimize the "prejudice and war-time fanaticism when he issued The Babel Proclamation on May 23, 1918 [only six months before the end of the war] ... which ban[ned] the public use of all foreign languages." In so doing Harding

[24] MacMaster 1921.   [25] Frese 2005.

Figure 9.4 1918 Liberty Bond posters with Germanophobic slogan

became the first and only governor in the United States to outlaw the public use of foreign languages.[26]

Official English / English Only / English First

As we have seen, assaults on speakers of other languages for speaking or using those languages has a long and distinguished history in the United States, going all the way back to "Founding Father" Benjamin Franklin before the American Revolution. A good number of these attacks on other languages and the rights of their speakers to use them can be attributed to the desire to expand or protect American (Anglophone) hegemony in and across North America. Up until the 1674, a century before Franklin wrote his anti-German screed, the British North American colonies consisted of two disconnected colonial enterprises – one centered on the Massachusetts Bay and one centered on the Chesapeake Bay – separated by the Dutch and Swedes and bounded on the north and south by the French and the Spanish, respectively. By 1700, having gained control of the entire Atlantic coast between Florida and Canada, British colonial competition was with France in the north and Spain to the south.

Franklin's stated hostility to colonies of (German) aliens may be seen in the larger context of English-speaking competition with the French at this time. When Franklin wrote against German-speaking settlers in Pennsylvania, things were already heating up between Britain and France. Only three years afterward, in 1754, the "French and Indian War" broke out between the British and French colonists (each supported by their respective American Indian allies). This war left British North America in a much more secure and expanded position, eliminating French sovereignty in continental North America.

After the American War of Independence, from 1783 on, ethnolinguistic conflicts were primarily (except for the contest between French and English speakers in New Orleans) with American Indian bands in the eastern half of the continent, arising as a consequence of expanded American settlement of the areas west of the Appalachian Mountains and east of the Mississippi River. However, these conflicts were mostly about treaties between the United States and the Indians, and negotiation for access to territory and resources. It wasn't until the latter half of the nineteenth century, after the Bureau of Indian Affairs was moved from the US War Department (i.e. Department of Defense) to the US Department of the Interior in 1849, that US Government relations with the Indians began to involve the elimination of their language rights and the imposition of assimilatory language policies of forced use of English (see Chapter 10).

[26] Frese 2005.

The next major linguistic conflict in the United States arose as a consequence of the Mexican–American War (1846–1848), in which the US came into possession of Mexican territories comprising current-day Texas, Utah, Nevada, New Mexico, Arizona, and California. This acquisition resulted, rather quickly, in conflict with the Spanish-speaking former residents of Mexico, and led to diminution and violation of their language rights (see Chapter 11).

Ensuing wars and geopolitical conflicts following this one have periodically led to assaults on the language rights of American residents who speak (or who are perceived to speak) the "language of the enemy," as noted in the Iowa World War I case, above. Since then, our history records discrimination against Japanese speakers in World War II, Russian speakers during the Cold War, and Arabic speakers more recently. Beginning in the 1980s, "conflict-instigated" English-only policies gave way to an "immigration-instigated" English-only movement. The immediate trigger for this was the passage of the Immigration and Naturalization Act of 1965, and the further irritant was the Immigration Reform Act of 1986. Up until the early 1960s, immigration to the United States was managed and constrained through quotas based on national origins, and the quotas were determined by each national group's representation in the US population. Thus, the system favored immigration on the part of nationalities that were already well established and well represented in US society (e.g. English, Irish, and Germans, over Chinese, Greeks, Mexicans, and Poles).[27]

The bias in favor of northern European immigrants over all others was quite overt and was seen, in the context of the Civil Rights Movement of the 1950s and 1960s, to be discriminatory, and in 1963 then-President John F. Kennedy spoke out against it, calling for immigration reform. By 1965 the US Congress passed the Immigration and Nationality Act (Public Law 89–236, enacted in 1968), which (among other things) did away with nationality-based immigration quotas.[28] The intended effect, as envisioned by those who drafted the law, was to open the door wider to immigrants from southern and eastern Europe. Once enacted, though, it resulted in a substantial influx from countries in South Asia, Southeast Asia, East Asia, Mexico and South America, and Africa.

Substantial amounts of illegal immigration to the United States during the 1970s and 1980s led to calls for tighter controls, and led to the passage of the Immigration Reform and Control Act of 1986 (Public Law 99–603). This law, intended to curb illegal immigration and control the movement of seasonal agricultural workers, also provided for legal status to be given to many illegal immigrants who had entered the United States and lived there continuously for

[27] History.com Staff 2010.   [28] United States Government Publishing Office 1965.

at least five years.[29] In practice, though, it had little effect on illegal immigration, but did provide amnesty and legal residency to some 2.7 million previously undocumented immigrants.[30] In this respect, the 1986 law might, in some quarters, have been seen as providing more of a boost to immigration than control of it. Regardless (or perhaps as a consequence) of the will of Congress, legal immigration to the United States from 1965 to 1995 amounted to some 18 million people (three times the number arriving during the thirty years prior), and by the 1990s only one in six arrivals were from Europe.[31]

American reaction to massive immigration on the part of non-European peoples took the form (in part) of a (hostile) reaction to the immigrants' language. Beginning in 1983, English-firsters began to coalesce into a language movement with the establishment of U.S. English, a "group dedicated to preserving the unifying role of the English language in the United States" by lobbying to make English *the* Official Language of the United States. The irony of U.S. English group's foundation was that its progenitor was Senator Samuel Ichiye "S. I." Hayakawa, a Canadian-born US immigrant of Japanese ancestry, and that its chairman/CEO is Mauro E. Mujica, "an immigrant from Chile."[32]

Another group, called English First, was founded shortly afterward, in 1986. This group (which appears to have become dormant in 2011), was a bit more radical than U.S. English, claiming to "lead the fight against bilingual education" (presumably on the basis of their belief that bilingual education reduces the need and motivation for immigrants to learn English).[33] Considering that "bilingual education" in the United States is principally Spanish–English bilingual education, it would be fair to say that English First was leading the fight against linguistic accommodations for Hispanic immigrants.

The most recently organized, and most active, of the English-language advocacy groups is ProEnglish, which was founded in 1994 under the name English Language Advocates in order to "work through the courts and in the court of public opinion to defend English's historic role as America's common, unifying language, and to persuade lawmakers to adopt English as the official language at all levels of government."[34]

It is worth noting that, despite issue-specific successes (in localized English-language conflicts and at the state level, thirty-two states having enacted English-only laws), the central goal of making English *the* official language of the United States has yet to be achieved, although legislation to make English the official language is currently under consideration by Congress.

[29] United States Government Publishing Office 1986.   [30] Wyloge 2009.
[31] History.com Staff 2010.   [32] U.S. English 2016a.   [33] English First 2011b.
[34] ProEnglish 2015.

On March 6, 2013, The English Language Unity Act of 2013 was introduced in Congress, with Congressman Steve King of Iowa as its chief sponsor (together with Senator James Inhofe of Oklahoma). It was not passed, and has been reintroduced (February 13, 2015) as the English Language Unity Act of 2015, with King again as primary sponsor. As of March 2015, it was referred to the Subcommittee on Immigration and Border Security and has not moved further.[35]

One might be led to ask why this is so, in light of the (possible) fact that "Eighty-four percent (84%) of Americans say English should be the official language of the United States."[36] An examination of these groups' assertions about English in the United States is enlightening in this regard. Whether lobbying for English to be *an* official language of the United States or *the* official language of the United States, the English advocacy movement is predicated on the premises that: (i) English is our "social glue"; (ii) immigrants refuse to learn English; (iii) people must be compelled to learn a language; (iv) communal leaders discourage immigrants from learning English; and (v) linguistic diversity leads to language conflict. The position taken by such groups (e.g. U.S. English) is that having English as the official language of the United States would promote unity, would empower immigrants, would be common-sense government, and would help protect English in the United States. Challenging these positions, the International Association of Teachers of English to Speakers of Other Languages (TESOL) has countered: (i) that only 4 percent of the US population speaks little or no English (i.e. lack of competence in English is not a problem in the United States); (ii) that immigrants are quite aware of the need to learn English and that what is needed are more resources to enable them to do so (i.e. there is no need for coercion in this regard); (iii) that very few taxpayer-funded resources are currently spent on bilingual services (i.e. non-English-speaking immigrants are not encumbering the US taxpayers in any substantial way); and (iv) English needs no special protections. It is perhaps on account of these factors that these English advocacy groups have not generated among the American electorate any perceptible urgency regarding the status of English as a national official language.[37]

---

[35] 114th Congress (2015–2016).   [36] English First 2011a.   [37] TESOL 2005.

Further Reading and Resources for Part II

Chapter 5

Edwards, John. 2009. *Language and identity: An introduction*. Cambridge University Press.

Erikson, Erik H. 1968. *Identity and youth crisis*. New York: W. W. Norton.

Joseph, John E. 2004. *Language and identity: National, ethnic, religious*. Basingstoke: Palgrave Macmillan.

Sapir, Edward. 1927. Speech as a personality trait. *American Journal of Sociology* 32: 892–905.

1933. Language. *Encyclopaedia of the Social Sciences* 9: 155–169.

Scott, Brian M., and Joshua Mittleman. 1999. A brief introduction to medieval bynames. www.s-gabriel.org/names/arval/bynames/

Türköz, Meltem. 2007. Surname narratives and the state–society boundary: Memories of Turkey's Family Name Law of 1934. *Middle Eastern Studies* 43: 893–908.

United Nations. 1959. United Nations Declaration of the Rights of the Child. www.un-documents.net/a14r1386.htm

Vygotsky, Lev. 1962. *Thought and language*. Cambridge, MA: MIT Press.

Chapter 6

American Dialect Society. 2016. 2015 word of the year is singular 'they.' www.americandialect.org/2015-word-of-the-year-is-singular-they

Joseph, John E. 2002. *From Whitney to Chomsky: Essays in the history of American linguistics*. Amsterdam: Benjamins.

Martin, Laura. 1988. "Eskimo words for snow": A case study in the genesis and decay of an anthropological example. *Americn Anthropologist* 88: 418–423.

Lord, Nancy. 1998. Native tongues. In Virginia Clark, Paul Eschholz, and Alfred Rosa (eds.), *Language: Readings in language and culture*, 19–25 (chapter 3). New York: St. Martin's Press.

Pullum, Geoffrey K. 1991. The great Eskimo vocabulary hoax. *The great Eskimo vocabulary hoax and other irreverent essays on the study of language*. University of Chicago Press.

2011. Pronoun agreement out the window. *Lingua Franca: The Chronicle of Higher Education*. December 16, 2011. http://chronicle.com/blogs/linguafranca/2011/12/16/pronoun-agreement-out-the-window/

Sapir, Edward. 1921. *Language*. Harcourt, Brace and World.
    1933. Language. *Encyclopaedia of the Social Sciences* 9: 155–169.
Whorf, Benjamin Lee. 1940a. Linguistics as an exact science. *Technology Review* 43: 61–63, 80–83. Reprinted in Carroll (ed.) 1956: 220–232.
    1940b. Science and linguistics. *Technology Review* 42: 229–231, 247–248. Reprinted in Carroll (ed.) 1956: 207–219.
Woodbury, Anthony. 1991. *Counting Eskimo words for snow: A citizen's guide.* http://linguistlist.org/issues/5/5-1239.html

Chapter 7

Coulmas, Florian. 1988. What's a national language good for? In Florian Coulmas (ed.), *With forked tongues: What are national languages good for?*, 1–24. Ann Arbor, MI: Karoma Publishers.
Faingold, Eduardo D. 2004. Language rights and language justice in the constitutions of the world. *Language Problems and Language Planning* 28: 11–24.
Fasold, Ralph. 1988. What national languages are good for. In Florian Coulmas (ed.), *With forked tongues: What are national languages good for?*, 180–185. Ann Arbor, MI: Karoma Publishers.
Harris, Roy, and Talbot Taylor. 1989. *Landmarks in linguistic thought: The Western tradition from Socrates to Saussure*. London: Routledge.
May, Stephen. 2012. *Language and minority rights: Ethnicity, nationalism, and the politics of language*. Routledge.
Myhill, John. 2006. *Language, religion and national identity in Europe and the Middle East*. Amsterdam: John Benjamins.
Wee, Lionel. 2011. *Language without rights*. New York: Oxford University Press.

Indonesia

Abas, Husen. 1987. *Indonesian as a unifying language of wider communication: A historical and sociolinguistic perspective.* Canberra: Department of Linguistics, Research School of Pacific Studies, Australian National University.
Alisbjahbana, S. T. 1974. Language policy and literacy in Indonesia and Malaysia. In Joshua Fishman (ed.), *Advances in language planning*, 391–416. The Hague: Mouton.
Dardjowidjojo, Soenjono. 1998. Strategies for a successful national language policy: The Indonesian case. *International Journal of the Sociology of Language* 130: 35–46.
Sneddon, James. 2003. *The Indonesian language: Its history and role in modern society.* Sydney: UNSW Press.

India

Das Gupta, Jyotirindra. 1970. *Language conflict and national development*. Berkeley: University of California Press.
Gandhi, M. K. 1956. *Thoughts on national language*. Ahmedabad: Navajivan Publishing.

Groff, Cynthia. 2007. Status and acquisition planning and linguistic minorities in India. *Working Papers in Educational Linguistics* 22: 15–41.

South Africa

Alexander, Neville. 2001. *Language education policy, national and sub-national identities in South Africa: Reference study.* Strasbourg: Language Policy Division DG IV – Directorate of School, Out-of-School and Higher Education, Council of Europe. www.coe.int/t/dg4/linguistic/Source/AlexanderEN.pdf
Beinart, William. 2001. *Twentieth-century South Africa.* Oxford University Press.
Davitt, Michael. 1902. *The Boer fight for freedom.* New York: Funk and Wagnalls.
Egerö, Bertil. 1991. *South Africa's Bantustans: From dumping grounds to battlefronts. Nordiska Afrikainstitutet Discussion Paper* 4. Uppsala: Nordiska Afrikainstitutet.
Frankental, Sally, and Owen Sichone. 2005. *South Africa's diverse peoples: A reference sourcebook.* Santa Barbara, CA: ABC-CLIO.
Kamwangamalu, Nkonko M. 2009. South African Englishes. In Braj Kachru, Yamuna Kachru, and Cecil Nelson (eds.), *The handbook of world Englishes*, 158–171. Hoboken, NJ: John Wiley and Sons.
Louw, P. Eric. 1992. Language and national unity in a post-apartheid South Africa. *Critical Arts: A Journal of Media Studies* 6(1): 52–60.
Mesthrie, Rajend. 2002. South Africa: A sociolinguistic overview. In Rajend Mesthrie (ed.), *Language in South Africa*, 11–26. Cambridge University Press.

Chapter 8

Coulmas, Florian. 1991. *Writing systems of the world.* Wiley-Blackwell.
    2003. *Writing systems: An introduction to their linguistic analysis.* Cambridge University Press.
Daniels, Peter T., and William Bright (eds.). 1996. *The world's writing systems.* Oxford University Press.
Goldwasser, Orly (2010). How the alphabet was born from hieroglyphs. *Biblical Archaeology Review* (Washington, DC: Biblical Archaeology Society) 36(2): 24–36.
Hockett, Charles F. 1960. The origins of speech. *Scientific American* 203: 88–96.
Sampson, Geoffrey. 1985. *Writing systems: A linguistic introduction.* Stanford University Press.
Sanders, Seth L. 2004. What was the alphabet for? The rise of written vernaculars and the making of Israelite national literature. *Maarav* 11: 25–56.

Chapter 9

Dorian, Nancy C. 1994. Choices and values in language shift and its study. *International Journal of the Sociology of Language* 110: 113–124.
Edwards, John. 1985. *Language, society, and identity.* Oxford: Blackwell.
    2003. Contextualizing language rights. *Journal of Human Rights* 2: 551–571.

Faingold, Eduardo D. 2004. Language rights and language justice in the constitutions of the world. *Language Problems and Language Planning* 28(1): 11–24.

May, Stephen. 2005. Language rights: Moving the debate forward. *Journal of Sociolinguistics* 9: 319–347.

2011. Language rights: The "Cinderella" human right. *Journal of Human Rights* 10: 265–289.

Mufwene, Salikoko S. 2002. Colonization, globalization and the plight of "weak" languages. *Journal of Linguistics* 38: 530–555.

Patrick, Peter. 2007. Linguistic human rights: A sociolinguistic introduction. priva tewww.essex.ac.uk/~patrickp/lhr/lhrlingperspex.htm

Phillipson, Robert, and Tove Skutnabb-Kangas. 1995. Linguistic rights and wrongs. *Applied Linguistics* 16: 438–504.

Romaine, Suzanne. 1994. From the fish's point of view. *International Journal of the Sociology of Language* 110: 177–185.

Skutnabb-Kangas, Tove, Miklós Kontra, and Robert Phillipson. 2006. Getting linguistic human rights right: A trio respond to Wee (2005). *Applied Linguistics* 27: 318–324.

UN Human Rights. 1996–2016. Office of the High Commissioner. www.ohchr.org/EN/Issues/Pages/WhatareHumanRights.aspx

Wee, Lionel, 2005. Intra-language discrimination and linguistic human rights: The case of Singlish. *Applied Linguistics* 26: 48–69.

2011. *Language without rights.* Oxford University Press.

Human Rights Declarations

American Convention on Human Rights (Organization of American States 1978) www.hrcr.org/docs/American_Convention/oashr.html

American Declaration of the Rights and Duties of Man (Organization of American States 1948) www.cidh.org/basicos/english/Basic2.American%20Declaration.htm

Draft American Declaration on the Rights of Indigenous Peoples (Organization of American States 1997) www.oas.org/en/iachr/indigenous/activities/declaration.asp

European Charter for Regional or Minority Languages (Council of Europe 1992) http://conventions.coe.int/Treaty/en/Treaties/Html/148.htm

Indigenous and Tribal Peoples Convention (No. 169) (International Labour Organization 1989) www.ilo.org/global/topics/indigenous-tribal/lang-en/index.htm

UN Declaration on the Rights of Indigenous Peoples (2007) http://undesadspd.org/IndigenousPeoples.aspx

UN Declaration on the Rights of Persons Belonging to National or Ethnic, Religious or Linguistic Minorities (1992) www.ohchr.org/Documents/Publications/GuideMinoritiesDeclarationen.pdf

UN International Covenant on Civil and Political Rights (1966) www.ohchr.org/en/professionalinterest/pages/ccpr.aspx

UN Universal Declaration of Human Rights (1948) www.un.org/en/universal-declaration-human-rights/

Universal Declaration of Linguistic Rights (1996) www.linguistic-declaration.org/index-gb.htm

English (Only or First) in the United States

English First. 2011a. The American public supports English First. www.englishfirst.org
/d/americapublicsupportsenglish
    2011b. The mission of English First. www.englishfirst.org
Frese, Stephen J. 2005. Divided by a common language: The Babel Proclamation and its
influence in Iowa history. *The History Teacher* 39(1): 59–88.
Linguistic Society of America Statement on Language Rights (1996) www
.linguisticsociety.org/sites/default/files/lsa-stmt-language-rights.pdf
Patrick, Peter. 2007. Linguistic human rights: A sociolinguistic introduction. priva
tewww.essex.ac.uk/~patrickp/lhr/lhrlingperspex.htm
ProEnglish. 2015. https://proenglish.org
TESOL. 2005. Position paper on English-only legislation in the United States. www
.tesol.org/docs/pdf/4162.pdf
U.S. English. 2016a. www.usenglish.org

Part III

A Typology of Language Conflicts

Introduction to Part III

The chapters in Part III are designed to apply the material presented thus far to a series of current and historical cases of language conflict and language rights issues. The cases presented in this part are organized according to an informal typology of language conflicts, which is designed to reveal and highlight similarities among conflicts that are distant in time and space, commonalities that might otherwise remain unnoticed.

Chapters 10 through 14 are named after the five categories of language conflict that comprise the typology: conflicts involving (i) indigenous minorities,[1] (ii) geopolitical minorities, (iii) migrant minorities, (iv) dialect minorities, and (v) competition for linguistic dominance. The disparate natures of these categories are mostly apparent from their names, but it is still worth spelling out what they mean in the context of this book.

Indigenous minority language conflict is, in our terms, an ethnolinguistic conflict involving some indigenous people and a dominant group that has settled in and appropriated their territory. The most salient example of this type of conflict would be that between English-speaking Americans/Canadians and the speakers of various tribal languages who were settled in North America long before the arrival of Europeans. Note that "indigenous" can be a relative term, and its application to a particular group occasionally open to debate. For instance, in our discussion of South Africa in Chapter 7, several waves of immigration and settlement were described, and one might contend that the Khoisan peoples were indigenous with respect to the Bantu incursion, that the Bantu were indigenous relative to the Dutch-speaking Boers, and that the Boers were indigenous in relation to the British. There is no clear demarcation that determines how long a group must reside in a territory before it can be considered indigenous to that territory, although one might expect at least a few hundred years of settlement for the term to be objectively applicable.

---

[1] There are, of course, colonial situations in which the indigenous group outnumbers the colonial group. However, in terms of the power dynamic, the indigenous group has a type of minority status. This was true in instances such as Australia and New Zealand. Of course, in those cases the indigenous groups did indeed become the minority as colonies grew into states.

The category of "geopolitical minorities" is intended to describe situations in which linguistic conflicts arise as a consequence of changed borders. These border shifts may be the result of war and conquest, post-war treaties, political unifications, or political dissolutions. In all such cases, though, the outcome of interest is that one linguistic group suddenly finds itself a minority in a country dominated by another linguistic group, without having moved anywhere. A classic case of this sort would be the language conflict and language rights issues that arose for the Mexican (Spanish-speaking) settlers in California who were living in Mexico at the beginning of 1846, but were in newly acquired American territory by 1848. It should be noted that the role of geopolitical linguistic minority is not necessarily fixed. A minority in one era might become a majority in the next, as has happened in the case of Slovaks and Hungarians. The former were a geopolitical minority within the Kingdom of Hungary until the post-World War I partitioning of Hungary in 1921. Today, since its independence in 1992, the Hungarians of Slovakia have been a geopolitical minority in that country.

Migrant minority language conflicts are those that arise when an ethnolinguistic group (or individuals from that group) moves into a territory dominated by a linguistically distinct population. On this view, English-speaking Americans moving *en masse* to Ontario or Manitoba in Canada would not be a migrant linguistic minority, but such a group moving to French-speaking Quebec would be so. There is, furthermore, no statute of limitations on being part of a migrant minority, so long as the group maintains its ethnolinguistic character and does not assimilate. We would thus consider the descendants of Koreans who immigrated to Japan in 1910 to belong to a Korean migrant minority of Japan, so long as they continue to speak Korean, identify culturally and ethnically as Korean, and are subject to linguistic impediments by the dominant Japanese culture.

Dialect minorities are sometimes more difficult to identify, in part because it can sometimes be difficult to determine whether two groups speak different languages or different varieties (dialects) of the same language. This issue was discussed in some detail in Chapter 4. That said, there are altogether too many cases of groups' speaking the "wrong" (i.e. stigmatized) variety of a language, and being punished (economically, socially, politically) for it. Individual cases of dialect minority language conflict are as varied as are the dialects themselves. There are instances in which a stigmatized dialect minority arises as the result of shifts in political power. For example, the western ('Kansai') dialects of Japanese maintained a good deal of prestige through the sixteenth century when Kyoto was the capital of Japan, and then became increasingly stigmatized as (first in 1603) the seat of government and (then in 1868) the emperor's residence were moved to Tokyo. There are instances in which speakers of another language (e.g. Okinawans in Japan) are presumed to speak a (stigmatized) dialect (of Japanese) and made to suffer for it. There are instances wherein the variety of a language spoken by an ethnic or racial minority (e.g. African Americans) is especially stigmatized on account of a generally negative disposition toward the minority group itself, rather than on account of any objective features of the dialect.

The final category, "competition for linguistic dominance," is reserved for cases in which two groups each hold sway in some region of a country, and their linguistic conflict is part of a struggle for the dominance of one group over the other, or a struggle on the part of one group for independence from the other. The French–English conflict in Canada generally and in Quebec specifically is a classic case of competition for linguistic dominance, and a determination of the winner in the conflict is dependent on how broadly or narrowly one defines the territorial space of the conflict. In Canada overall, it is apparent that English has won the day (even acknowledging accommodation to French) and that Canada is de facto an English-speaking country (60 percent of Canadians are English speakers, and over 95 percent outside the provinces of Quebec and New Brunswick). In Quebec Province though, French has won the competition, in that 80 percent of the residents are native speakers of French and 95 percent have it as a first or second language. In some cases, competition for dominance is resolved through legislation (as in Canada). Sometimes there is no resolution and the conflict continues as a stalemate (as in Belgium). In some instances, the competition leads to war (as happened in Sri Lanka).

It should be acknowledged again that these categories are provided as a matter of convenience, and as an informal but useful way of talking about language conflict. Furthermore, we would not expect that every case of language conflict would fit neatly into one or another of these categories. Many conflicts incorporate aspects of more than one category, and some conflicts might belong to one category at a particular moment in time and to a different category somewhat later. And some conflicts might, in certain areas and in certain contexts, belong to several categories at once. The ongoing language conflict between Spanish speakers in the United States and the dominant English-speaking culture is one such example. If we take the Spanish speakers of New Mexico, many of them descended from Spanish settlers when it was part of Mexico, we are looking at a geopolitical linguistic minority. But Mexicans living and working in Chicago would be classed as a migrant linguistic minority, and Puerto Ricans living in New York might be considered, to the extent that they have developed their own (stigmatized) dialect of English (a.k.a. Spanglish), to be a dialectal minority.

Each of the following five chapters will focus on one of the five language conflict categories, present the historical and linguistic background for two or three ethnolinguistic conflicts pertaining to that category, and examine the language rights issues that have arisen in each case. We will identify some commonalities arising from a comparison of cases within each. At the end of each chapter are short synopses of three additional cases that readers might explore on their own.

10 Indigenous Minorities

This chapter presents cases of indigenous minority language conflict, that is to say, ethnolinguistic conflicts which involve the fate of some indigenous people at the hands of a dominant group that has settled in and appropriated their territory. The fully developed cases presented here are those of the Sámi in Norway, the Ainu of Japan, and the Native Americans in the United States. Additional cases for the reader to explore are: Māori in New Zealand, Aboriginals in Australia, and the Basque in Spain and France.

Sámi in Norway

The first case in this chapter takes up the fortunes of the Sámi people of northern Scandinavia. Their fate in the face of European nationalism and Norwegian expansion represents a fairly classic case of indigenous peoples' struggles.

Historical background

The Sámi[1] (or Saami) are considered to be the oldest extant peoples indigenous to the Scandinavian Peninsula (Fennoscandia), having inhabited the area since roughly 8000 BCE. As is true of many indigenous groups, the origin of the Sámi people has been controversial. Early theories, now widely believed to be incorrect, suggested that the Sámi (and Finns) are of Asian stock and moved into the Scandinavian Peninsula as recently as 2,000 years ago. However, this theory was based primarily on linguistic evidence – the Sámi and Finnish languages are not Indo-European, and thus not related to most European languages, but are related to languages of Central Asia. However, recent

---

[1] The Sámi are also sometimes known as the Lapps, or Laplanders. However, the term is now considered pejorative. *Lapp* means 'a patch of cloth for mending' in Norwegian and Swedish, suggesting that the Sámi's traditional clothing was in need of repair. Note that there are a variety of spellings used for the *Sámi*. In addition to *Sámi*, one also finds *Sami* and *Saami*. For the sake of consistency we have rendered the term *Sámi*, even in quoted sources where another spelling is used.

Figure 10.1 Homeland of the Sámi people

DNA evidence shows that the Sámi and Finns are genetically Caucasoid[2] and may well have originated in the area between the Danube and Ukraine and followed the retreating glaciers into their present location some 10,000 years ago.[3,4]

The Sámi homeland, referred to as Sápmi, comprises the area north of the Arctic Circle spread over the four modern states of Finland, Norway, Sweden, and Russia, stretching southward in Norway and Sweden (see Figure 10.1). There is a long history of discrimination against the Sámi dating back to at least the eighteenth century, with governments variously attempting to assimilate the

[2] Niskanen 2002.   [3] Julku 2002.
[4] However, other DNA evidence suggests the Sámi should not be bound too tightly with Finns as they have a distinct mitochondrial gene pool. Sajantila et al. (1995) argue that "the Sámi have a history distinct from that of other groups in Europe."

Sámi or eradicate Sámi culture, notably their language. Here we focus on the situation in Norway.

Largely unmolested by other Europeans for centuries, the Sámi lived a semi-nomadic life as hunter-trappers and fishers. Some Sámi were primarily nomadic, following the reindeer herds that roamed in the area. Others were more sedentary, living in small villages in specific areas, in part supporting the nomadic group. Aside from the household, a basic unit of organization was the *siida*, a group of households usually made up of an extended family. The siida exercised authority over issues related to use of pastureland, migration, organization and exercise of herding knowledge, and resolution of disputes.[5] Later, as the reindeer population dwindled due to overhunting, some Sámi domesticated the reindeer and became herders in the interior of Finnmark, while others settled along the western coast of Norway. While sometimes paying taxes to Norse chieftains, the Sámi led a comparatively isolated existence until the end of the Middle Ages, when Germanic kingdoms in the southern peninsula consolidated power, the Kingdom of Norway entering the Kalmar Union with Denmark and Sweden. During this period, Norwegian settlers began moving into Sámi areas, pushing the Sámi more northward and westward. But early settlers largely learned from the Sámi how to survive in the area and adopted some aspects of their lifestyle.

More and more settlers moved into the area in the early 1700s, many in the form of missionaries, wishing to convert Sámi from their traditional shamanistic religion to Christianity in an effort to "civilize" them. As the number of Norwegians grew, Sámi livelihood was increasingly compromised as their traditional lands, fisheries, and industry were slowly absorbed by outsiders. Figure 10.2 illustrates typical Sámi people at the beginning of the twentieth century.

Linguistic Background

The Sámi "language" is actually a group of languages (ten varieties are identified by *Ethnologue* 2015) that stretch across Sápmi in a dialect continuum, including Akkala, Inari, Kildin, Lule, North, Pite Skolt, South, Ter, and Ume. Several of these are now extinct or soon will be, and not all are mutually intelligible, for example, North and South Sámi. Of these North Sámi has by far the largest number of speakers, estimated at 20,000 or slightly more.[6] Sámi is a member of the Finno-Ugric branch of the Uralic language family and is most

---

[5] Brännlund and Axelsson 2011.

[6] The precise number of Sámi can be difficult to pin down. According to *Ethnologue* there are currently approximately 100,000 Sámi. The CIA *World Factbook* estimates the population in Norway is nearly 60,000 (www.cia.gov/library/publications/the-world-factbook/geos/no.html).

Figure 10.2 Sámi people, 1900–1920

closely related to languages such as Finnish, Estonian, and, slightly more distantly, Hungarian. Finno-Ugric languages are typically highly inflected, and Sámi is no exception. Nouns are marked for number (singular vs. plural) and occur in seven different cases in three distinct lexical classes (depending upon the number of syllables in the citation form of the noun). Verbs occur in five different moods and two distinct tenses (past, present) and are conjugated for three persons (first, second, third) and three numbers (singular, dual, plural). Additionally, like nouns, there are three different conjugation classes on the basis of the number of syllables in the base form. An example of a North Sámi sentence is given in (1), which includes four different cases: nominative, accusative, locative, and illative.

(1)   Máhtte   adda   Márehii   gova   alddis.
       Máhtte.nom   give.ind.pres.3s Máret.illative   picture.acc   self.3s.loc
       'Máhtte gives Máret a picture of himself.'

Table 10.1 presents a chart showing the form of Sámi third-person pronouns declined for number and case. Note that there is no grammatical gender distinction (masculine/feminine). The context in which the sentence is used provides that information.

Norwegian is a North Germanic language, a member of the Indo-European language family, while Sámi is a Uralic language, related to Finnish and Hungarian. While there is some variation among dialects, Norwegian nouns are inflected for number (singular, plural) and definiteness (definite, indefinite), and there are three gender classes (masculine, feminine, neuter). Verbs are conjugated for tense (past, present future), mood (indicative, imperative,

Table 10.1 *Sámi third-person pronouns*

	Singular	Dual	Plural
Nominative	son	soai	sii
Genitive–accusative	su	sudno	sin
Locative	sus	sudnos	sis
Illative	sutnje	sudnuide	sidjiide
Comitative	suinna	sudnuin	
Essive	sunin	sudnon	sinin

Table 10.2 *Sámi–Norwegian lexical correspondences*

	Sámi	Norwegian
'cow'	burru	kveg
'dog'	beana	hund
'deer'	goddi	hjort
'horse'	heasta	hestur
'I'	mun	jeg
'you'	don	du
'he'	son	han
'she'	son	hun

subjunctive), and voice (active, passive). There are finite and nonfinite forms. Sámi is somewhat more complex in its inflection, but, more importantly, the two languages make very different inflectional distinctions, for example, case (Sámi) versus definiteness (Norwegian) for nouns. A quick look at a few lexical items makes it clear that the languages are not closely related:

Thus, we can conclude that the two languages are quite distinct.

Events Leading up to the Conflict/Situation

While there were social and political issues for the Sámi in Norway, language had not been an important factor in these issues. The Christian missionaries were in the vanguard of settlement in the area and made no attempt to impose the Norwegian language, instead actively advocating the use of Sámi in religious contexts.[7] Although missionaries and priests advocated using Sámi,

---

[7] Again and again, one finds that missionaries, among the first to arrive in the course of colonization, invariably advocated the use of local languages in their work. As their goal was to convert indigenous people to Christianity, they recognized the need to make their teaching understandable in the language of the people they hoped to convert.

things began to change as more Norwegian colonizers moved in and the government sought more and more to create a cohesive state. Caught up in the wave of nationalism that was sweeping Europe, thoughts turned not only to educating the Sámi but assimilating them into the Norwegian nation, which, of course, meant adoption of the national language and suppression of the Sámi culture. Thus, from the mid nineteenth century until the end of World War II, the government embarked on a campaign of "Norwegianization." In his endorsement of the Norwegianization program, the first prime minister of the new parliamentary government, Johan Sverdrup, is reported to have said, "for the Lapps, the only salvation lies in their assimilation into the Norwegian nation,"[8] a sentiment toward indigenous peoples pronounced in many nationalist movements.

This Norwegianization push, with its roots in social Darwinism, took various forms. In a number of cases, including the Ainu in Japan, Native Americans in the United States, and the Māori in New Zealand, governments have used the education system to attempt to suppress local languages with the stated aim of assimilating indigenous people to the state founded by colonial powers. So the Norwegian government did with the Sámi. While schools in the Sámi homeland had largely used Sámi as the language of instruction, from the mid nineteenth century on (and at times before), Sámi was slowly but steadily eliminated from the classroom. For example, at various times, it was decreed that instruction in Sámi schools must be in Norwegian, and teachers were incentivized by a system of bonuses that rewarded teachers who were particularly successful in this regard.[9] Again, as happened in the United States in the attempt to suppress Native American languages, in the late nineteenth and early twentieth centuries, boarding schools were established for Sámi children, in part "to keep them away from their Sámi environment."[10] Additionally, while Sámi had been allowed as a "helping language" in schools, it was removed from this status in 1889.[11]

In the same effort, an 1898 law passed by the Norwegian Parliament reaffirmed that all instruction in schools must be in Norwegian; this law was not repealed until 1959.[12] Education was by no means the only domain in which the Sámi language was suppressed or treated unequally. Language also figured into Parliament's passage in 1902 of the Land Sales Act. This law stipulated that land could only be owned by those who could read and write Norwegian. The effect of this was that many Sámi were dispossessed of their land and thousands of others adopted Norwegian names[13] and promised to speak Norwegian in their homes.[14]

---

[8] Bucken-Knapp 2003.   [9] Magga 1994.   [10] Bull 2002: 32.   [11] Bucken-Knapp 2003.
[12] Bucken-Knapp 2003.   [13] Grenersen 2012.   [14] Magga 1994.

The civil service was conducted in Norwegian. While Sámi was not strictly forbidden, documents written in Sámi had no legal standing and had to be accompanied by Norwegian translations. Sámi individuals, groups (such as siidas), and other organizations had to address authorities in Norwegian. Place names were also actively suppressed. A royal decree in 1876 (which was reissued in 1895) mandated that all farms be given Norwegian names, only allowing existing Sámi names to be included in brackets. Beginning in 1900, Sámi place name were in many instance removed from official maps and replaced with Norwegian.[15]

By most accounts, the Sámi were unable to mount an effective opposition to the repressive measures. Among the failed efforts at resistance were "the establishment of Sámi language newspapers in northern Norway that ran frequent editorials calling for equal rights to be given the Norwegian Sámi; repeated efforts of Southern Sámi activists to obtain separate Sámi schools; and attempts at founding a national Sámi organization that would have served to provide a common front against the Norwegianization activities."[16]

The effect of these actions was devastating for Sámi language and culture and had important economic repercussions. Many Sámi children were never educated in their mother tongue, which led them to either take on Norwegian as their language of choice or remain undereducated, which stifled their economic mobility. Also, as in other language rights cases we will look at, parents opted for their children to be educated in Norwegian even when there was a choice, as they recognized that Norwegian was the language of opportunity. Things basically continued in this vein until the end of World War II.

Developments after World War II

After World War II, there was a gradual shift in attitudes toward minorities across Western and Northern Europe, and the same was true in Norway. This had begun a little before the war; for example, the 1936 Education Act had reinstated the use of Sámi as a helping language and Norway had participated in discussions of minority rights in the League of Nations. However, having suffered harshly under the control of the German hegemony, the Norwegian government continued to ameliorate its policies toward the Sámi. Much of this gradual shift occurred in education, where state-sponsored suppression had been most active. Although the use of Sámi in schools was not officially reestablished as a legal language of instruction until 1959, the Parliament (known as the Storting) approved funds for the publication of textbooks in both Norwegian and Sámi in 1948 and set up a subcommittee to address Sámi

[15] Sandvik 1993.   [16] Bucken-Knapp 2003: 121.

education in 1949; a Sámi Committee was set up by the Department of Church and Education in 1956 to advise the Storting regarding economic and cultural measures that would better the lives of the Sámi.[17] Among the recommendations was that Sámi children be bilingual in Norwegian and Sámi. The goal at the time was integration of the Sámi into Norwegian society but in a way that respected Sámi norms. The passage of the 1969 Primary School Law provided that parents could request that their children attend school in Sámi if they regularly spoke the language.

Nonetheless, the Norwegian government and majority citizens did not fully embrace Sámi linguistic and cultural rights. The International Labour Organization Convention no. 107, adopted in 1957, guaranteed among other things the language and property rights of indigenous people and obligated signatories to "respect and promote" the relevant resources. Despite being a signatory, the Storting did not ratify the Convention. At the time the Norwegian government continued to deny the existence of minorities within its borders.

Although progress was slow at first and met some resistance from Norwegians, the Sámi Committee was established by the Department of Church and Education in 1956 to consider Sámi cultural and linguistic issues. In the report it submitted in 1959, the committee asserted among other things that the maintenance of the Sámi language was integral to sustaining Sámi culture. However, the recommendations of the committee were met with strong opposition in the Storting and most were never implemented. Those that were had little effect. However, a new generation of Sámi activists arose, in part due to greater educational opportunities and a greater international emphasis on the rights of indigenous peoples. New Sámi organizations developed, including the Nordic Sámi Council (made up of groups from Norway, Sweden, and Finland), and regular conferences were held, one of which resulted in a declaration of rights and resource management.[18] The new activism and participation in the founding of the World Council of Indigenous Peoples in 1974 created new hope and opportunities. But it was the controversy over the building of the Alta Dam that brought the plight of the Sámi to the attention of the Norwegian people.

In the 1970s, the Norwegian government was making plans to build a hydroelectric dam across the Kautokeino-Alta River, which runs through traditional Sámi lands. The project would have completely inundated the Sámi community of Máze and disrupted reindeer migration and salmon fishing. Sámi organizations petitioned the government to abandon the project and did manage to

---

[17] Bucken-Knapp 2003.   [18] Minde 2003.

convince them to pursue a smaller-scale project that would result in less disruption of people and wildlife.

In 1979, when the project was set to begin, activists blocked the heavy machines at the construction site and staged a hunger strike outside the Storting building, thus delaying the dam for a further two years. Protesters who had chained themselves to the fence at the construction site were forcibly removed by a large contingent of police. National news coverage (and international reaction) alerted the Norwegian public to the plight of the Sámi, which lead to recognition of the Sámi as a national minority and set in motion significant reforms.

The Sámi Act

The outcome of the Alta Dam incident was the establishment of the Sámi Rights Commission and the Sámi Cultural Commission, both of which made sweeping recommendations. On the basis of the Sámi Rights Commission report, the Storting passed a constitutional amendment in 1987 that obligates the government to safeguard and promote Sámi rights:

§ 110a [Minority Rights of the Sámi]
It is the responsibility of the authorities of the State to create conditions enabling the Sámi people to preserve and develop its language, culture and way of life.

The Sámi Act, also passed in 1987, provides for the establishment of a Sámi parliament, the Sámeting or Sámediggi, but more generally states: "The purpose of the Act is to enable the Sámi people in Norway to safeguard and develop their language, culture and way of life" and asserts "Sámi and Norwegian are languages of equal worth." Included in the Act are extensive provisions for the Sámi language and the rights of its speakers. These include:

- provisions for translation of laws and government documents into Sámi,
- the right of a Sámi speaker to receive correspondence from government entities in Sámi,
- the right to use Sámi in all aspects of the judicial system,
- the right to use Sámi in public health and social institutions,
- the right to education in Sámi,
- the use of Sámi in municipal administration,
- the establishment of the Sámi Language Council, and others.

Most of the provisions of the Sámi Act are intended to apply only to six Sámi majority authorities in Finnmark (the Sámi area in the interior of Norway) and Tromsø. Another key provision of the Sámi Act was the formation of a Sámi parliament, the Sámediggi. Made up of 39 representatives (increased to 43 in 2005) elected solely by Sámi voters, it was established as an advisory body, which at its inception had limited legal or executive power. The Sámediggi was officially inaugurated in 1989.

The constitutional amendment and the Sámi Act are formulated to ensure extensive language rights to the Sámi people and obligate the state of Norway to provide the necessary structure to guarantee their enforcement. These were in keeping with the evolving governmental position regarding indigenous minorities. In 1990, Norway became the first country to ratify the International Labour Organization Convention no. 169 Concerning Indigenous and Tribal Peoples in Independent Countries, which safeguards the rights of indigenous peoples, including specific reference to language rights.

- "Children belonging to the peoples concerned shall, wherever practicable, be taught to read and write in their own indigenous language or in the language most commonly used by the group to which they belong."
- "Measures shall be taken to preserve and promote the development and practice of the indigenous languages of the peoples concerned."

Other developments during this era include the founding of Sámi Allaskuvla (Sámi University College) in Kautokeino. Its original mission was to train Sámi teachers, but this has expanded to also include instruction in Sámi language and culture. In 2005, it merged with the Nordic Sámi Institute, which had been established in 1973. The Norwegian Ministry of Church, Education, and Science issued new curriculum guidelines in 1997, which for the first time introduced two national curricula, one for Sámi areas and one for the rest of the country. In 2000, the Sámediggi officially took limited responsibility for the Sámi school system.

Of course, as was discussed in Chapter 9 with respect to various international declarations, constitutions, and state laws, there can be a wide gulf between the intent of such statements and their implementation. For many Sámi, movement toward realization of their rights has been slower than desired. Magga (1994) outlines the limitations of the Sámi Act and the fact that initially the resources made available were inadequate. The drive for full implementation of Sámi rights has continued, including convening a conference on Sámi self-determination in 2008.

Recognition of Sámi language rights can still stir controversy among the general Norwegian population. In 2011, the municipal council in Tromsø applied to join the Sámi Language Administrative Area. This would entail making Sámi an official language of the city and including Sámi names on street signs and other designations of public space. Opposition parties made it an issue in the following election and there were reports of threats against pro-Sámi politicians and harassment of people in Sámi garb. Nonetheless, Tromsø made a cooperative agreement with the Sámediggi in 2013 and continues to hold an annual week-long Sámi celebration.

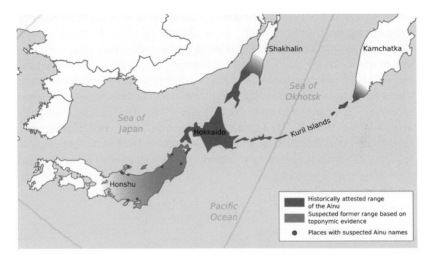

Figure 10.3 Historic range of the Ainu people

Ainu in Japan

The Ainu, much like the Sámi, are a northern-latitude people whose traditional lifestyle and language did not hold up very well in the face of Japanese hegemony. They fared rather worse than the Sámi, when all was said and done.

Historical Background

The origin of the Ainu is somewhat obscure, though it has been claimed on the basis of DNA-type evidence that both the Ainu and the Ryūkyūans are descended from a group (the Yayoi) believed to have arrived in northern Japan/ Hokkaido some 14,000 years ago, originating in southeast Asia.[19] The Ainu are indigenous to Japan's northern territories, including northern Honshu (possibly), Hokkaido, the Kuril Islands, and Sakhalin Island (the latter two areas having been lost to the Soviets following World War II). Figure 10.3 shows their historic range.

Traditionally hunter-gatherers who lived in *kotan* (small villages) of people directly related by blood, the Ainu were animists who believed in spirits associated with natural phenomena (wind, fire, water), parts of nature (animals, plants, mountains), and material culture (boats, pots), and whose rituals included bear hunting, animal sacrifice, and tattooing the lips, hands, and arms of girls when they reached puberty.

---

[19] Hanihara 1991.

Although there had been earlier contact, regular trade with the Japanese only began during the 1400s, with the establishment of small Japanese trading settlements in southern Hokkaido. The Japanese themselves considered the Ainu to be barbarians, and this led to an uneasy relationship from the start and to repeated efforts on the part of the Ainu to expel the Japanese from their lands. After a few centuries of sporadic conflict, including the last "pan-Ainu" uprising against the Japanese in 1669 (Shakushain's War), the territory essentially came under the control of the Japanese. Competition between the Japanese and Russians for control of Ainu lands officially ended in 1855 with the signing of the Treaty of Shimoda (*nichiro tsūkō jōyaku*), under which the Japanese gained sovereignty over Hokkaido. After this point, Japanese control of the island grew progressively tighter.

Linguistic Background

Despite various proposals attempting to establish a genetic relationship between Ainu and Japanese,[20] it is widely accepted among linguists[21] that Ainu belongs to no established language family. Although some superficial similarities between Ainu and Japanese exist, these are generally grammatical traits common to most languages having Subject-Object-Verb word order. Thus, the same traits are shared not only by Ainu and Japanese, but also by other completely unrelated languages such as Hindi, Tamil, Choctaw, and so on. Much more striking are their dissimilarities.

First, the sound systems of the two languages are distinct. Perhaps the most noticeable difference is the fact that, whereas Japanese has voiceless and voiced pairs of (certain) consonants, Ainu only has the voiceless member of each pair, so there is no /b, d, g, z/, as shown in Table 10.3.

Table 10.3 *Oral obstruent consonants in Japanese and Ainu languages*

		Bilabial	Alveolar	Velar	Glottal
Japanese	Stop	p b	t d	k g	
	Fricative		s z		h
Ainu	Stop	p	t	k	ʔ
	Fricative		s		h

[20] Batchelor 1905; Hattori 1964.   [21] Kindaichi 1937; Shibatani 1990.

Second, Ainu grammatical inflections and case marking are quite distinct from Japanese. Unlike Japanese, Ainu verbs have no inflection for tense and aspect, and thus temporality is interpreted solely on the basis of context. Nouns are not marked to indicate the grammatical relations such as subject, object, or indirect object, whereas Japanese includes postpositions for this purpose (i.e. *ga, o, ni*). Thus word order can be a crucial indicator of who is doing what to whom in a clause, as seen in (2). Japanese would have much freer word order, with subjects and objects signaled by *ga* and *o*, respectively.

(2)   a. Kamuy aynu rayke.   b. Aynu   kamuy rayke.
           bear person kill   person   bear   kill
           'The bear killed the man.'   'The man killed the bear.'

Additionally, Ainu first- and second-person subjects and objects are cross-referenced on the verb with prefixes. In contrast, Japanese has no such agreement system.

(3)   a. ku-i-kore   b. e-en-kore
           1SING(ULAR)-2HON(ORIFIC)-give   2SING-1SING-give
           'I give you (HON).'   'You give me.'

Language Rights Issues

Language rights issues for the Ainu "officially" began in 1869 when the island of Ezochi was renamed Hokkaido by the newly formed Meiji government. Local administrative development systems were set up, and the Meiji government embarked on a policy of (forced) assimilation – a policy whose ultimate aim was to eradicate Ainu culture. Under this regime, the Ainu were systematically stripped of any Ainu identity and were "made" Japanese.

The official "registration" of Ainu occurred in 1871, at which time the Ainu were designated "commoners," and were forced to assume Japanese names.[22] Laws passed at around this time were designed to prevent or curtail many Ainu traditions, including salmon fishing and deer hunting, the practice of burning a family's house and moving elsewhere after the death of a family member, the tattooing of girls at puberty, and men wearing earrings. Also imposed at this time were many restrictions concerning the use of the Ainu language:

---

[22] Irish 2009.

- **Naming:** The Ainu were forced to take Japanese names, and names in the public domain had to be Japanese.
- **Restrictions on public use:** The use of Ainu in public, including the government and the legal system, was prohibited.
- **Education:** Aside from naming, education in one's native language is widely considered to be a fundamental language right. From the time of registration, Ainu children were forced to attend schools that were conducted solely in Japanese as the use of Ainu in education was banned by law.

Thus began the decline of the Ainu language. This was also a period of dramatic decline in the Ainu population. A government survey in 1807 estimated that there were more than 26,000 Ainu living in Hokkaido. By 1873, it was estimated that the population was roughly 16,000, and the Ainu made up only 14.6 percent of the population of the island.[23] Thus the Ainu had minority status after only a short period of time. Among the causes for the dramatic decline were the spread of diseases (e.g. smallpox, measles, and syphilis) brought by the colonists and the breakup of families due to forced labor.[24]

In the late 1870s, as part of the promulgation of the myth of Japanese ethnic unity, the Ainu were officially designated "former aborigines" and their land was expropriated by the government. An influx of ethnic Japanese continued apace, propelled in part by government offers of land to the Japanese colonists. Naturally, as the population of Japanese settlers from Honshu increased, the Ainu became increasingly marginalized. A photograph in Figure 10.4 shows a typical Ainu group at the beginning of the twentieth century. Linguistically, the Ainu continued to decline through (i) the coercion of the government, (ii) the belief among the Ainu that the use of the Japanese language would make life better for their children, and (iii) intermarriage with Japanese settlers.

The next major event in the cultural and linguistic decline of the Ainu came in 1899 with the signing of the Hokkaido Former Aborigines Protection Act (*hokkaido kyūdojin hogohō*). At this time (possibly due to insecurity about its control over the northern territories), the Japanese government redoubled its efforts at assimilating the Ainu into Japanese society and eradicating Ainu culture. Under the Act, Ainu families were granted small plots of land, in order to transform them from hunters into (more easily managed) farmers. Much of the best farmland had already been claimed by Japanese settlers. In the end, most of the Ainu farmland reverted back to the government, as they themselves lacked the desire or the skills to be successful farmers.

The Regulations for the Education of Former Aboriginal Children, which reinforced the education repression of the Ainu, were established in 1901.

[23] Siddle 1996.   [24] Walker 2001.

Figure 10.4 A group of Sakhalin Ainu, *c.* 1903

Under this regime, Ainu children were compelled to attend (mostly) segregated schools, where the focus was on learning Japanese language skills,
rather than science, math, or other subjects. They were thereby denied both
the right to be educated in their native language as well as a decent education. So, despite the fact that over 90 percent of Ainu children attended
school by 1910,[25] most received a greatly inferior education, and were cut
off from their heritage. As the Ainu continued their descent into poverty and
disadvantage, the Ainu language itself continued its path toward near-
extinction.

The first organization devoted to Ainu issues was established immediately
after the end of World War II. Beginning in 1946, the Ainu Association of
Hokkaido (later renamed Hokkaido Utari Association) focused its attention
on pressing economic issues and attempted to increase wealth in Ainu
communities. There were more public works initiatives in the 1960s, but
the Ainu themselves remained less well educated and on the cultural and

[25] Ishikida 2005.

economic margins of Japanese society. For example, in 1972, barely over 40 percent of Ainu youth attended high school.[26] Other statistics are equally bleak, although the economic status of the Ainu has reportedly improved in recent years.

During the 1960s and 1970s, a general awakening of indigenous human rights efforts worldwide spurred the Ainu and their supporters to increased activism, which led to a reawakening of the culture. Shigeru Kayano championed the effort to open the first Ainu nursery school in Nibutani (80 percent Ainu) in the early 1980s, where the Ainu language was taught to preschoolers. Under his leadership, a number of additional community-based Ainu-language schools opened.[27] Despite these efforts, the Ainu language has not been successfully revived, and may be beyond rescue. Various reports place the current number of speakers of the only remaining Ainu language (the Hokkaidō variety) at anywhere from 15 to about 100.

The Japanese government has only recently acknowledged the official existence of the Ainu as an ethnic minority. Only following the ratification of the UN-sponsored International Covenant on Civil and Political Rights in 1979, and after international pressure and some domestic activism, did the government renounce its official claims of ethnic homogeneity for the region. But even then, official recognition of the Ainu as an ethnic minority did not occur until 1991. Starting in the mid 1980s, the Hokkaido Utari Association (with Kayano as its inspiration) started to agitate for the repeal of the 1899 Act and the establishment of a new one.

A key element in the eventual recognition of the Ainu as an indigenous people distinct from the ethnically Japanese population was the Nibutani Dam controversy. In 1989 the Japanese government expropriated land in Hokkaido to construct a dam on the Saru River. A lawsuit was filed by Kayano and another landowner claiming the government had illegally seized the land. Although the dam project was completed in 1997, that same year the District Court of Sapporo ruled that the Ainu were indigenous to Hokkaido and were eligible for protection under the Japanese constitution and international law. The decision was the first time Japanese authorities had recognized the Ainu as an indigenous people and raised public awareness of the plight of the Ainu.[28]

On the heels of the decision, in 1997 the Act on the Encouragement of Ainu Culture and the Diffusion and Enlightenment of Knowledge on Ainu Tradition (also referred to as the Ainu Culture Promotion Act) was passed.[29] The Act included provisions for non-discrimination, political activity, economic

---

[26] Siddle 1996.   [27] Sjöberg 1993.   [28] Maruyama 2012.
[29] Despite these developments, the Japanese government did not officially recognize the Ainu as an indigenous people until 2008.

development (i.e. fishing, agriculture), and the formation of an advisory committee. But at the heart of the Act was the promotion and preservation of Ainu
culture through teaching, research, and other efforts (focusing on language as
well as traditional arts, such as music, drama, oral tradition). At one point, there
was an annual Ainu Oratorical Contest (1998–2004) in which students from the
various language schools came together for Oral Literature and Oratory competitions, but this has been discontinued.

So, in fact, few Ainu speak the Ainu language or follow the traditional way
of life. Given this, the Ainu identity is likely to become a "symbolic ethnicity,"
with Ainu culture and heritage being transmitted to future generations of the
Ainu through schools, museums, and annual festivals.[30]

Conclusion

For the Ainu, being an aboriginal people meant that the very existence of their
ethnicity and culture was antithetical to the Japanese notions of manifest
destiny and their claim to being the first civilization on the islands. This was
handled by determining them to be "uncivilized" or "savages." Thus, while
they might be "earlier" inhabitants of the land, they did not constitute an
"earlier civilization." Secondly, they were remade into Japanese, by replacing
their language and other cultural identifiers with that of the dominant
civilization.

American Indians in the United States

The plight of American Indians is widely known, and we do not intend to
rehearse the sad and shameful tale of their treatment at the hands of the
European immigrants. However, one part of that history is particularly germane
to the issue of language rights and has many parallels with the story of other
indigenous minorities.

Lest the reader imagine that European settlers encountered some singular
ethnic group, that they styled "American Indians," it should be pointed out that
the pre-colonial linguistic diversity of the North American continent was
logarithmically larger than that of Europe. Native peoples in North America
consisted of some twenty-nine distinct language families (which contained
over 250 distinct languages), plus another two dozen language isolates.
By comparison, the six dozen or so languages of Europe can be grouped
(with the lone exception of Basque) into a mere three language families (Indo-
European, Uralic, and Turkic).

[30] Ishikida 2005: 24.

Of the many language families indigenous to North America, the Na-Dené, Algic, and Uto-Aztecan families contain the greatest number of languages. Some of the better-known languages are: Navaho (a Na-Dené language spoken in northwestern Arizona), Hopi (an Uto-Aztecan language, also spoken in northwestern Arizona), Cherokee and Mohawk (two Iroquoian languages, spoken in New York and other areas east of the Appalachians), Cheyenne (an Algonquian language, spoken in the northern Plains region), Choctaw (a member of the Muskogean language family, spoken in the American southeast), and Seminole (another Muskogean language, spoken in Florida).

Historical Background

During the 1800s, the United States was making its drive to the west by the political philosophy that came to be known as Manifest Destiny.[31] By the end of the 1830s most of the Indians in the southeast had been killed or forced to move westward to present-day Oklahoma along the Trail of Tears. Based on its control of territory ceded by Mexico at the conclusion of the Mexican–American War in 1848, the United States laid claim to lands stretching west to the Pacific Ocean.[32] The run-up to the Civil War delayed expansion westward.

Up until the Civil War most Western-type education of the Indians was in the hands of missionaries. The missionaries set up schools – usually with the blessing of the tribe – and taught in the language of the people being educated,[33] much as was done by early missionaries in Norway. Of course, their basic goal was conversion of the Indians, which they reasoned could best be accomplished in the mother tongue. The ultimate desire was to "civilize" and assimilate or acculturate the Indians, but it was done in a manner that was relatively linguistically respectful. Some tribes even set up their own Western-type schools, as was true of the Choctaw starting in 1833.[34] The Federal government had not been much interested in working with Indian education, and were busy taking their lands and eventually setting up the system of reservations, which was started during Ulysses S. Grant's presidency.

After the Civil War, when the government's attention turned toward the west, the friction between American settlers and the Indians, who had no desire to have their lands taken, was severe. The Indian Wars moved west. Confronted

---

[31] The term was coined in 1845 by John L. O'Sulllivan in his article "Annexation" published in his *United States Magazine and Democratic Review*. O'Sullivan was arguing for the annexation of Texas in the piece.
[32] See Chapter 11 for a discussion of the Mexican–American War and its aftermath.
[33] Fear 1980.   [34] Debo 1975.

with this situation, thought again turned toward the "Indian problem." People had various motives, some of them comparatively high-minded but many decidedly not. Thinking at the time was strongly influenced by the theory of the evolution of human society as a continual progression from primitive through civilized. Most believed that White American culture had evolved to the highest condition while the American Indians remained in the primitive phase. The more humanistic (the so-called "friends of the Indian") felt that the American Indians could evolve as well but in order to do so they must develop the core values of individualism, industry, private property, and the Christian doctrine. Such people sought to assimilate the American Indians into American culture. Others just sought to eradicate the them. Neither seemed willing to leave the Indians unmolested.

However, even assimilationists used some extremely harsh rhetoric. Not atypical were comments like that of the Commissioner of Indian Affairs Carl Schurz, who in 1881 saw the situation this way: "Indians can choose extermination or civilization." In 1882, Henry Pancoast, a Philadelphia lawyer who co-founded the Indian Rights Association advocacy group, stated plainly, "We must either butcher them or civilize them, and what we do we must do quickly."[35] *The Report of the Secretary of the Interior* (1887) summed things up in the following way, "the only alternative presented to the Indian race is absolute extinction or a quick entrance into the *pale* of American civilization" [emphasis added].[36] At the same time, reformers and philanthropists were optimistic that assimilation was possible and that the Indians could fully assimilate into American society. Their efforts took a couple of different forms.

The Dawes Act

The system of reservations first established by Congress in the 1850s and pursued aggressively during the Grant presidency was seen by many as aiding the continuation of the communal life that was part of the philosophy and heritage of many tribes inasmuch as the reservations were granted to tribes as a whole and not to individuals. Some also argued that it fostered dependence on the government, which provided a limited amount of aid. In an effort to counteract the communality of tribal organization and to instill the values of personal property and individual responsibility, in 1887 the Congress passed the General Allotment Act, more familiarly known as the Dawes Act after its author, Senator Henry Dawes of Massachusetts. The Act took the communally held lands and split them into smaller parcels that were allocated to individuals within the tribe, and granted US citizenship to the Indians, making them subject

---

[35] Adams 1995.   [36] Atkins 1887.

to federal laws. Under the Act, the head of household was allotted 160 acres, single males over the age of 18 and orphans under 18 received 80 acres and others under 18, 40 acres. If after twenty-five years the individual landholders were not successfully farming the land, it would revert to the government and could be sold to white settlers. Inasmuch as many Indians were not interested in the agrarian lifestyle and others were unsuccessful, American Indians lost even more of their lands, that which had been set aside by the government as reservation and had been owned collectively.[37] Thus, the appropriation of Indian land simply continued under a different guise. The Dawes Act (and later the Burke Act) remained in force and was not overturned until 1934, when Congress passed the Indian Reorganization Act re-establishing tribal owner-ship of reservation lands.

Language Rights Issues

The Dawes Act failed to assimilate American Indians into White American culture, and it is unclear that all who supported the Act were necessarily interested in assimilation. It was not the only effort though. As in the case of the Sámi and the Ainu, education was seen as a way to forcibly assimilate Indians.

Efforts to educate the Indians had largely been left to Christian missionaries. But as public education developed in the 1800s, the government took an active role. Many saw the education of Indian youth as a means of teaching them the white man's ways and considered adults as not educable in the same way. Attempts through on-reservation day schools proved unsuccessful as the chil-dren would "unlearn" what they had been taught when they returned home in the evening. Not surprisingly, language was considered a linchpin in the assimilation process. If Indians were to effectively assimilate into American society, they would have to abandon their native language and learn English. The Social Darwinism underpinning the opinion that cultures evolved toward the most civilized was also applied to language, so Indians' languages were viewed as primitive and unable to express the sophisticated concepts available in English. Thus the belief of many missionaries that education through the native language was the most effective way to help people understand new ideas was rejected. A prevailing view was voiced by J. D. C. Atkins, Commissioner of Indian Affairs, in his 1887 report, "This language [English], which is good enough for a white man and a black man, ought to be good enough for the red man."[38]

Around this time, Lt. Richard Pratt, who was engaged in the western Indian Wars, was charged with transporting seventy-two Indian prisoners from

[37] Ruppel 2008.   [38] Atkins 1887.

western territory to St. Augustine, Florida. Pratt shared the opinion that Indians could be educated, and so rather than operating a standard prison, he taught the prisoners English, Christian ideals, and practical skills. Three years later, in 1878, sixty-two Indians from his prison enrolled in Hampton Institute in Virginia, a teacher-training school established with federal funds in 1863 for black freemen and freed slaves. People took note of Pratt's work, and in 1879 the federal government granted him permission to open a school for Indians, the United States Training and Industrial School, in an abandoned fort in Carlisle, Pennsylvania. At what became known as the Carlisle School, Pratt brought Indian children from midwestern and western tribes and taught them English and vocational trades (largely manual labor and domestic skills). The children wore military-style dress and lived a regimented life. It was important that the children came from far-off tribes so that they could be removed from the influences of their home life. In 1892, Pratt summed up the philosophy behind his educational mission thus, "Kill the Indian, save the man."[39]

Pratt's apparent "success" in his mission convinced others of the educability of Indians and led to the establishment of government-sponsored, off-reservation Indian boarding schools through Congress's approval of a large outlay of funds in 1882. At times parents willingly allowed their children to attend, but at others children were forcibly removed from their homes. Upon arrival at the schools, the children would have their long hair cut, be given Western dress, and be assigned English names – all effectively stripping them of their Indian identities. Having their hair cut was particularly painful and shameful for some as in many tribal traditions long hair has religious significance, and cutting one's hair is done when mourning the death of a close relative.[40] Language was an important focus at the schools, and using one's native language was forbidden. Students were often severely punished if caught speaking their mother tongue. Life was difficult for many of the students: in addition to demanding labor and an extremely regimented life, children were subject to harsh discipline, physical and sexual abuse, and a lack of sufficient food and health care. The photo in Figure 10.5 is illustrative of the transformation imposed upon these children.

The deplorable conditions of the boarding schools were brought into sharp focus in the Meriam Report of 1928, entitled *The problem of Indian administration*. A study that investigated all aspects of the assimilation effort (the effects of the Dawes Act, living conditions on reservations, disease and death rates, and conditions in the boarding schools), the report laid bare the inadequate diet for the children, the lack of adequate medical care, overcrowding, excessive labor, the overly regimented life of the children, harsh discipline and more.[41] The report eventually led to the Indian Reorganization Act, which,

[39] Pratt 1964.   [40] Johnstone 1998.   [41] Meriam et al. 1928.

Figure 10.5 Chiracahua Apaches from Fort Marion, 1886–1887 (before and after)

among other things, re-established Indian governance of tribal lands. After the publication of the Meriam Report many of the boarding schools were closed, though some continued for many more years. The fact that some are still in operation is a testament to the fact that some reforms took place and some Indians felt and still feel that they benefited from their experience.

However, while for the most part failing to assimilate Indians into American society, the Indian boarding school experience succeeded in robbing many of the children of their native language and their heritage. Many American Indian languages have disappeared and the majority of those still spoken today are endangered.[42]

The 'experiment' was replicated with the First Nations indigenous people in Canada with the same disastrous results. Residential schools became active after the Indian Act of 1876 and further took hold when the Act was amended in 1894 when attendance at day schools, industrial schools and residential schools was made mandatory for First Nations children. Although the last of the schools closed in 1996, the attitudes that engendered them appear to live on: in 2016 it was alleged that Nunavut students were told that they could face suspension if they spoke Inuktitut in school.[43]

Summary: Comparison of Cases

The similarities between the histories of the Ainu and the American Indians in the United States are unmistakable. Both groups were subject to internal colonization: for the Ainu, by the Japanese moving up from the south, and for the Plains and Western Indians, by American settlers coming from the east. Both were subject to forced assimilation policies. Just as the Dawes Act (1887) provided land to American Indians to encourage an agrarian livelihood, so the Hokkaido Former Aborigines Protection Act (*hokkaido kyūdojin hogohō*, 1899) gave land to every Ainu man for purposes of homesteading. Education played an important role in the assimilation policies. For the Ainu, the Regulations for the Education of Former Aboriginal Children (1901) ensured that Ainu children went to government-sanctioned schools where one of the primary foci was learning Japanese. In the United States, the Indian Boarding School movement of the late 1880s and early 1900s took children from their families to be educated including "a thorough knowledge of the use of the English language."[44] Finally, just as the Ainu were registered under Japanese names (1871), so were the American Indian children given Western names when they entered school. In both cases, children who spoke in their native language were punished. The strategies of both the Japanese and

---

[42] Part IV takes up the topic of language vitality and endangerment.
[43] Skura and Konek 2016.   [44] Lamar 1886: 4.

US governments, while not actually ensuring assimilation, did ensure the loss of native culture and the precipitous decline of the languages of the indigenous populations.

Aboriginals were deemed to be "uncivilized" or "savages." Thus, while they might be "earlier" inhabitants of the land, they did not constitute an "earlier civilization." Secondly, they were remade into Japanese or into Americans, by replacing their language and other cultural identifiers with that of the dominant civilization.

Additional Cases for Exploration

Māori in New Zealand

The Māori are the aboriginal people of New Zealand – Aotearoa 'Land of the Long White Cloud' in the Māori language. A Polynesian people, they migrated to an unpopulated New Zealand from eastern Pacific islands in the vicinity of Tahiti 800–1,000 years ago. They settled coastal areas on both the northern and southern islands where they lived unmolested by outsiders for centuries, living on a bounty of fish and large land birds (many of which were hunted to extinction), and cultivated Polynesian plants they brought with them. The Māori language is an eastern Oceanic Polynesian language most closely related to Fijian, Tahitian, and Hawaiian. Though there was no threat from outsiders, the Māori developed a warrior culture and clashed with rival tribal groups. The name Māori means 'the local/original people.'

The first contact with Europeans was around 1640, when a Dutch ship landed off the north island. The majority of the crew was killed. Tales of this kind kept European contact relatively infrequent for a number of years, though Māori acted as crew on American and British whaling and sealing ships. The British began to arrive in significant numbers during the 1830s, at which point the estimated population of Māori was 125,000 and the British around 2,000. Early settlers and traders conducted business with the Māori in Māori, but they began to arrive in large numbers and assumed sovereignty over the lands in the 1840 Treaty of Waitangi. As in other cases, the colonists considered Māori language and culture substandard, and the British adopted English-language policies. The use of Māori declined to the point that around 1960 only 26 percent of the indigenous population were native speakers. Fearing the loss of their native language, there was a reawakening starting in the 1960s and 1970s; the Māori took action on their own to revitalize the language, through the development of language nests (like those of the Sámi), in which small children were taught by their elders, and agitation that gained some concessions from the government, including the use of Māori in courts and the eventual recognition of Māori as a national language.

Aboriginals in Australia

It is generally agreed that the indigenous people of Australia have been living on the continent for at least 50,000 years. Despite their popular designation as simply Australian Aborigines, there is actually great diversity among the different indigenous communities. Although all hunter-gatherers, each group adapted its society to the environment which it inhabited. It is esti-mated that there are nearly thirty different language families and isolates, precise numbers being a continuing controversy among linguists. As Australia is well known for its unique plant and animal species due to its separation from other land masses for tens of thousands of years, it comes as no surprise that the Aborigines lived unmolested by invading cultures for millennia. They first came in contact with Europeans in the seventeenth century and avoided any colonization until after Captain Cook claimed the east coast of the island for Great Britain in 1770. British colonization began as the eighteenth century came to a close.

Some 770,000 people spoke an estimated 250 languages (with many vari-eties) at the time of large-scale European invasion. By the twenty-first century, that number had dropped to less than 150 languages, the vast majority of which are endangered with twenty or fewer currently being learned in the home by children. The process mirrored what we have seen in most colonial situations: at first relations between the Aborigines and English were relatively peaceful, but they quickly deteriorated as more English settled, eventually methodically suppressing the languages and cultures of the indigenous people through legislation, the educational system, and brute force (and at times genocide). The population had decreased to between 93,000 and 117,000 in 1900 but has since rebounded and is projected to be around 720,000 in 2021. In recent years, some attempts have been made by the government to make amends, with linguistic results at best mixed.

Basques in Spain and France

The Basque people of Spain and France are probably the most aboriginal of all of Europe's peoples, and have inhabited the northern and southwestern border regions of Spain and France, respectively, for thousands of years. They were there before the Roman Empire conquered the Celtic people of Gaul, and they were there before the Celtic people of western Europe moved into the region. The Celtic languages (Irish, Welsh, Breton, and Manx) and the Romance languages (Portuguese, Spanish, Catalan, Occitan, French, etc.) are all sub-families of Indo-European whose ancestors migrated (or flooded, depending on one's theory) into Europe some 4,000 years ago. The fact that the Basque language (called "Euskara" by its speakers) is unrelated to, and pre-dates, these, suggests that these indigenous people have an ancient claim to the Iberian regions that they inhabit.

For many, many centuries, the Basques continued unperturbed by outside conquest or by events in European history generally. However, the rise of European nationalism changed their fortunes quite radically, in much the same manner that nationalism affected indigenous peoples in other regions (e.g. Norway and Japan). In 1882, keen to standardize their own national language, the French required all students in the French Republic, including the Basque ones, to acquire high levels of proficiency in Standard (i.e. Parisian) French. In the aftermath of the Spanish Civil War of the 1930s, the fascist Spanish dictator Francisco Franco actively suppressed the use of all regional dialects (e.g. Galician, Catalan, etc.) and languages (i.e. Basque), in favor of Standard (Castilian) Spanish. By 1959, suppression of Basque language, culture, and autonomy by the Spanish central government gave rise to a violent, radical independence movement called Euskadi Ta Askatasuna (ETA). Today, the Basques in Spain have achieved some measure of autonomy and some accommodations of their language and culture, and the violence of the 1980s and 1990s has receded. In France, Basques were not subject to the same level of repression in the twentieth century as they were in Spain, and a violent quest for autonomy did not arise. The fact that there are only one-tenth as many Basques in France (250,000) as there are in Spain (2.4 million) has also most likely contributed to the disparity in ethnolinguistic agitation on opposite sides of the Spanish–French border.

11 Geopolitical Minorities

This chapter presents cases in which language conflict and language rights issues have arisen in the aftermath of the creation of a geopolitical minority as a consequence of changed national boundaries. Some of these changes are the outcome of war, some result from political unification, and others stem from political dissolution. Each case, though, involves a linguistic group finding itself a minority in a country dominated by another linguistic group, without having moved anywhere. The cases featured in this chapter are Hungarians in Slovakia, Hispanics in the southwestern United States, and Kurds in Turkey. Three extra cases presented at the end of the chapter for the reader to explore are the Tetum in Timor Leste, the Amazigh (Berbers) in the Maghreb region of Africa, and the Tibetans in China.

Hungarians in Slovakia

The Hungarians and Slovaks have a joint history that spans more than 1,100 years. It might not be an exaggeration to say that virtually each one of those years has been contentious, and understanding past events and the linguistic background of their previous interactions helps make the present conflict more understandable.

Historical Background

The Slovaks and the Hungarians have very different origins. Slavs settled around the Danube River in what is present-day Slovakia sometime during the fifth century CE, prior to which the area had been controlled by Germanic tribes. The first notable Slavic principality was created when Samo (reputedly a Frankish merchant) united several Slavic tribes during the seventh century. He ruled what has become known as Samo's Empire from 632 to 658 CE. By the end of the eighth century, the Principality of Moravia came into existence. At the beginning of the ninth century, to the south of Moravia, the Principality of Nitra was established by other Slavic tribes, ruled by Prince Pribina. Mojmor I, the prince of Moravia, conquered Nitra and united the two

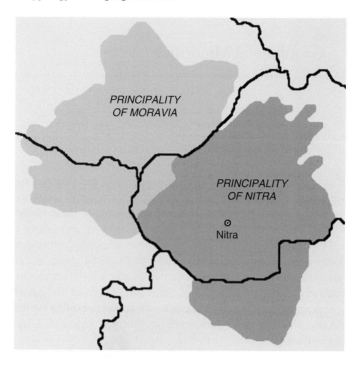

⬤ Principality of Nitra during Prince Pribina's reign

◯ Principality of Moravia during Prince Mojmir I's reign

— Borders of modern countries

Figure 11.1 Principalities of Moravia and Nitra in the early ninth century (until 833 CE)

principalities in 833 (as shown in Figure 11.1), establishing Great Moravia. Great Moravia was conquered by the Magyars in the early tenth century.

The provenance of the Magyars (the Hungarian term for their people) is the matter of much scholarly debate. It is, however, known that they did not enter the Carpathian Basin (which includes present-day Hungary and Slovakia) until a little before the turn of the tenth century.[1] There is some consensus that they originated in the Eurasian steppes, east of the Ural Mountains, and slowly migrated westward. One hypothesis is encapsulated in Figure 11.2.

---

[1] Magocsi 1993: 12.

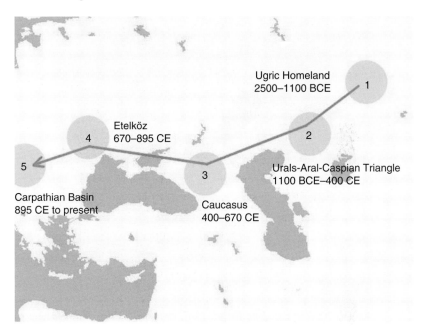

Figure 11.2 Origins of the Magyar people

It is believed that the Magyar migrated to Etelköz, north of the Black Sea and east of the Carpathian Mountains, sometime during the first half of the ninth century. From there, Árpád led a confederation of Magyar tribes over the mountains around 895 CE and conquered the Carpathian Basin, including Great Moravia. Except for incursions by the Ottoman Empire, from that time until 1918, the Slovaks were ruled by the Magyar, their homeland part of the territory referred to as Upper Hungary in the Kingdom of Hungary for most of the Middle Ages and during the Habsburg period.

In the mid sixteenth century, the territory came under the rule of the Habsburg Empire (later the Austrian Empire), which included the Kingdom of Hungary until 1867 (see Figure 11.3). After a number of years of dissatisfaction with Habsburg rule and experiencing the nationalistic fervor that was sweeping much of Europe, the Kingdom of Hungary waged an unsuccessful war of independence in 1848–1849.

Later, as the power of the empire waned, and after defeats in both the Franco-Austrian and Austro-Prussian wars, the Austrian Habsburgs signed the Compromise of 1867, under which they agreed to share power with a separate Hungarian government, dividing the territory of the former Austrian Empire between them, and Hungary once again had complete sovereignty over its own

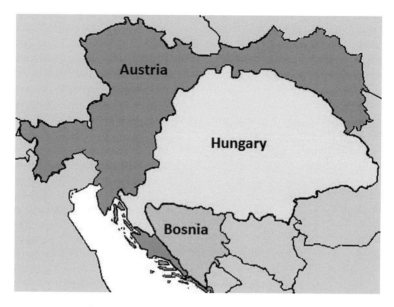

Figure 11.3   The Habsburg Empire 1867, including the Kingdom of Hungary

territory, which included much of present-day Slovakia. The Slovaks remained under Hungarian rule until the end of World War I, at which point the Austro-Hungarian Empire was dissolved.

Linguistic Background

As so often in cases of language conflict, the two languages in this conflict are linguistically unrelated. Slovak is a Slavic language, most closely related to Polish and other Slavic languages such as Bulgarian and Russian. Hungarian is a Finno-Ugric language, and so is related to Finnish, Sámi, and Estonian.

As is true of Sámi, Hungarian has rich inflection on nouns, marking number (singular, plural) and case (there are between 17 and 27 cases).[2] Verbs are inflected for tense and mood and person and number. Additionally, there are two sets of person markers depending on the definiteness of the direct object. Hungarian is an agglutinating language, meaning that words are formed by

---

[2] Kenesei, Vago, and Fenyvesi 1998. According to these authors, the number of cases that others identify differs among authors, some analyzing some suffixes as derivational word formation affixes that others identify as inflectional case. Regardless of the precise count, it is an unusually high number of case categories, and certainly much higher than found in Slovak.

adding affixes in a regular order one after the other to a root, as in the verb forms below:[3]

(1)   meg-ír-t-ad
        PERFECT-write-PAST-DEF.2SG
        'you have written (it)'
(2)   meg-csinál-t-a
        PERFECT-do-PAST-DEF.3SG
        'he/she has done (it)'
(3)   Hány-ban   szület-t-él?
        how.many-INESSIVE be.born-PAST-INDEF.2SG
        'When were you born?'

Note in (1) and (2) that each of the morphemes for perfect, verb root, past tense, and the person endings is easily identified. Comparing (1) and (3) illustrates how the second-person singular verb agreement marker is sensitive to the definiteness occurring as -ad in (1) (with an unexpressed definite pronoun) and él in (3) where there is no definite object.

Slovak nouns are also inflected for case (there are six), grammatical gender (masculine, feminine, neuter), and number (singular, plural). Unlike Hungarian, much of Slovak morphology is fusional, meaning the indications of case, gender, and number are not distinct affixes as in Hungarian but are combined into a single morpheme. In some instances the form of the noun changes as well.

Table 11.1 illustrates the declension for feminine nouns whose roots end in a consonant. While it is fairly easy to identify the root, kosť-/kost-, the suffixes include the information about case, number, and gender. For instance, the suffix ou carries the information that the noun is feminine, singular, and in the instrumental case. For a neuter class noun, such as dievča 'girl,' the suffix ťom carries the information that the noun is neuter, singular in the instrumental case

Table 11.1 *Declension for Slovak feminine noun* kosť *'bone'*

	Singular	Plural
Nominative	kosť[4]	kosti
Genitive	kosti	kostí
Dative	kosti	kostiam
Accusative	kosť	kosti
Locative	kosťou	kosťami
Instrumental	kosti	kostiach

---

[3] Data from Kenesei, Vago, and Fenyvesi 1998.
[4] The symbol ť represents a voiceless palatal stop [c].

Table 11.2 *Comparison of Hungarian and Slovak number terms (1–5)*

	Hungarian	Slovak
1	egy	jeden (jedno (neuter), jedna (feminine))
2	ketto	dva (dve (neuter, feminine))
3	három	tri
4	négy	štyri
5	öt	pät'

dievčat'om. Slovak verbs are inflected for tense (present, past, future), person (first, second, third) and number (singular, plural). In addition there are different conjugation classes for verbs, which take distinct sets of inflectional affixes.

Additionally, in Table 11.2 the numbers 1–5 illustrate the distinctiveness of the vocabularies of each language.

Language Rights History: Hungarian Hegemony

During the majority of the time from 1000 CE until the mid nineteenth century the official language of the Kingdom of Hungary was Latin, both under independent Hungarian rule and the Habsburg and Austrian Empires. Both German and Hungarian were official languages for brief periods, but Hungarian was made the official language in 1844. This was solidified after the Compromise of 1867. It is noteworthy that at that time there were actually fewer Hungarians living in the kingdom than other ethnic groups, a situation that did not change until 1900. Initially the language rights of these minorities were explicitly protected. The 1868 Nationality Act declared each citizen regardless of ethnicity to be "a member in equal rights." That same year, the Education Act contained provisions for children to receive state-sponsored education in their native language and for ethnic minorities to conduct local government in their own language.[5] Such policies ended just a few years later during a drive to transform Hungary into a nation-state on a par with the emerging nation-states of Europe, an effort referred to as Magyarization

Magyarization was a coercive policy designed to assimilate ethnic minorities to Hungarian language and culture.[6] The policy affected various domains, but as is so often the case, it took dead aim at education. In 1875–1876 many Slovak secondary schools were shut down. The 1879 and 1883 Education Acts included Hungarian-language requirements for teachers, extended compulsory education in Hungarian, and curbed the use of minority languages. By 1900, the

---

[5] Bideleux and Jeffries 1998.   [6] Lyon 2008.

success of the effort was evident, as more than 80 percent of primary schools were Hungarian-medium and nearly 85 percent of primary school teachers spoke Hungarian. And the numbers were equally high or higher for secondary and post-secondary schools. This Magyarization of schools not only had the unfortunate effect of alienating ethnic minorities; it also resulted in their children receiving substandard educations as students learned neither Hungarian nor their minority language well, and studying Hungarian took time away from other subjects.[7]

Naming practices were affected as well. Non-Hungarians were pressured by the government and private societies such as Központi Névmagyarositó Társaság ('the Central Society for Name Magyarization') to Magyarize their names, particularly persons employed in public service. In the late 1890s, minority draftees had their names converted to Magyarized spelling and non-Hungarian place names were replaced even when inside predominantly minority areas.[8] After the defeat of the Austro-Hungarian Empire in World War I, the landscape changed significantly.

Language Rights History: Slovak Hegemony

The Treaty of Trianon, signed in 1920, officially ended World War I between the Kingdom of Hungary and the Allies (including France, Great Britain, the United States, and others). As a result of the redrawn state boundaries, the territory of Hungary shrank by about 70 percent (see Figure 11.4).

The Prague National Committee had proclaimed an independent republic of Czechoslovakia in October 1918, and the Slovak National Council, representing the weaker, outnumbered Slovaks, acceded to the Prague proclamation. The new borders resulted in a sizable minority of ethnic Hungarians suddenly living in Czechoslovakian territory, roughly 30 percent of the Slovak population at the time. As can be imagined, Hungarian language rights were generally impacted during the period between the two world wars.

The situation became more acute after World War II. Many Hungarians in Czechoslovakia were expelled or forced into labor in Bohemia. Hungarian (and German) schools were closed and the language was not permitted in public.[9] Hungarian place names were changed to Slovak, as were all road signs. After the Soviet takeover of Czechoslovakia in 1948, radical language restrictions were ameliorated significantly (though not completely eradicated) until the collapse of the Soviet Union in 1989.

---

[7] Jaszi 1929.   [8] Karady 2002.   [9] Daftary and Gál 2000.

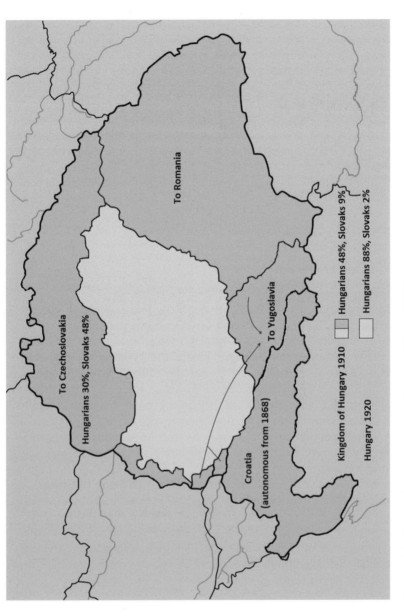

To Romania

To Czechoslovakia

Hungarians 30%, Slovaks 48%

To Yugoslavia

Croatia
(autonomous from 1868)

Kingdom of Hungary 1910   Hungarians 48%, Slovaks 9%

Hungary 1920   Hungarians 88%, Slovaks 2%

Figure 11.4 Hungary before and after the Treaty of Trianon (1920)

Ethnic groups in 1910

☐ *Hungarians*   ▨ *Slovaks*

━━━━━━━━━━━

Present-day borders of Hungary and Slovakia

Figure 11.5 Slovakia/Hungary: present-day borders superimposed over pre-World War I ethnic data

Through deportation and migration, the Hungarian population in Slovakia dwindled to roughly 10 percent (see Figure 11.5).[10] The ethnic Hungarians are concentrated in the south of the country near the Hungarian border, where they have lived for centuries. In some municipalities, they constitute a majority of the population. As we will see shortly, while the laws governing the mandatory use of Slovak in these areas make certain allowances for municipalities in which a particular minority make up at least 20 percent of the population, Slovak is mandated nonetheless. (In 2001, this

---

[10] According to the 2011 census, a little over 500,000 Slovakian citizens have Hungarian as a mother tongue.

20 percent rule led to gerrymandering by the state government, which enacted legislation orienting districts north–south rather than east–west, thereby reducing the number of districts meeting the 20 percent threshold.)[11]

Fall of the Soviet Union and Independent Slovakia

The fall of the Soviet Union in 1989 ushered in a new era in Slovakia, one that included a strong nationalist surge, with its concomitant repression of ethnic minorities – particularly Hungarians; for some it was time for retribution. After the 1990 elections in the Slovak Republic (which at that point was still in a federation with the Czech Republic), one of the early orders of business was setting a language policy. The Slovak National Council adopted the 1990 Act on the Official Language of the Slovak Republic in October, which established the Slovak language as the only official language of the Slovak Republic, claiming that a single official language was crucial to fostering "democracy and culture for the Slovak nation and the national minorities in the Slovak Republic" and the "strengthening of tolerance, humanity, and international unity in the domain of human rights."[12] The law provided that Czech could be used in official contacts, and minorities could use their language in municipalities in which they made up at least 20 percent of the population. However, all government business, records, and publications and public signage had to be in Slovak; state and municipal employees need not be able to use the minority language. Additionally, increased teaching of Slovak was forced upon Hungarian-medium schools.

Understanding of the intent of the law is illustrated by the fact that in October 1991, a deputy in the Slovak Ministry of the Interior issued a statement that all bilingual municipal signs even in heavily populated Hungarian areas were illegal and had to be taken down. There was resistance on the part of the mayor of one such town who sent police out to the town limits to prevent anyone removing the signs inasmuch as such signs were not explicitly banned by the law.[13]

The next important milestone occurred in 1992, at the time of the break-up of Czechoslovakia when it was necessary to adopt a constitution for the soon-to-be-independent Republic of Slovakia. With the 1990 law still in force, the adopted constitution of the Slovak Republic asserted in Article 6:
1. Slovak is the state language on the territory of the Slovak Republic.
2. The use of other languages in dealings with the authorities will be regulated by law.
Of course, the 1990 law severely restricts the use of other languages, and so section 2 is of cold comfort to speakers of minority languages. In specific

[11] O'Dwyer 2008: 113–114.   [12] Schwegler 2008.   [13] Kontra 1995/1996.

reference to the rights of national minorities and language use minorities are granted "the right to master the state language," "the right to disseminate and receive information in their mother tongue," "the right to education in their own language," among others. Clearly these seem like desirable guarantees and may have been included as they are with an eye toward entry in the then Council of Europe, which indicated particular standards for membership. However, each of these rights is governed "by law" – again the 1990 law which greatly restricts these rights.

From 1990 to 1993, the Slovak government had been formed by a coalition of two political parties – the Movement for a Democratic Slovakia and the Slovak National Party, both with strong nationalistic tendencies. For a brief interlude during 1994, a more moderate government was in place, which relaxed some of the language restrictions. However, this period of moderation was short-lived and a new, stronger language law was approved.

The 1995 Slovak State Language Law

Both the 1990 language law and the language provisions in the constitution engendered strong and swift reactions from the country's minorities, particularly the Hungarian community, and from the international community, particularly in Europe, where the documents were seen as clearly violating principles of the Council of Europe. Conversely, some hardliners in Slovakia had been critical that the 1990 law had not been strong enough. In 1995, the Slovak National Council upped the ante, debating and passing an even more comprehensive law that governed the use of Slovak more stringently and set a schedule of fines for violations. It was the strongest legal statement of Slovak nationalism to date, fully embracing the philosophy of one nation, one language, one state.

The preamble to Law no. 270/1995 on the State Language of the Slovak Republic states very strongly the connection between language and the identity of a people:

the Slovak language is the most important feature of the individuality of the Slovak nation, the most precious value of its cultural heritage and the expression of sovereignty of the Slovak Republic and the universal communication means for its citizens, that ensures their freedom and equality in dignity and rights on the territory of the Slovak Republic ...[14]

The law goes on to specify measures to protect the integrity of the Slovak language and govern its use in a variety of domains, including official contacts, education, the mass media and public meetings, the armed forces and fire

---

[14] Passages quoted here come from a translation of the law included in Kontra 1995/1996.

department, the judicial system, and the economy, service and health care. Included is the assertion that the law does not regulate minority languages, the use of which "is determined by other laws."

The law ensures that all contact with government officials (oral and written), all official documents, and all official names of towns, streets, and public lands must be in the Slovak language and that all state employees meet competency standards in Slovak. The law makes Slovak the obligatory medium of instruction in schools and imposes the requirement of fluency in spoken and written Slovak on teachers. All TV, radio, and newspapers must be in Slovak or include translation. Cultural and educational events conducted in other languages must "first take place in the State language." Court proceedings, communications, and records must be in Slovak although translation is possible for persons "not competent in the State language." Contents on packages, employment documents, and health care records are to be kept on in Slovak. Translations of public signage, advertisements, and announcements in other languages are permissible, but only if the Slovak precedes and is no smaller than the other language. The law is breathtaking in its coverage and includes an extensive schedule of hefty fines, which for some infractions can be as high as half the fine levied for endangering Slovakia's nuclear safety.[15] Included are numerous provisos that the use of other languages in education, textbooks, print media, courts, and elsewhere, is governed by separate laws; however, at the time of the passage no such laws were on the books.[16]

Reaction was swift and strong. There were calls from the Council of Europe, the United States, and the Organization for Security and Co-operation in Europe to amend the law and make clear what minority language rights would be. Hungary–Slovakia relations grew strained. And in February of 1996, a month after the law came into force, opposition parties in the National Council submitted the law to the Slovak Constitutional Court, which ruled that it violated the Slovak constitution. The government ignored the court's ruling and calls for it to rescind or modify the law. In July of 1997, Slovakia was denied candidacy for the European Union.[17]

Motivated by a desire to join the EU, with a new, less nationalistic coalition government in place after 1998 elections, a law on minority languages in 1999 was passed by the Slovak Parliament. The law appeared to reverse some of the provisions of the 1995 law, but dealt primarily with official contacts with local governments, the conduct of meetings in minority languages, public signage, and the use of minority languages by officials. It also canceled the schedule of fines included in the 1995 law. However, the law did not address the courts, education and culture, or local

---

[15] Kontra 1997: 7.   [16] Schwegler 2008.   [17] Daftary and Gál 2000.

promotion of minority languages, explicitly stating that these were subject
to other laws and regulations, and was mute on mass media, public meeting,
commerce, and the health care system. As is typical of many such documents, the law included plenty of wiggle room, many provisions including
the words *may, on request*, or *if all present agree*, all of which allow
discretion regarding implementation. The law was greeted with protests by
the Hungarian minority (including Hungarian members of parliament voting
against) and some skepticism by the international community. Nonetheless,
Slovakia was allowed to apply for EU membership in 1999 and in 2004
entered the European Union.

The 2009 Slovak Language Law

Entry in the EU did not signal an end to the language conflict in Slovakia.
In 2006, a new, more nationalist government was formed, and in 2009 the
parliament passed a law amending the 1995 law, but in this case strengthening
some of the provisions. The new law reaffirmed the primacy of Slovak, and
reinstituted a schedule of heavy fines for violations of the law – up to €5,000 for
using "incorrect" Slovak. Included in the law are provisions that Slovak must
be used to conduct business; books, journals, and scientific proceedings must
be published in Slovak; the Slovak must be used first at cultural events even if
only minorities are present; inscriptions on monuments must be in Slovak; and
that minority-language schools must keep records in Slovak as well as the
minority language.[18] Once again reaction was swift, with criticism from the
Organization for Security and Co-operation in Europe, the European Bureau
for Lesser-Used Languages, and others. Protests were launched by the National
Committee of Hungarians (in Slovakia), the Hungarian Human Rights
Foundation, and the Hungarian American Coalition. A protest held at the
soccer stadium in the Hungarian-majority city of Dunaszerdahely drew
between 6,000 and 10,000 participants. The 2009 law also gained the attention
of international media, among them the *Economist*, the *New York Times*, and
NBC News. Since passage, Hungarian–Slovakian relations have been strained,
with politicians in both countries using the language situation to drum up
political support in their country.[19]

Despite a 2010 document setting out the principles of interpretation issued
by the Slovak government intended to soften the law, the language conflict in
Slovakia remains a highly charged, divisive issue. In 2012 the Hungarian
government offered ethnic Hungarians living in other countries the opportunity
to apply for dual citizenship, which prompted a Slovakian response that would

[18] Wardyn and Fiala 2009. [19] Groszkowski and Bocian 2009; Wardyn and Fiala 2009.

strip anyone of Slovakian citizenship who applies for citizenship in another country.[20]

Conclusion

In the case of the Hungarians living in Slovakia, a shift in borders can practically overnight take a population that had been part of a dominant majority and make it a minority. The case is instructive as it illustrates one of the motivations for suppressing the language rights of a group: retribution. Now that they controlled the government, the Slovaks took their opportunity to even the score with the Hungarians for what they viewed as centuries of oppression of their basic civil and linguistic rights. This theme emerges in a number of the cases we examine in later chapters.

Hispanics in the Southwestern United States (California)

By the time of the Mexican–American War of the nineteenth century, the Spanish-speaking settlers of Mexico, like their English-speaking neighbors to the north and east, had separated themselves from their European overlords and forged for themselves a new nation. Begun in 1810 with the exhortation of priest Miguel Hidalgo y Costilla to local residents to "recover from the hated Spaniards the land stolen from your forefathers," the Mexican War of Independence concluded in 1821 with the presentation of the Treaty of Córdoba, which Spain refused to sign (not recognizing Mexican independence until 1836). The short-lived Mexican Empire established immediately after independence was replaced in 1823 by a democratic government.

Historical Background

During the early period of the democracy (up until 1848), Mexico continued the settlement of California as the Spanish colonial government had done before it. Beginning in the 1780s, the Spanish colonial government had fostered settlement of the sparsely populated province of Las Californias (later divided into Alta California and Baja California) through the granting of large tracts of lands referred to as *ranchos* for grazing rights and settlements near the missions, presidios, and pueblos that had already been established. Independent Mexico (shown in Figure 11.6) greatly accelerated these grants, especially after secularization of the missions in 1834, at which time the Mexican government took control of the lands and left the priests the mission churches and smallholdings. By 1848 individuals had title to over 800 ranchos, and the Mexican population

---

[20] BBC 2012.

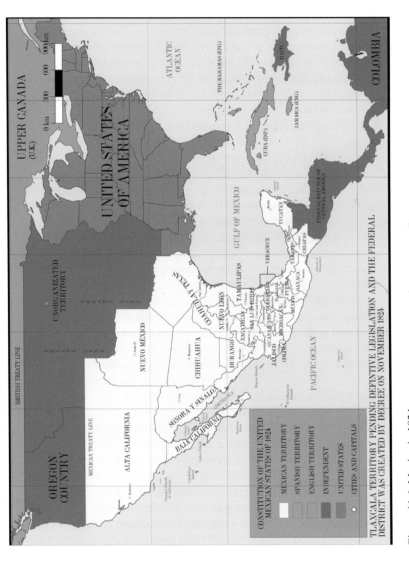

Figure 11.6 Mexico in 1824

in Alta California had risen to 1,500 Mexican males and their wives and native-born children, who numbered 6,500.[21]

During the same period, settlement of Texas accelerated. In the early 1800s, the non-native population of Texas was roughly 7,000.[22] Seeking to colonize the area more completely, the Spanish colonial government granted Moses Austin permission to settle in the territory with some 300 Catholic families. After Austin died without realizing his ambition, Stephen Austin, his son, received the identical grant and settled in the eastern part of Texas with 300 American families recruited through advertisements in New Orleans. Receiving no protection from the Mexican government, the colony established its own code of justice and militia, and by 1835 the population of Texas had swelled to 30,000 Americans compared to 8,000 Mexicans. Disputes and disillusionment with the Mexican government led to revolution in 1835. After a brief war, Texas declared its independence and formed the Republic of Texas. The United States government recognized the republic in 1837 (shown below in Figure 11.7), setting the stage for the Mexican–American War and the eventual annexation of much of the northern Mexican territory.

In 1845 the United States annexed Texas, which became the twenty-eighth state. A dispute over the western border of Texas and US designs on the territory stretching to the Pacific Ocean (an attempt to purchase the territory from Mexico had been refused) erupted into the Mexican–American War in 1846. At the start of the war, the recognized borders of Mexico and the United States coincided with the borders agreed upon by the United States and Spain in the Treaty of Adams-Onís in 1819, which had been adopted by Mexico in 1828 with the signing of the Treaty of Limits, except for the territory of the State of Texas which stretched from the Nueces River east to Louisiana and Arkansas.

A little over a year and one-half after it began (and four months after cessation of hostilities), the Mexican–American War officially concluded with the signing of the Treaty of Guadalupe Hidalgo on February 2, 1848. The terms of the treaty included Mexico's ceding the territory of Alta California and Nuevo Mexico and relinquishing all claims to Texas, setting the border at the Rio Grande River, as shown in Figure 11.8. In return the United States agreed to pay $15 million to Mexico for the ceded land and over $3 million owed to Texans by the Mexican government.

In addition, the treaty guaranteed the property rights and civil rights, including the language rights, of Mexicans living in the new US territory. Mexican residents were given one year to decide whether they wanted to be relocated in Mexico or become US citizens with a guarantee of full voting rights; 90 percent chose to remain in the United States. When the US Congress ratified the treaty, it struck the article guaranteeing Mexican's land grants and amended the treaty

[21] www.liquisearch.com/history_of_california/history_of_california_to_1899/mexican_period
[22] Texas Historical Society 2010. https://tshaonline.org/handbook/online/articles/ulc01

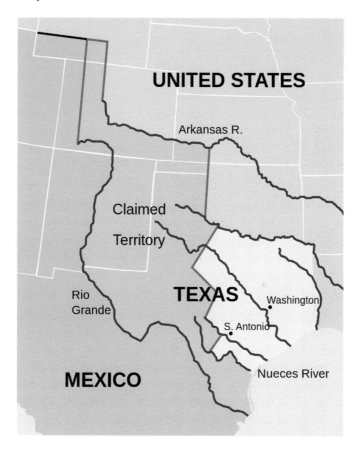

Figure 11.7 The Republic of Texas, 1836–1845

so that Mexican citizens would "be admitted at the proper time (to be judged of by the Congress of the United States)" instead of "admitted as soon as possible."

Language Rights in California under American Rule

While not explicitly stated, the property and civils rights guaranteed in the Treaty of Guadalupe Hidalgo also included language rights for Mexicans remaining in the new US territories. The first California constitution, in fact, does guarantee some language rights for Spanish-speaking citizens. Section 21 of the constitution of the State of California (1849) states:

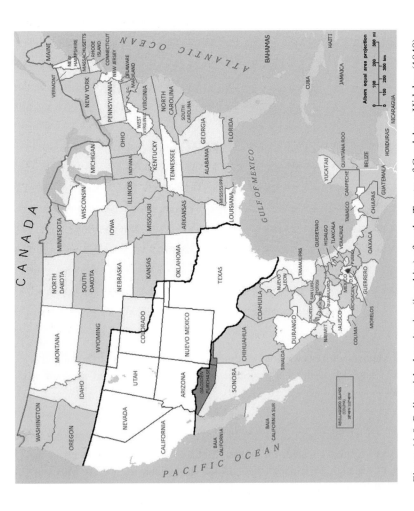

Figure 11.8 Relinquished territories (in white) after the Treaty of Guadalupe Hidalgo (1848)

All laws, decrees, regulations, and provisions, which from their nature require publication, shall be published in **English and Spanish**.

Apparently section 21 applied to the constitution itself, as a Spanish translation, *Constitucion del Estado de California*, was released simultaneously. However, there was a major demographic shift that would soon induce a concomitant shift in the language rights for Spanish-speaking Californians, known as Californios.

In 1846 at the start of the Mexican–American War, estimates are that there were approximately 6,000–8,000 Californios living primarily on ranchos, 700–2,000 largely American foreigners, and perhaps 150,000 Native Americans (although estimates vary widely).[23] After the discovery of gold in 1848 (just days before the signing of the Treaty of Guadalupe Hidalgo), the rush of fortune-seekers brought the non-native population to approximately 100,000 in 1849.[24] The population of San Francisco alone expanded from about from 1,000 in 1848 to over 20,000 by 1850.[25]

One of the guarantees of the treaty had been protection of property rights of the Californios. However, it was necessary to issue titles to landholders, which required adjudication of claims. Due to the very large number of claims to examine, in 1851, the US Congress, which was responsible at the time for processing land claims, passed the California Land Act. The Act established a three-member Board of Land Commissioners to pass on claims, and Commission decisions could be appealed in the courts. Incomplete documents and widespread fraud contributed to the process being long and cumbersome.[26] Additionally, lawyers' fees for claimants were significant, and many landholders were forced to sell portions of their lands to pay the fees.[27] One result was that many Californios lost their ranchos or significant portions of them. Among the causes were poor translations of Mexican titles (where they existed) and the testimony of the Spanish-speaking claimants. Unscrupulous interpreters also were a factor in the problem. Added to that was the mood of the country and the fact that some felt that the United States was in the process of giving back lands it had fought for. The burden of proof was thus placed on the Mexican residents.

Language rights setbacks occurred in education in the 1850s as well. In 1852, the State Bureau of Public Instruction prohibited religious schools from getting state funds. Most of the schools affected were Spanish Catholic schools. Soon afterward, in 1855 the Bureau decreed that all schools must teach

---

[23] PBS 2006.
[24] The 1850 US Census put the non-Native American population of California at 92,597 (Seventh Census of the United States: 1850). However, not included in those numbers were San Francisco, Santa Clara, and Santa Rosa counties.
[25] PBS 2006.   [26] Gates 1971.   [27] Perez 1982.

exclusively in English. This was followed up in the California State Legislature, which passed a law in 1870 that all schools in the state must be English-language-medium schools.[28]

As in other cases we have examined, the justice system was another domain in which language rights have been an issue. The constitution of 1879 includes a requirement that mandates the use of English in the courts. The requirement is part of a provision that nullifies Article 21 of the 1849 constitution regarding publishing announcements in both English and Spanish. Article IV section 24 of the 1879 constitution applies to all three branches of government:

All laws of the State of California, and all official writings, and the executive, legislative, and judicial proceedings shall be conducted, preserved, and published in no other than the English language.

While this is clearly a tremendous step backward for the language rights of all non-English speakers, its harshest outcome was to remove a right previously held by the state's formerly Mexican Spanish speakers. The new constitution reflected the changing mood of the state's white population in other ways as well. For example, while the constitution did not affect the voting rights of Spanish speakers, it did deny suffrage to Chinese.[29] Article II section 1 states, "no native of China ... shall ever exercise the privilege of an elector in this state."

But the winds of change were stirring. In 1891, citing "corrupting influences of the disturbing elements ... from abroad," A. J. Bledsoe proposed in the California State Assembly an amendment to the constitution that would impose an English-language literacy requirement on eligible voters.[30] The amendment was initially voted down. However, the public reacted strongly to the outcome; voicing its support for the action, the legislature passed the bill, which it put up for a general vote in the 1894 election. The voters approved the measure, amending Article II section 1 to read in part:

no native of China, no idiot, no insane person, no person convicted of any infamous crime, no person hereafter convicted of the embezzlement or misappropriation of public money, and **no person who shall not be able to read the constitution in the English language and write his or her name**, shall ever exercise the privileges of an elector in this state.

When voting on a women's suffrage amendment in 1911, and becoming the sixth state in the country to extend voting right to women, the literacy requirement was retained in the constitution.[31]

---

[28] Leibowitz 1971.
[29] This occurred before the passage of the Chinese Exclusion Act signed into law by President Chester A. Arthur in 1882, designed to end the immigration of Chinese to the United States.
[30] Tucker 2013.
[31] The provision "no native of China" was later amended to "no alien ineligible to citizenship."

More Recent Language Rights Issues

In 1900 the Mexican population in California was roughly 100,000. Due largely to immigration, that figure leapt to 1.5 million by 1930. At that point there were social changes afoot in the United States. In comparatively rapid succession, the US Congress passed and the President signed into law the Civil Rights Act (1964), the Voter Rights Act (1965), and the Bilingual Education Act (1968).

Despite these developments since the voting amendment was approved in 1894, language rights issues have arisen. The literacy test remained in the constitution for many years, even after the passage of the Voting Rights Act in 1965. In fact, it was not until the California Supreme Court ruled in 1970 on the case of *Castro* v. *State of California* that the literacy test was expunged from the California constitution. The 1967 suit involved Genevevo Castro and another plaintiff who were denied the right to register to vote. The Supreme Court determined that the restriction on voting rights violated the fourteenth amendment of the US constitution guaranteeing equal protection under the law. Justice Raymond L. Sullivan's ruling stated flatly, "It is obvious that fear and hatred played a significant role in the passage of the literacy requirement."[32]

However, it is clear that many voters in California wanted an English requirement in elections. Despite the Castro ruling, in 1984 California voters approved Proposition 38, which required the governor "to deliver to the President of the United States, the Attorney General of the United States, and all Members of Congress" a statement urging the federal government to enact an amendment to federal law "so that ballots, voters' pamphlets, and all other official voting materials shall be printed in English only." The measure passed with 70.5 percent of the vote. Two years later, Californians voted by an even higher margin (73.2 percent) to make English the official language of the state. This resulted in Article III section 6 of the constitution of California, which includes:

(a) English is the common language of the people of the United States of America and the State of California. This section is intended to preserve, protect and strengthen the English language, and not to supersede any of the rights guaranteed to the people by this Constitution.

(b) English is the official language of the State of California.

The article also enjoins the legislature to "take all steps necessary to insure that the role of English . . . is preserved and enhanced" and to "make no law which diminishes or ignores the role of English." California thus became the ninth state to declare English its official language.

Education is the other domain that has a long history with respect to use of English. Recall that English was mandated as the sole language of instruction

---

[32] Sullivan 1970.

by the State Bureau of Public Instruction in 1855 and by the legislature in 1870. This remained in place for decades, and during that time school performance and completion among Hispanics (and other minorities) was noticeably compromised. When the US Bilingual Education Act became law in 1968, things changed rapidly and radically. Bilingual and English as a Second Language instruction became a major focus for the California Department of Education and there was much discussion among education administrators, teachers, and lawmakers regarding the best means of implementing programs. In 1969–1970, twenty-six bilingual programs began operation with some state funding.[33] California made a major commitment to bilingual education in 1976 when the legislature passed the Bilingual–bicultural Education Act. Under the Act, California Education Code section 52165 laid out the broad reach, guaranteeing bilingual education for all students who were identified as needing it:

Each pupil of limited English proficiency enrolled in the California public school system in kindergarten and grades 1 to 12, inclusive, shall receive instruction in a language understandable to the pupil that recognizes the pupil's primary language and teaches the pupil English.

There was a range of program types that emerged, and, as was true across the country, there was controversy regarding the effectiveness of the programs.[34]

This controversy reached a boiling point in the 1990s in California. The result was the passage of Proposition 227 in 1998. Also known as the English Language in Public Schools Statute, this proposition mandated that Limited English Proficient (LEP) students be taught only in English. Approved by 61.3 percent of the voters, the proposition directed the legislature to pass a law that largely ended bilingual education in the state, and mandated that students take special classes in English to learn English, and that they move from these to mainstream classes as soon as possible, usually in a year or less.

Recent events show that the issue was not necessarily decided with the passage of Proposition 227. In 2014, the California lawmakers passed a bill (SB 1174) that would decidedly alter the law. It would strip out of the law any language indicating California public schools are ineffective at educating LEP students, the provision that all LEP students be taught English in English, and other key components. It would allow parents to choose the type of language programs they wanted for their children and provide additional opportunities for monolingual English students to achieve proficiency in an additional language. On November 8, 2016, California voters passed ballot initiative Proposition 58 with an overwhelming majority, 73.5 to 26.5 percent; SB 1174 became law and bilingual education was no longer legally restricted.

---

[33] Tay 1971.   [34] Duignan 1998.

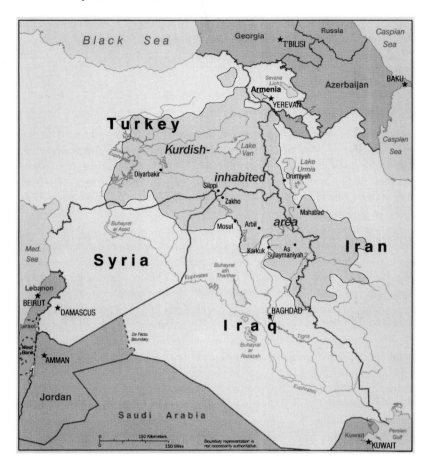

Figure 11.9 Kurdish-inhabited area

Regardless of the outcome of the vote, the history of language conflict and language rights in California certainly will not be put to rest. We expect that there will be further developments in years to come.

The Kurds in Turkey

The next example we take up is the case of the Kurds, a people who inhabit territory primarily in the countries of Iran, Iraq, Syria, and Turkey, with smaller populations in several other states, as amply illustrated in Figure 11.9.

The area labeled "Kurdistan" in Figure 11.10 represents a hypothetical rather than actual political state. In fact, with a current population of roughly 27 million,[35] the Kurds are often referred to as the world's largest nation without a state.[36]

Historical Background

While details are debated, the consensus is that the Kurds have inhabited the area fairly steadily for at least the past two millennia (having been mentioned in the fifth-century BCE text *Anabasis*, by the Greek warrior and historian Xenophon), and most likely have their origins in northwestern Persia (Iran).[37] Of Indo-Iranian stock, the Kurds were until modern times primarily a nomadic people. There is speculation that the term "Kurd" derives from Middle Persian *kwrt*, a term commonly used to refer to "nomads" or "tent dwellers"[38] – a term firmly established during the Muslim conquest of Persia in the seventh century CE. While there were a number of powerful Kurdish principalities and dynasties that flourished in the tenth to the twelfth century, the Kurds for the most part have had a long and tumultuous history of domination by the various Persian and Arabic empires that ruled the region, a situation which resulted in frequent movement of the Kurds and the boundaries of their lands. At the same time, because their traditional territories were remote and mountainous, the Kurds still managed to maintain a certain degree of autonomy.

Their autonomous status began to change in the first half of the nineteenth century when the rulers of Ottoman Turkey started to centralize their power across this region. Up until this time, the Kurds (as well as other groups within the Ottoman Empire) were immune to the nationalism that had started sweeping across Europe. And it remained so until the late 1800s when stirrings for a Kurdish nation-state first emerged and grew steadily, culminating in a Kurdish nationalist movement at the end of World War I.

Linguistic Background

Kurdish is an Indo-European language (like English and Hindi), most closely related to languages such as Farsi (Iran) and Pashto (Afghanistan). However, rather than there being a standard Kurdish language, the Kurds' wide geographic distribution across the territories of different empires and states led to the development of several, very distinct, Kurdish dialects (which, despite some differences, still largely share grammatical properties). In Turkey, the area we are concerned with in this section, the prevalent Kurdish variety is the

---

[35] *CIA Factbook* 2015.   [36] Gallaher, Dahlman, and Gilmartin 2009.   [37] Zaken 2007.
[38] Kreyenbroek and Sperl 1992.

Northern Kurdish dialect Kurmanji, which is also spoken in northern Iraq. As is so often true of the cases we examine, Turkish, the language of the dominant group, is not related to Kurdish and is a Turkic language, closely related to Mongolian and perhaps distantly related to Korean.[39] While both Kurdish and Turkey are SOV languages, this is no measure of their relatedness since, as we have seen, SOV word order is a feature of languages belonging to many distinct language families.[40]

Morphological differences between Kurdish and Turkish amply demonstrate how different they are. While nouns in both Kurdish and Turkish can distinguish between SINGULAR and PLURAL number, Kurdish nouns are also distinguished on the basis of MASCULINE and FEMININE gender, with gender here being of the type found in Romance languages such as French, Italian, and Spanish. While nouns in both languages are marked for case, Kurdish distinguishes only two cases, referred to as ABSOLUTIVE and OBLIQUE. On the other hand, Turkish displays six case forms: ABSOLUTIVE, ACCUSATIVE, DATIVE, GENITIVE, ABLATIVE, and LOCATIVE.

Verbs in the two languages have morphology identifying agreement with person and number of the subject at least some of the time. And while they are also marked for tense, mood, and aspect, the tense, mood, and aspectual categories for each language are quite different. The following sentences illustrate some of the salient differences.

(4)   Kurdish[41]
        Min   ji   te   re gul   dan.
        I.OBL to   you   to rose.ABS   give.PST
        'I gave you a rose.'

(5)   Turkish[42]
        Sema   lokanta-da   Hasan-a   kitab-ı   ver-di.
        Sema.ABS   restaurant-LOC   Hasan-DAT   book-ACC   give-PST.3SG
        'Sema gave the book to Hasan in the restaurant.'

In the Kurdish sentence in (4) the subject *min* 'I' occurs in its oblique case form, the direct object *gul* 'rose' occurs in its absolutive case form, and the indirect object *te* 'you' occurs in between two prepositions, *ji* and *re*, which combine to

---

[39] There is some disagreement among linguists regarding the precise categorization of Turkish, with some identifying Turkish as a Turkic language with a small number of related languages and others identifying it as belonging to the larger Altaic family, which includes a larger number of languages. Regardless of the precise categorization, Kurdish and Turkish belong to distinct language families.

[40] SOV has been identified as the most common word order among the world's languages – roughly 45 percent of the sample. The remaining possible orders are distributed as follows: SVO (45%), VSO (9%), VOS (3%), and OVS and OSV (both 1% or less).

[41] Aygen 2007: 80.   [42] Özkaragöz 1986.

Table 11.3 *Comparison of Kurdish, Farsi, Pashto, and Turkish number terms (1–5)*

	Kurdish	Farsi	Pashto	Turkish
1	yek	yak	yaw	bir
2	du	du	dwa	iki
3	se	se	dre	üc
4	chwar	char	tsalor	dört
5	penj	panj	pindze	bes

form the meaning 'to.' In the Turkish sentence in (5) there is a very different alignment of cases and nouns. The subject *Sema* is in its absolutive form, the object *kitab* 'book' takes the accusative case marker, and the indirect object *Hasan* takes dative case. Additionally, the location *lokanta* 'restaurant' is in the locative. Locations in Kurdish take prepositional marking.

As might be expected, the vocabularies of languages are very different, the Kurdish lexicon being similar to related Indo-European languages but quite distinct from Turkish, as illustrated in the comparison of numbers words in Table 11.3.

A "popular" poem captures the neighboring people's attitudes toward the Kurds (from the Kurdish Academy of Language):

> Arabic is the Alpha and Omega,
> Persian is (as sweet as) sugar,
> Turkish is a work of art,
> Kurdish is a donkey's fart.[43]

Of course, this was answered with a Kurdish poem:

> Although it's said that Persian's sweet as sugar,
> For me is Kurdish sweeter still.
> Clearly, in this perfidious world,
> Everyone is happiest with his own mother tongue.

With these linguistic differences firmly in mind, we next turn to the events leading up to the denial of Kurdish language rights by the modern state of Turkey.

Language Rights History

From the late 1800s right up to World War I, the political and military power of the Ottoman Empire was in steep decline. The period also saw a concomitant

---

[43] Nebez 2000.

rise in Turkish ethnic nationalism (as well as in nationalism among Albanians, Armenians, Circassians, Kurds, and other groups), culminating in a 1908 revolution in which the Community of Union and Progress (CUP; mainly composed of Ottoman military officers, also known as the Young Turks) took control of the government. Increasingly under pressure, the CUP embarked on a campaign referred to as Turkification, which aimed to establish a Turkish "nation-state" (with Turkish as the only recognized state language) and which led to the harsh repression of minority groups. This was accomplished in part by banning non-Turkish political and social groups and their publications, but in the more extreme cases including the relocation and the genocide of some minority groups (e.g. Armenians, Assyrians, Greeks, etc.).[44] These events are what set the stage for the rise in Kurdish nationalism.

After its defeat in Worl War I, the remainder of the Ottoman Empire was broken up and its constituent territory divided by the victorious Western powers into several new states and colonial territories and protectorates. The Treaty of Sèvres, signed in 1920, was the first attempt at redrawing the map. In addition to determining borders for Turkey, Armenia, Iraq, and others, the treaty included provision for an autonomous Kurdish state, Kurdistan, as illustrated in Figure 11.10.

From 1922 to 1924, a semi-autonomous Kingdom of Kurdistan was recognized in northern Iraq, roughly the territory designated "Kurdish-inhabited areas" in Figure 11.10.

However, the idea of a state of Kurdistan vanished in 1923 with the signing of the Treaty of Lausanne. Turkey had steadfastly refused to sign the Treaty of Sèvres, unhappy with the boundaries and other provisions set by the treaty. The Treaty of Lausanne was drawn up to placate the Turkish nationalist government, and in so doing annulled the Treaty of Sèvres and with it any provision for a Kurdish state. Thus, as we saw in Figure 11.10, the area identified as Kurdistan simply marks the territory inhabited by Kurds in the states of Turkey, Iran, Iraq, and Syria, but not a Kurdish state. Provisions were also made for minorities in the treaty. But, as was the case in the late Ottoman Empire, the Turkish nationalists recognized only non-Muslims as having the prerogative of belonging to minority groups. Hence, while the Armenians, the Greeks, and the Jews were recognized minorities, all Muslims were officially counted as Turks. And since this included the Kurds, they were thus not only denied a state but also a national identity.

Under the leadership of Mustafa Kemal Atatürk, who became the first president, the newly formed secular Turkish government set about the task of creating the new nation-state. With the nationalism that helped topple the Ottoman Empire firmly in mind, the new government adopted a radically

---

[44] Üngör 2008.

Proposed boundaries of independent Kurdistan

Areas to be given choice to join Kurdistan after August 1922

Figure 11.10 The borders of Kurdistan as prescribed in the Treaty of Sèvres

nationalistic and anti-clerical philosophy, one guided by the ideal of one nation, one state, one language. Other than the minorities identified in the Treaty of Lausanne, the state denied the existence of any minorities within its border. The Kurdish minority was deemed not to exist, and the government decreed that they were to be referred to as "mountain Turks" and the area they inhabited as "the East." Thus the government pursued an assimilationist agenda with regard to the Kurds and all Muslim ethnic varieties, much as was attempted with the Sámi in Norway, the Native Americans in the United States, the Ainu in Japan, and countless other cases. (See Chapter 10.)

As one of the most essential components of the nation-building process, the Turkish language was the object of numerous laws and decrees, as well as declarations in the constitution. The effects of these laws and regulations pervaded all of Turkish life, as did the language rights issues they engendered.

As part of the push to Westernize and secularize their new nation, a new Roman alphabet was introduced, officially replacing the Arabic-based script that had been used for centuries. Additionally, as we have seen in other cases of establishing a national language (e.g. Indonesian), a language academy (the Turkish Language Academy or Turk Dili Akademisi) was instituted in 1926 to modernize and intellectualize the language, which involved the addition of many technical and scientific terms to the vocabulary.[45] Such changes affected not only minority groups but also ethnic Turks.

For the Kurds and other Muslim minorities there was much more. In addition to the 1924 constitution declaring Turkish to be the official language, Atatürk issued a decree that prohibited the use of the Kurdish language in public and private domains. As recently as 1982, a new constitution granted the government extensive powers as regards the promotion of national unity, and on this basis legislation was enacted that made Turkish the "mother tongue" (as opposed to merely the "official language") of all Turkish citizens.[46] This 1983 law (No. 2932 "The Law Concerning Publications and Broadcasts in Languages Other than Turkish") declared further that "It is forbidden to claim that there exist minorities in Turkey," and that "It is forbidden to protect or develop non-Turkish cultures and languages."[47] Thus were the ethnic identities of Muslim minorities stripped away in stages.

Domains of Turkish Interference in Kurdish Language

The history of Turkish government repression of the Kurds from the birth of the modern state to the present day is a long and tortured one, there being an ebb and flow of stricter periods and more liberal periods. During this time, there were three military coups (1960, 1971, and 1980), three constitutions (1924, 1961, and 1982), and a succession of governments. Language has played a critical role through this time, with many governments revising and reissuing laws and decrees governing language. These laws applied to domains of public and personal life familiar to the reader from other cases we have considered: personal and public naming, education, publication and broadcasting, politics, and the judicial and penal systems.

Of course, nothing can be stronger than an outright ban on the use of a language in both public and private realms. While public use is relatively easier to control than private use, this category of restrictions were reinforced by various laws for various domains.

Private Naming   One such law is the Surname Law, discussed briefly in Chapter 5. It was often the case that people did not have a family name.

---

[45] Aytürk 2008.   [46] Watts 1999: 635.   [47] Skutnabb-Kangas and Bucak 1994: 356.

In 1934, not only was it mandated that people had to take on family names (if they didn't yet have one), but it was also stipulated that names had to conform to Turkish tradition and to fit into the phonology of the Turkish language (i.e. only consist of sounds that are present in Turkish). As Turkish and Kurdish have different sound systems, many traditional Kurdish names were outlawed as being unpronounceable in Turkish. A later law addressed given names. To understand the situation that the Kurds faced, one might imagine an English speaker on the Indonesian island of Madura attempting to give their child an English name that conforms to the sound system of Madurese. Since Madurese lacks the English consonants [f] (as in *father*), [v] (as in *victor*), [θ] (as in *thistle*), and [ð] (as in *those*), the English names Fred, Steven, and Martha would be ruled out, along with many others.

Public Naming   For similar reasons, names of towns, geographical landmarks, and so on have been changed by law, much as we saw with the renaming of Hungarian locations in Slovakia, and Ainu places in Japan, among others. The 1949 Provincial Administrative Law declared: "Village names that are not in Turkish and give rise to confusion are to be changed in the shortest possible time by the Interior Ministry ... "[48] Many names in Kurdish areas were changed as a result. A similar law was passed in 1960, and during the 1980s, 2,842 Kurdish village names were officially renamed in Turkish.[49]

Education   As we have seen previously, the educational system is a common locus of government efforts to suppress minority languages. If children are only able to attain an education in a national or official language, they must learn that language and become proficient in it. As a result, they frequently lose their mother tongue, sometimes with the encouragement of their parents (who see it as an economic necessity). Turkish laws required that the language of education was Turkish only, with the 1982 constitution stating that "No language other than Turkish may be taught as a native language to citizens of Turkey in instructional and educational institutions" (Article 42 paragraph 9). Throughout the years, this has been reinforced by various additional items of legislation, such as a 1992 law which stipulated that Turkish be the language of instruction, with some exceptions made primarily for English, French, and German, and secondarily for Arabic, Chinese, Italian, Japanese, and Russian, but not Kurdish.[50] As described for Ainu and Sámi in Chapter 10, children are disadvantaged if their early education is in a language they cannot speak, thus limiting their education early on, and leading to their facing acute social and economic challenges as adults. This was certainly the case for many Kurds as well.

[48] Panico 1999: 121.   [49] Hassanpour 1992.   [50] Panico 1999.

Other Domains There were also laws that banned the use of any language but Turkish in other domains. For example, it was illegal to publish or record materials (including sound recordings) in Kurdish; and there were laws pertaining to the courts and the penal system as well. Many times these provisions are couched in terms of "no language prohibited by law." For example, the 1982 constitution states that "No publications or broadcasts may be made in any language prohibited by law" (Article 26, paragraph 2). This is comparable to the case of Slovakia's language law discussed above. Those who broke any of these laws were dealt with harshly, through stiff fines and imprisonment.

Further Development of Kurdish Language Rights Difficulties

The story of Kurdish language rights does not end here. As alluded to above, there have been numerous attempts by the Kurds to secure political and language rights. "Insurrections" in the 1920s and 1930s were quickly quelled by the Turkish military, and the Kurdish areas saw a more robust government presence following these. Periods of rigorous government control ebbed and flowed, and the 1970s were a time of relative liberalism and resurgence of Kurdish nationalism. In the late 1970s, the Partiya Karkerên Kurdistanê (PKK), the Kurdish Workers' Party, was formed and took up the struggle for a Kurdish state. By the early 1980s, the PKK took up arms against the government in the wake of renewed repression of minority language and political rights, as laid out in the 1982 constitution and in a series of laws, including the Language Ban Law. The PKK was deemed a terrorist group by the Turkish government, and in that context speaking and publishing in Kurdish were then treated as terrorist acts that threatened the unity of the state and which were punished with heavy fines and imprisonment. From 1984 to 1991 roughly 2,500 lost their lives in the conflict, but in the early 1990s the conflict intensified and in the span of four years some 20,000 perished as the military took control of Kurdish areas in the southeast. Over 3,000 Kurdish villages were destroyed during this period and nearly 380,000 Kurds were displaced.

Perhaps ironically, this repression came on the heels of the official repeal in 1991 of the Language Ban Act. Speaking Kurdish in public and some Kurdish publications were no longer illegal. However, Kurdish was still banned in schools, in radio and television broadcasts, and for use in political activities, with these declared terrorist acts. In that same year, Leyla Zana, the first Kurdish woman elected to the Turkish parliament, broke the law by speaking the last sentence of her oath of office in Kurdish. But because she was a member of parliament, she had immunity from prosecution. However, in 1994, after her Kurdish political party was declared a terrorist organization, she was arrested for separatism (due to her alleged membership of the PKK), and sentenced to fifteen years in prison along with three other Kurdish members of parliament. Ten years later, after years of pressure from the European Union, she and the others were released at the prosecutor's request.[51] In another incident, in 2009, a state-run television station stopped a live broadcast of a session of parliament when another Kurdish MP, Ahmet Turk, started speaking Kurdish during a speech to the legislature. These are just two examples of linguistic suppression of the Kurds. Among many others are:

- the 1999 arrest and conviction of a taxi driver for listening to Kurdish music;
- the arrest of two local mayoral candidates for campaigning in Kurdish;
- the 2010 arrest of the musician Rodja for singing a Kurdish song at a public event;
- the 2012 arrest and imprisonment of the mayors of thirty-two villages;
- the 2014 closing of three Kurdish-medium primary schools.

Note that all of these incidents occurred after the Turkish government had lifted the ban on the private use of Kurdish in 1991. Other reforms adopted by the government included the limited lifting of the ban on broadcasts in 2002,[52] the opening of the first private Kurdish language school in 2004, offering Kurdish as an elective class in Turkish public schools, allowing Kurdish to be used in court (although speakers must pay for translators themselves), and others. There was even a 2004 amendment to the constitution in which a provision against discrimination in the law included language:

All individuals are equal without any discrimination before the law, irrespective of **language**, race, colour, sex, political opinion, philosophical belief, religion and sect, or any such considerations.

Despite these apparent advances in language rights in Turkey and a call by jailed leader Abdullah Ocalan in 2013 for PKK fighters to lay down their arms, in 2015 there is as yet no ceasefire between the PKK and the Turkish government. It is clear that the conflict is far from over and language rights are far from guaranteed. After the 2015 parliamentary election, Leyla Zana's oath of office was deemed invalid because she spoke Kurdish, and folk singer Nudem Durak was imprisoned for singing a Kurdish song. And so, the Kurds' struggle for language rights continues to this day.

Summary: Comparison of Cases

The conflicts presented in this chapter each have a distinct provenance and a different direct cause. The present Hungarian situation in Slovakia arose from the peaceful dissolution of Czechoslovakia. The fate of Hispanics in the

---

[51]   Also, Zana was sentenced to ten years in prison in 2012, again on charges of separatism, for a series of speeches she gave in Kurdish in 2007–2008.

[52]   Rodriguez, Avalos, Yilmaz, and Planet 2013.

southwestern United States was determined by a war. And the circumstances of the Kurds emanates from a centuries-old conflictual relationship between the Kurds and their Turkic neighbors. The superficial motivations for the conflicts are also distinct, at least superficially. In the southwestern United States, the Spanish-speaking Mexicans were just bystanders in a competition for hegemony in the western parts of North America between the English-speaking and Spanish-speaking post-colonial enterprises of the United States and Mexico. In Slovakia, the Hungarians are the ethnolinguistic remnant of a time when Hungary was a much greater power in Central Europe, and currently pay the heaviest linguistic price in Slovakia's quest to distinguish itself from the Czech Republic. Finally, in the case of the Kurds, they (along with several other nationalities) were caught short in the post-World War I transformation of the multinational Ottoman Empire into an ethnically oriented Turkish nation-state.

All this said, it is nevertheless the case that the consequences of these conflicts and the uses made of language in subjugating each linguistic minority are quite similar. In each circumstance, language use and the restriction of linguistic rights became a tool with which to assert power and control over the minority group. In California, restrictions on Spanish were explicitly used to deprive the Spanish speakers of the land which they had bought and owned. In Slovakia, language laws were used to disenfranchise to the extent possible the ethnic Hungarians in the south, and were certainly felt on both sides to be "payback" for similar depredations suffered by Slovaks when the lands were controlled previously by Hungary. In the case of Turkey, the Kurds are a far-too-numerous minority occupying the southeastern quarter of the Anatolian Peninsula and posing a threat to Turkish sovereignty there. Forcing (or trying to force) them to become more "Turkish" (in their language use and in their naming practices) was designed in part to make them into Turks, irrespective of their actual ethnic heritage, and to secure Turkish rule in those lands.

Additional Cases for Exploration

Tetum in Timor Leste

The island of Timor lies at the far eastern edge of the Indonesian archipelago. The west side of the island is part of Indonesia, and in the eastern part of the island is the independent country of Timor Leste (East Timor). The indigenous population of Timor Leste is descended from various groups that have inhabited the area for over 40,000 years. Prior to European colonization, different ethnic groups lived in small kingdoms, speaking a variety of languages from both the Austronesian and the Trans-New Guinea families. Intergroup communication was carried out through Tetum, a contact or trade language based largely on the Tetum languages spoken on the island. The Timorese conducted business with Indian and Chinese traders, exporting sandalwood, honey, and wax during the fourteenth century, and maintained autonomy. The landscape changed in the 1500s with the arrival of Europeans.

The Portuguese arrived and set up outposts beginning in the sixteenth century, establishing a permanent settlement in the eastern part of Timor in 1769, while the Dutch claimed the west side of the island as part of its Indonesian holdings. The Portuguese used Tetum to communicate with the indigenes during the early period of decentralized colonial rule, but that changed in the twentieth century, at which time Portuguese became the man-dated language of instruction in government-funded schools and the Catholic church, bestowing economic and social advantage for Timorese educated in Portuguese. A political crisis in 1975 led to the Indonesian invasion and annexation of East Timor and establishment of a brutally repressive regime in which Indonesian was declared the sole language of education and govern-ment. During this time, Tetum became a language of resistance and identity (Portuguese having been outlawed by the Indonesian government). Securing its independence in 2002 after a fierce civil war, Timor Leste has declared Portuguese and Tetum as official languages, but many rights and language planning issues persist.

Amazigh (Berbers) in the Maghreb Region of Africa

The Berber peoples of western and Saharan Africa (the Maghreb region – northwestern Africa) have inhabited the lands included in present-day Morocco, Algeria, Tunisia, Libya, Western Sahara, Mauritania, Mali, and Niger for several thousand years. These people, whose numbers are greatest in Morocco, Algeria, and Libya, style themselves as "Amazigh" (meaning 'freeborn') and speak languages that are only distantly related to the Semitic language of Arabic. The Amazigh peoples, through their early history, were variously independent (e.g. the Numidian kingdom of 202–46 BCE) and subject (e.g. to the Phoenicians and then the Romans). They, in their different tribal groups, practiced a variety of religions (including Judaism, Christianity, and various local and regional traditions), before being invaded by Islamic armies late in the seventh century. Alongside their submission to Islam, the Berber people were subjected to Arab rule, which involved the gradual dom-ination of Arabic over the regional Amazigh languages.

The relative ethnic, linguistic, and political domination of Arab over Berber people has depended, to a large extent, on their relative population in the various countries in which they live. In Morocco the Berber population is about half of the total, and in Algeria it is between one-fifth and one-third of the total. In contrast, Libya's Amazigh population numbers only about 4 percent of the population. As might be expected, the circumstances of Libya's Amazigh have, in recent times, been far more difficult than any of the others. Thus, while Berber is an official language of Morocco and a national language in Algeria, Amazigh in Libya were forbidden to use Amazigh or to write it (using the Amazigh script, Tifinagh) for forty years under Gaddafi's rule. Unsurprisingly, the Amazigh of Libya were a key constituency in the 2011 uprising against, and overthrow of, Gaddafi's rule.

Tibetans in China

Roughly 15,000 feet above sea level on the Tibetan plateau between India and China and flanked by the Himalayas live the indigenous people of Tibet, descendants of a group that has inhabited the area for some 3,000 years. Stretching back to the seventh century, Tibetan history is closely entwined with Buddhism, which was introduced at that time at the beginning of the Tibetan Empire and which is an integral part of Tibetan identity. After a period of rule by warlords following the collapse of the empire in the ninth century, first the Mongols and then the Qing Dynasty in China controlled the area, though the people remained largely isolated and Tibetan religion and culture flourished. In modern times, the Dalai Lama asserted Tibetan independence in 1913. Related to Chinese as a member of the greater Sino-Tibetan language family, the Tibetan language is more closely related to Burmese and Newari (spoken in Nepal), and though tones are an important phonological device, as they are in Chinese, it has a much richer morphology, with case marking on nouns and some inflection on verbs.

Since the early eighteenth century the Chinese have laid claim to the area, initially through the Qing Dynasty, and in 1950, the Communist Chinese invaded in order to "liberate" Tibet. Following a period of relative peace, symbols of Tibetan Buddhism and culture came under attack by the Chinese, there was a military crackdown, and the Dalai Lama fled into exile in India in 1959. With the stated intent of bringing stability and modernity, China tightened its control and carried out a full assault on Tibetan culture by many of the means we have discussed in other cases, while encouraging mass immigration by Han Chinese, maintaining a robust military presence, and closing the territory to outsiders. Tibetans have resisted the imposition of the Chinese language in public life and education, by means of protests that have been brutally suppressed, as well as self-immolation by Buddhist monks and others, a practice the Chinese have banned as illegal. Since 2008, there has been a surge in resistance to Chinese rule.

12 Minorities of Migration

This chapter focuses on migrant minority language conflicts, which are those that arise when an ethnolinguistic group (or individuals from that group) moves into a territory dominated by a linguistically distinct population. The migrant minority cases presented in full detail in this chapter are those of the Roma in Europe, Koreans in Japan, and Puerto Ricans in the United States. In addition, at the end of the chapter, the reader will find (for further exploration) synopses of the following immigrant communities: Russians in Israel, Turks in Germany, and Chinese in Vancouver.

Roma in Europe

This section of the chapter addresses the status of the Roma people as our first and central case of "minorities of migration." We feature the Roma here, in part because they are immigrants of the longest standing, having entered Europe some 900 years ago, and are still being treated as immigrants in many countries where they reside even today. The Roma are, however, somewhat different (and more disadvantaged) than most other immigrant groups, in that they are non-territorial. That is, most modern immigrant groups come from somewhere else, and have at least an idealized connection with a foreign land (if not an actual one). For the Roma, whatever connection they may have had with their place of origin is long forgotten, and there is no "native land" to call home to (even in their imagination). They are, thus, permanent immigrants wherever they go, a nation set adrift in the world with nowhere to sail back to.

Historical and Linguistic Background

The Roma people go by several different names across Europe, calling themselves *Roma* or *Romani* in Eastern Europe, *Kale* ("black") in Scandinavia and Spain, *Sinti* in Germany and northern Italy, *Manush* in France and Belgium, and *Romanichal* in England. Confusing things further, they are referred to by others as *Dom* (in reference to their origins), *Gypsies/ Gipsies* (a derogatory name for the group in English-speaking countries),

Travelers (in reference to their traditionally nomadic life-style), *Gitano* (in Spain), and *Zigeuner* (in Germany, with variants of this term across Europe). In this chapter, we will use the term *Roma* to refer to the people themselves and *Romani* to refer to their language and culture.

That the Roma are known by so many different names is reflective of their origins, as well as their historical tribulations and current plight, for the Roma can be said to be the last major ethnic group to make their way into Europe in premodern times. Their arrival in Europe (beginning in the twelfth century) followed by at least 200 years the arrival of the Hungarians (the last people to establish an ethnically based national territory in Europe). Unlike the Hungarians, though, they arrived into Europe as wanderers and migrant refugees from other parts, rather than as a tribal group fighting for territorial possessions.

The origins of the Roma have, for centuries, been somewhat shrouded in mystery and colored by improbable folklore and legends. For instance, the name *Gypsy* itself refers to a belief that the Roma people originally came from Egypt (supposedly, on some accounts, having been expelled from there for having sheltered the baby Jesus).[1]

Their actual origins were determined in the early twentieth century to have been somewhere in India, through comparative linguistic studies showing that their language is most closely related to Indo-Aryan.[2] More recently, these conclusions have been validated and sharpened by genetic research. The genetic research – a Y-chromosome study that matched European male Roma to groups of low-caste Dalits (untouchables) from northwestern India – confirmed a hypothesis that the Roma people's origins lie in the northwestern parts of India.[3]

The largest cohort of Roma is hypothesized to have entered the Punjab region of present-day Pakistan between 1001 and 1026 to fight on behalf of Hindu rulers against incursions of the Islamic Ghaznavid dynasty.[4] Their motivation for doing so may have been a promise of promotion in caste (having at that time been associated with the Dalit caste, i.e. "untouchables"). The Ghaznavid dynasty is known to have defeated its Hindu adversaries in these battles, and to have carried off many thousands of captives to the seat of their empire in what is present-day Iran. In this way, it is theorized, the Roma entered Persia, and then moved further westward into the domains of the Byzantine Empire in Anatolia.

During their sojourn in the Byzantine Empire, during the eleventh through thirteenth centuries, the Romani language was greatly influenced by Byzantine Greek, borrowing extensively from the Greek lexicon as well as absorbing features of Greek phonology and syntax. The list of words for numerals in

[1] Fraser 1992.   [2] Turner 1926.   [3] Mendizabal et al. 2012.   [4] Hancock 2007b.

Table 12.1 *Numerals in Romani, Hindi, Persian, and Greek*[a]

	Romani	Hindi	Persian	Greek
1	ekh, jekh	**ek**	yak, yek	*ena*
2	duj	**do**	**du, do**	*dio*
3	trin	**tīn**	se	*tria*
4	štar	**cār**	čahār	*tessera*
5	pandž	pāñc	**pandž**	*pente*
6	šov	che	**šaš, šeš**	*eksi*
7	ifta	sāt	haft	***efta***
8	oxto	āṭh	hašt	***okto***
9	inja	nau	nuh, noh	***enia***
10	deš	**das**	dah	*deka*
20	biš	**bīs**	bist	*eikosi*
100	šel	**sau**	sad	*ekato*

[a] Based in part on Hancock 2007b.

Table 12.1 illustrates Romani's Indo-Aryan origins, as well as Persian and Greek influence on the language.

Migration throughout Europe and Outsider Status

In subsequent centuries and for a variety of reasons (e.g. in response to the devastations of the Black Death in the fourteenth century and the defeat of the Byzantine Empire in the fifteenth century), the Roma dispersed throughout central, western, and northern Europe.

In the Roma's wanderings, depicted in Figure 12.1, their language evolved into many very different dialects, with some of these dialects mixing heavily with other European languages and sometime disappearing altogether. The diffusion of dialects is so extreme, that it is difficult in some ways to characterize any single Romani language to which any of these dialects can be considered heteronomous.[5] The reasons for the "confusion" of Romani dialects are several (and we will explore these below), but regardless of why it is the case, the fact that the "language" is in such disarray has important ramifications for the linguistic fortunes and rights of the Roma people.

As we noted above, the Roma people did not arrive in Europe until sometime in the eleventh or twelfth century, settling first in areas under Byzantine rule – most notably in the Balkans. Unlike other groups that entered Europe earlier in its history (e.g. Hungarians, Bulgars, Turks, etc.), the Roma did not arrive as

---

[5] *Heteronomy* is the state of a dialect belonging to a larger language category. For example, Southern American English is heteronomous to American English, Yorkshire English is heteronomous to British English, and Singaporean English is heteronomous to neither of these.

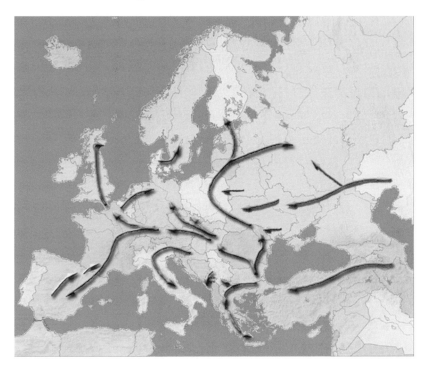

Figure 12.1 Migrations of the Roma people

a conquering people, displacing others from their lands. Rather, they arrived as migrants, and perhaps refugees, from lands further east, and from the fourteenth century on they dispersed widely across the European continent.

Today, there are Roma living in every European country, with the largest numbers of them residing in the eastern Mediterranean, the Balkans, Spain and France. The size of the wheel in Figure 12.2 represents absolute population numbers, and the darker shades on the map represent higher proportions in the overall population.

The Roma were, everywhere they went, religiously, ethnically, racially, and linguistically quite distinct from their host populations, and having no established territorial security, government, or other civic structures with which to protect themselves, they were persecuted and victimized pretty much everywhere they went. They brought no distinct, organized religion with them to Europe and, apart from a few Hindu traditions, appeared to have no religion. This, of course, did not endear them in any way to Christian Europeans, or bring them any favor or mercy. They were racially distinct from Europeans as

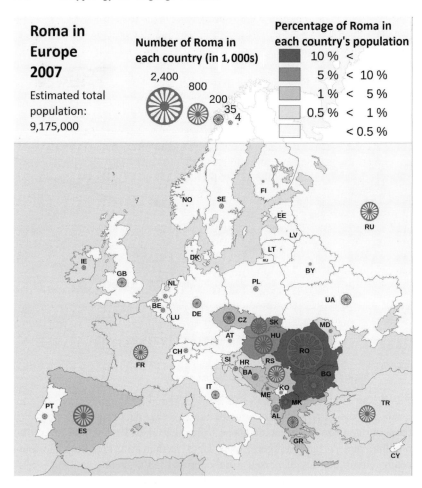

Figure 12.2 Distribution of Roma throughout Europe

well, more closely resembling (if anything) the Turkic and Mongol peoples who periodically invaded Europe in these times. So, if Roma looked like anything at all, they looked like an enemy.

Almost from their first entrance into Europe, the Roma were treated as second-class people (and less). In the Balkans, the Roma were enslaved by the Vlachs/Romanians in what is present-day Romania and Moldova, from the middle of the fourteenth century right up until the beginning of the nineteenth century. The invasion of the Balkans by the Ottoman Turks in the fifteenth century resulted in many Roma being forced to flee into central and northern

Europe. But in so doing, they were (mistakenly) taken to be Turks (or affiliated with them), and were thus persecuted as hostile and unwelcome strangers. Wherever they went (Spain, Germany, France, Holland, etc.), the most frequent response to them was banishment.

In describing the Roma people's circumstances, Friedman (2005) characterizes them as stateless, non-territorial, and lacking in any native literary tradition. In this way, their situation has consistently been worse than the Armenians in Cyprus, who have no territory in Cyprus but who have a state elsewhere (i.e. Armenia, an independent republic in the Caucasus Mountains), worse than the Kurds, who are stateless (for the moment) but who occupy a distinct territory, and worse than Yiddish-speaking or Ladino-speaking Jews, who were (until the last century) stateless and non-territorial, but who did have literary traditions and institutions.

The fate of Roma in some ways paralleled that of the Jews. Drawing support from many non-Nazi Germans who harbored social prejudice toward Roma, the Nazis judged Roma to be "racially inferior." Under the Nazi regime, German authorities subjected Roma to arbitrary internment, forced labor, and mass murder. While exact figures or percentages cannot be ascertained, historians estimate that the Germans and their allies killed around 25 percent of all European Roma. Of slightly less than 1 million Roma believed to have been living in Europe before the war, the Germans and their Axis partners killed up to 220,000.

Migration and Dialect Formation

In some three and a half centuries following their migration out of the Balkan region (between the late fourteenth and the early eighteenth centuries), Roma groups in their many regions developed a "proliferation" of dialects. This vast number of dialects is thought to have arisen at least in part from "the antisocial pressures from the host societies that continue to divide the Romani-speaking populations."[6] Varieties of the Romani language were influenced by the dominant language everywhere they went, with Turkish, Romanian, Hungarian, German, and various Slavonic languages exerting the greatest influence, collectively.[7]

Romani dialects fall into two or three major groups: Balkan dialects (spoken in Greece and regions surrounding the Black Sea), Vlax (i.e. Wallach) dialects (developed in the region where the Roma suffered four centuries of enslavement by the Romanian/Wallachian people), and Northern (NE and NW) dialects (which evolved after the Roma migrated out of the Balkans into central and western Europe).

---

[6] Hancock 2007a.   [7] Matras 2015.

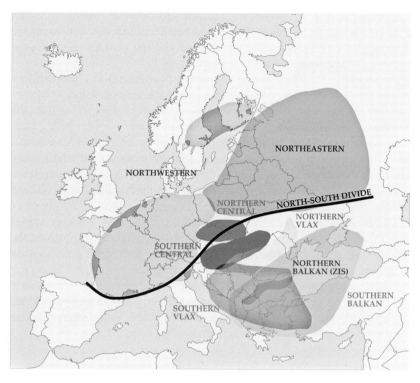

Figure 12.3 Dialects of the Romani language

As a result of the extensive movement throughout Europe (forced and otherwise) of the Roma people, and given the lack of a territorial homeland or a written/liturgical tradition, many Roma groups have given up the Romani language. This includes some Traveller communities (e.g. English Romanichals, Welsh Kaale, and Swedish Tattare), along with Spanish and Portuguese Gitanos. These groups were descended from Romani-speaking populations, but "due to various historical circumstances (such as bans on the use of their language, or intermarriage with indigenous groups) gave up their language and shifted to that of the surrounding majority population."[8] Among such groups, what typically remains of their use of Romani is a specialized and limited lexicon of some 500 (insider) Romani words which are used when speaking their adopted language among themselves. Figure 12.3 shows the several Romani dialect regions, as well as the major north–south dialect divide (black line on the map).

[8] Matras 2005.

And even in areas where the Roma form a large segment of the population, relatively few speak it. For example, in Romania, which counts 3.3 percent of its population as Roma (621,000, which is one-quarter as many as counted in Figure 12.2), only 40 percent of these (244,000) are native speakers of Romani (Institutul Naţional de Statistică 2011). In Macedonia, where 11 percent of its citizens are Roma (250,000), only 15 percent (38,000) speak Romani.[9]

Roma People and Human/Language Rights Violations

Roma have historically been treated, throughout Europe, as unwelcome strangers. Being different from Europeans in every imaginable way (ethnically, religiously, culturally, racially, and linguistically) does not help. Unlike other stateless European minorities, such as the Basques (who are an indigenous people living in the northeastern corner of Spain and the southwestern corner of France), the Roma have no contiguous territorial base of settlement. Another consequence of their being non-territorial (in combination with their having no literary traditions) is that there is no monolithic (i.e. standard or majority) Romani language that one might point to as deserving of recognition. This leaves the Roma in each country of residence with their own local variety of Roma, or (as is the case with the English and Spanish Roma groups) no variety at all.

Recall as well (from Chapter 9) that the Universal Declaration of Language Rights (unenforceable though it is) distinguishes indigenous *language communities* from *language groups*, which may be comprised of immigrants, refugees and others, defining a language group as "any group of persons sharing the same language which is established in the territorial space of another language community but which does not possess historical antecedents equivalent to those of that community." By this definition, even given their many centuries of residence in countries across Europe, the non-territorial Roma form a language group (or a collection of language groups), rather than a language community. So, the Roma are at a disadvantage in comparison to nearly every other linguistic minority in Europe.

This situation leads some, who are in positions of responsibility in this matter, to suggest that "The Roma have no language" (said by the director of a Czech NGO).[10] What is meant, in this instance, is that the Roma are perceived (somewhat accurately) to have lost their own ethnolect and that they are also not sufficiently competent/fluent in the national language of the countries in which they reside. Of course, if one believes that the Roma don't have a language to which language rights need be applied, then there is no language rights issue to contend with. Attitudes such as this are pervasive throughout

---

[9] Friedman 2005.   [10] New 2014: 166–168.

Europe. In Bulgaria, in 2006 the National Agency for the Accreditation of University programs closed the only university program in the country for the training of teachers who could teach Romani in the classroom. The reason given was that the "Romani language does not exist."[11]

Of course, even if one does recognize that the Roma have their own ethnolect/language, one might still determine that there is no point in preserving it and teaching it to children. This is the position taken by some Bulgarian education officials, as reported by an observer of an international consortium on the "Decade of Roma Inclusion 2005–2015" (see further below).[12] He relates a conversation with a Romani language expert from the Bulgarian Ministry of Education, who stated that integration [into Bulgarian society] is the "the most important thing for the Roma children," and that "if they study Romani it will create obstacles for their integration."

Decade of Roma Inclusion 2005–2015

Purportedly for the purpose of eliminating discrimination against Roma and closing the unacceptable gaps between Roma and the rest of society, a "Decade of Roma Inclusion 2005–2015" (www.romadecade.org) was initiated by a dozen (mostly Eastern) European governments. The participant countries were: Albania, Bosnia and Herzegovina, Bulgaria, Croatia, the Czech Republic, Hungary, Macedonia, Montenegro, Romania, Serbia, Slovakia and Spain. The priority areas of focus identified by this international consortium were: education, employment, health, and housing. The stated goals of this effort were "to eliminate discrimination against Roma and close the unacceptable gaps between Roma and the rest of society." However, even in this otherwise beneficent context, barriers to Romani language were still maintained.[13] It is rather clear from the statements of participant country officials, as well as from some of their actions, that a large part of the effort to eliminate discrimination involved efforts to assimilate the Roma minority in their host countries, more than to protect and end discrimination against Roma culture and language. In many respects, these efforts bear an uncomfortable similarity to historical efforts on the part of many nations (e.g. the United States vis-à-vis American Indians, and Japan vis-à-vis the Ainu) to assimilate their indigenous minorities by assimilating them to the national majority (see Chapter 11).

These regrettable attitudes toward the Roma and the unwillingness of European nations to address or accommodate their linguistic rights continue to have negative repercussions on their fortunes and welfare throughout Europe. Roma children are often segregated into special classes because they

---

[11] Kyuchukov 2009: slide no. 8.   [12] Kyuchukov 2009.   [13] Kyuchukov 2009.

are not sufficiently proficient in the language of instruction of the country in which they live. At the same time, there is little interest on the part of their host countries (as the comments above show) in providing them with education in their own language. This leads to the majority of Roma students leaving school early, without completing their education, which only reinforces their continued social and economic exclusion from the societies in which they live. All this puts "Roma children in a double bind when it comes to gaining an education and fashioning a life they have reason to value."[14] For these and other reasons, the Decade of Roma Inclusion had less than lustrous results for the intended beneficiaries, the Roma themselves.

Romani: Creating a Language out of Dialects

As was noted previously, there is a wide profusion of dialects throughout the Roma world and no recognized standard which might be used internationally as a vehicle for literacy and a tool for education. This situation has a number of negative ramifications, the most salient among them being that the large number of differing Romani dialects stands as a major obstacle to the attainment of political and cultural unity among the widely scattered Roma groups throughout the world. The resulting lack of communication among the Roma, on account of their having no common vernacular, impedes reunification and hinders efforts made to improve their status across Europe. This was recognized as far back as 1992 in the European Charter for Regional or Minority Languages, and elaborated in 2000 by a European Committee of Ministers that declared "in countries where the Romani language is spoken, opportunities to learn in the mother tongue should be offered at school to Roma/Gypsy children."[15]

Given these circumstances, it goes without saying that the Roma would be helped immeasurably if they were able to establish a common dialect. However, the creation of such a standard variety faces several obstacles and might not solve the problem at hand:[16]

- No single dialect spoken anywhere is so close to the common protoform spoken upon arrival in Europe that it may be adopted with no modification.
- The propagation of such a standard would be very unevenly achieved. Sedentary, literate Roma (i.e. those in Eastern Europe) are better positioned to acquire a standardized dialect than illiterate and nomadic Roma elsewhere.

The adoption of an "international standard" by all Roma is unlikely, and it would lead to a "linguistic elite" of only those who have learned to use it. Hancock himself proposes a means by which such a standard might be brought about. His well-articulated prescription for the creation of a standard Romani

[14] New 2014.   [15] Matras 2005.   [16] Hancock 2007a.

follows the observed and accepted protocols for the establishment of any standard variety: selection, elaboration, codification, and restriction:

- Selection of Romani dialects from the most widespread or numerically most important branches: Vlax (such as Kalderaš), Balkan (such as Erli), Central (such as Bašaldo), and Northern (such as Sinti).
- Removal of non-Romani elements, followed by codification of important features of each, and standardization of the lexicon.

In looking for positive signs of progress in the Roma world, one might point to the positive and beneficial effects that can accrue simply by having Romani gain official recognition in a country where Roma live. Recall that the Roma in the Republic of Macedonia constitute about 11 percent of the total population of the country (about 250,000 out of ~2 million), but that only some 1/6 of these (~40,000) are counted as Romani speakers.

Nevertheless, Romani is recognized as an official minority language in Macedonia's constitution, and this has led to its use in the public sphere (in radio broadcasts and the trilingual newspaper *Roma Times* from 2001). Thus, the prospects for the natural development of a local Romani language in Macedonia, out of a non-territorial language with no literary tradition, are greatly enhanced as a result of official recognition and government sanction.[17]

Koreans in Japan

Another immigrant minority case worth examining, one that emerged some ninety years ago rather than 900, is that of Koreans living in Japan. Unlike the Roma, there are no questions regarding their origin, there are no questions about the nature of their language or culture (which is in no danger of disappearing), and they are not very far from their homeland (Korea is separated from Japan by a mere 125 miles of the Japan Sea). As is not infrequently the case, the migration of Koreans to Japan is a direct consequence of Japanese imperialism and conquest in the late nineteenth and early twentieth centuries. In this section, we will examine the history of this migrant minority and analyze the role that language rights issues have played in diminishing their fortunes in their adopted home.

Historical Background

Contact between the Korean peninsula and the Japan archipelago most likely dates back several thousand years. The earliest verifiable contact would have been some 2,400 years ago when agrarian Yayoi people crossed from Korea, bringing with them rice cultivation. Several hundred years later, in the sixth

---

[17] Friedman 2005.

century CE, the Korean peninsula served as the conduit for the introduction of Buddhism into Japan. From a linguistic perspective, this contact brought Chinese Buddhist texts and the introduction of the Chinese orthographic system to Japan.

A thousand or so years later, in 1592 and 1597, Japan (under the late sixteenth-century leadership of the unifying Imperial Regent Toyotomi Hideyoshi) attempted to invade and subjugate Korea. While the invasions ultimately failed, in great measure on account of the military intervention of the Chinese Ming Empire, Japan and Korea returned to a normal regime of trade for the next two centuries. However, Hideyoshi's invasions – with the explicit aim of extending Japanese military supremacy far out beyond the archipelago – presaged developments three centuries later.

It was in the latter half of the nineteenth century that Japan (having been forced by the United States to open itself up to trade in 1854 and taking its cues from European imperial powers) once again began to assert itself beyond the traditional four main islands. During this period, Japan consolidated its control over Hokkaido and the Ainu aboriginals (see Chapter 11), and sought complete control over the Ryūkyū Islands to the south (see Chapter 14). Also around this same time (in 1876), Japan took advantage of some Korean internal instability, and forced an unequal trading treaty (the Japan–Korea Treaty of Amity) upon the Korean Empire.

Consolidation of control in the north (Hokkaido) and the south (Ryūkyū Islands) did much to embolden Japan in its relations with its near neighbors. The 1880s saw increasing tensions between Japan and the Chinese Qing Empire regarding their respective influence over Korea. The Chinese Empire having been weakened economically and militarily by European colonial powers, it was a much less formidable opponent than it would have been a century earlier, and Japan saw little reason to fear the Chinese. These tensions, inflamed by several diplomatic and military confrontations, ulti- mately led to the Sino-Japanese War (1894–1895), in which Japan utterly defeated the more numerous but less well equipped or trained Chinese forces. The outcome of the war put Japan in control of Taiwan, and eliminated any remaining Chinese influence over Korea (leaving Japan with more or less complete military and economic power over the peninsula).

With the elimination of Chinese sea power, the Russian Empire, seeking to fill this vacuum and enlarge its influence in eastern Asia (specifically in Manchuria, Korea, and northeastern China), came into direct conflict with Japan. Several years of unfruitful negotiations and maneuvering followed, until Japan (fearing a massive Russian military build-up in Manchuria) struck the first blow and initiated hostilities by attacking the Russian fleet at Port Arthur (1904). Russia did not take its Asian military opponent seriously, and by underestimating the Japanese contributed to their own defeat. In the treaty that

Figure 12.4 The Japanese Empire following the Russo-Japanese War

ended the Russo-Japanese War (1904–1905), Russia ceded to Japan the southern half of Sakhalin Island (north of Hokkaido), evacuated its forces from
Manchuria, and recognized Korea as falling within Japan's official "sphere of
influence." This last outcome set the stage for the annexation of Korea into the
Japanese Empire in 1910, shown in Figure 12.4.

The incorporation of Korea into the Japanese Empire at the beginning of the
twentieth century led, inevitably, to the transmission of Japanese culture and
language to Korea and to the movement of population between the two (with
Japanese military, administrators and teachers going in one direction, and
Korean laborers going in the other). On the Korean side of the Japan Sea,
schools were established to teach "Japanese language and culture, and to instill
loyalty to the Japanese emperor."[18] This intensified in the 1930s in the run-up to
World War II, with policies designed to instill the unity of Korea and Japan
(*naissen ittai*), declarations of loyalty to the emperor, and the adoption of
Japanese names.

Koreans migrated in great numbers to Japan, to work in factories, construction, and mining. By the start of World War II, there were some 700,000
Japanese living in Korea and about 1.2 million Koreans living in Japan.
By the end of the war, due in part to forced conscription of Korean laborers
to help the war effort, the Korean population of Japan had mushroomed to over
2 million out of a total population of 72 million (about 3 percent). Over two-
thirds of this number (i.e. over 1.5 million) returned to Korea immediately after
the end of the war, leaving about 600,000 Koreans in Japan by 1948. This
number has increased over the past 50–60 years to about 850,000 (with many
newly arrived Korean immigrants coming in the 1980s and 1990s). Most
Korean residents of Japan live in the Kansai area (Osaka, Kyoto, and Hyōgo
Prefectures) and the Tokyo metropolitan areas such as Tokyo and Kanagawa
Prefectures.

Following World War II, the General Headquarters of the Supreme
Commander for the Allied Powers (GHQ) deemed as "Japanese nationals"
any Koreans who refused to be repatriated to Korea, although for the Japanese,
these individuals were considered "resident aliens" and not accepted as having
the right to Japanese nationality.

The end of World War II brought with it a change of status for Korea as well.
The Russians (now Soviets) declared war on Japan five days before the
Japanese announced their surrender to the Allies on August 15, 1945. This
enabled them to get some payback from the Japanese for their defeat forty years
prior, as the Red Army marched into Japanese-occupied Korea and took
possession of the northern half of the peninsula (down to the thirty-eighth
parallel). With the Japanese surrendering the southern half of the Korean

---

[18] Ishikida 2005: 50.

peninsula directly to the United States, Korea was effectively split into two post-war occupation zones, which ultimately transitioned in 1948 into the contemporary states of North (Democratic People's Republic of) Korea and South (Republic of) Korea.[19]

The surrender of Japan, the division of Korea, and the 1950–1953 Korean War greatly complicated the situation for the Korean residents of Japan. In 1952, with the enforcement of the San Francisco Peace Treaty (in which Japan formally renounced any claims to Korea), Koreans "who came to reside in Japan for various reasons during 36 years (1910–1945) of Japan's so-called rule over Korea" lost their Japanese nationality, and remained in Japan with the status of "Special Permanent Resident."[20] These Korean permanent residents, having been stripped of their citizenship, were also not well accepted or welcomed in a shrunken, post-imperial Japan, either. Although most of them had their origins in the southern parts of the Korean peninsula, a great number of them strongly identified with the socialist vision of the North Korean republic, since they were largely working-class, poor, uneducated, and under-privileged economically and socially. With the Korean War having turned the North into a "pariah" state, the Korean permanent residents of Japan found themselves a suspect population in the reviving capitalist society of American-allied and American-protected Japan.

Language Rights Issues

One of the most difficult issues for Koreans in Japan has been, and remains, the preservation of their language and culture. Because the two largest Korean associations in Japan (the Chōren and the Minsei) were communist-dominated (for reasons described above), they were dissolved in 1949 upon the outbreak of the Korean conflict, and this led to cultural and educational deficits that would be difficult to overcome. Up until the outbreak of hostilities in Korea, these two associations had established nearly 600 elementary schools, six middle schools, ten "youth schools," and two vocational schools, serving over 50,000 students. The dissolution of the supporting Korean associations, coupled with an order from the GHQ that the Korean language could only be taught in extracurricular classes, resulted in a sharp fall in the number of Korean children receiving any ethnic or Korean-language education. Only

---

[19] A short-lived People's Republic of Korea was established in September 1945 and lasted until January 1946. This independent entity was quickly suppressed in the South by the Americans, but its institutions were continued in the North in some fashion until the end of Russian occupation.

[20] Ministry of Foreign Affairs of Japan. 1999. "International Convention on the Elimination of All Forms of Racial Discrimination (First and Second Report)" (www.mofa.go.jp/policy/human/race_rep1/)

20,000 continued their ethnic and language training in private Korean schools, while some 40,000 transferred to Japanese schools or dropped out.[21]

The 1950–1960s saw a temporary recovery in the area of Korean ethnic and language education, with the establishment of the Chongryun (the General Association of Korean Residents in Japan), affiliated with North Korea. By 1966, "there were more than 140 schools with 14 branch schools, 30 ethnic classes, 208 afternoon and night classes, with a total of 40,000 students."[22] Over the next forty years though, the number of students in these schools declined (by 2003) to just over 11,000, with the decreasing enrollments putting further pressure on the schools (as they are private and self-supporting).

One of the ongoing problems with Korean-heritage education concerns the official Ministry of Education policies that impede it. These ethnic schools do not have official status. Japanese educational policy provides free public education, but only if the medium of instruction is Japanese. This means, among other things, that "students from Korean national schools are prevented from receiving the same treatment as those from Japanese schools in terms of candidacy for university entrance examinations; and Korean schools do not benefit from Government subsidies and tax exemptions."[23] Since Korean language and culture are not taught in public schools, and since Korean-heritage schools must therefore be private, there are strong economic and educational disincentives for ethnic Koreans to attend such schools. This had led, naturally, to a decline in enrollments in these schools, and to a gradual loss of ethnic identity, cultural knowledge, and linguistic aptitude among younger Korean-Japanese. It is noted that the overwhelming majority of ethnically Korean youth use Japanese names "rather than their given Korean ones" in order to avoid being labeled as Korean.[24]

There is, however, some indication that things are in fact changing for the better. Beginning in 2004, the Japanese Ministry of Education began to allow colleges and universities to independently assess the academic credentials of their applicants and, in 2005, revised the examination that high school students take to enter college, such that graduates from Korean ethnic schools now have the same status vis-à-vis the exam as do graduates of Japanese public high schools. It is also the case that Japanese youth sports associations have begun to allow Korean ethnic schools to participate in intermural sports competitions. Whether this will change the trend, or whether it is too little, too late, remains to be seen. But it is clear that these changes are in the right direction.

[21] Lee 1999: 139–145, as cited in Ishikida 2005.   [22] Ishikida 2005; Lee 1999: 150.
[23] Hatori 2005: 48.   [24] Hatori 2005; Ishikida 2005.

Conclusion

Problems affecting Korean residents of Japan, including the domain of language and language rights, are effectively a subset of the problems affecting any non-native ethnic group in Japan. As a 2008 US Department of State report states:

Despite legal safeguards against discrimination, the country's large populations of Korean, Chinese, Brazilian, and Filipino permanent residents – many of whom were born, raised, and educated in Japan – were subject to various forms of deeply entrenched societal discrimination, including restricted access to housing, education, and employment opportunities.[25]

That Korean residents of Japan have these problems, after over 100 years of residence, is quite remarkable, although not unthinkable.

The Korean case, involving what is clearly acknowledged to be a distinct national group, is somewhat different from these other two. Complete eradication and absorption is not an option (as with the Ainu), since the Korean nation remains a distinct national entity, irrespective of the conditions of Koreans in Japan proper. Also, while it might have once been imaginable during Japan's imperialistic heyday, the idea that Koreans would be absorbed into Japan, and their language and culture replaced by Japanese, ceased to be a possibility after 1945. They are acknowledged, but also deemed to be "alien" and kept from positions of power and influence through the diminution of, and constraints upon, their language and culture.

Puerto Ricans in the United States

The treatment of Korean residents of Japan by the Japanese government and by Japanese society at large might seem unfair and uncharacteristic of a modern nation-state. However, the Korean experience in Japan has uncomfortable parallels with that of Hispanic citizens of the United States, and when examined closely, the similarities are undeniable. The closest case for comparison is that of Puerto Ricans.

Just as the Japanese occupation of Korea emanated from its expansionist wars with China and Russian, the American acquisition of Puerto Rico came as the result of the 1898 war between the United States and Spain, after which the United States occupied the former Spanish possessions of Cuba (until 1902), the Philippines (until 1946), Guam (still), and Puerto Rico (still). The colonial expansion of the United States into the Caribbean and the Pacific was contemporaneous with Japan's expansionism in East Asia (at the time, one might say that "everyone was doing it"). Unlike Korea, Puerto Rico remains

---

[25] United States State Department 2008.

a US territory to this day, but much like the Korean residents of Japan, Puerto Rican Americans (who are in fact US citizens) are also subject to "various forms of deeply entrenched societal discrimination, including restricted access to housing, education, and employment opportunities."[26]

Much of this discrimination, like that against Koreans in Japan, finds its expression in resistance to culture and obstacles to the use of language. Also, while there are many areas in which Puerto Rican citizens have full access to Spanish language services, their need for such services is still marked as an immigrant problem, even though they are clearly not immigrants in any sense of the term. We will, here below, take a brief look at the historical and linguistic background of this conflict situation, and its current status.

Historical and Linguistic Background

As noted above, the island of Puerto Rico (shown on the map in Figure 12.5) became a territorial possession of the United States as a consequence of the 1898 Spanish–American War, after over 400 years of being a Spanish colony (from 1493). In the December 1898 "Treaty of Peace Between the United States and Spain," Spain relinquished sovereignty over the island of Cuba, but ceded to the United States the colonies of Guam, Philippines, and Puerto Rico.[27] Unlike Puerto Rico, Cuba had been actively engaged in a military struggle for independence from Spain since 1895, and the Spanish relinquishing sovereignty after the war set the stage for Cuban independence in 1902, following a four-year US military occupation.[28] In Puerto Rico's case, the island's incipient independence movement was far less robust or organized, and cession to the United States converted its status to that of a US territory (as it remained until 1952).

In 1917, the US Congress passed a law (the Jones Act) extending US citizenship to all the native residents of the island, creating an elected bicameral legislature (with the island's governor appointed by the US President), and exempting the islands' residents from taxation.[29] In 1950, another law was enacted (Public Law 81–600)[30] which allowed Puerto Rican citizens to elect their own governor and to write their own constitution. This constitution, ratified in 1952, established the island as a "commonwealth" or "Estado Libre Asociado" (Free Associated State).[31] This commonwealth status is in fact not much different from that of a territory, leaving the island neither independent nor a state. One of the odd consequences of Puerto Rico's

---

[26] United States State Department 2008.   [27] Lillian Goldman Law Library 2008.
[28] Note that the Cuban constitution, adopted at independence, allowed the United States to intervene in Cuban financial affairs and foreign relations. This provision precipitated two additional occupations of Cuba by the United States (in 1906–1909 and again in 1917–1922).
[29] United States Congress 1917.   [30] United States Congress 1950.
[31] Constitution of the Commonwealth of Puerto Rico 1952.

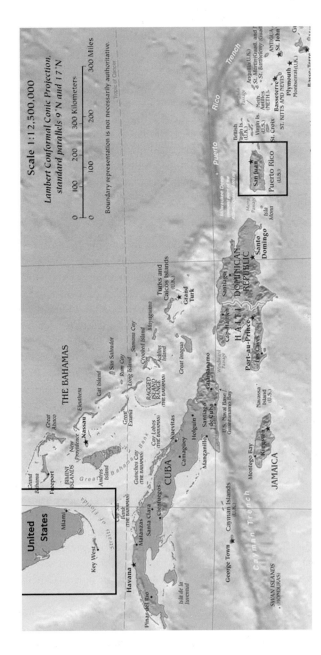

Figure 12.5 Puerto Rico in relation to the United States

commonwealth status is that citizen residents of the island cannot vote in federal elections. This includes native Puerto Ricans, as well as any US citizen from the mainland who takes up residence there. On the other hand, Puerto Ricans who move to the US mainland, being US citizens, can indeed vote in federal elections.

The (continuing) "in-between" status of Puerto Rico (being neither independent nor one of the US states) has long been a divisive issue, both for Puerto Ricans themselves and for the rest of the United States, and it is clear that language plays a role in the perseveration of this matter. Puerto Rico, having been a colony of Spain for 400 years before becoming a US territory, was and remains an island where 95 percent of the population speaks Spanish. Only 20 percent of the population speaks English. Official business of the courts is conducted in Spanish, as is public school instruction and most commerce.

Language has been a contentious issue on the island since 1902, when a Language Law declared both Spanish and English to be "official languages" of the island. At the same time, pressure to impose English-language culture on the island began early in the first third of the twentieth century (1900–1930). US authorities, with the aim of "Americanizing" the island, applied pressure to transition to English-language instruction in public schools, coupled with "intense teaching of American history." Alongside this were efforts to celebrate American holidays, encouraging students to use English outside the classroom, and naming buildings after American heroes. The intensity of the Americanization efforts was typified by the US Education Commissioner in Puerto Rico, in 1921, referring to the Puerto Rican flag as an "enemy flag." These American efforts are quite similar to those of Japan in the Ryūkyūan Islands (as will be discussed in Chapter 14).[32]

These efforts at cultural and linguistic "imperialism" were resisted, effectively, by the Puerto Rican population. In 1913, Puerto Rican legislators (unsuccessfully) attempted to make Spanish the required language of instruction in public schools. This was attempted again in 1933, by the Puerto Rican Teachers' Association, and in 1947, by the Puerto Rican legislature. In each of these instances, the efforts were vetoed by the US-appointed governor or the US president. Despite these failures to mandate Spanish language instruction, Spanish has nonetheless remained the de facto medium of public school instruction throughout Puerto Rico.[33]

Various factors have, for over a century, led both to US resistance to allowing Puerto Rico to become independent and to limited Puerto Rican enthusiasm for it. The United States has seen the island both as a strategic asset for projecting power in the Caribbean, as well as a means of exerting economic influence in the area. For the Puerto Ricans, US federal subsidies and exemption from

---

[32] Muniz-Arguelles 1988.   [33] Muniz-Arguelles 1988.

taxation have created a situation wherein independence would present a bitter economic pill to swallow, leaving the island on an economic plane with Cuba and the Dominican Republic. In various status referenda over some fifty years, the number of Puerto Ricans voting for independence has never exceeded 6 percent of the electorate.

The remaining two options, continuation as a commonwealth or joining the United States as a fifty-first state, have typically split the vote, with a slight preference for the former. One of the major impediments to Puerto Rico's becoming a US state has been, and remains, the linguistic divide. And it is not an exaggeration to say that discomfort with that prospect has emanated from both the American and Puerto Rican sides of the issue. As we noted above, pressure from US authorities to "Americanize" the island (i.e. instill loyalty to the United States and turn the island into an English-speaking territory) lasted for a very long time, and many Puerto Ricans still fear the prospect of losing the Spanish-language character and culture of the island, if it were to become a state. On the American side of the divide, many in the United States are uncomfortable with the prospect of, and the problems inherent in, admitting a monolingual Spanish-speaking state to the Union. For some, the prospect of admitting a state whose official and functional language is not English would endanger English as the "national" language of the United States, and force it to at once become a de facto bilingual country.[34] It would be fair to say that, if Puerto Rico were an English-speaking territory (or commonwealth) of the United States, it would long ago have been admitted to the Union as a state.

These attitudes are soon to be tested, first by the Puerto Rican electorate and soon after by the US government. In 2012, the three-choice ballot, specifying (i) commonwealth status quo, (ii) independence, or (ii) statehood – none of which had ever achieved a majority of the vote – was replaced with a two-step voting process. In the first part of this, voters rejected their current status as a US commonwealth by a 54 to 46 percent margin, and then in a separate question, 61 percent chose statehood as the alternative, compared with 33 percent for the semi-autonomous "sovereign free association" and 6 percent for outright independence.[35] In June 2017, a fifth congressionally mandated referendum was held, offering only two options: "Statehood" and "Independence/ Free Association." It was the first referendum not to offer the choice of "Commonwealth." As expected, the "Statehood" option carried the day, with 97 percent of the voters choosing statehood over independence. However, voter participation was astoundingly low, with only 23 percent of registered voters going to the polls. Whether a landslide vote by a small minority of the island's voters is taken to be a reliable mandate will depend on the US Congress, when it

[34] U.S. English 2016.   [35] Castillo 2012.

takes up the issue of whether the United States is prepared to admit a Spanish-speaking state into the Union.

Puerto Ricans as "Immigrants" in the US Mainland

As the scare quotes in the section title suggest, Puerto Rican islanders living on the US mainland are not immigrants, any more than are New Yorkers living in California or Alaska. From 1917 on, Puerto Ricans have had US citizenship, unlike Hispanics immigrants from Cuba or Mexico, and can come to New York (or elsewhere) freely and legally by simply buying passage on a boat or a domestic flight. In this respect, the migration of Puerto Ricans to the continental United States (largely for economic reasons) is quite comparable to the movement of Koreans to Japan between 1910 and Word War II, in that each group was moving from occupied territory to the occupying country. Of course, in the case of Koreans, they were not accorded citizenship, and those remaining in Japan after the war became foreign residents.

Also, unlike the case of Koreans in Japan (who came to Japan in great numbers before World War II), Puerto Rican migration to the United States was rather anemic until after the war. There were some 2,000 Puerto Ricans in the United States in 1910, and only a little more than 40,000 in 1930. In the ten years following World War II, driven by poor economic conditions on the island and a manufacturing boom in the continental US, some 700,000 Puerto Rican migrants arrived.[36] Subsequent waves of migration lifted the Puerto Rican population further, such that by 2013 there were some 5.1 million Puerto Ricans living in the continental United States (1.5 million having been born on the island and 3.6 million having been born in the 50 US states).[37]

Puerto Ricans constitute the second most numerous Hispanic group in the United States, behind Mexicans (numbering ~35 million in 2013) and ahead of Cubans (numbering ~2 million in 2013).[38] What stands out more than anything else about this number is the fact that Puerto Ricans living in the continental United States far outnumber those living on the island itself, whose population stands at ~3.5 million (for comparison, there are 122 million Mexicans living in Mexico proper, and 11 million Cubans living on that island). It can be fairly assumed that this difference from the migration patterns of other Hispanic nationals is due to Puerto Ricans being US citizens. In this way, the movement of most Puerto Ricans off the island is no different from any other large-scale internal migration in the United States (e.g. the migration out of the Dust Bowl (Great Plains) states during the 1930s, or the emptying of the Rust Belt cities of

---

[36] Library of Congress.   [37] Pew Research Center 2015.
[38] United States Census Bureau 2015.

the Northeast and upper Midwest following the decline of heavy industry in the 1970s and 1980s).

It is also clear that Puerto Ricans' status as American citizens greatly confounded and problematized their situation as migrants in the continental United States. As non-whites who spoke a language other than English, they were viewed as "foreign" and on a par with other actual immigrants (e.g. Chinese, Haitians). In fact, "Puerto Ricans' U.S. citizenship was widely misunderstood or unknown by the public and even many officials in the United States," and this made them in some ways more to be feared than actual non-white non-English-speaking immigrants, since they couldn't be deported even if they committed a crime and they could (as residents of their respective states) vote and exert political power. As a good number of them were politically left-leaning, there was great suspicion in their regard, especially during the post-Korean War anti-Communist paranoia of the 1950s.[39]

Fear and loathing of Puerto Ricans was most acutely (and almost exclusively) felt in New York City, the destination of probably 90 percent of the island's migrants during this period. Some of this angst is captured in the 1961 musical play (and later, movie) *West Side Story* (by Arthur Laurents and Leonard Bernstein), a Romeo-and-Juliet story set in New York's upper West Side, featuring a struggle between a white ethnic (Italian American) gang, The Jets, and their Puerto Rican counterparts, The Sharks. They were seen as politically and socially subversive both racially and linguistically. As poor non-whites, and non-immigrants, they were seen to make common cause with the African American underclass, and as Spanish speakers, they were natural allies of other Hispanic immigrants, albeit with more potential political power at the polls.

It is clear from surveys of their language proficiency and use that linguistic-inspired discrimination against Puerto Ricans has been driven more by fear of their language than by fact. Fully five out of six Puerto Ricans living in the continental United States (83 percent) are proficient in English (as compared with two-thirds of Hispanics overall), with 40 percent being English-dominant (as compared with 25 percent of Hispanics overall). Of those Puerto Ricans born in the continental United States, over 60 percent are English-dominant.[40] If anything, Puerto Ricans in the United States are at the leading edge of Hispanic assimilation to the English language, rather than a drag on it. Nevertheless, it is clear from the fear and the facts that the perception of being the linguistically "wrong class" of citizen is as powerful in motivating discrimination and conflict as is the "fact" of being so.

---

[39] Thomas 2015.   [40] Pew Research Center 2015.

The fact of speaking Spanish as their primary language presented difficulties for and barriers to Puerto Rican migrants from the island to the continental United States, much more so than those experienced by English-speaking migrants from any part of the United States to any other part of the country. Among other things, "the language barrier sometimes made it difficult to find well-paying work or to navigate government agencies or other English-speaking institutions."[41] Additionally, during the height of Puerto Rican migration to the Northeast and Midwest regions of the United States, Puerto Rican children of these migrants (many of whom had learned Spanish as their first language) faced a daunting lack of accommodation of their need for English-language instruction in the public school systems.[42]

However, even Puerto Ricans born in the continental United States have faced significant linguistic discrimination. As noted above, 83 percent of the 5 million Puerto Rican residents of the continental United States are proficient in English, with half of these using English as their dominant language. That said, 60 percent of these Puerto Ricans are either Spanish speakers or Spanish-dominant bilinguals. Accordingly, within the Puerto Rican migrant community there is an ongoing need to communicate with each other in Spanish or in a mixture of Spanish and English (vernacular forms of Spanish mixed with English that have evolved in the community, sometimes referred to as Spanglish or (in New York) Nuyorican). Even among those Puerto Ricans who communicate primarily in English, Spanish-tinged English accents and the use of Spanish loan words in their English discourse mark them as distinct from their English-speaking neighbors. And these differences in language use often result in overt and covert discrimination.

In using Spanish-influenced English accents, Puerto Ricans often faced discrimination in their quests for jobs and housing. This was shown in an article depicting how speakers of non-standard English suffered (racial and ethnic) discrimination even when responding to apartment ads over the telephone.[43] Puerto Rican (and other) speakers of Spanish and Spanish–English mixed varieties often experience complaints about using their (stigmatized) language in public. English speakers are frequently known to complain about the "unfairness" of having to hear Spanish spoken in the workplace or in public spaces, such that even in the absence of rules forbidding the use of their language, there is often substantial negative social pressure applied to suppress it.[44]

---

[41] Library of Congress.   [42] Thomas 2015.
[43] Purnell, Idsardi, and Baugh 1999. While this article focused on African Americans and Mexican Americans in northern California, the findings are equally applicable here. For a detailed discussion of the article, see Chapter 13.
[44] Urciuoli 1996.

Summary: Comparison of Cases

Migrant ethnolinguistic minorities, as we have seen in this chapter, can arise for as many different reasons as people have for moving from one place to another. They might be political, economic, ethnic, or religious refugees. The United States in particular has historically attracted all three. Political refugees have included Hungarians fleeing the 1956 Soviet invasion of Hungary, Cubans fleeing Castro, and Mexicans fleeing from the upheavals of the 1910 revolution there. Economic refugees have come pouring into the United States as well, in each generation. Where many of today's economic refugees tend to come from Mexico and Central America, 150 years ago the multitudes were fleeing the Irish potato famine. Ethnic and religious refugees to the United States have included (Protestant) Moravian refugees from Catholic Czech lands, Armenian survivors of the Turkish genocide, Catholic Vietnamese refugees following the Vietnam War, and always, from too many different places, Jews.

Reasons for migration aside, one common obstacle for most refugees is that of language. Depending on the language spoken by a refugee group, they might be more or less accommodated in their new place. In the case of the Roma, there have been somewhat conflicted approaches to their language. Their host countries have variously tried to keep them apart, thus reinforcing the Roma's desire to maintain their linguistic differences, and tried to assimilate them, thus attempting to eliminate their language and culture as a divisive factor. In the case of Koreans in Japan, we saw that Japan was not trying to assimilate them at all, but also not providing for their linguistic and cultural accommodation, at once forcing them to maintain Korean names and refusing to provide them with education in their native language. For American Puerto Ricans, the general attitude has been that they should learn to function in English (although English-speaking Americans are shown to be displeased with the Puerto Rican Spanish-tinged English that they wind up speaking).

One further factor that is worth noting is that a migrant minority may, if they are not accepted, accommodated, or assimilated, remain an ethnolinguistic minority long past their time of entry into their new country. This is to say that the children of migrants will still, de facto, belong to a migrant ethnolinguistic culture, if they continue to speak the language of their parents, maintain their community's culture, and live primarily or exclusively among members of their own group. The Roma lived in this manner in their adopted Balkan homelands for hundreds of years, and some of the descendants of Korean immigrants to Japan are still, effectively, members of a migrant minority some several generations removed from their immigrant ancestors. In many modern cases, however, when a migrant group is accepted and provided with opportunities to assimilate, their children rapidly assimilate to the domi-nant culture (even if they maintain linguistic and cultural traditions of their parents) – as we noted, five-sixths of the 5 million Puerto Rican residents of the United States are proficient in English (which is no small number).

Additional Cases for Exploration

Russians in Israel

Perhaps one of the most interesting cases of migrant minorities is that of Russian speakers in modern Israel. Far from being (unwanted or unwelcome) refugees in the common sense of the word, Russian Jewish immigrants to Israel were (at least officially) sought after. After World War II, the number of Jews in the Soviet Union stood at a bit under 2.5 million, with about two-thirds of these residing in the Ukraine and in Russia proper. Official and officially sanctioned anti-Semitism in the Soviet Union led to a great clamor on the part of many Jews to be allowed to leave, and while the Soviet Union did not make it easy for them to do so, about 10 percent of them managed to emigrate in the 1970s and early 1980s (with about 125,000 of these winding up in Israel). It was the collapse of the Soviet Union in 1991, though, which led to the greatest exodus of Jews (and some non-Jews) from Russia to Israel – approximately 900,000 in total.

From a demographic perspective, this influx was huge for such a small country whose entire population was about 5 million at that time, with Russian speakers quickly coming to represent some 16 percent of the population overall and about 20 percent of its Jewish population. Thus, the number of Russian native speakers in Israel in the 1990s outnumbered the native speakers of every other language in this relatively cosmopolitan state except for Hebrew and Arabic. Regardless of their being generally welcomed and not being the target of discrimination (at least initially), their sheer number entailed that they found it difficult to assimilate and that Israel found it difficult to absorb them. One-quarter of these immigrants do not speak fluent Hebrew some twenty years on, and on account of this it is hardly surprising that they suffer more unemployment than other groups, that they have come to be seen as "immigrants" with the stigma that goes along with it, and that they are rather ghettoized (e.g. 85 percent of the population of the coastal town of Ashdod are now immigrants or descendants of immigrants from the former Soviet Union).

Turks in Germany

Currently some 3 million Turks or people of Turkish descent reside in Germany, nearly 4 percent of the population. Of these, roughly half are German citizens, many of whom have dual German-Turkish citizenship. The large Turkish population has its roots in the guest work program begun in the 1960s, which brought unskilled and semi-skilled laborers to meet the needs of the booming West German economy. Initially designed to have the workers return to Turkey after two years, the return policy was dropped to circumvent the need (and expense) for business to constantly recruit and train new workers. Also there were few incentives for the workers to give up jobs they considered far better than their prospects in Turkey, and so the population increased further with the immigration of workers' family members and additional guest workers.

Assimilation of the Turkish guest workers was not initially encouraged, nor, given the presence of translators at work, was the acquisition of German-language skills. As a result, enclaves in which one's life could be conducted completely in Turkish grew up in these industrial areas, and Turkish children attended schools designed to facilitate their return to Turkey. The effect of these policies and expectations was that they received inadequate instruction in both German language and Turkish language. This in turn led inevitably to low educational achievement and high unemployment. The fall of the Soviet Union and the reunification of Germany brought additional conflict as the Turkish population, who were Muslim and culturally distinct, were vilified by some former East Germans who felt left behind by the progress and affluence of West Germans. The result has been continued language and cultural conflict, exacerbated by a renewed influx of refugees from the recent Middle East conflict.

Chinese in Vancouver

Chinese immigrants began arriving in Canada in 1858, first as gold prospectors and then as laborers for the completion of the Canadian Pacific Railway. For much of the time they have been in Canada, the Chinese have been anything but warmly welcomed. A "head tax" was instituted for Chinese immigrants in 1885 as a reaction to an economic downturn during which it was feared that the lower wages paid to Chinese laborers would take jobs from struggling white Canadians. The tax on Chinese immigrants became increasingly onerous (to the point of reaching the equivalent of two years' wages for each immigrant in 1903) but proved ineffective, and the Chinese Immigration Act (Chinese Exclusion Act) was passed in 1923. On the books until 1947, the Act successfully stemmed the flow of Chinese immigrants.

Things changed for the better after World War II, but lately language issues have surfaced in Vancouver, the city with the highest concentration of Chinese residents. The time preceding the return of Hong Kong to China in 1997 saw a dramatic rise in Chinese immigration to Vancouver, as well as mainland Chinese more recently. These wealthy immigrants are seen as responsible for steep increases in real estate prices and have had a marked presence in Vancouver (which has been variously referred to as "Hongcouver" and the most Asian city outside Asia), which has engendered resentment among some white residents. Recently this resentment has focused on the appearance of business signs (including land development and financial services) including only the Chinese language. Citing the traditional English and French identity of Canada, some have petitioned local governments to mandate inclusion of English on such signage, and there have been disputes regarding some tenant meetings being conducted solely in Mandarin. The nearby city of Richmond advertised as recently as December 2015 for a position dedicated to convincing Chinese businesses to voluntarily adopt bilingual signage.

13   Intra-Linguistic (Dialectal) Minorities

In this chapter, the reader will find discussion of cases involving dialect minorities. The two featured cases are Okinawan speakers in Japan and African American English (AAE) speakers in the United States. Each case presents the story of a group speaking the "wrong" (i.e. stigmatized) variety of a language, and being punished (economically, socially, and politically) for doing so. The former case involves speakers of a language that is not Japanese (i.e. Ryūkyūan) being presumed to speak a (stigmatized) dialect of Japanese and being made to suffer for it. In the second case, we find the language variety of English spoken by African Americans to be especially stigmatized on account of a generally negative disposition toward the minority group itself, rather than on account of any objective features of their dialect. At the end of the chapter, in the section on extra cases for further exploration, the reader will find synopses on Occitan in France, Singaporean English and local Chinese dialects in Singapore, and Landsmål/Bokmål in Norway.

Ryūkyūan and Japanese

Before taking up the matter of dialectal minorities in Japan, it is instructive to situate Japanese linguistically in its region and to understand the nature of, and motivations for the promotion of, Standard Japanese over regional dialects. Interactions of the Japanese with the Okinawans, as we shall see, have been guided by how the Japanese view their own language and the Ryūkyūan/ Okinawan language of the Ryūkyūan archipelago.[1] Ideas, among the Japanese themselves and others, regarding where Japanese comes from are key to understanding these interactions.

---

[1] For the purposes of this chapter, the terms Ryūkyūan and Okinawan are used interchangeably. In fact, however, Okinawa is the largest island in the Ryūkyūan archipelago (which itself is called the Okinawan Prefecture). Okinawa is at times used to refer to the entire island chain, since it is the largest of the several hundred islands in the chain (comprising some 25 percent of the entire land area) and because over 85 percent of the island chain's population lives on this one island. Okinawan is also the name of one of the several Ryūkyūan languages native to the islands.

There is a range of theories regarding the origin of Japanese; however, no firm consensus exists regarding any single one of them. The most linguistically plausible classification for Japanese groups it, along with Korean, as an Altaic language (a group whose members include: Turkish and related Turkic languages, Mongolian and related Mongolic languages, and other disparate languages of central and northern Asia). Other theories of origin (basing themselves on features of the language that don't appear Altaic-like) include connecting Japanese with Malayo-Polynesian languages (a language family that includes Indonesian, Philippine, and South Pacific island languages). Some (primarily a small number of Japanese scholars) hypothesize that Japanese is a language "isolate" – namely, that it is related to no other language or language family. This last conjecture, while satisfying to those focused on the uniqueness of Japanese history and genealogy, is highly implausible.

Several things are clear from discussions in the literature that help explain the lack of consensus.[2] First, the split of Japanese from its linguistic relatives took place much longer ago than did that of the Romance language descendants of Latin (e.g. Spanish, French, Portuguese, etc.), which was only 1,000–1,500 years ago. This, combined with the absence of any written records such as we have for Latin, makes the historical reconstruction of the Japanese language much more difficult. Second, Japanese scholars have tended not to use scientific methods of linguistic reconstruction with particular rigor, thus making the results of many comparisons somewhat suspect. This may be in part due to a belief (alluded to above) about the special nature of Japanese, in comparison with other languages. Miller states that, for Japanese scholars, "foreign languages, Western languages, perhaps even Chinese, have genetic relationships (*shin'en kankei*) that can be and often are established by rigorous methods of linguistic reconstruction.[3] However, for these same scholars, Japanese is, in this respect as in so many others, 'unique,' in that it has only a *keitō* [(family) lineage], which must, by terminological definition, remain forever obscure."

Although some of the more remote linguistic relationships between Japanese and larger language families are unsettled (such as whether Japanese belongs to the Altaic and/or the Malay-Polynesian language families), some parts of the origins picture, such as the connections between Japanese and Korean, and between Japanese and Ryūkyūan, are fairly secure. However, proposals differ with respect to these relationships as well.

For example, some consider Japanese and Korean to have developed from different subfamilies of the Altaic language family, while taking Japanese and

---

[2] See Miller 1974; Shibatani 1990; Holmberg 2010.   [3] Miller 1974: 94–95.

Ryūkyūan to be more closely related (i.e. the sole members of the Japonic language group).[4] On the other hand, there are those who claim that Japanese, Korean, and Ryūkyūan all developed from a single common ancestral language, exclusive of others.[5] Yet others do not accept the suggestion that "Middle Korean, Old Japanese, and Ryūkyūan [are] sisters on a par," but take the position that "the Japanese–Ryūkyūan connection is far more transparent than that between Japanese and Korean."[6] As such, Shibatani would most likely agree with Robbeets on this matter over Miller, but would go further in claiming that Ryūkyūan is merely a "dialect (group) of Japanese." This claim will be assessed further as we consider the historical and linguistic relationship between Japanese and Ryūkyūan, but for now we take the position that Ryūkyūan and Japanese are closely related and that Korean and Japanese are somewhat less closely related.

Turning to the issue of Standard Japanese and Japanese dialects, it is important to note that the geography of Japan (i.e. its numerous islands and mountainous interior) lends itself to a high degree of linguistic diversification, leading to a situation in which many of the various dialects of Japanese are not mutually intelligible.[7] For example, as Shibatani says, "speakers [from] the southern island of Kyūshū would not be understood by the majority of the people on the main island of Honshu … [and] northern dialect speakers from … Aomori and Akita would not be understood by the people in the metropolitan Tokyo."[8]

This linguistic reality led to an effort by the Meiji government in Tokyo in the nineteenth century to attempt to impose a national standard variety (called *hyōjun-go*, or "Standard Language") that would unify the nation linguistically. The enforcement of a national standard was historically imposed through the educational system (as described later on). Teaching the Tokyo dialect as the standard throughout Japan had the effect, Shibatani notes, of fostering feelings of inferiority among speakers of non-standard dialects. The enforcement could be, at times, rather cruel, as when a *hōgen huda* (dialect tag) was hung around the neck of any student who used their home dialect in school. This policy and practice continued through the end of World War II, when the concept of *kyōtū-go* (common language) was introduced. This variety of Japanese (used by speakers of different dialects to communicate with each other) is much more malleable than "Standard/ Tokyo Japanese," possessing many of the features of the standard, but also "retains dialect traits, such as accentual features."[9] With this in mind, we take up the case of Ryūkyūan.

---

[4] Robbeets 2005.   [5] Miller 1971.   [6] Shibatani 1990.   [7] Shibatani 1990: 185–186.
[8] Shibatani 1990: 185.   [9] Shibatani 1990: 186.

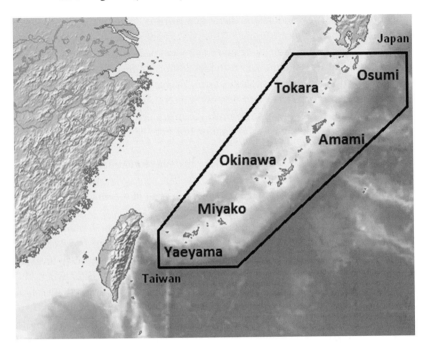

Figure 13.1 Ryūkyū Islands

Ryūkyūan Languages/Dialects

As the title of this section indicates, we are noncommittal as to whether Ryūkyūan is a language with many dialects or a small family of related languages. We are sure, however, that Ryūkyūan is not a dialect of Japanese, as asserted by Japan in the nineteenth and twentieth centuries.

Historical Background

With a population of some 1.5 million and an area amounting to somewhat less than 2,000 square miles, the 100 islands of the Ryūkyū Island chain extend about 650 miles, from the southern main island of Kyūshū to within 75 miles of Taiwan, as shown in the map below. This is nearly half the north to south distance of Japan's four main islands (i.e. from the northernmost tip of Hokkaido to the island of Kagoshima adjacent to Kyūshū).

The physical location and range of these islands are as important as their history to an understanding of their current status. If, as Shibatani maintains, the numerous islands and mountainous interior of Japan lend themselves to a high degree of linguistic diversification such that Japanese speakers from

Hokkaido would not understand their compatriots from Kyūshū, then one might expect much more linguistic diversification in an island chain strung out over 650 miles and isolated from the major Japanese islands.

The history of the island chain provides important insights into our understanding of the linguistic situation here. It has been suggested that the Ryūkyūans are descended from Jōmon hunters, gatherers, and fishermen, who had settled in the Japanese archipelago many centuries before the arrival of the agrarian Yayoi peoples, who immigrated from North Asia through Korea some 2,400 years ago.[10]

Regardless of their origins, it is clear that the Ryūkyūans comprised an autonomous nation from the end of the twelfth century right up until their incorporation into the Japanese nation-state at the end of the nineteenth century. The first recorded Ryūkyūan dynasty (the Shunten Dynasty) was founded in 1187, at about the same time as the Kamakura shogunate (which marks the end of the Heian classical period and the beginning of feudal Japan). The Ryūkyūan kingdom started attracting the (perhaps less than welcome) attention of its more powerful Chinese and Japanese neighbors beginning in 1372, when the Ryūkyūan King Satto was compelled to begin paying tribute to the first emperor of the Chinese Ming Dynasty.

At the beginning of the seventeenth century, Japanese feudal rulers got into the act. Upset that the Ryūkyūans refused to provide conscripts for a Japanese invasion of Korea, and taking advantage of a succession struggle in the Ryūkyū kingdom, the Satsuma rulers in Kyūshū invaded and defeated the Ryūkyūans in 1609. Deciding that a life well taxed was preferable to a life cut short, the Ryūkyūans wound up paying double tribute (to China and to the Satsuma) for another century. Toward the end of the nineteenth century, though, as China was slipping irretrievably into the losers' column of the colonialist–colonized equation, Japan stepped up to claim the Ryūkyūs as a province, making them the Okinawa Prefecture of the Meiji state in 1879. China, after having been soundly beaten by Japan in the Sino-Japanese War, was finally forced to officially renounce its claim to the islands in 1895.

Thus, from 1879 until its defeat in 1945, the Ryūkyū Islands were ruled directly by Japan. Following Japan's defeat in World War II, the islands were under a US military government until 1950, and then ruled by an indigenous government (though still subject to US oversight) until 1972. In 1972, the Ryūkyū Islands were returned to Japan. Adding up the years, then, the Ryūkyū Islands have been an actual part of Japan for only about one of the past eight centuries. This is a significant point in understanding the current context.

---

[10] Ishikida 2005.

Figure 13.2 Aikwa Kindergarten in the Ryūkyūan capital, Shuri, Okinawa, c. 1907

Linguistic Background

In order to understand the linguistic situation in the Ryūkyū Islands, some discussion of the language(s) spoken there is in order. As noted earlier, the linguistic relationship between Japanese and Ryūkyūan is a matter of contention, and there is a wide divergence of opinion on whether they are languages separate from Japanese, or "merely" dialects of Japanese.

Some have claimed that "Middle Korean, Old Japanese, and Ryūkyūan [are] sisters on a par," which would surely make them distinct languages.[11] Others, such as Robbeets, while placing Korean at a further distance from Japanese than Ryūkyūan, also consider Japanese and Ryūkyūan to be distinct languages. On the other side of the debate, there are many Japanese scholars who would classify the varieties spoken on the Ryūkyū Islands as "dialects" of Japanese. Shibatani notes that "the relationship between Ryūkyūan and Japanese is something like that between Spanish and Italian or between French and Italian," and then goes on to say that "unlike these Romance languages, the Ryūkyūan dialects are often mutually completely unintelligible among themselves, let alone to the speakers of any mainland dialect."[12] Figure 13.2 shows Ryūkyūan children in a Japanese-language kindergarten in Okinawa at the beginning of the twentieth century.

[11] E.g. Miller 1971.   [12] Shibatani 1990: 191.

At issue is whether to consider Ryūkyūan varieties as belonging to the larger class of Japanese dialects or whether to see Ryūkyūan and Japanese as two families of related but distinct languages. For his own part, Shibatani dismisses the issue, saying: "Once a genetic relationship is established between two languages, it is a moot point whether to regard them as two languages or as two dialects of one language."[13] But it is not a moot point at all. Whether the Ryūkyūans have their own language and linguistic traditions, or whether they all speak rustic (and by popular implication, inferior) dialects of Japanese, has enormous implications for them and for their linguistic culture.

As discussed in Chapter 4, in most (at least Western) contexts, considering two varieties of a language to be dialects entails that they be mutually intelligible to some extent. This is apparent with British and American English, whose speakers can readily converse with each other in their respective standard dialects, usually with no difficulties other than the occasional challenges presented by lexical differences (e.g. British *lift* for American *elevator*, etc.). In Asia, the term "dialect" is often used to refer to pairs of mutually unintelligible languages – e.g. Shanghai and Beijing "dialects" of Chinese, which are in fact distinct Chinese languages – and at other times to refer to what Western linguistics would acknowledge as true varieties (i.e. dialects) of a single language.

With respect to the Ryūkyūan–Japanese situation, the two languages are not mutually intelligible. In contrast, the various dialects of Ryūkyūan are mutually intelligible, relatively speaking, and so are the various dialects of Japanese proper. In assessing Ryūkyūan as a Japanese dialect, it has been asserted that "the Hirara dialect (of Ryūkyūan) is sufficiently close to Standard Japanese for its speakers to be able to create a good proportion of the standard vocabulary by applying sound changes to dialect words."[14] But what is this evidence of? One could make the same claim regarding Italian and Spanish, or about Russian and Bulgarian. Clearly such a metric is not really informative.

However "transparent" the relationship between Ryūkyūan and Japanese, it is nonetheless the case that "the Ryūkyūan stock split from the mainstream Japanese language at the latest around 6 A.D."[15] From an historical perspective, this would suggest a split at, or shortly after, the arrival of the agrarian Yayoi people in the Japan archipelago (i.e. around the time of the formation of a separate ethnic Japanese people). From a linguistic perspective, calling Ryūkyūan and Japanese dialects of the same language would be no different from calling English, German, and Icelandic dialects of the same language

---

[13] Shibatani 1990: 191.   [14] Chew 1976.   [15] Shibatani 1990: 193.

(whatever language that might be).[16] Thus, while it might be advantageous to Japan to consider Ryūkyūan languages as mere varieties (i.e. dialects) of Japanese, such an assessment does not carry much linguistic or historical weight (Shibatani's characterization of "moot points" notwithstanding).

Beginning with its 2009 edition, the United Nations Educational, Scientific and Cultural Organization (UNESCO) *Atlas of the World's Languages in Danger* includes, alongside Ainu, the following Ryūkyūan languages of Japan: Amami, Hachijō, Kunigami, Miyako, Okinawan, Yaeyama, and Yonaguni.[17] By classifying Ryūkyūan as a group of endangered languages, the UNESCO document thus affirms their status as autonomous languages, and as objects worthy of study and preservation.

The UNESCO classification serves as a challenge to "the long-standing misconception of a monolingual Japanese nation state that has its roots in the linguistic and colonizing policies of the Meiji period."[18] It is also notable that Japanese society laid claim to the Ryūkyūan people and language as a part of Japan and the Japanese language, and simultaneously categorized them and their language as inferior and contemptible. It has also been maintained that the Ryūkyūan people are deemed by main island Japanese to be "backward, lazy, inefficient, prone to insanity, irrational and unhygienic ... Japanese, in contrast, [are] modern, hardworking, efficient, sane, rational, and clean."[19]

Language Rights Issues

One of the central issues of concern, as noted, is the preservation of the Ryūkyūan languages. While there was some acknowledgement of local Ryūkyūan culture and language at the outset of Japanese de facto control over the territory in 1872, this did not last long. From the time of its administrative incorporation into Japan in 1879, there was a deliberate and focused effort at making the Ryūkyūans Japanese. This effort primarily took the form of disseminating the (standard) Japanese language through the public educational system.

The motivations for this are, to some degree, understandable. The Ryūkyū Islands stand at the southwestern extremity of the Japan archipelago and extend out into the vulnerable space between Japan and its larger Asian neighbor, China. The pressure to incorporate this space into the Japanese nation took on

[16] "According to results employing the lexicostatistics method (Hattori 1976), the Ryūkyūan languages share only between 59 and 68 percent cognates with Tokyo Japanese. These figures are lower than those between German and English (Bairon, Brenzinger and Heinrich 2009).
[17] The interactive atlas can be found at www.unesco.org/culture/languages-atlas/index.php?hl=enandpage=atlasmap
[18] Bairon, Brenzinger and Heinrich 2009.   [19] Barclay 2006: 120.

greater urgency after the 1895 Sino-Japanese War, as Japan was facing threats from the north, from Russia, which shortly thereafter culminated in the 1905 Russo-Japanese War. It was in this same year (1895) that Japan occupied both Taiwan and Korea, making the Ryūkyūans the most closely related peoples in Japan's recently acquired territories. In this context, and given the mutual unintelligibility of Japanese dialects to begin with, it is not a surprise that the Ryūkyū Islands became an extension of the Ministry of Education efforts to standardize Japanese throughout the empire. As far as the policy-makers were concerned, Ryūkyūan languages appeared to be nothing more than dialects of Japanese, and were consequently treated as such.

What this meant for the Ryūkyū islanders, at the start of the twentieth century, was that "efforts to spread [standardized] Japanese increasingly employed coercive measures."[20] In 1907, with the passage of the Ordinance to Regulate Dialects (*hōgen torishimari-rei*), children were now prohibited from speaking their native Ryūkyūan languages in school. As Japan's imperial ambitions increased, so did the pressure on Ryūkyū islanders to conform to the national(istic) model of Japanese language and culture. In 1931, Japan invaded and occupied Manchuria (China's northeasternmost territory), and on the island of Okinawa established the Movement for Enforcement of the Normal Language (*fūtsūgo reikō undō*). Under this movement, debate societies were established to promote the use of Japanese. At these gatherings, "speaking a Ryūkyūan language ... was considered an unpatriotic act, and children taking part in debate circles risked being penalized if they failed to speak Japanese."[21]

While Japan lurched toward the expansion of military conflict throughout East Asia and the Pacific in the mid 1930s, there was an effort throughout the nation to promote loyalty, patriotism, and national unity. In this milieu, "active measures to suppress Ryūkyūan increased ... [and] speaking Ryūkyūan in the private domain came to be seen as an obstacle to the spread of Standard Japanese."[22] This period saw a marked increase in the use of the infamous *hōgen huda* (dialect tag) which was hung around the neck of any student who used their home dialect in school. Heinrich notes that punishments for speaking Ryūkyūan were not limited to shaming, but included many other punishments, such as being tasked with extra clean-up duties after school. It is also reported that, at one school, children had to sing "using dialect is the enemy of the country" (*hōgen tsukau wa kuni no kateki*) during morning assemblies.[23] One author reports that when he was at school, "there was a clothes-line in the classroom on which colored paper in the shape of laundry was hung. If a student spoke Ryūkyūan, the expression used was written on a paper and symbolically cleansed."[24]

[20] Heinrich 2005.   [21] Heinrich 2004.   [22] Heinrich 2004: 158.   [23] Nishimura 2001: 176.
[24] Tanaka 2001: 12 cited in Heinrich 2004: 8.

By 1939, the suppression of Ryūkyūan had been extended well beyond the classroom. A law was passed requiring the use of Standard Japanese in all government offices and institutions. Customers who used Ryūkyūan in these places would be denied service and any employees who spoke Ryūkyūan were fined. As the war progressed toward its inevitable catastrophe, the situation only got worse for the Ryūkyūans. Heinrich characterizes the attitude toward Ryūkyūan as "hysterical," such that by 1945, during the Battle of Okinawa, the Japanese army stationed there ordered anyone found using Ryūkyūan to be considered a spy. Remarkably, there were instances in which the order was executed and individuals found speaking Ryūkyūan were shot or stabbed to death.

Heinrich also points out, accurately, that "language ideology is always also ideology about something other than language." In this light, the ideology of the Standard Japanese (national language) movement is about the projection of political power from the capital region of the country (i.e. Tokyo/Yokohama) where standard dialect is spoken. The Ryūkyūan languages have been measured (along with many true Japanese language dialects) against the "correct" national standard, and under the mistaken assumption that Ryūkyūan is a variety of Japanese, the Ryūkyū Islands stand out "as the region in which (perceived) embarrassing language behaviour [is] most pronounced."[25]

After the end of the World War II, there were attempts on the part of the American occupiers (in concert with local Ryūkyūan activists and scholars) to promote the distinct culture and language of the Ryūkyūan Islands. However, resentment of US occupation served to enhance Ryūkyūan islanders' affinity with Japan, and to cause them to agitate for reunification. Since 1972, the incursion of Standard Japanese into all forms of communication (public and private) and the diminution of Ryūkyūan languages has proceeded unrelentingly, to the point that the entire group of the Ryūkyūan languages is about to disappear.

While the UNESCO recognition is long overdue and welcome, it is unclear whether it has perhaps come about too late to effect any meaningful preservation of Ryūkyūan languages and culture. There is some reason to be mildly optimistic though. As Heinrich reports, the establishment of a Society for Spreading Okinawan (*uchinaguchi fukyū kyōgikai*) has begun to exert a positive influence, through the establishment of dialect classes in public schools and the introduction of a standard orthography for the language. A recent "dialect boom" throughout Japan may also have the effect of making Ryūkyūan languages more fashionable as well.

---

[25] Heinrich 2005.

Conclusion

The Ryūkyūan case is one involving (for the Japanese, at least) an intra-ethnic minority. In this regard, the Japanese imposed the same regionally dictated chauvinist solution as was promulgated for all "dialect"-speaking subgroups. To promote national unity, one variety of Japanese would have to be officially favored, and be esteemed over all others. In this model, the Ryūkyūans were simply deemed to speak a different dialect of Japanese, and one that was judged "clearly" inferior to all the others.

African American English in the United States

In this section, we turn to a dialect familiar to the vast majority of Americans, as well as to many English speakers worldwide – African American English (AAE). This variety of English, which has been also been referred to as African American Vernacular English (AAVE), Black English, and Ebonics, is a dialect with a long and complex history, and one which has garnered more attention (positive and negative) than any other American English dialect, excepting perhaps Southern American English. Since this is an ethnic dialect, as opposed to a regional one, we will examine the history of African Americans in the United States, as well as the origins and nature of their dialect. This section will also consider conflicts between African American and Mainstream American Englishes, as they have emerged in Oakland, California and the San Francisco Bay area.

Historical Background

To understand the linguistic and ethnic origins of African Americans, one must understand the history of the slave trade within and from Africa, since this is the means by which African Americans came to be in the United States. The story of North American slavery is, though, a very small part of the totality of modern slavery and its depredations in the world. Trade in African slaves, long before the Europeans came into the picture, was dominated by Arabs and other Muslim tribes, beginning in the eighth century and lasting at least until the rise of the European Atlantic slave trade. In those medieval times, African slaves (largely from Bantu-speaking tribes) were transported and traded across Saharan northern Africa, and along the east African coast of present-day Somalia, Kenya, and Tanzania.[26] European involvement in the worldwide

---

[26] Slavery remains a problem in northern Africa and Arabia to this day (although the incidence of twenty-first-century slavery is higher in South and Southeast Asia). "The West African nation of Mauritania . . . [has] the highest prevalence [of slavery], with an estimated 4% of its population in bondage. Other offenders include Uzbekistan (3.97%), Haiti (2.3%) and Qatar (1.35%)." CNN, November 17, 2014 (www.cnn.com/2014/11/17/world/walk-free-global-slavery-index-2014/).

slave trade began with the Portuguese, and didn't really begin in earnest until the fifteenth century, when Portugal established a permanent trading post at El Mina, in what is present-day Ghana. The immediate motivations for establishing a presence on the west African coast was to bypass the Arab traders and gain direct access to gold, ivory, and spices. It wasn't long after, with the sixteenth-century establishment of plantations in the New World with their labor-intensive crops, that the need for cheap (i.e. slave) labor propelled the Portuguese (and other European nations, eventually) into the slave trade, once again bypassing the Arab traders and their routes.

The depredations of the slave trade upon the African continent were extreme by any objective measure, but put into the context of its time, the human catastrophe was astounding. Some 11 million Africans were transported by European slave traders across the Atlantic Ocean from the western coasts of Africa, and an additional 2 million souls died in transit. To this, one must add some 14 million slaves traded to South Asia and within Africa (including north Africa) and the estimated 4 million who died in the process of enslavement.[27] The effect of 30 million slave-trade victims over two centuries (1650–1850) upon the fortunes of Africa is even more shocking when compared with world population figures of that time. During the 100-year period from 1750 to 1850, primarily as a consequence of the slave trade, the population of Africa rose by less than 5 percent (see Table 13.1). This was during a time when the populations of every other continent increased dramatically: Asia 60 percent, Europe 68 percent, Latin America/Caribbean 138 percent, and North America 1300 percent. Put another way, the slave trade affected a number of people equivalent to over 25 percent of the population of the African continent, which would represent some 200 million people in present-day terms.

Data depicting the routes and human traffic of the Atlantic slave trade place the North American traffic in its broader context. During the period 1650–1860, 500,000 African slaves were taken across the Atlantic Ocean from the western coastal regions of sub-Saharan Africa (primarily from the slave trade regions of present-day Senegal, Sierra Leone, Ghana, Benin, Cameroon, Congo, and Angola). These half million slaves, brought to British North America, represented a mere 5 percent of the total number of African slaves delivered to the New World (about 11 million). This means that some twenty times as many African slaves (10 million) were brought to Latin America and the Caribbean, with about 4.5 million being imported into the West Indies and about 5 million being carried to Brazil. Unsurprisingly, they (and their descendants) represented a much larger portion of their region's 38 million inhabitants than did the slaves who were brought to British North America.

---

[27] Manning 1992: 119–120.

Table 13.1 *World population by continent, 1750–2000*

World population (in millions)						
Year	1750	1800	1850	1900	1950	1999
World	791	978	1,262	1,650	2,521	5,978
Africa	**106**	**107**	**111**	133	221	767
Asia	502	635	809	947	1,402	3,634
Europe	163	203	276	408	547	729
Latin America and the Caribbean	16	24	38	74	167	511
Northern America	2	7	26	82	172	307
Oceania	2	2	2	6	13	30

Source: www.un.org/esa/population/publications/sixbillion/sixbilpart1.pdf

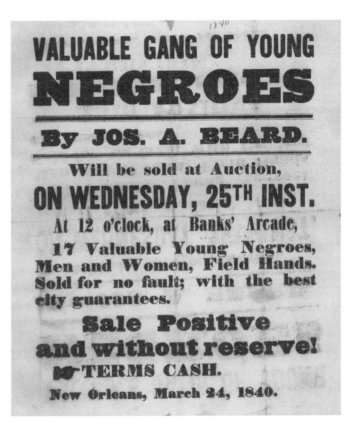

Figure 13.3 Handbill advertising a slave auction, New Orleans, Louisiana, 1840

The slaves brought to North America largely ended up in the present-day southeastern United States, which is where they were most useful to the cash-crop plantation economies that sprang up there. In any case, the British abolished the slave trade in 1807 and abolished slavery altogether in 1833, throughout the British Empire. By the middle of the nineteenth century, as illustrated by the advertisement for a New Orleans slave auction here above, the only African slaves in North America were in those states in the United States that allowed it (i.e. primarily in the states that would secede from the Union to form the Confederacy beginning in 1860).[28] By 1860, at the beginning of the American Civil War, the black population of the United States (consisting of the African slaves and their descendants) numbered 4.4 million and accounted for 14 percent of the US population. Some 90 percent of these were slaves in the slave-holding states, as shown in Figure 13.4. Of the approximately 500,000 free blacks, more than half of those also lived in the slave-holding states.

At the end of the Civil War and for some time afterward, the slaves who had been emancipated mostly remained in the states of the former Confederacy. During the Reconstruction Era of the 1860s and 1870s, African Americans in the southern states had some reason to hope that their conditions would vastly improve in the place of their former slavery. However, the departure of US Federal troops from the newly "reconstructed" states led quickly to a revanchist takeover of local governments and civil institutions by white-supremacist Radicals, who overturned and reversed any accommodations that had been made to the recently liberated slaves.

Each year, people who had been able to vote or ride the train where they chose found that something they could do freely yesterday, they were prohibited from doing today. They were losing ground and sinking low in status with each passing day, and, well into the new century, the color codes would only grow to encompass more activities of daily life as quickly as they could devise them.[29]

While conditions had deteriorated rapidly, it wasn't until the beginning of the twentieth century that African Americans began to find opportunities (in the Northeast, Midwest, and Far West) that allowed them to leave the Southeast. From 1910 until 1970, over 5 million African Americans migrated out of the South, with over 50,000 per year leaving in the first thirty years and over 110,000 per year moving out from 1940 until 1970.[30]

---

[28] At the founding of the United States in 1789, eight of the former thirteen Colonies allowed slavery. These were, from north to south: New York, New Jersey, Delaware, Maryland, Virginia, North Carolina, South Carolina, and Georgia. By 1800, New York had abolished slavery and Kentucky and Tennessee had joined the Union as slave-holding states. New Jersey abolished slavery in 1804, and was the last of the original slave-holding states to do so before the advent of the American Civil War.

[29] Wilkerson 2010: 42.   [30] Kopf 2016.

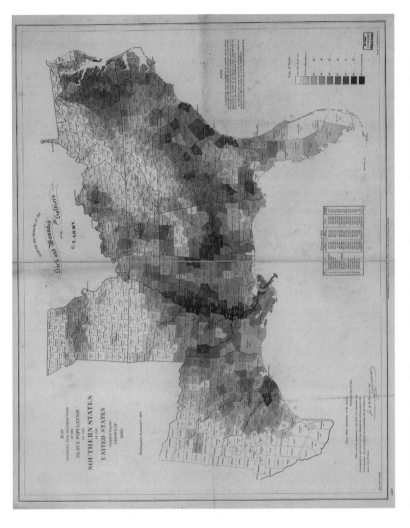

Figure 13.4 Distribution of slave population in the southern states of the United States, 1860

African Americans have moved over the past 100 years far beyond their original concentrations of settlement in the American South, and comprise significant portions of the population in most states in the Northeast, Midwest, and Far West. Their concentration into major urban population centers in all these areas is also significant. However, while African Americans are much more widely settled across the United States, their representation in the US population has not increased at all. In fact, where 4.4 million blacks comprised 14 percent of the US population in 1860, this country's current population of 42 million African Americans constitutes only 13 percent of the population in 2010 (some 150 years later).

One effect of this dispersion (which was not accompanied by any increase in African Americans' proportional representation among the populous) has been the increased degree of linguistic and cultural contact between African Americans and the white population of the United States. In 1860, it was likely that the vast majority of (white) Americans, and nearly all those outside the South, had few occasions ever to see, much less interact with, a black person. Black slaves at that time were concentrated in areas in which they were often a majority, and in which they typically had contact only with the whites who owned and supervised them. In this context, their variety of speech would not be something that Americans outside the plantation culture would have any awareness of. And they themselves would have been less likely to have consciousness of their "dialect" as a marker of their identity. After all, their dialect was simply how they themselves spoke, and was in the main pretty much all they heard (except when communicating with the whites they were required to interact with).

The Great Migration out of the South brought African Americans into close and regular contact with the majority of other Americans, especially so in the largest American cities, where the African American population increased anywhere from seven to 100 times, as illustrated in Table 13.2.

Table 13.2 *Four US cities with the largest African American population in 1970*

	1910	1940	1970
New York	142,000	661,000	2,347,000
Chicago	58,000	346,000	1,328,000
Philadelphia	119,000	346,000	836,000
Los Angeles	7,000	76,000	767,000

Source: Kopf 2016.

Table 13.3 *AAE phonological variation*

ask/aks alternation	*I aks him a question*
-ing/-in' alternation	*He's runnin' fast*
final consonant reduction in clusters	*fine* for *find; han* for *hand*
final consonant devoicing	*bat* for *bad*
/s/ as [d] before /n/	*idn't* for *isn't; wahn't* for *wasn't*
stress shift from second to first syllable	*POlice; UMbrella*

Source: Based on data from Charity 2008.

And while racism and discrimination certainly impeded contact between African Americans and the rest of the citizenry, white Americans have, over the past 100 years, been increasingly exposed to African American cuisine, music, and vernacular English. This plays a role in our discussion of AAE here below.

Linguistic Background

Before the Great Migration, AAE was an isolated subvariety of English, spoken by a particular ethnic group (African Americans) in a particular region (the American South). Many features of this dialect were shared with Southern American English (the prevalent dialect of white speakers in that region). As a consequence of migration, this English dialect was carried to all parts of the United States and became a marker of ethnic identity for African Americans wherever they went.

This is not to say that all African Americans speak AAE. They don't. Nor is it the case that only African Americans speak AAE. Furthermore, AAE is not monolithic. It is not spoken the same way by all speakers at all times. There are regional differences. There are socio-economic distinctions in the variety that is used, as well as situational differences in how and when it is used. Nevertheless, there are some very well-known features of AAE that are common to most subvarieties of it. Table 13.3 lists some features common to AAE pronunciation (focusing here on consonants).[31]

In addition to its phonology of AAE (i.e. the AAE "accent"), the variety has its own characteristic lexicon and syntax (like any other dialect). Well known among these features (at least to linguists) are the complementary phenomena of "zero copula" and "habitual *be*," which are exemplified here alongside their Mainstream American English (MAE) equivalents (notice that MAE does not make any distinction between these two uses of the verb *be*):

---

[31] It should be noted that other dialects of English exhibit some of these same features.

AAE: She workin' late.   MAE: She is working late.
AAE: She be workin' late.   MAE: She is working late.

The first of these (with "zero copula" – i.e. the omission of the copula verb *is*) means that she is presently, at this time, working late. The second (with the uninflected form of the verb *be*) means that she often, or habitually, works late. Thus, in AAE it would be acceptable to say *She be workin' late most of this year*, but not **She workin' late most of this year*. Likewise, it would be fine to say *She workin' late tonight*, but not **She be workin' late tonight*.

More central to our discussion of AAE are its origins and the attitudes that speakers of AAE themselves and speakers of MAE have, respectively, to it. As is pointed out by Preston and Robinson, "It is perhaps the least surprising thing imaginable to find that attitudes toward languages and their varieties seem to be tied to attitudes toward groups of people."[32] Accordingly, individuals who have negative attitudes toward a group of people will also have negative attitudes toward the dialect of that group (attitudes that are provably unconnected to the actual linguistic features exhibited by the dialect). Unsurprisingly, it is also the case that groups of people have attitudes toward their own dialect. In this regard, it has been observed that members of an economically and socially dominant group typically have positive attitudes toward their own patterns of speech, while members of a minority group will variously (depending on the individual and the circumstance) display either positive or negative attitudes toward their own dialect. With respect to AAE, we know (and will discuss further below) that MAE speakers oftentimes display very negative attitudes toward the dialect, and that these attitudes have negative real-world consequences for AAE speakers' opportunities to prosper educationally, socially, and economically in the larger society.

The attitudes of AAE speakers toward their own dialect vary widely. Some African Americans take pride in using it, seeing it as an integral part of their ethno-cultural identity, while some avoid using it to the extent that they are able, considering it to be an impediment to their success. As might also be expected, some AAE speakers use or avoid using the dialect depending on the context. Thus, an AAE speaker might be careful to avoid features of the dialect in a professional setting, but would utilize all the dialect features at a family function or among close friends (this is, in fact, typical of speakers of just about any non-mainstream dialect of any language). Thus, the decision to use or not to use it is an intensely personal one. African Americans who eschew their

---

[32] Preston and Robinson 2005.

dialect are often judged by their peers to be inauthentic, and non-African Americans who adopt AAE (or its linguistic features) can be branded as imposters (this has been observed in regard to the performance language of some white hip-hop artists). For many in the African American community, it is difficult to express oneself fully and authentically without it. As Toni Morrison writes in her 1970 work *The Bluest Eye*,

> The language, only the language . . . it is the thing that black people love so much – the saying of words, holding them on the tongue, experimenting with them, playing with them. It's a love, a passion. Its function is like a preacher's: to make you stand up out of your seat, make you lose yourself and hear yourself. The worst of all possible things that could happen is to lose that language. There are certain things I cannot say without recourse to my language. (Toni Morrison, 1970, *The Bluest Eye*, p. 54)

One factor with the potential to influence African Americans' attitude toward their own dialect is the matter of its origins. An examination of this issue will help explain why. There are three main (and competing) theories on the origins of the AAE dialect, which are commonly labeled: (i) the Substratist position, (ii) the Anglicist position, and (iii) the Creolist position.

The first of these, the Substratist position, claims that AAE is very heavily influenced by West African languages spoken by the slaves that were brought over to British North America, with marginal input from English. Supporters of this theory have noted lexical and grammatical similarities between AAE and varieties of West African English that are spoken in Nigeria and Ghana. The idea behind this is that if the speakers of AAE and West African English exhibit similar linguistic features, then these could not have arisen in the United States by virtue of their contact with English-speaking slaveholder whites.

The second, Anglicist, position holds that AAE is a British-dialect-based variety of English with little or no outside influence from African languages. Support for this theory comes from the records of several African American communities in Nova Scotia and the Dominican Republic whose dialect (presumably) has remained constant throughout the years, along with study of other older English dialects. This position holds that many of the features that have come to be associated with AAE can be found as regular, rule-governed features of other English dialects, and attested in older forms of English.[33] In the United States, supporters of this theory attribute the documented similarities between AAE and Scots-Irish varieties as due solely to contact.

The Creolist position (or hypothesis) suggests that AAE exhibits patterns that are similar to the general phenomena associated with creole formation. According

---

[33] Poplack 2000: 27.

to this view, AAE developed from a mix of both African languages and English. During the time of the slave trade, a lot of different African peoples without a common language were forced together and their need to communicate resulted in a *pidgin* language which cobbled together aspects of many languages. This pidgin was simplified and incomplete until it was '**creolized**' and began to have native speakers who perfected the grammatical forms of the language. The English influence comes from the white slaveholders, and all of these influences led to a language with a unique grammatical structure and vocabulary.[34]

How do these different theories reflect on the speakers of AAE, and how do they affect the way that AAE is valued in African American society? Marcyliena Morgan discusses this issue in some detail, noting that "when two or more languages come together, two or more peoples have come together and the result is always about power and identity."[35] She suggests that each of these theories brings with it a different perspective. The Anglicist hypothesis, according to Morgan, incorporates the notion that "trans-Atlantic slavery left African Americans with no cultural roots worth mentioning," making AAE out to be nothing more complicated than wholesale imitation and borrowing from (and corruption of) British English. The Creolist hypothesis, for its part, suggests that the language of the African slaves is the newly formed language of a "conquered people who never got back home." The Substratist hypothesis, in contrast to the others, is built upon the notion that African languages (along with traditions, beliefs, and culture) made the crossing together with the slaves that carried them, and that this cultural wealth was transmitted down through the generations. On this view, the new language encodes traces of the original land from which the slaves were brought. Irrespective of which hypothesis is correct (and in truth AAE possesses features attributable to each one of them), one can see how AAE speakers' beliefs about their own dialect might affect their attitudes toward it. If AAE is a relic of slavery, a souvenir of those depredations, then perhaps it is something to be rid of, as a reminder of a painful time. On the other hand, to the extent that AAE preserves in itself elements of the African languages spoken by the free ancestors of the enslaved peoples, it is a legacy of that time and place, and worth preserving.

Recalling that attitudes toward language varieties are tied to attitudes toward the people who speak them, we turn now to two cases which demonstrate how African American speakers are judged (and discriminated against) on the basis of the language they speak. The first case illustrates how the use of AAE (as much as physical appearance) can be used to identify and discriminate against African Americans. The second case

---

[34] Shousterman et al. 2009.   [35] Morgan 2002.

Table 13.4 *Racial composition of Greater San Francisco areas (percentages)*

	Geographic area				
Population	East Palo Alto	Oakland	San Francisco	Palo Alto	Woodside
African American	42.9	43.9	10.9	2.9	0.3
Hispanic	36.4	13.9	13.9	5.0	3.8
White	31.7	32.5	53.6	84.9	94.7

Sources: US Census Bureau 1990; Purnell et al. 1999.

reveals just how deep-seated are the negative attitudes that people can have toward the dialect.

The first case involves an experiment conducted by a group of scholars in the 1990s which followed from the experience that one of them, John Baugh, had trying to get an apartment.[36] Baugh, an African American visiting scholar at Stanford looking for a place to live, had called several landlords and had been having trouble getting appointments to see them. He and his research team wondered whether his difficulty might be related to the AAE dialect he speaks. The experiment involved having speakers of three different varieties of American English – MAE, AAE, and Chicano (Mexican) American English (CAE) – respond to apartment listings in five San Francisco Bay area neighborhoods. The five neighborhoods differed greatly in the number of minority residents, with East Palo Alto having the lowest percentage of white residents and the highest percentage of African American and Hispanic residents, and Woodside being the "whitest" neighborhood (with fewer than 5 percent minority residents). Table 13.4 above shows the population distribution, based on 1990 census figures. Table 13.5 illustrates what happened when inquiries were made by speakers of MAE, AAE, and CAE.[37]

Nearly 1,000 calls were made, with the caller in each case following a prepared and identical script. Notice that an AAE-speaking caller was offered an appointment nearly 80 percent of the time when phoning East Palo Alto, but less than 30 percent of the time when phoning Woodside. White MAE speakers were offered interviews 70 percent of the time in calls to Woodside listings, and nearly 60 percent of the time when phoning up listings in East Palo Alto. Often, after telling the AAE-speaking caller that the apartment was already rented, a landlord would offer a white MAE speaker an appointment to see the same apartment. What is overwhelmingly clear from the experiment is that (i) people can very accurately identify speakers of other dialects on the basis of a very

[36] Purnell, Idsardi, and Baugh 1999.   [37] Purnell et al. 1999.

Table 13.5 *Confirmed appointments to view apartments (percentage) by race of caller*

	Geographic area				
Dialect guise	East Palo Alto	Oakland	San Francisco	Palo Alto	Woodside
AAE	79.3	72.0	63.5	48.3	28.7
CAE	61.9	58.3	53.2	31.9	21.8
MAE	57.6	68.7	71.9	63.1	70.1
Total calls per locale	118	211	310	263	87

Source: Purnell et al. 1999.

small sample of phonetic information, and (ii) people's attitude toward a dialect (and the speakers of it) affects their behavior.

The second case involves an effort some twenty years ago (in 1996) by the Oakland Unified School District in California to help the AAE-speaking majority of children in their district. They proposed recognizing AAE (which they called Ebonics) as the native language of the pupils who spoke it, their purpose being to be able to accommodate them in English and other subjects. Their rationale for doing this can be understood in its context. At that time, significant resources were being used to ameliorate English Language Arts deficits of Hispanic students who were not English native speakers. Recognizing that Hispanic students spoke a language different from English, educators were providing bilingual instruction and extra help in learning (Mainstream American) English as a second language. The Oakland School Board reasoned (correctly) that AAE-speaking students also had "non-native-speaker-like" language deficits on account of their speaking a variety of English that is quite different from MAE. And since African American students had similar difficulties bridging the gap between their dialect and MAE, recognizing AAE as a distinctive variety would help.

It would be an understatement to say that the reaction to this attempt to address a real problem was extremely hostile. And this reaction was character-istic of the white society at large, as well as the African American community leaders themselves. In his 1997 column on this matter, linguist Geoffrey Pullum states that the nation was scandalized by the proposal "to recognize the native tongue of most of its (African American) pupils as a language."[38] And while all linguists agree that AAE is a dialect of American English, and not a separate language, the controversy was more about what this variety

---

[38] Pullum 1997: 321.

represented than its linguistic status. AAE, Pullum said, was "described as if it were English with mistakes and omissions ... commentators clarified little except the deep hostility and contempt whites feel for the way blacks speak ..., and the deep shame felt by Americans of African descent for speaking that way (a *Los Angeles Times* column by Eldridge Cleaver, a former Black Panther party official, compared the official acknowledgement of AAE with condoning cannibalism)." Reverend Jesse Jackson's (initial) reaction to the proposal was (stereo)typical, stating: "I understand the attempt to reach out to these children, but this is an unacceptable surrender borderlining on disgrace ... It's teaching down to our children and it must never happen."[39]

However, as Pullum suggests, most Americans do not realize that AAE is not merely "bad English," but (as has been shown by numerous linguists) is the same as any other human language, having a unique grammar and pronunciation rules.[40] "There is no more reason for calling it bad standard English," Pullum says, "than there is for dismissing western dialects of English as bad eastern speech, or the reverse."[41] What we can take away from this is that there is a general popular misunderstanding about the nature of dialects, and a tendency, based on this misunderstanding, to respond viscerally to speakers of them rather than to the dialects themselves.

Summary: Comparison of Cases

We return here to Ryūkyūan and a comparison of that case with the AAE situation just described. Recall that, to promote national unity, the Japanese government determined that one variety of Japanese would have to be officially favored, and be esteemed over all others. In this model, the Ryūkyūans were simply deemed to speak a different dialect of Japanese, but one that was "clearly" inferior to all the others. In this regard, the American attitude toward African American English is worthy of comparison (in that many Americans regard African American vernacular as the worst of the non-standard varieties).

While Ryūkyūan languages are indeed distinct from Japanese and do not fall into the category of dialects, similarities of Japanese attitudes toward them and American attitudes toward non-standard varieties of American English, more notably African American English, are striking.

The fallacies evident from the Ebonics controversy are reflected in attitudes accompanying some of the local resistance to a revival of Ryūkyūan languages. Heinrich reports the following comment in a letter to the editor of the *Okinawa Times* from December 3, 2004. The letter-writer, a government official opposed to a Ryūkyūan language revival or having these languages taught in the schools, wrote:

---

[39] Harris 1996: A02.   [40] Bailey et al. 1998.   [41] Pullum 1997: 321.

I have come across the misunderstanding that the Okinawa dialects are believed to constitute language systems of their own because terms such as Okinawan or island language and the like exist. As a matter of fact, they are merely instances of corrupt accents and Old Japanese words which have not vanished but continue to be used in Okinawa ... Although there have recently been voices calling for teaching the dialects as languages to children, such a practice would be dreadful. What is the idea of teaching corrupt accents? If pupils are not taught to speak proper Japanese, they will face humiliation when grown up because of the language barrier.[42]

The author of this letter has many like-minded allies in the United States, whose attitudes toward Standard American English are equally unenlightened and linguistically flawed. Educating individuals such as this is no easy task, and one that must be undertaken across linguistic borders.

Additional Cases for Exploration

Occitan in France

Occitan is a language spoken by some 1.5 million people in southern France. It encompasses a number of varieties that eventually arose from Vulgar Latin following the fall of the Roman Empire. Variously referred to as Langue d'Oc and Provençal and some of the other local varieties, it is famously the language of the French troubadours, the wandering minstrels of the late medieval period, and was, as such, an established literary language. Although the area was subsumed in the Kingdom of France in the thirteenth century and French declared the language of government and state affairs, in practice government and court documents were translated into local varieties of Occitan. There was a major shift following the French Revolution, at which point Parisian French was declared the official language of the new republic of France, viewed as a vehicle for the establishment of a unified French nation. However, despite the fact that French became the language of free education, government, the courts and public signage, Occitan was still used as the language in the home, business, and art.

Pressure on minority languages continued to increase in the late nineteenth and early twentieth centuries. Primary education in languages other than French was not sanctioned by the state and efforts were made to eradicate local languages even in the schoolyard. French was reasserted as the language of the French Republic. The result was a significant decrease in the number of speakers, virtually all of whom were also native speakers of French. In the 1950s the teaching of Occitan was allowed in schools, but not beyond the primary level. The issue of Occitan and language rights for its speakers has

---

[42] Heinrich 2005.

been brought to the fore by recent attempts at some revival (e.g. bilingual signage) and by France's signing in 1999 (but not ratifying) the European Charter for Regional and Minority Languages. The continued decline of Occitan and other local varieties continues to be a contentious issue.

Singaporean English and Local Chinese Dialects in Singapore

Lying just off the southern tip of the Malay Peninsula, the island city-state of Singapore recognizes four official languages – Mandarin Chinese, Malay, Tamil, and English – a reflection of its complex history and inhabitants. Despite its multilingual heritage, Singapore has experienced language conflict, in part owing to its economic aspirations and its bilingual policy which required each student to be able to speak English and their home language.

The Chinese population traced its ancestry to diverse regions of China and largely spoke Hokkien, Cantonese, Teochew, and Hakka varieties. In 1979, the Singapore government launched its Speak Mandarin Campaign to encourage the use of Mandarin in public with an eye toward economic development, promoting Chinese cultural identity, and facilitating communication among its Chinese residents. Use of Mandarin was mandated for government employees (except when speaking with residents over 60 years of age) and for service industry workers under the age of 40. Some complained that many children were in practice compelled to learn two second languages in school, English and Mandarin, and that communication between children and 'dialect-speaking' elders was hampered. The Speak Mandarin Campaign continues to this day.

For years under British rule, English was well established in Singapore. However, Singaporean English, or Singlish, is a creolized variety that incorporates features from Hokkien, Malay, and other local languages and is distinct from British (or American) Standard English. Citing economic concerns and the need to communicate with the global community, the government launched the Speak Good English Movement in 2000, in an effort to reduce if not eradicate the use of Singlish, discouraging its use in broadcast and print media, in educational settings, in the service industry and elsewhere. However, many consider Singlish to be an integral expression of what it means to be Singaporean, an expression of their postcolonial experience, and suppression of the language is suppression of personal and cultural identity. In some respects, the Speak Good English Movement has strengthened the resolve of speakers of Singlish and is used by some politicians to help build their constituency. The Movement remains an ongoing program of the Singapore government.

Landsmål/Bokmål in Norway

Sitting along the North Sea coastline adjacent to Sweden, Norway is a relatively "new" country, having become independent (for the second time) only in the twentieth century. Norway had been an independent kingdom previously for some 500 years (872–1380) until it was absorbed by the Danish crown, as a consequence of being greatly weakened demographically and economically by the Black Death of the fourteenth century. After over 400 years of Danish rule, followed by some ninety years of Swedish rule, Norway became once again an independent monarchy in 1905 via a peaceful dissolution of its union with Sweden. This union, for diplomatic, economic, and cultural reasons, had outlived its usefulness to both nations, and Norway was once again able to seek its own fortunes.

One of the central conflicts in Norway's resurgence into nationhood concerned language. The language of the first independent Norwegian monarchy had been Old Norse, but after 400 years of Danish rule, Old Norse had fallen into disuse as an official language, having been replaced by the local urban elites with a local variety of Danish (called Riksmål, 'idiom of the realm,' or Bokmål, 'idiom of the book'). Old Norse itself had slowly evolved into a collection of local rural dialects. For urban Norwegians, Riksmål was a language that allowed them to distinguish themselves from the Swedes, from whom they had recently become independent. However, for others Riksmål was not "Norwegian" enough, and there was a strong desire to restore the Old Norse language with a newer version, called Nynorsk ('New Norse') or Landsmål ('idiom of the land') by its proponents. Those who wished to bring Nynorsk into use believed it to be a more "authentic" language for the nation. Those who opposed it felt that Nynorsk was merely a collection of rustic and crude dialects, and that using it would make it more difficult for Norwegians to communicate with their Scandinavian neighbors. Norway has had, since 1917, a law that permits children to use their own spoken variety of Norwegian in the classroom and encourages teachers to accommodate it – making Norway a far more accommodating place for regional varieties than many other nations (including the United States).[43] It is nonetheless the case that disputes over what should be used as an "official" Norwegian language persisted through the twentieth century.

[43] Trudgill 2016: 42–43.

14   Competition for Linguistic Dominance

In this final chapter on the typology of language conflicts, the reader will find cases of "competition for linguistic dominance," in which two groups each hold sway in some region of a country, and are struggling for dominance or independence, with language rights playing a part in the articulation of that struggle. The featured cases are (i) Flemish versus Walloons in Belgium (where no resolution is in sight), (ii) Tamils versus Sinhalese in Sri Lanka (where the former group was crushed in a civil war with the latter), and (iii) French versus English in Canada (where legislation has achieved a more-or-less livable stasis). The extra case synopses presented at the end of the chapter are: French versus Wolof in Senegal, Chinese, Cantonese, and English in Hong Kong, and Hebrew versus Arabic in Israel.

Flemish versus Walloons in Belgium

The competition between the Flemish and the Walloons in Belgium is note-worthy as a smaller version of the international competition between German and French speakers in Western Europe, and as an example of how a sectarian conflict can diminish in intensity, only to be replaced by ethnic-linguistic conflict. As we shall elaborate on below, Flemish is a Germanic language and a regional variety of Dutch, Walloon is a regional variety of French, and Belgium's linguistic conflict is between these two ethnically distinct groups of speakers. The fact of these two groups becoming constituent parts of a single country is attributable, in part, to the Roman Catholic–Protestant conflict that preceded and led to Belgian independence.

The Rise of Belgium: Historical and Linguistic Background

The northern portion of what is now Belgium includes the historically prosperous region called Flanders. This area is the southern part of a region occupied before the sixth century by Frankish tribes who spoke Lower Franconian (Nederfrankisch), a language which evolved into Modern Dutch. As Figure 14.1 shows, the area occupied by this group includes present-day

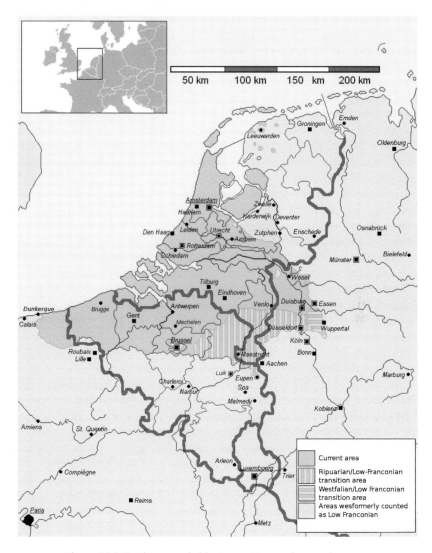

Figure 14.1 Region occupied by Lower Franconian speakers

southern Netherlands and northern Belgium. In contrast, the southern half of Belgium, known as Wallonia, is a French-speaking region that has historically been part of the Romance-speaking world since the time of the Roman Empire.

One might, on seeing this map and understanding the nature of this centuries-long ethnic-linguistic divide, wonder how it came to be that the Walloons and the Flemish wound up occupying the same country, and how it is that the Dutch were split between the two. To understand this, we must go back to the four-teenth century. In the last part of that century, the Low Countries (present-day Belgium, the Netherlands, and Luxemburg) came under the sway of two successive external dynasties – first under the Dukes of Burgundy (from 1384 until 1477) and then under the Habsburgs, a royal house from Switzerland that married and battled its way to possessions and power across Europe over the course of several centuries. By 1547, at the peak of Habsburg power in Europe, all of present-day Belgium and the Netherlands were con-solidated under Habsburg rule after their decisive victory at Mühlberg in 1547 over a league of Protestant German princes.

Collecting all the Dutch-speaking people under one rule, as the Burgundians and Habsburgs did, had unintended consequences. For one thing, the Dutch were now more inclined to work in concert than they had been when they were divided into numerous duchies and bishoprics. Two more or less concurrent sets of circum-stances conspired to ignite a rebellion against (Spanish) Habsburg rule in 1566, less than two decades after they vanquished the Protestant rebels at Mühlberg.

First of all, the Dutch (whose economic activity was substantial and success-ful) had been turned into a lucrative source of tax revenue by the Spanish Habsburg king, Philip II (whose own royal purse was empty and who had already declared bankruptcy twice before this in 1557 and 1560). Being taxed more heavily than other areas of the empire and more heavily than they could bear united the Dutch in their opposition to the Spanish crown.

Secondly, and perhaps more importantly, northern Europe (inclusive of the Netherlands) had been awash with the rebellions of the Protestant Reformation from the beginning of the sixteenth century. And while the Catholic king of Spain may have vanquished a confederation of German princes in 1547, resentment of the Catholic Church and the temporal rulers who served it was not at all dampened in the Dutch provinces. In 1566, a small but significant (to Philip II) Catholic Church was invaded and destroyed by an anti-Catholic mob. This incident quickly spread across the Calvinist Dutch provinces, becoming a Beeldenstorm (literally: 'image or statue storm') that swept across the Low Country. Protestant mobs burned churches, destroyed artwork, and smashed statues (in keeping with their biblically inspired hostility toward "graven images"). From this beginning, a full-fledged revolt against Spanish Habsburg rule was initiated, a war of Dutch Revolt that is also, appropriately, named the Eighty Years' War, lasting as it did from 1568 until 1648 (punctuated by a decade of truce in 1609–1619). The second installment of the Eighty Years' War (1619–1648) coincided with, and was a part of, the European continent-wide Catholic–Protestant conflagration known as the Thirty Years' War (a conflict which cost as many as 8 million lives and drastically reduced the population of the participant nations – Germany lost 25–40 percent of its population).

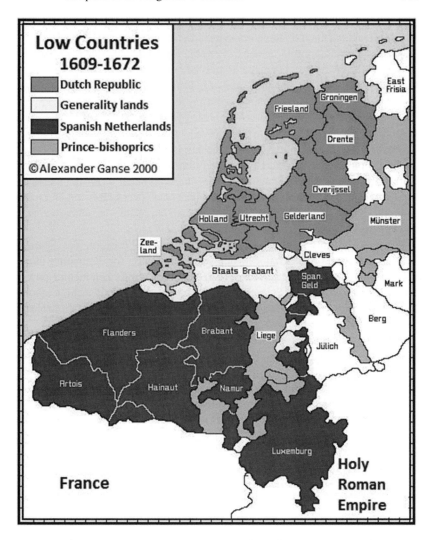

Figure 14.2 Low countries 1609–1672, including the Dutch Republic and Spanish Netherlands

The outcome of this decades-long struggle was that the Protestant-majority northern Dutch-speaking provinces (also styled as the United Provinces) won their independence from the Spanish crown, and the Catholic-majority southern Dutch-speaking provinces remained under Catholic Spanish rule as the Spanish Netherlands, as shown in Figure 14.2. From this point onward (excepting for a brief fifteen-year period, 1815–1830), the Flemish Dutch and the Netherlands Dutch lived on opposite sides of an international border.

Turning our attention more squarely to the Spanish Netherlands, it is interesting to discover that language issues began brewing nearly as soon as Catholic rule was consolidated and the Protestant Dutch were contained north of the border. Unsurprisingly, during the seventeenth century, French was the language used by the government first under Habsburg rule, as the French language had by this time evolved into a regional "lingua franca." However, the Spanish and Austrian Habsburgs had no especially ideological connection to French, and there were therefore no laws prohibiting the use of Dutch in areas where Dutch speakers predominated (i.e. in Flanders, Luxemburg, and other northern provinces). Nevertheless, the Dutch Catholics had to deal with the fact that their own language was not particularly usable outside their own language community, and was subordinate to French.

For most of this period and into the eighteenth century, the Spanish Netherlands was a battleground which saw competition for dominance along its margins and sometimes into its core among various continental power configurations – e.g. the Protestant Dutch and English against the Catholic Habsburgs, the Austrian Habsburgs against the French, and the French and Dutch against the English.

These many decades of steady, but predictable instability came to a close with the French Revolution. In 1790, French armies overran the southern (formerly Spanish, then Austrian) Netherlands, and subsequently declared war on everyone that they weren't already at war with (adding to their established list of enemies – Austria and Prussia – their new adversaries: Holland, England, and Spain). Recovering quickly after an initial setback before the Austrian armies, France invaded the United Provinces in 1795, ran off their Dutch rulers (to England), and incorporated this territory into the French Empire.

Napoleon's empire being distinctively and consciously French, the French language was no longer just a useful tool of government in the territories of the former Spanish/Austrian Netherlands and in Holland. It was, rather, the ideological vehicle of the French Revolution and the instrument of its advancement. After imposing the French language on the southern Netherlands, in the spirit of their "one nation, one language" policy, the French government promulgated an edict in 1803 across its territories (including the newly acquired Holland) which declared that only French could be used in official documents commencing in 1804. This also being the year in which Napoleon himself was crowned emperor, one might imagine (with tongue in cheek) that the 1803 language decree left those who didn't know French unaware that Napoleon was now their emperor, since they would not have been able to read the French-only proclamation. Thus began, in the Napoleonic period, "a directed language policy against press, literature, and theatre in Dutch."[1]

Napoleon's defeat at Waterloo in 1815, and the Congress of Vienna that followed it, set the stage for a return to the old order, and for the compensation of those nations, such as Holland, who had fought against the French Revolution and its offspring empire. The Dutch, therefore, found themselves reunited briefly (until 1830) in a linguistically coherent Kingdom of the Netherlands, under their exiled king's son, William I, who also ruled over the Catholic Dutch in the southern Netherlands and over Luxemburg (as shown in Figure 14.3). This arrangement, despite William's otherwise enlightened rule, did not ultimately go down well in the Catholic south. William, a Calvinist, was not naturally well disposed toward Catholics and was rather belligerent toward the Catholic Church and its clergy. In the nearly 200 years since the end of the

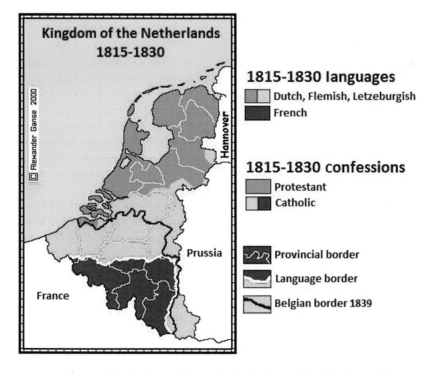

Figure 14.3 Kingdom of the Netherlands 1815–1830, with 1839 Belgian border

[1] de Groof 2002: 121–122.

Catholic–Protestant wars of the seventeenth century, the relative importance of sectarian divisions compared to linguistic and ethnic ones had not receded sufficiently for the king of the Netherlands to be kind to his Catholic subjects, or for those Catholic subjects to be content with a Calvinist king. As linguistically put-upon as the Dutch speakers of the French Empire might have been under Napoleonic language laws, they chafed ever so much more under their anti-Catholic monarch.

The July Revolution of 1830 against the French king, Charles X, helped to instigate a similar uprising a month later in August against the king of the Netherlands. Resistance to northern Dutch rule was stiff enough that the "Belgians" were able to declare their independence by November of that year. The war with the northern Kingdom of the Netherlands rattled on for another eight years (until 1839), but in the end, the Catholic lands of the Dutch-speaking Flemish and French-speaking Walloons reverted to their former separation from the Protestant Netherlands, and Belgium was born.

The Rise of the Belgian Language Conflict

Once the Catholics of Belgium were safely ensconced in their own nominally sectarian state and the Calvinists were pushed to the other side of a border, it did not take long for them to find something else to fight about. The Catholic Belgian state emerged, as it were, almost as an afterthought or endnote to centuries of European Protestant–Catholic religious strife. But it emerged in a century in which various nationalisms were being birthed all across the continent. Germans in Austria, Czechs in Bohemia, Magyars in Austria–Hungary, Poles in Galicia, Italians in Lombardy and Venice, and Slavs in Balkan reaches of Austria–Hungary were all finding their "nationhood" and with it their "national languages." So, the Belgians having created a state, in part to protect their confessional preferences, immediately found themselves to be a binational and bilingual state – something which most definitely went against the emerging grain of nineteenth-century Europe.

The foundational problem for Belgium, coming on the scene in a period when pent-up nationalism was breaking out all over, was that there was no Belgian nation, per se. The French-speaking elite papered over this problem by manufacturing a sense of national identity – compensating for the lack of any real cultural unity with "shared historical experience," "mutual interests," and "an invented territorial past."[2] Although Dutch speakers have always outnumbered French speakers in Belgium, and did so at the time of Belgium's founding (2.4 million Dutch speakers to 1.8 million French speakers in 1846),[3] French dominated from the start. This was on account of the fact that both the

---

[2] O'Neill 2000: 115.   [3] Mnookin and Verbeke 2009: 157.

Wallonian and Flemish bourgeoisie spoke French, it having long been used as the language of government (de facto until 1795 and de jure afterward). The capital region of Brussels and seat of political power, therefore, was (and still is) overwhelmingly populated by French speakers. Thus, while the Belgian constitution of 1831 allowed freedom of language choice, the Dutch language was only tolerated.

The French-speaking areas of Belgium, outside the capital, were also economically dominant in the nineteenth century. The textile industry in Flanders, having failed to industrialize, was in decline, and heavy industry in Wallonia was burgeoning, buoyed along by the region's substantial coal reserves. The rural Flemish of the north were thus reduced to subsistence farming, with many of them migrating to the south for factory jobs, and subsequently assimilating to the French-speaking population there. Belgium's language policy was designed "at the outset, simply to suppress the minor language, to create the new State on the basis of one language, and to impose a policy of assimilation through legal and economic influence."[4]

In 1840, soon after the signing of the 1839 Treaty of London (which ended the conflict with the Netherlands and settled the Belgian borders), the Dutch Flemish minority was agitating for Dutch language rights. The 1840 petition called for greater cultural contact with the Dutch Netherlands, and for spelling reform to align Flemish Dutch with Netherlands Dutch.[5] The protests were answered in 1856, officially, with the establishment of a Commission on Grievances, which "recommended bilingualism in Flanders and unilingualism in Wallonia."[6] Unfortunately, the Commission's recommendations were not taken up in the form of legislation, and the situation for Dutch speakers continued to get only worse.

The suppression of Dutch in the Flanders region was rather excessive in this period, especially in the justice system, education, and health care. One egregious consequence of this policy was a travesty of justice involving two Flemish laborers, Jan Coucke and Pieter Goethals. The two men "were tried [in 1860] for the murder and robbery of an elderly widow ... Their trial was conducted entirely in French ... and even the defense attorney was unilingual [French]. The evidence against them was circumstantial, turning primarily on a remark between the two men overheard by a jailer and allegedly mistranslated by the court interpreter. Nonetheless, both were found guilty and guillotined in November 1860. Several months later, the case took a dramatic and unexpected turn when another suspect confessed to complicity in the murder" and they were posthumously declared innocent.[7] In the realm of education, the neglect of the Dutch language in the northern provinces of Belgium had the effect of reversing the significant gains in Dutch literacy achieved under William I

---

[4] Huysmanns 1930: 680.   [5] Vos 1993: 134.   [6] O'Neill 2000: 116.   [7] McRae 1986: 24–25.

during the 1815–1830 Kingdom of the Netherlands. By 1900, Belgium had a higher percentage of non-literate people than any of its neighbors. This is unsurprising in light of the dearth of Dutch-language schools (in 1910, apart from one private school in Antwerp, there was not a single Dutch-language secondary school in the country). In health care as well, abuses abounded. A 1911 newspaper report (*Het Laatste Nieuws*, May 30, 1911) tells of two nurses in a Brussels hospital who were disciplined for speaking Dutch to each other. The director of the hospital is reported to have commented, "It is already bad enough that we have to tolerate the patients speaking in Flemish."[8]

The outcry following the miscarriage of justice in the 1860 court case, as well as other similar injustices and indignities, led to some reforms. Through the efforts of pro-Flemish members of parliament, several language laws came into effect, such as the right to use Dutch or French in the courts (1873), in administration (1878), and in secondary education (1883). Later on, the Dutch language was symbolically recognized through the introduction of bilingual coins (1886), banknotes (1888), and postage stamps (1891).[9]

It is important to understand that the laws of accommodation (in courts, government services, and education) applied to Flanders only; that is, they only permitted Dutch to be used in the courts in Dutch-speaking areas, but not in the southern French-speaking region. French, of course, was permitted everywhere. Note also that these were laws of linguistic tolerance, not linguistic promotion. They simply allowed Dutch to be used, but did not require anyone to provide for it. There were plenty of government officials in Flanders who only spoke French, and the new laws did not require them to know Dutch or to use it. By 1898, however, pressure on the part of the Flemish Movement had become significant enough to force parliamentary passage of the "Equality Law," which set Dutch and French "on an equal footing for parliamentary debates and for the promulgations of laws."[10]

Beginning in 1921 and culminating in 1963, efforts were made to accommodate the bilingual realities of Belgium by applying different language rules to different areas of the country in recognition of the language composition of each area. The 1921 law essentially extended the administrative legislation passed in 1878 by recognizing Dutch as the official language of the Flemish region and requiring that Dutch be used in government communications at the provincial level (but allowing French to continue to be used in such, optionally). One extremely progressive aspect of this law was the requirement that officials in the central government (and other sensitive positions) attain basic fluency in Dutch. This part of the law raised some hackles among Belgian officialdom, over 90 percent of whom did not have fluency in Belgium's new, second official language and who most likely resented being told to make this

---

[8] Belien 2005.   [9] Vos 1993: 134.   [10] Beheydt 1995: 51.

accommodation. Of course, the very fact that Flemish only constituted 6 percent of all Belgian central government officials (from 1830 until 1930) points to how enormously underserved was that 60 percent of Belgium's population.[11]

A language law passed in 1932 continued and strengthened aspects of the 1921 law, more stringently imposing administrative unilingualism in Flanders and Wallonia, and compulsory bilingualism in Brussels and areas/communities in which minority speakers exceeded 30 percent of the population. The 1932 law also set aside some of the individual requirements for personal bilingualism for central government officials, allowing those departments to assign officials to tasks according to linguistic criteria and (presumably) making sure that there were sufficient staff to handle the needs of both language communities.[12]

Finally, a law passed in 1963 served to elaborate all the requirements of the 1932 law, "sought to apply the principles more stringently, to close loopholes, to strengthen the mechanisms for application and surveillance, and to remedy the absence of sanctions in the earlier law." While the 1932 law constituted six pages of text in each language, the 1963 law required forty, followed in 1966 by thirty-four additional pages that articulated ten "decrees of execution" emanating from the 1963 law.[13] One imagines that some of this obsessive attention to detail served as fine practice for Belgian officialdom to train themselves for their eventual role as the bureaucrats of Europe.

Figure 14.4 illustrates the official language border as defined since 1963. The municipalities with language facilities are shaded darker. These municipalities are required to offer services to French-speaking residents if in the Dutch region, and services to Dutch-speaking residents if in the French region. All of the German area has language facilities for both Dutch and French speakers. Brussels is, by law, bilingual. Outside these exceptions, all Dutch and French areas are respectively unilingual.

A Reversal of Fortunes and Sharpening of the Conflict

The Flemish, and their Dutch-speaking compatriots to the north, had been quite economically successful from the twelfth century through the fifteenth, when Burgundian and then Habsburg rulers and their imposition of high taxation began to sap their economic strength. Being at the crossroads of so many European conflicts and wars didn't help advance their fortunes greatly either. And from the beginning of the seventeenth century, with the exception of a brief interlude imposed by the Congress of Vienna, the fortunes of Flanders and the lives of the Flemish came under the increasing sway of their French-speaking neighbors to the south (both the Wallonian French and the French

[11] McRae 1986: 190.   [12] McRae 1986: 191.   [13] McRae 1986: 191.

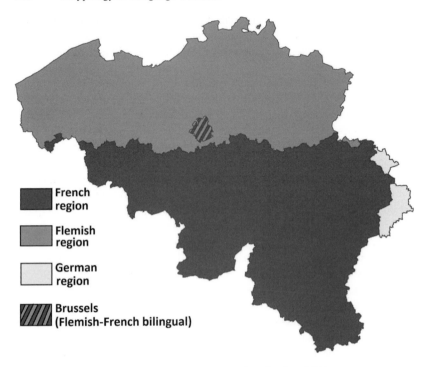

French
region

Flemish
region

German
region

Brussels
(Flemish-French bilingual)

Figure 14.4 Language partition of Belgium by the 1963 law

themselves). By the founding of Belgium, and for at least 100 years afterward, the Flemish were pretty much reduced to being second-class citizens in their own country. They were separated from their Dutch compatriots by a border, underserved by their own government, and left to flounder in an economic backwater.

This situation remained pretty much the status quo through the middle of the twentieth century, with those Flemish that wished to advance themselves forced to move south into the prosperous, heavy industrial zone of the south, and to assimilate to the French-language culture there. This situation began to change after World War II, as Wallonia's economic engine began to run down. In a manner similar to that of the United States, the 1960s, 1970s and 1980s saw the heavily unionized iron and steel industry become outmoded and outrun by newer economic powerhouses such as China, Korea, India, and Brazil (Belgium ranked ninth in steel production worldwide in 1967, thirteenth in 1980, fifteenth in 1990, eighteenth in 2000, and twentieth in 2010). At the same time, Flanders was returning to its former prominence as a center for freight transfer (ports and rail), as a diamond market, and as a center for chemical industries.

The economic fortunes of Flanders and Wallonia (outside Brussels) have by now been reversed. In 1948, Flanders' per capita GDP was 83 percent that of Wallonia.[14] In 2006, Wallonia's per capita GDP was 72 percent that of Flanders. Other economic indicators are similar: "Unemployment in Wallonia is mainly structural, while in Flanders it is cyclical. Flanders' unemployment level equals only half that of Wallonia. The southern region continues a difficult transition out of sunset industries (mainly coal and steel), while sunrise industries (chemicals, high-tech, and services) dominate in Flanders."[15]

This circumstance, in which the Flemish Dutch find themselves heavily taxed in order to support social and economic services for the welfare of others (i.e. the Flemish in the south), is somewhat reminiscent of the last time (350 years ago) that an over-taxed Dutch community rebelled against its rulers (the Habsburgs). While the likelihood of an armed uprising is quite minimal, it is the case that the recent economic resurgence of the Flemish, together with their overly long domination by the French, has led them to assert themselves even more forcefully in the matter of cultural parity and linguistic rights. The Walloons, for their part, being used to the privilege of being French, do not always respond positively or charitably to Flemish assertiveness, preferring perhaps the comfort of "status quo."

The impatience of each side with the other, and the sharpening of differences over the past couple of decades, has made it increasingly harder for the two constituencies to agree on anything. Nationalistic movements on both sides have agitated for devolution of their respective regions, or at least for a solution that is more confederal in nature, with each region gaining independence and autonomy. Each region is, in keeping with these developments, less willing to compromise on linguistic matters. In recent years, Flemish authorities have been pressing back on French communities in the Flemish region, on occasion forcing everyone in a town to do their business in Flemish, even though no one speaks it, simply because the law says they must.[16] It might not be wrong to think that these current attitudes and actions are, to some degree, retribution for centuries of French mistreatment of the Flemish. In April 2010, the government of Belgium fell apart over the legality of a bilingual voting district in the outskirts of Brussels (the courts declared that it could not remain so), and Belgium remained without any government for nearly two years on account of it.[17]

Were it not for the location and linguistic composition of Brussels, Belgium might have devolved into two separate states several years ago. Brussels is a

[14] McRae 1986: 75.   [15] United States State Department 2012.   [16] Daley 2010.
[17] Blenkinsop 2010.

bilingual city, but it also has an overwhelming majority of French speakers. So, one might imagine that it would become part of Wallonia, should the two regions separate. However, Brussels is a valuable national resource, economically, and it is well inside the Flemish region (surrounded on all sides by it). The Flemish would be highly unlikely to allow Brussels to become part of Wallonia, and the Walloons would be just as unlikely to allow the Flemish to keep it. So, if Brussels is the brilliant offspring of Belgium's two parts, it appears that the "parents" are staying together on account of the child.

Tamils versus Sinhalese in Sri Lanka

The case of Sri Lanka (known as Ceylon under British colonial rule) and the language conflicts arising in the aftermath of its independence are quite interesting, when compared and contrasted with the situation in neighboring India. In many, many ways, the two nations' situations – both pre- and postcolonial – were quite similar. Yet, in one or two respects, they were different enough to lead to widely different results – the imposition of severe language restrictions on the Tamils and a devastating civil war in Sri Lanka, compared with much less destructive outcomes in India.

Historical Background

While there is some evidence of prehistoric settlement of the island of Sri Lanka, it is likely that such settlement was very sparse. The first historical records (i.e. written evidence of civilization) found in Sri Lanka date from 600–500 BCE, and consist of pottery inscriptions written in Middle Indo-Aryan script, suggesting migration to the island from northern India around that time. There is no evidence of Dravidian writing from that period. From that time onward, the establishment of Buddhism and the spread of agriculture on the island led to its main city being one of the most populous in south Asia by the third century BCE.[18]

The first of numerous Tamil invasions (from the modern-day region of Tamil Nadu) took place in the mid third century BCE, and involved two Tamil leaders, Sena and Guttika, who overthrew a Buddhist ruler Suratissa in 236 BCE. During this period, Hindu worship from south India was introduced to previously Buddhist-only Sri Lanka.[19] Figure 14.5 shows Tamil Nadu and the modern-day distribution of Tamil speakers in Sri Lanka.

From the second century BCE until early in the tenth century CE, the central political unit in Sri Lanka was the Sinhalese kingdom of Anurādhapura. From the capital, Anurādhapura, in north central Sri Lanka, the kingdom developed a

---

[18] Deraniyagala 1996.   [19] Abeykon 1884: 83.

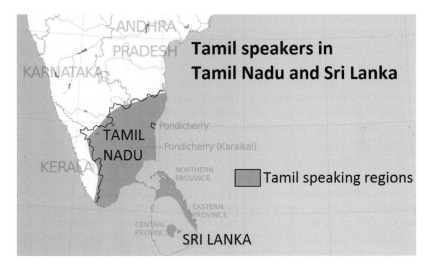

Figure 14.5 Tamils in Sri Lanka and Tamil Nadu state

high level of art and architecture, along with complex and sophisticated irriga-
tion systems (due in part to its location in the dry northern parts of the island).
Over the course of its existence, control of Anurādhapura changed hands many
times and saw several different dynasties – resulting both from struggles for
dominance among different Sinhalese clans and invasions from southern India.
Partly on account of invasions from southern India, Anurādhapura was abandoned as the seat of the kingdom in the late eleventh century (1070) and moved
eastward to the city of Polonnaruwa, where it remained for 150 years, until
early in the thirteenth century. During the long fourteenth-century period of the
Anurādhapura–Polonnaruwa kingdoms, the kingship was "essentially
Brahmanic (hereditary within the priestly social class), with strong Buddhist
influences; all the kings were practicing Buddhists and patrons of Buddhist
institutions."[20]

Toward the end of the twelfth century, the Polonnaruwa kingdom fell into the
hands of non-Sinhalese rulers from southern India, principally Kalingas and
Pandyas (the latter being Tamil). A particularly brutal forty-year reign (1214–
1255) of a Kalinga king, Magha, spelled the end of unitary Sinhalese control
over the island. From that point on, various Sinhalese kings ruled their own
cities and local areas in the southern parts of the island, while the north was
dominated by the Tamil kingdom of Jaffna. The political weakness and disunity
of Sri Lanka during the thirteenth through fifteenth centuries made the island

___

[20] Arasaratnam and Peiris 2016.

particularly vulnerable to foreign invasions – from southern India, from China, and ultimately from Europe.[21]

The colonization of Sri Lanka by European powers resulted from the combination of (i) a politically divided and weak island, (ii) the fractious nature of Sri Lankan politics, and (iii) a European desire to establish and control trading outposts. The basic formula, repeated more than once, was that some party to a political or military struggle on the island would enlist the aid of a European nation, the European power would come along and help that party to victory, and then the European power would take over.

In 1505, a Portuguese fleet happened upon the west coast port of Colombo (Sinhalese *Kolamba*) due to a storm. The Portuguese were welcomed, the port seemed promising, and the Portuguese built a fort and began trading. In 1518, the three sons of the king of Kotte (just inland from Colombo) murdered their father and divided the kingdom among themselves into three smaller realms: Kotte (along the coast in the western third of the island), Sitawaka (in the southern central highlands), and Raigama (in the southwestern quarter). As one might have predicted, given the nature of the protagonists, one of the three murderous sons (the ruler of Sitawaka) decided he would like a larger portion of the whole (a piece of Kotte, in this case). The ruler of Kotte enlisted Portuguese support.[22]

Ever-increasing dependence on the Portuguese through the sixteenth century resulted in ever-increasing concessions by the kingdom of Kotte to the Portuguese, until, by 1597, Kotte belonged to the Portuguese. From there, the Portuguese pursued the conquest of the rest of the island, and the conversion of its inhabitants to Christianity. They were mostly successful in this, coming to possess the western and northern parts of the island (i.e. everything except the Kingdom of Kandy) by 1619. Portuguese pressure on Kandy led that king to find common cause against the Portuguese with the Dutch (who had already established trading posts by the beginning of the seventeenth century). After some fits and starts, the Dutch took on the Portuguese in 1638, in a battle for possession of the island (purportedly to help the Kandyans), and completed their conquest in 1658. The Dutch, who were much more benign rulers in matters of religion, culture, and traditions than the Portuguese had been, remained in control of Sri Lanka until the arrival of the British in 1796.[23]

Although the British had had designs on the Dutch Sri Lankan possessions during the eighteenth century, the immediate impetus for British involvement in Sri Lanka had less to do with Sri Lanka itself than with British trepidation regarding the possibility that Sri Lanka might fall into French hands (the French having conquered and occupied the Netherlands in 1795).[24] From

[21] Arasaratnam and Peiris 2016.   [22] Pieris 1920: 42–46.   [23] Arasaratnam and Peiris 2016.   [24] Pieris 1918: 139.

exile in England in February 1795, the deposed Dutch ruler, Prince William V of Orange, wrote to the Dutch governor of Colombo, requesting that he admit into the colony British troops and ships, and that he consider them as "belonging to a Power that is in friendship and alliance with their High Mightinesses, and who come to prevent the Colony from being invaded by the French."[25] The prince did not, perhaps, consider the possibility that the British (once allowed in) would be loath to leave, as they indeed turned out to be. By 1815, the British had secured control and possession of the entire island, eliminating the last resistance of the Kandyan kingdom in 1817. From then, until independence in 1948, the British ruled the island.

Linguistic Background

Recall that the languages of southern India belong to the Dravidian language family, which is wholly distinct and unrelated to languages of the Indo-European language family in the north. Tamil is one of the former and Sinhala is one of the latter.

The term *Dravidian*, to refer to the entire family of (mostly) south Indian languages, was coined by Robert Caldwell (1856: 26) as a derivative of *drāviḍa*, a Sanskrit word historically used to refer to the Tamil themselves. The language family consists of four major literary languages of south India – Kannada, Malayalam, Tamil, and Telugu – along with some twenty other minor languages, some of which are distributed in northern India and Pakistan. The origins of Dravidian language speakers is unknown, but linguistic and historical evidence confirms that they were broadly spread across the Indian sub-continent (north and south) by the time that Aryan (i.e. Indo-European) peoples migrated into the northern half of the subcontinent about 3,500 years ago (~1500 BCE). Some speculate that Dravidians arrived in India 2,000 years before that (~3500 BCE), although even those who have suggested this acknowledge that they are not certain.[26] After Indo-Aryan peoples moved into the sub-continent, the Dravidians were gradually pushed further and further southward, such that the vast majority occupy the southern third of the subcontinent. The largest numbers of Tamils, the group with which we are concerned here, occupy the southeastern-most parts of India (about 64 million in Tamil Nadu) and northern Sri Lanka (about 3 million). See Figure 14.6.

Regardless of when the Dravidians arrived, it is clear that their languages are unrelated to any other family of languages in the world. This an important factor to keep in mind when one is assessing the difficulties engendered in a conflict between Sinhala (an Indo-Aryan language) and Tamil (a Dravidian one). Dravidian languages have been profoundly influenced by Indo-Aryan

[25] Anthonisz 1907: 138.   [26] Zvelebil 1990: 123.

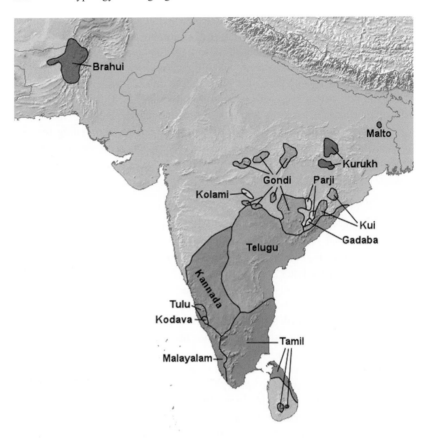

Figure 14.6 Dravidian language family

languages, and vice versa, their speakers having coexisted and interacted with each other for millennia. As Murray Emeneau noted, "in a multilingual area like the [Indian Language Area], the question of autonomy of one language/dialect from another is difficult to ascertain."[27] Nevertheless, despite centuries of contact, the two languages are quite distinct and mutually unintelligible.

Looking at the differences, one first notes a marked difference in their phonology. Tables 14.1 and 14.2 lay out the inventory of consonants for each language, showing only contrastive sounds (and not allophones).

One of the first things one sees is the difference in the number of consonants: Tamil has 18 and Sinhala has 25. Tamil has no voiced/voiceless (e.g. [p]/[b]

[27] Shiffman 1982: 186.

Table 14.1 *Tamil consonants*

	Labial	Dental	Alveolar	Retroflex	Palatal	Velar
Plosives	p	t̪	t	ʈ	t͡ɕ	k
Nasals	m	n̪	n	ɳ	ɲ	ŋ
Tap				ɾ		
Central approximants	v			ɻ	j	
Lateral approximants		l̪		ɭ		

Source: https://en.wikipedia.org/wiki/Tamil_language#Phonology

Table 14.2 *Sinhala consonants*

		Labial	Dental/ Alveolar	Retroflex	Palatal	Velar	Glottal
Nasal		m	n̪	ɳ	ɲ	ŋ	
Plosive	voiceless	p	t̪	ʈ	tʃ	k	
	voiced	b	d̪	ɖ	dʒ	g	
	prenasalized	ᵐb	ⁿ̪d̪	ⁿɖ		ᵑg	
Fricative			s				h
Rhotic			r				
Approximant		ʋ	l		j		

Source: https://en.wikipedia.org/wiki/Sinhalese_language#Phonology

contrast), while Sinhala does. Sinhala, but not Tamil, also has a series of prenasalized consonants, such as [ᵐb] (pronounced as though one was trying to have an [m] before a [b]). Sinhala also has a couple of fricative consonants, [s] and [h], where Tamil does not. Tamil, but not Sinhala, distinguishes between dental and alveolar consonants (the dental "t" sound [t̪] is similar to the French pronunciation, e.g. *tête* 'head,' while the alveolar "t" sound [t] is similar to the English pronunciation in *top*).

Tamil and Sinhala word morphology also displays numerous and fundamental differences, the most basic of which is that Tamil (like all Dravidian languages) is agglutinative, which means that complex words are formed by the addition of strings of stable affixes that do not (much) alter in spelling or pronunciation from one context to another. In this regard, Tamil is similar to Hungarian, Turkish, and Japanese, which all exhibit agglutinative morphology.

A good example of a (mostly) stable affix is the Tamil pluralizing suffix for nouns. In contrast with English which has a variety of options (*cat/cats, bush/*

Table 14.3 *Singular to plural "additive morphology" in Tamil*

Singular	poonai	muyal	puththakam	singam
Plural	poonai**kal**	muyal**kal**	puththakan**gal**	sinkan**gal**
Gloss	*cat(s)*	*rabbit(s)*	*book(s)*	*lion(s)*

Source: Data from http://mylanguages.org/tamil_plural.php

Table 14.4 *Singular to plural "subtractive morphology" in Sinhala*

Singular	pothə	reddə	kantho:ruvə	sathiyə	busekə
Plural	poth	redi	kantho:ru	sathi	bus
Gloss	*book(s)*	*cloth(es)*	*office(s)*	*week(s)*	*bus(ses)*

Source: https://en.wikipedia.org/wiki/Sinhalese_language#Number_marking

bushes, child/children, goose/geese, deer/deer), Tamil only has the suffix *-kal* (or *-gal* after [n]) as Table 14.3 shows.

Sinala has nothing as simple as this. In fact, many (inanimate) nouns in Sinhala have a singular affix which is removed to make a plural. Table 14.4 shows that this affix can be *-ə, -də, -və, -yə,* or *-ekə*.

Other significant differences include the Tamil organization of noun classes, absent any equivalent in Sinhala. Tamil nouns are classified into two classes, "rational" and "irrational." These two major classes each have subclasses. The "rational" class contains the subclasses "human" and "deity," while the "irrational" class has the subclasses "animal," "object," and "abstract."[28]

The lexicon of both languages also exhibits great differences, even though Dravidian and Indo-Aryan languages have borrowed words from each other for centuries. Consider the names for the numbers 1 through 5, in Table 14.5. The lexical similarity between the Indo-Aryan Sinhala and Sanskrit is apparent, as is the difference between these and Dravidian Tamil.

Finally, we note that the dramatic differences in the writing systems of the two languages pose an additional hurdle. Both Sinhala and Tamil use abugida orthographies, syllabic writing systems in which each symbol is an initial consonant coupled with a vowel diacritic. That said, they could not otherwise be more different. What this means for the two language communities is that, even if one were to learn the phonology, morphology, and lexicon of the other, they would still not be able to read each other's writing (e.g. road signs, advertisements, notices, etc.).

---

[28] Caldwell 1875: 133–137.

Table 14.5 *Names for the numbers 1–5 in Sinhala, Sanskrit, and Tamil*

Number	Sinhala	Sanskrit	Tamil
1	eka	éka	onnu
2	deka	dvá	rendu
3	tuna	trí	moonu
4	hatara	catúr	naalu
5	paha	páñca	anju

Tamil and Sinhalese Language Conflict from 1948

During British rule of Sri Lanka, access to English language instruction and literacy was higher in the northern (Tamil-speaking) parts of the country (in the northernmost parts of the island and along the east coast, as shown in the map below). This was at least in part due to the English language educational system established in the north by American missionaries.[29] Access to education was so much higher in the northern region that levels of literacy in the Northern Province were higher by 1930 than anywhere other than the capital city of Colombo.[30]

This was one of the (several) important factors leading to disproportionate representation by minority Tamils in the elite Ceylon (i.e. Sri Lankan) civil service, the judicial service, and higher education. In 1946, just two years before independence, the Tamils (who constituted only 11 percent of the population) accounted for "33% of the civil service and 40% of the judicial service ... [as well as] 31% of the students in the university system."[31] This, together with the marginalization of the Buddhist and Sinhala-speaking majority by the British (in keeping with their often-utilized "divide-and-rule" policies), generated a great deal of resentment among the Sinhalese in the years leading up to independence. The *Swabasha* ('self-language') movement, which campaigned to replace English with ethnic languages (both Tamil and Sinhala), was not initially used to polarize ethnic relations before independence. But after independence, Sinhalese Buddhist nationalists began to demand that *swabasha* favor the use of Sinhala only.[32]

Unlike the case of India, in which the more numerous Hindi-speaking population had substantially more power at the time of independence than did any of the Dravidian language-speaking minorities, Sri Lanka's Dravidian minority had much more power than the Sinhalese. In this context, the use of language to effect retribution and a redistribution of power is not surprising.

---

[29] DeVotta 2003: 115.   [30] DeVotta 2004: 46.   [31] DeVotta 2004: 46–47.
[32] DeVotta 2003: 113–116.

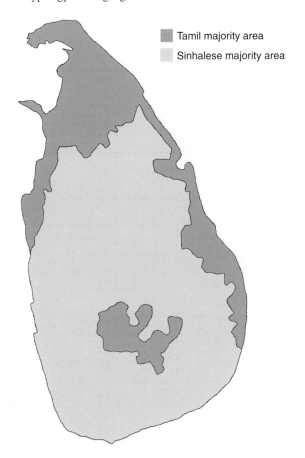

Tamil majority area

Sinhalese majority area

Figure 14.7 Sinhala- and Tamil-speaking areas of Sri Lanka

In 1949, the Sri Lankan government acted to revoke the citizenship of some 500,000 Indian Tamils (these were Tamils recently immigrated to Sri Lanka to work on the tea plantations in the central highlands). In 1956, after eight years of rule by the United National Party, the first prime minister from the Sinhalese nationalist Sri Lanka Freedom Party came to power. This prime minister, S. W. R. D. Bandaranaike, had promised to enact (retributive) language reforms in favor of the Sinhala-speaking majority and, shortly after coming to power, had enacted the Sinhala Only Act (also called the Official Language Act no. 33 of 1956). This law, in one stroke, eliminated both English and Tamil as official languages. The Act declared "the Sinhala language as the one official language of Ceylon," allowing for the continued use of English and Tamil only where it is "impracticable to commence the use of only the Sinhala language" and that only until "the 31st day of December, 1960."[33]

By 1978, Tamil objections to official discrimination against their language led the Sri Lankan government to provide some minimal recognition, and accommodation, of Tamil in the new constitution. Chapter IV of the constitution, in addition to maintaining that "The Official Language of Sri Lanka shall be Sinhala," also stipulates that "The National Languages of Sri Lanka shall be Sinhala and Tamil." The document goes on to provide that government officials "shall be entitled to perform [their] duties and discharge [their] functions . . . in either of the National Languages." It also provides that people can be educated in either of the national languages, and that laws be published in both national languages, together with an English translation. It restricts the language of administration and the courts to the official language (i.e. Sinhala), but provides that Tamil can also be used for these purposes in the Northern and Eastern Provinces.[34]

Even though some concessions were made, the 1978 constitution "still tilted toward favoring the Sinhalese, and in that sense was hardly an ethnically impartial document"; furthermore, by this time, a Tamil "separatist movement had already taken shape."[35] So, the intended effects of the Sinhala Only Act, enforced for over twenty years before any constitutional change was implemented, were accomplished. From 1956 on, the Tamil minority were increasingly excluded from many if not most jobs in the state civil service because of linguistic preferences, and by the 1970s the Tamils were seriously underrepresented in the civil service."[36]

After the 1978 constitution was enacted, constitutional amendments in the late 1980s, brought about through Tamil political pressure, further reduced the language inequities. A 1987 amendment (the thirteenth) revised the codification of "Official Language" to:

1. The Official Language of Sri Lanka shall be Sinhala.
2. Tamil shall also be an official language.
3. English shall be the link language.[37]

Thus, Tamil ("an official language") was raised almost level with Sinhala ("the Official Language," and official provisions were made for the use of English (as "the link language"). The sixteenth amendment, enacted in 1988, further elaborated, clarified, and codified the enhanced status of Tamil in the country.

However, one might aver that the reforms (gradually reversing thirty years of linguistic discrimination and language rights violations) had taken too long and come too late. The transfer of political and economic power from the Tamils to

[33] Official Language Act (No. 33 of 1956).   [34] Parliament of Sri Lanka 2013.
[35] DeVotta 2004: 8, 44.   [36] de Varennes 2010: 462–463.
[37] Presidential Secretariat of Sri Lanka 2008.

the Sinhalese was already complete, and the "postcolonial payback" policies of the Sri Lankan government had already led to civil war (by 1983). This conflict, initiated by the Liberation Tigers of Tamil Eelam (LTTE, aka Tamil Tigers), lasted for twenty-five years (concluding in 2009), caused great economic hardship for the entire country, and resulted in the loss of over 60,000 (and as many as 100,000) lives – a high price to pay for linguistic discrimination by any calculus, although language (really) was not the sole issue.

French versus English in Canada

Canada is often held up as a country in which bilingualism works, in that English and French are indeed recognized in the constitution and by law as official languages on equal footing with respect to government (use in Parliament and government offices) and the courts.[38] According to the 2011 census, 58.5 percent of Canadians responding reported that English was one of or their only mother tongue, while 22 percent reported French as such. The remainder reported speaking a non-official language.[39] The majority of French speakers live in the provinces of Quebec, Ontario, and New Brunswick, but only in Quebec are French speakers a majority, where 81.5 percent of Quebecers report French as their mother tongue. While both languages are official, nationally, the equilibrium that has been reached has been difficult to achieve and remains somewhat uneasy.

Historical Background

Among the European countries hoping to discover a western sea route to the Pacific Ocean and wanting to lay claim to fishing rights on the eastern coast of what is now Canada, the English were among the first to explore the area, beginning with John Cabot's first voyage there in 1497. However, aside from the establishment of a few fishing stations in present-day Newfoundland, the English did not create much of a footprint in terms of settlements and exploration, focusing more on establishing the thirteen colonies to the south, in the territory which became the United States. While this lack of northern focus on the part of the British changed in later years, the French took a much more active interest in the area.

In 1524, France's King Francis I sent the Florentine Italian explorer Giovanni da Verrazano in search of a route to the Pacific Ocean, a voyage that took him from Florida in the south to Newfoundland in the north. Jacques

---

[38] There is a recent movement to recognize as official the languages of the First Nations people (the Canadian term for Native Americans). As it stands, currently two provinces – Nunavut and the Northwest Territories – have given official status to some First Nations languages.
[39] Statistics Canada 2016.

Cartier, a French explorer from Breton, headed up France's next organized attempts at exploration with the first of his voyages in 1534. Cartier explored the coast of Newfoundland and along the St. Lawrence River, claiming territory for France and declaring the territory New France (Nouvelle-France) when he planted a cross on the Gaspé Peninsula at the mouth of the St. Lawrence. While subsequent efforts at establishing settlements in the area failed, the French did establish a successful fur trade, cooperating with the Hurons and other Algonquin First Nations peoples.

More territory in the North American interior (Great Lakes, Midwestern United States) was opened up for the French with the expeditions of Samuel de Champlain and others, and the first "permanent" settlements were established in the early 1600s, in Port Royal in Acadia (the territory north of Maine – present-day Nova Scotia) and in Québec in the St. Lawrence Valley. But raids by the English and their Iroquois allies (themselves enemies of the Algonquin tribes that cooperated with the French), along with the fact that the territory was controlled by a trading company that relied more heavily on indigenes than on French workers, conspired to keep these settlements extremely small. By 1628, the French population in New France amounted to a mere 207 settlers. By the 1665–1666 census, even though the French government had itself assumed control of New France, the population had still only risen to 3,215,[40] an extremely small number compared with the British colonies to the south, whose estimated population was around 70,000.[41]

English presence in this northern territory remained relatively modest through the seventeenth century: there were small settlements in Newfoundland and attempts to take over Acadia, and in 1670 the Hudson Bay Trading Company set up outposts for its fur trade. However, the Treaty of Utrecht, signed in 1713 at the conclusion of the War of Spanish Succession, firmly established England's claims in Canada, as France ceded to the English Newfoundland, the Acadian colony of Nova Scotia, and land claimed by the Hudson Bay Company. The map below depicts the area still held by France in the mid eighteenth century.

For a time, into the mid eighteenth century, New France prospered. More permanent settlements were established, and by 1755 the population had grown to around 75,000.[42] But as the French pushed farther into the Great Lakes region and the Ohio River Valley, there were increasing conflicts with the British colonists established to the southeast, who wished to expand their own thirteen colonies westward. These conflicts, as well as heightened tensions between the British and French (and their respective allies) in Europe and elsewhere, eventually led to the attenuation of France's presence in North America. Beginning in the mid 1750s, the British and French fought what is

[40] Statistics Canada 2008.   [41] Site for Language Management in Canada (SLMC) 2016a.
[42] Site for Language Management in Canada (SLMC) 2016a.

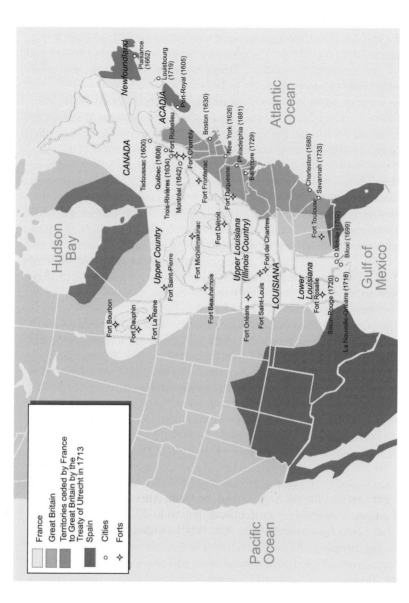

Figure 14.8 Map of New France about 1750

variously known as the "Seven Years' War" (from the British perspective), the "War of Conquest" (from the French Canadian perspective) or the "French and Indian War" (from the American colonial perspective). The crowning blows against the French in North America were the fall of Quebec in 1759 and Montreal in 1760. Regardless of the perspective taken, the outcome of the war was a full rout of the French, and the conditions of the Treaty of Paris (1763), which ended the conflict, included France's cession to Great Britain of all claims to Canadian territory.[43] Thus began the British rule of Canada and the cultural and linguistic conflict of Francophone and Anglophone Canadians.

This cultural and linguistic conflict had actually begun prior to the Seven Years' War. Ever since gaining control of Nova Scotia through the Treaty of Utrecht (1713), the British colonists had pressured the French-speaking Acadians to pledge loyalty to Great Britain, something they steadfastly refused to do. Beginning in 1755, under the British governor of Nova Scotia Charles Lawrence, the British began the deportation of what ultimately amounted to about three-fourths of the French Acadian population (~12,000 people). Many of these were relocated to France, a good number to the (then) Spanish colony of Louisiana (New Orleans), and some others to the western parts of Canada. Initially, the British attempted to impose their language and culture on the French Canadians with the goal of assimilation to an English society. Also looming large was the question of religion, the English being Protestant and the French Catholic. The Royal Proclamation of 1763 imposed English common law on the new territory and required all government employees to take a Test Oath that included pledging allegiance to the British crown and renouncing the Pope, neither of which was problematic for the Anglophone population but would require Francophones to renounce Catholicism.[44] This had little impact on Nova Scotia from which most of the Francophone population had already been expelled, but the sizable Francophone majority remaining in the St. Lawrence Valley neither understood English common law nor the language in which it was written and adjudicated. The French Canadians there, unsurprisingly, proved most uncooperative. The governor, in order to be able to govern at all, was forced to allow the Catholic Church to operate as it had prior to British rule and exempted those Francophones whose skills were needed for government service from having to take the Oath. Although the Anglophone population objected, this became official policy in 1774 when the British Parliament promulgated the Quebec Act. While language was not explicitly mentioned, the Act abolished the Test Oath, reintroduced French civil law, gave tithing power to the Catholic Church, and expanded the boundaries of the Province of Quebec.[45] However, due to laws requiring that commerce be

[43] Bélanger 2005.   [44] Site for Language Management in Canada (SLMC) 2016d.
[45] Site for Language Management in Canada (SLMC) 2016c.

conducted only through British companies, the Anglophone minority continued to dominate trade.

Neither the Anglophone nor Francophone populations of Quebec were truly satisfied with the governmental structure, so in 1791 the Constitutional Act of Parliament divided Quebec into Francophone Lower Canada (which included territory in present-day Quebec) and Anglophone Upper Canada (which included territory in present-day Ontario).[46] Each colony had its own legislature and governor and reflected the language and culture of its constituent majority. There was tension still nonetheless, as the Anglophone minority continued to wield economic power in Lower Canada. Regardless of how it was received, this arrangement lasted barely fifty years; and following rebellions in both Upper and Lower Canada, the British Parliament reunited the two into a single colony of Canada, with a single legislature and government. Once again, British policymakers hoped that the rapidly growing Anglophone population would overwhelm and hasten the assimilation of the French Canadians; especially since English remained the primary language used in administration, business, the economy, trade, and industry. Needless to say, the British intentions were transparent to the French Canadians, whose mistrust of British rule and resistance to assimilation continued unabated.[47]

The union of Upper and Lower Canada was a union in name only. Relations between the French and English were so bad and the political atmosphere was so fraught with tension that the legislature was virtually unable to act and the province proved extremely difficult to govern.[48] Spurred by politicians in both linguistic communities, the province of Canada was once again divided, this time into Ontario and Quebec, and under the British North America Act of 1867 these two were confederated with the colonies of Nova Scotia and New Brunswick as the Dominion of Canada, as shown in Figure 14.9.

The British North America Act of 1867 (years later renamed the Constitution Act of 1867) created a national parliament and the office of prime minister. In addition, it provided for a provincial government for each of the constituent states, which included for each a vice governor and legislative bodies. While touted by some Anglophones as an opportunity to create a "unified English America," John Alexander Macdonald, the first Canadian prime minister, saw things differently: "I disagree with the viewpoint expressed in certain quarters that we must somehow attempt to suppress one language or place it in an inferior position with regard to the other; any such attempt is doomed to failure, and even were it possible, would be foolish and petty."[49] The British Parliament agreed, as the

[46] The designations Upper and Lower refer to orientation with respect to the St. Lawrence River. The headwaters were in Upper Canada and thus upriver, and the mouth of the river was in Lower Canada.
[47] Tattrie 2014.   [48] Tattrie 2014.
[49] Site for Language Management in Canada (SLMC) 2016d.

Canadian provinces

Other territories
controlled by the UK

North-Western
Territory

Colony of
British
Columbia

Labrador
(dependency of
Newfoundland)

Colony of
Newfoundland

Rupert's Land

Colony of
Prince Edward
Island

July 1, 1867
Dominion of Canada formed
(Ontario, Quebec, New Brunswick, Nova Scotia)

Ontario

Quebec

New
Brunswick

Nova
Scotia

Figure 14.9 Dominion of Canada, 1867

question of language was, in fact, directly addressed in the Act. While stopping short of declaring English, French, or both to be official languages (but clearly presaging official bilingualism), section 133 of the Act explicitly set out provisions that members could address the Canadian parliament and the legislature in Quebec in either English or French, as could individuals in pleadings before Canadian federal courts or any courts in Quebec. Additionally, the section mandated that all Acts of Parliament and the Quebec legislature should be printed and published in both languages. The provincial government of Quebec, in combination with the Catholic Church, was seen as a means of ensuring continuation of French–Canadian culture and language in the newly formed confederation, which by then had a solid Anglophone majority.

However, in spite of section 133, linguistic parity was difficult to achieve. Due to the sizable Anglophone majority and the absence of simultaneous translation, English became the de facto working language of Parliament, which for all intents and purposes required aspiring Francophone members to be bilingual. Laws were for the most part drafted in English and subsequently translated – frequently imperfectly – into French. Francophones also faced challenges in the Supreme Court, which was largely made up of English monolingual justices, and in the ultimate court of appeal in Great Britain, which was conducted solely in English. Outside Quebec, Francophone minorities faced challenges in education, as provisions in the Act were ineffective in the face of political pressure by Anglophone majorities. There were tensions in the military as well, where English was again dominant. All in all, then, aside from some hard-fought victories, such as bilingual stamps (1927), bilingual currency (1934), and bilingual government checks in Quebec (1945), Canada was a linguistically (and culturally) divided country during the first century of the Confederation.

The Rise of Bilingualism in the Federal Government

The first 100 years of the Confederation was marked by a status quo of the dominance of the English-speaking majority, with little inclination toward bilingualism. However, the second half of the twentieth century saw a dramatic shift, spurred in significant measure by Quebec's "Quiet Revolution." During the 1950s and 1960s, Quebec was transformed by modernizing forces from being largely rural and heavily influenced by the Catholic Church into a more urban, secular society seeking increased economic and political power for the Francophone majority. There was a rise of political parties such as the Parti Québécois (formed in 1968) and cultural organizations which favored increased autonomy for Quebec and the preservation of Quebec's cultural and linguistic identity.[50] In 1961, the Office Québécois de la langue Française was established to promote and standardize Quebec French.

Developments in Quebec coupled with Francophone minority demands in other provinces pushed the federal government into action. A commission to study bilingualism in the government was appointed, as was a civil service commission, charged with establishing a language training center. In 1963, Prime Minister Lester Pearson formed the Royal Commission on Bilingualism and Biculturalism (the Laurendeau–Dunton Commission). The Commission ordered wide-ranging studies to determine the linguistic and cultural landscape of the country and make recommendations for addressing those deficiencies. Among other things, the Commission recommended declaring both English and French to be official languages, making federal institutions more bilingual, and establishing both languages as official in Ontario and New Brunswick as well as other provinces that had at least a 10 percent Anglophone or Francophone minority. In education, the Commission declared that parents should be granted the right to have their children educated in the official language of their choice (provided there were sufficient numbers to warrant it).

---

[50] Linteau 2006.

In 1969, the Canadian Parliament passed the Official Languages Act, which took up many of the Commission's recommendations, declaring English and French the official languages of Canada, mandating their equal status in the federal government, and creating the Office of the Commissioner of Official Languages. In 1988, the Act was thoroughly revised to accord with the Canadian Charter of Rights and Freedoms (1982). The revised Act included provisions for promoting the equal status of English and French in (i) legislation, (ii) the judiciary, (iii) communication with and provision of services to the public, (iv) use in federal government work places, (v) active promotion of English and French in federal institutions, and (vi) the functions of the Commissioner of Official Languages.[51] This legislation was quite ambitious both in its scope and in its optimism.

French in Quebec

Federal legislative enthusiasm for bilingualism and biculturalism was not matched by much enthusiasm on the part of the public. Nor were bilingual and bicultural initiatives applied evenly in federal institutions (e.g. some government service agencies, airport services, the military) or by provincial governments. In fact, in Quebec itself, there was quite the opposite reaction to the national efforts in favor of bilingualism/biculturalism. Nationalistic tendencies in Quebec had grown substantially in the 1960s. It was during this period that talk of secession arose in the province, the militant Front de Libération du Québec (Quebec Liberation Front) operated (1963–1970), and the independence-minded Parti Québécois was formed (1968). The Parti Québécois gained control of the Quebec government in 1976 and, per its party platform, pushed for sovereignty.[52] Following the recommendations of the Gendron Commission (charged to investigate the status of French in Quebec), the provincial government passed its own Official Language Act in 1974, declaring French to be the sole official language of Quebec. This Act had far-ranging implications for the conduct of government and private business, education, and more.[53] Three years later, it was superseded (and broadened) by the Charter of the French Language (also known as Bill 101). The goal of the Charter was to make French the pre-eminent language of Quebec in all areas, as made clear in the preamble:

the National Assembly of Québec recognizes that Quebecers wish to see the quality and influence of the French language assured, and is resolved therefore to make of French the language of Government and the Law, as well as the normal and everyday language of work, instruction, communication, commerce and business ...[54]

---

[51] Government of Canada 2016.
[52] Votes to declare independence in 1980 and 1995 were unsuccessful, though the 1995 initiative failed by only 4 percent.
[53] Busque 2006.   [54] Gouvernement du Québec 2016.

While the majority of Francophones were pleased, the strength of the Charter's provisions angered most of the Anglophone minority in Quebec, as well as many Anglophones elsewhere in Canada (giving rise to the English-language advocacy group Alliance Québec, which was active from 1982 to 2005).[55] Many of the provisions of the Charter were challenged in court.

- Under the Charter, French was made the sole language of legislation and the courts. Laws were to be translated and published in English at the end of the process. The Supreme Court of Canada ruled this to be unconstitutional in 1979, as it violated section 133 of the British North America Act. The Charter was eventually amended to permit the use of English in legislation (and the courts).
- Under the original Charter, "Public signs and posters and commercial advertising must be in French."[56] This, too, was ruled unconstitutional (in 1988), which led to the section eventually being amended, allowing other languages to be used in advertising, provided that the French print was larger.
- Education was also tightly controlled. The Charter mandated that French be the language of instruction, but under very limited exceptions allowed for instruction in English. The Supreme Court judged this provision to have violated the Canadian Charter of Rights and Freedoms in 1984, resulting in a broadening of situations in which children were permitted to receive English-language instruction.[57]

---

[55] Behiels and Hudon 2013.   [56] Gouvernement du Québec 2016.
[57] The original Charter included the following restriction:

73. The following children, at the request of one of their parents, may receive instruction in English:
(1) a child whose father or mother is a Canadian citizen and received elementary instruction in English in Canada, provided that that instruction constitutes the major part of the elementary instruction he or she received in Canada;
(2) a child whose father or mother is a Canadian citizen and who has received or is receiving elementary or secondary instruction in English in Canada, and the brothers and sisters of that child, provided that that instruction constitutes the major part of the elementary or secondary instruction received by the child in Canada;
   Subsequent to 1984, the following was added:
   86.1. In addition to the cases provided for in section 73, the Government, by order, may, at the request of one of the parents, authorize generally the following children to receive their instruction in English:
(a) a child whose father or mother received the greater part of his or her elementary instruction in English elsewhere in Canada and, before establishing domicile in Québec, was domiciled in a province or territory that it indicates in the order and where it considers that the services of instruction in French offered to French-speaking persons are comparable to those offered in English to English-speaking persons in Québec;
(b) a child whose father or mother establishes domicile in Québec and who, during his last school year or from the beginning of the current school year, has received primary or secondary instruction in English in the province or territory indicated in the order;
(c) the younger brothers and sisters of children described in subparagraphs a and b.
(Gouvernement du Québec 2016)

There have been more challenges and more amendments of the Charter of the French Language over the past three decades, but suffice to say that French remains predominant in Quebec, and the Anglophone minority continues to press its case.[58]

Bilingualism Today

Bilingualism in Canada has had an uneven history. When two distinct linguistic groups lay claim to the same territory (even when neither is truly native to the land), conflicts inevitably arise. Some of the cultural and economic tensions between English-speaking and French-speaking Canadians have (predictably) manifested in language conflict. Though the government's mandate of bilingualism has not always been fully embraced in all government institutions, Canadian citizens have come to be increasingly supportive of the idea. In 1988, when the Official Languages Act was enacted, only 44 percent of Anglophones were in favor of bilingualism for all of Canada, and this figure declined to a low of 32 percent in 1991 during a period of particularly acute political tension between Quebec and the rest of the country. However, since then, that figure has risen dramatically according to a 2006 report issued by the Office of the Commissioner of Official Languages. At that time, fully 72 percent of all Canadians backed national bilingualism, including 65 percent of Anglophones and 90 percent of Francophones, with only 26 percent dissenting. Furthermore, the increasing acceptance of bilingualism seems likely to continue, as about 81 percent of younger people surveyed (18–34-year-olds) were found to favor bilingualism. This does not imply that this number of Canadians aspire to be bilingual nor that they expect others to. But one might surmise that Canadians have come to accept, and perhaps be proud of, their country's bilingual status, whether or not they themselves are bilingual. As the Commissioner of Official Languages Graham Fisher explained in 2012, "The policy was never to make all Canadians bilingual. Instead, what it guarantees is that no matter which language you speak – English or French – you can get the same level of service."[59]

This service extends to access to a glass of lemonade on a warm summer day. In a recent incident, two girls 5 and 7 years of age were issued a special permit to operate a lemonade stand on public property (with proceeds going to charity). One of the conditions of the permit was they have signs in both official languages.[60]

---

[58] As of 2015, the Quebec Community Groups Network, an organization linking English-speaking groups in Quebec, is a center of "evidence-based expertise and collective action on the strategic issues affecting the development and vitality of English-speaking Quebec" (Quebec Community Groups Network 2016).
[59] Baluja and Bradshaw 2012.   [60] Hurley 2016.

Summary: Comparison of Cases

Competition for linguistic dominance, as we have seen in this chapter, is often acted out using traditional mechanisms of power politics, from the making and enforcement of laws to the exercise of military force. As with any sort of conflict, the results are unpredictable. In the Sri Lankan case, the Tamils were ultimately crushed militarily, and have essentially been turned into a permanently oppressed linguistic minority. One would say about Sri Lanka that, since 2009, there is no longer any sort of "competition" for dominance (of any kind). In Belgium's case, the power pendulum has swung one way and then the other over the course of a century, with the present domination of the Flemish over the Walloons as a modern development. It is too early to say whether the balance of power might again shift back to the Walloons, or whether this conflict will ever find a resolution satisfactory to all parties to it. Canada presents the most successful case in terms of relatively acceptable solutions for all parties (although there are still many Francophone residents of English-speaking Canada and many Anglophone residents of Quebec who would beg to differ). Nevertheless, the linguistic accommodation and compromises are now enshrined in law, and are unlikely to change in any radical fashion from here on.

In the cases we've examined, the key common ingredient for conflicts in this category is the possession of some definable territory on the part of each group. The Tamils were well established (for centuries) in the northern and eastern parts of the island of Sri Lanka. The Flemish and Walloons of Belgium each, with the exception of Brussels, inhabit their own region of the country, rarely venturing into each other's realms. And the Francophone community of Canada is, with few exceptions, still confined to the range that constituted Canadian parts of Nouvelle-France.

There are certainly cases of linguistic competition that have been resolved through dissolution, thereby ending the competition entirely, from a national or nation-building perspective. The Slovak people might have had an ongoing linguistic competition with the Czech people, had they not seceded from Czechoslovakia. But having done so, there is nothing to say about them in this chapter. Likewise, the breakup of Yugoslavia in 1991–1992 (into Slovenia, Croatia, Bosnia and Herzegovina, Macedonia, Serbia, and Montenegro) averted a competition for linguistic dominance that would have taken this entire chapter to describe.

Additional Cases for Exploration

French and Wolof in Senegal

Senegal is a former French African colony on the extreme western coast of the African Sahel. It is geographically unique in that it surrounds another African country, Gambia (a former British colony), on three sides. Islam reached this black African area in the eleventh century, and today is the religion of 90 percent of the population. In the two centuries before the fifteenth-century arrival of European traders (and then colonists), the area of present-day Senegal was part of the West African Mali Empire (which stretched from east of Timbuktu to the Atlantic Senegalese coast). The lands of the Senegal area (or parts of it) were variously controlled by the Portuguese, British, Dutch, and French. By the middle of the eighteenth century, the French had the upper hand in this part of Africa, and by 1848 extended French citizenship to the inhabitants of the four major communities in the area. French colonial rule of Senegal ended in 1960, when Senegal became independent.

The language problems of Senegal are, unsurprisingly, related to its colonial history. The country includes many ethnically and linguistically distinct peoples, with the largest two groups, the Wolof and Puular, comprising about two-thirds of the total (representing 43 and 24 percent of the population, respectively). Given further that Wolof is spoken by over 75 percent of the population, one might guess that Wolof, or that Wolof and Puular, would be counted among Senegal's official languages. In fact, the only official language of Senegal is French, a language spoken by only 15 percent of the country's population (and by only 2 percent of its women). Despite internal pressure on the part of the Senegalese themselves to replace French with Wolof, or some combination of local languages, French remains today the country's official language. Some reasons for this may be: (i) the utility of French as an international language of business and trade; (ii) the advantages that knowledge of French provides to the current Senegalese ruling class; and (iii) possible resistance on the part of those who are not themselves Wolof to making Wolof the dominant national language.

Chinese, Cantonese, and English in Hong Kong

Hong Kong ('Xiang Gang' in Mandarin Chinese) is a port region in southern China whose territory presently consists of 1,000 sq. miles of land and water in southeastern China, adjacent to Canton ('Guang Dong') Province and 400 miles east of China's border with Vietnam. With a population of over 7 million people, it would be the 100th most populous country in the world (with more people than Bulgaria and fewer than Switzerland). Hong Kong was a part of China from about 111 BCE (when it was conquered by the Han Dynasty). The present-day territory of Hong Kong is comprised of a series of forced colonial concessions from China by the British, beginning with the acquisition (in perpetuity) of the 30 sq. mile Hong Kong Island following China's defeat in the First Opium War. Further acquisitions by the British that make up the territory were the Kowloon ('Jiu Long') Peninsula in 1860, and the New

Territories in 1898. Aside from the Japanese takeover of Hong Kong in the Second World War (1941–1945), British colonial administration of the territory lasted until 1997, when sovereignty was transferred to China in accordance with a Sino-British Joint Declaration of 1984. The territory is currently a special administrative district within the People's Republic of China, allowing for it to maintain a degree of political and economic independence from the mainland.

For nearly a century, English was the sole official language of the British colony. This changed in 1974, when Chinese was made a co-equal official language of the territory, and the official language designation for Chinese and English has been retained since the 1997 transfer of sovereignty to China. Today, English is spoken by less than 5 percent of the population, and while Chinese is the other "official language," the de facto language used by nearly 90 percent of the population is Cantonese – a Sinitic language whose spoken forms are as different from Mandarin Chinese as English is from German. While written Standard Mandarin Chinese is usable throughout China, the spoken Chinese languages are often mutually unintelligible, and Hong Kong is in this respect a linguistically special place – where an official European language, a regional variety of Chinese, Standard Mandarin Chinese, and mixtures of all three can be heard.

Hebrew and Arabic in Israel

The State of Israel, before its independence in 1948, was part of the British Protectorate of Palestine. This territory, assigned to the United Kingdom by the League of Nations after World War I (and after the partitioning of the Kingdom of Jordan), included Israel, the area commonly known as the "West Bank," and the area known as the Gaza Strip. This same area, until the end of World War I, had been part of the Ottoman Empire for 300 years (since 1516).

During the Ottoman period, throughout the Ottoman Empire, the official language of administration was Ottoman Turkish, but as most areas outside Anatolia proper had non-Turkish majorities, people were generally free and used to using their old local languages for everything except official dealings with the government. In 1922, the British, in recognition of (i) the majority of Arabic speakers in the territory, (ii) the growing population of Jews, and (iii) the fact that the British themselves had to administer the area, promulgated Article 82 of the Palestine Order, establishing Arabic, English, and Hebrew as official languages. Upon gaining independence, the new State of Israel revised the British official languages policy by removing English as an official language, and by requiring some knowledge of Hebrew for citizenship.

Today, in the pre-1967 areas of Israel, a little over 50 percent of the people are native speakers of Hebrew and about 25 percent are native speakers of

Arabic. In addition, some 15 percent are native Russian speakers. The status of Arabic, once the language of a majority and now the minority, has suffered during much of the state's history, with issues such as language of education, official signage, and language use in the media and the government all being central issues. Recent accommodations as a result of political pressure and (in some instances) court cases have improved the situation of minority Arabic speakers in some respects.

Further Reading and Resources for Part III

Chapter 10

Sámi in Norway

Bucken-Knapp, Gregg. 2003. *Elites, language and the politics of identity: The Norwegian case in comparative perspective*. Albany: State University of New York Press.

Bull, Tove. 2002. The Sámi language(s), maintenance and intellectualization. *Current Issues in Language Planning* 3(1): 28–39.

Magga, Ole Henrik. 1994. The Sami Language Act. In Tove Skutnabb-Kangas and Robert Phillipson (eds.), *Linguistic human rights: Overcoming linguistic discrimination*, 219–233. Berlin: Mouton de Gruyter.

Minde, Henry. 2003. Assimilation of the Sami: Implementation and consequences. *Acta Borealia: A Nordic Journal of Circumpolar Societies* 20:121–146.

Sandvik, Gudmund. 1993. Non-existent Sámi language rights in Norway 1850–1940. In Sergij Vilfan (ed.), *Comparative studies on governments and nondominant ethnic groups in Europe, 1850–1940*, vol. 3: *Ethnic groups and language rights*, 129–150. New York: NYU Press.

Ainu in Japan

Batchelor, John. 1905. *An Ainu–English–Japanese dictionary (including a grammar of the Ainu language)*. Tokyo: Methodist Publishing House.

Dubinsky, Stanley, and William D. Davies. 2013. Language conflict and language rights: The Ainu, Ryūkyūans, and Koreans in Japan. *Japan Studies Review* 17: 3–27.

Irish, Ann B. 2009. *Hokkaido: A history of ethnic transition and development on Japan's northern island*. Jefferson, NC: McFarland and Company.

Ishikida, Miki Y. 2005. *Living together: Minority people and disadvantaged groups in Japan*. iUniverse.

Maruyama, Hiroshi. 2012. Ainu landowners' struggle for justice and the illegitimacy of the Nibutani Dam project in Hokkaido Japan. *International Community Law Review* 14: 63–80.

Shibatani, Masayoshi. 1990 *The languages of Japan*. Cambridge University Press.

Siddle, Richard. 1996. *Race, resistance and the Ainu of Japan*. London: Routledge.

Sjöberg, Katarina. 1996. *The return of the Ainu: Cultural mobilization and the practice of ethnicity in Japan*. Amsterdam: Harwood Academic Publishers.

Umeda, Sayuri. 2009. *The education of non-native language speaking children: Japan. Report for the Law Library of Congress.* www.loc.gov/law/help/non-native-education/japan.php

United States State Department. 2008. *Country reports on human rights: Japan.* Bureau of Democracy, Human Rights, and Labor. www.state.gov/g/drl/rls/hrrpt/2008/eap/119041.htm

Walker, Brett L. 2001. *The conquest of Ainu lands: Ecology and culture in Japanese expansion, 1590–1800.* Berkeley: University of California Press.

American Indians in the United States

Atkins, J. D. C. 1887. *Annual report of the Secretary of the Interior,* vol. 1. Washington, DC: Government Printing Office.

Adams, David Wallace. 1995. *Education for extinction.* Topeka: University of Kansas Press.

Debo, Angie. 1975. *The rise and fall of the Choctaw Nation.* Norman: University of Oklahoma Press.

Fear, Jacqueline. 1980. English versus the vernacular: The suppression of Indian languages in reservation schools at the end of the nineteenth century. *Revue française d'études américaines* 9: 13–24.

Lamar, Lucius Q. C. 1886. *Annual report of the Secretary of the Interior.* Washington, DC: Government Printing Office.

Meriam, Lewis, Roy A. Brown, Henry Roe Cloud, Edward Everett Dale, Emma Duke, Herbert R. Edwards, Fayette Avery McKenzie, Mary Louise Mark, W. Carson Ryan, and William J. Spillman. 1928. *The problem of Indian administration.* Baltimore, MD: Johns Hopkins University Press.

O'Sullivan, John L. 1845. Annexation. *The United States Democratic Review* 17 (5): 5–10.

Pratt, Richard H. 1964. *Battlefield and classroom: Four decades with the American Indian, 1867–1904.* New Haven: Yale University Press.

Ruppel, Kristin T. 2008. *Unearthing Indian land: Living with the legacies of allotment.* Tucson: University of Arizona Press.

Chapter 11

Hungarians in Slovakia

BBC. 2012. Slovaks retaliate over Hungarian citizenship law. March 12, 2012. www.bbc.com/news/10166610

Daftary, Farimah, and Kinga Gál. 2000. The new Slovak language law: Internal or external politics. *ECMI Working Paper # 8.* European Centre for Minority Issues (ECMI).

Groszkowski, Jakub, and Mariusz Bocian. 2009. The Slovak–Hungarian dispute over Slovakia's language law. *OSW Commentary* (Issue 30). Warsaw: Centre for Eastern Studies. www.isn.ethz.ch/Digital-Library/Publications/Detail/?id=110682andlng=en

Jaszi, Oscar. 1929. *The dissolution of the Habsburg Monarchy*. University of Chicago Press.
Kontra, Miklós 1995/1996. English only's cousin: Slovak only. *Acta Linguistica Hungarica* 43: 345–372.
   1997. On the right to use the language of one's choice in Slovakia. *Canadian Centre for Linguistic Rights Bulletin* 4(1): 5–8.
   1998. Language rights arguments in Central Europe and the USA: How similar are they? In Douglas A. Kibbee (ed.), *Language legislation and linguistic rights*, 142–178. Amsterdam and Philadelphia: John Benjamins.
Schwegler, Brian A. 2008. Confronting the devil: Europe, nationalism, and municipal governance in Slovakia. PhD dissertation, University of Chicago.
Wardyn, Łukasz, and Jan Fiala. 2009. The 2009 Amendment of the Slovakian State Language Law and its impact on minority rights. *Polish Yearbook of International Law* 29: 153–173.

Hispanics in the Southwestern United States

Constitution of the State of California 1849. California Secretary of State Alex Padilla www.sos.ca.gov/archives/collections/constitutions/1849/
Constitution of the State of California 1879. Sacramento: State Office. www.sos.ca.gov/archives/collections/constitutions/1879/
Constitution of the State of California. State Constitution. www.citizensinchargefoundation.org/files/California Constitution.pdf
Gates, Paul. 1971. The California Land Act of 1851. *California Historical Quarterly* 50: 395–430.
Leibowitz, Arnold H. 1969–1970. English literacy: Legal sanction for discrimination *Notre Dame Lawyer* 45: 7–67
   1971. *Educational policy and political acceptance: The imposition of English as the language of instruction in American schools*. Washington, DC: ERIC Clearinghouse for Linguistics, Center for Applied Linguistics.
Macías, Reynaldo F. 2001. Minority languages in the United States, with a focus on Spanish in California. In Dürk Gorter and Guus (eds.), *The other languages of Europe*, 331–354. Clevedon: Multilingual Matters.
Perez, Cris. 1982. Ranchos. Excerpted from *Grants of land in California made by Spanish or Mexican authorities*. California State Lands Commission report. http://vm136.lib.berkeley.edu/EART/rancho.html
SB-1174. 2014. English language education. California State Legislative Information. http://leginfo.legislature.ca.gov/faces/billNavClient.xhtml?bill_id=201320140SB1174
Sullivan, Raymond L. 1970. *Castro v. State of California*, 2 Cal.3d 223 http://scocal.stanford.edu/opinion/castro-v-state-california-27547
Tucker, James T. 2013. *The battle over bilingual ballots: Language minorities and political access*. London: Ashgate.

Kurds in Turkey

Aytürk, İlker. 2008. Politics and language reform in Turkey: The "Academy" debate. *Wiener Zeitschrift für die Kunde des Morgenlandes* 98: 13–30.

Cemiloglu, Dicle. 2009. The dilemma of the Kurdish language in Turkey: A case study on language policy between 1924–2009. Honors thesis, University of Pennsylvania.

Hassanpour, Amir. 1992. *Nationalism and language in Kurdistan, 1918–1985*. San Francisco: Mellen Research University Press.

1999. Language rights in the emerging world linguistic order: The state, the market, and communication technologies. In Miklós Kontra, Robert Phillipson, Tove Skutnabb-Kangas, and Tibor Várady (eds.), *Language: A right and a resource. Approaching linguistic human rights*, 223–241. Budapest and New York: Central European University Press.

Kreyenbroek, Philip and Stefan Sperl (eds.). 1992. *The Kurds: A contemporary overview*. London: Routledge.

Kurdish Academy of Language. The history of the Kurdish language. www .kurdishacademy.org/?q=node/37

Nebez, Jemal. 2000. The Kurdish language from oral tradition to written language. Kurdish Academy of Language. www.kurdishacademy.org/?q=node/135

Panico, Christopher. 1999. *Turkey: Violations of free expression in Turkey*. New York: Human Rights Watch.

Skutnabb-Kangas, Tove, and Sertar Bucak. 1994. Killing a mother tongue: How the Kurds are deprived of linguistic human rights. In Tove Skutnabb-Kangas and Robert Phillipson (eds.), *Linguistic human rights: Overcoming linguistic discrimination*, 347–370. Berlin: Mouton de Gruyter.

Üngör, Uğur Ü. 2008. Seeing like a nation-state: Young Turk social engineering in Eastern Turkey. *Journal of Genocide Research* 10: 15–39.

Watts, Nicole F. 1999. Allies and enemies: Pro-Kurdish parties in Turkish politics, 1990–1994. *International Journal of Middle East Studies* 31: 631–656.

Chapter 12

Roma in Europe

Fraser, Angus. 1992. *The Gypsies*. Oxford: Blackwell.

Friedman, Victor. 2005. The Romani language in Macedonia in the third millennium: Progresss and problems. In Dieter W. Halwachs, Barbara Schrammel, and Gerd Ambrosch (eds.), *General and applied Romani linguistics: Proceedings from the 6th International Conference on Romani Linguistics*, 163–173. Munich: Lincom Europa.

Hancock, Ian. 2007a. Issues in the standardization of the Romani language: An overview and some recommendations. RADOC. www.radoc.net/radoc.php? doc=art_c_language_recommendationsandlang=enandarticles=true

2007b. On Romani origins and identity. RADOC. www.radoc.net/radoc.php? doc=art_b_history_originsandlang=enandarticles=true

Kyuchukov, Hristo. 2009. The importance of Romani language in the cognitive development of Roma children. 17th International Steering Committee Meeting (Decade of Roma Inclusion 2005–2015). September 22–23, 2009, Spisska Nova Ves, Slovakia.

New, William. 2014. Regulating Roma language and culture in Central Europe. *Journal of Language and Cultural Education (JoLaCE)* 2(2): 165–181.

Koreans in Japan

Hatori, Reiko. 2005. Policy on language education in Japan: Beyond nationalism and linguicism. *Second Language Studies* 23(2): 45–69. Manoa, HI: Department of Second Language Studies, University of Hawai'i.

Ishikida, Miki Y. 2005. *Living together: Minority people and disadvantaged groups in Japan*. Lincoln, NE: iUniverse. www.iuniverse.com/bookstore/BookDetail.aspx? BookId=SKU-000027958.

Ministry of Foreign Affairs of Japan. 1999. *International Convention on the Elimination of All Forms of Racial Discrimination (First and Second Report)*. www.mofa.go.jp /policy/human/race_rep1/

United States State Department. 2008. *Country reports on human rights: Japan*. Bureau of Democracy, Human Rights, and Labor. www.state.gov/g/drl/rls/hrrpt/2008/eap/ 119041.htm

Puerto Ricans in the United States

Constitution of the Commonwealth of Puerto Rico 1952. Wikisource. https://en .wikisource.org/wiki/Constitution_of_the_Commonwealth_of_Puerto_Rico

Pew Research Center. 2015. *Hispanics of Puerto Rican origin in the United States, 2013: Hispanic trends.* www.pewhispanic.org/2015/09/15/hispanics-of-puerto-rican-origin-in-the-united-states-2013/

United States Congress. 1917. An act to provide a civil government for Porto Rico, and for other purposes. 64th Congress, Session II, Chapter 145: 951–968. *Statutes at Large* 39 (1915–1917): 951–968. www.legisworks.org/congress/64/publaw-368.pdf

1950. An act to provide for the organization of a constitutional government by the people of Puerto Rico. 81st Congress, Session II, Chapter 446: 319–320. *Statutes at Large* 64 (1950–1951): 319–320. http://legisworks.org/congress/ 81/publaw-600.pdf

Urciuoli, Bonnie. 1996. *Exposing prejudice: Puerto Rican experiences of language, race, and class*. Boulder, CO: Waveland Press.

U.S. English. 2016. Puerto Rico: The 51st state? www.us-english.org/view/899

Chapter 13

Okinawans in Japan

Bairon, Fija, Matthias Brenzinger, and Patrick Heinrich. 2009. The Ryūkyūs and the new, but endangered, languages of Japan. *Asia-Pacific Journal* 19(2). www.japanfocus.org/articles/print_article/3138. Reproduced in *OGMIOS Newsletter* 38: 6–12.

Barclay, Kate. 2006. Okinawan identity. *Nations and Nationalism* 12(1): 117–137.

Heinrich, Patrick. 2004. Language planning and language ideology in the Ryūkyū Islands. *Language Policy* 3(2): 153–179.

2005. Language loss and language revitalization in the Ryūkyū Islands. *Asia-Pacific Journal: Japan Focus* 3(11). www.japanfocus.org/-Patrick-Heinrich/1596.

Ishikida, Miki Y. 2005. *Living together: Minority people and disadvantaged groups in Japan*. Lincoln, NE: iUniverse. iuniverse.com/bookstore/BookDetail.aspx?Bookl d=SKU-000027958.
Miller, Roy Andrew. 1971. *Japanese and the other Altaic languages*. University of Chicago Press.
1974. The origins of Japanese: Review of Murayama Shichiro and Obayashi Taryo, *Nihongo no Kigen. Monumenta Nipponica* 29(1): 93–102.
Robbeets, Martine I. 2005. *Is Japanese related to Korean, Tungusic, Mongolic and Turkic?* Wiesbaden: Otto Harrassowitz.
Shibatani, Masayoshi. 1990. *The languages of Japan*. Cambridge University Press.

African American English in the United States

Bailey, Guy, John Baugh, Salikoko S. Mufwene, and John R. Rickford. 1998. *African-American English: Structure, history, and use*. London: Routledge.
Baugh, John. 1999. *Out of the mouths of slaves: African American language and educational malpractice*. Austin: University of Texas Press.
2000. *Beyond Ebonics: Linguistic pride and racial prejudice*. New York: Oxford University Press.
Charity, Anne Harper. 2008. African American English. In H. Neville, B. Tynes, and S. Utsey (eds.), *Handbook of African American psychology*. Thousand Oaks, CA: Sage.
Labov, William. 1970. *The logic of nonstandard English*. Champaign, IL: National Council of Teachers of English.
Morgan, Marcyliena. 2002. The African American speech community: Culture, language ideology, and social face. In *Language, discourse, and power in African American culture*, 10–29. Cambridge University Press.
Poplack, Shana (ed.). 2000. *The English history of African American Vernacular English*. Malden, MA, and Oxford: Blackwell.
Preston, Dennis, and Gregory Robinson. 2005. Dialect perception and attitudes to variation. In Martin Ball (ed.), *Clinical sociolinguistics*, 133–149. Oxford: Blackwell.
Pullum, Geoffrey K. 1997. Language that dare not speak its name. *Nature* 386: 321–322.
Purnell, Thomas, William Idsardi, and John Baugh. 1999. Perceptual and phonetic experiments on American English dialect identification. *Journal of Language and Social Psychology* 18:10–30.
Shousterman, Cara, Ayesha Baez, Nicole Holliday, and Renée Blake (African American English blog team). 2009. The origins of AAE. *Word: The Online Journal on African American English. Wordpress*. https://africanamericanenglish.com/2009/04/16/the-origins-of-aae/
Weldon, Tracey. 2000. Reflections on the Ebonics controversy. *American Speech* 75: 275–277.
Wolfram, Walt. 1998. Language ideology and dialect: Understanding the Oakland Ebonics controversy. *Journal of English Linguistics* 26(2): 108–121.

Chapter 14

Flemish versus Walloons in Belgium

Beheydt, Ludo. 1995. The linguistic situation in the new Belgium. In Sue Wright (ed.), *Languages in contact and conflict: Contrasting experiences in the Netherlands and Belgium*, 48–64. Avon: Multilingual Matters.

Belien, Paul. 2005. *A throne in Brussels: Britain, the Saxe-Coburgs and the Belgianisation of Europe*. Exeter: Imprint Academic.

Daley, Suzanne. 2010. The language divide, writ small, in Belgian town. *New York Times*, July 15, 2010. www.nytimes.com/2010/07/16/world/europe/16belgium.html

de Groof, Jetje. 2002. Two hundred years of language planning in Belgium. In Andrew Linn and Nicola McLelland (eds.), *Standardization: Studies from the Germanic languages*, 117–134. Amsterdam: John Benjamins.

Huysmanns, M. Camille. 1930. The Flemish question. *Journal of the Royal Institute of International Affairs* 9(5): 680–690.

McRae, Kenneth Douglas. 1986. *Conflict and compromise in multilingual societies 2: Belgium*, 3rd edn. Waterloo, ON: Wilfrid Laurier University Press.

Mnookin, Robert, and Alain Verbeke. 2009. Persistent nonviolent conflict with no reconciliation: The Flemish and Walloons in Belgium. *Law and Contemporary Problems: Group-Conflict Resolution: Sources of Resistance to Reconciliation* 72 (2): 151–186.

O'Neill, Michael. 2000. Belgium: Language, ethnicity and nationality. *Parliamentary Affairs* 53(1): 114–134.

Vos, Louis. 1993. Shifting nationalism: Belgians, Flemings and Walloons. In Mikulas Teich and Roy Porter (eds.), *The national question in Europe in historical context*, 128–147. Cambridge University Press.

Tamils versus Sinhalese in Sri Lanka

de Varennes, Fernand. 2010. Political participation and power-sharing in ethnic peace settlements. In Marc Weller and Katherine Nobbs (eds.), *Political participation of minorities: A commentary on international standards and practice*, 453–474. Oxford University Press.

DeVotta, Neil. 2003. Ethnolinguistic nationalism and ethnic conflict in Sri Lanka. In Michael E. Brown and Šumit Ganguly (eds.), *Fighting words: Language policy and ethnic relations in Asia*, 105–140. Cambridge, MA: MIT Press.

2004. *Blowback: Linguistic nationalism, institutional decay, and ethnic conflict in Sri Lanka*. Stanford University Press.

Official Language Act (no. 33 of 1956). Sri Lanka Consolidated Acts. Commonwealth Legal Information Institute. Australasian Legal Information Institute. www.commonlii.org/lk/legis/num_act/ola33o1956180/

Parliament of Sri Lanka. 2013. 1978 Constitution. www.parliament.lk/constitution/19 78-constitution

Presidential Secretariat of Sri Lanka. 2008. Thirteenth Amendment to the Constitution. Policy Research and Information Unit. www.priu.gov.lk/Cons/1978Constitution/ AMENDMENTS.html#Thirteenth Amendment

Schiffman, Harold F. 1982. Review of *Language and linguistic area: Essays by Murray B. Emeneau.* Selected and introduced by Anwar S. Dil. Stanford: Stanford University Press, 1980. *Language* 58: 185–193.

French versus English in Canada

Behiels, M. D., and R. Hudon. 2013. Bill 101 (Charte de la langue française). *The Canadian encyclopedia.* Toronto: Historica Canada. www.thecanadianencyclopedia.ca/en/arti cle/bill-101/

Busque, Anne-Marie. 2006. Québec language policy. *The Canadian encyclopedia.* Toronto: Historica Canada. www.thecanadianencyclopedia.ca/en/article/quebec-language-policy/

Gouvernement du Québec. 2016. C-11 – Charter of the French language. Légis Québec. Québec: Les Publications du Québec. http://legisquebec.gouv.qc.ca/en/ShowDoc/cs/C-11

Government of Canada. 2016. Official Languages Act (R.S.C., 1985, c. 31 (4th Supp.)). Justice Laws Website. http://laws-lois.justice.gc.ca/eng/acts/o-3.01/FullText.html

Linteau, Paul-André. 2006. Québec since confederation. *The Canadian encyclopedia.* Toronto: Historica Canada. www.thecanadianencyclopedia.ca/en/article/quebec-since-confederation/

Site for Language Management in Canada (SLMC). 2016a. Canada at the time of New France. University of Ottawa. https://slmc.uottawa.ca/?q=canada_new_france
  2016b. The Constitution Act of 1867 and the language question. University of Ottawa. https://slmc.uottawa.ca/?q=bnaa_linguistic_question
  2016c. The Québec Act of 1774 and tentative linguistic duality. University of Ottawa. https://slmc.uottawa.ca/?q=quebec_act_1774
  2016d. The Royal Proclamation of 1763 and the Use of Languages. University of Ottawa. https://slmc.uottawa.ca/?q=canada_new_france

Tattrie, Jon. 2014. Québec and confederation. *The Canadian encyclopedia.* Toronto: Historica Canada. www.thecanadianencyclopedia.ca/en/article/quebec-and-confederation/

Part IV

Language Endangerment, Extinction, and Revival

15 Endangered Languages: Taxonomy, Ecology, and Ownership

This chapter will first introduce issues that need to be fully apprehended before one can even begin to discuss the practical matters of specific language preservation or revival. Specifically, we need to understand how one can usefully identify as autonomous, languages that are endangered or in need of preservation. Our Chapter 4 discussion on the differences between "languages" and "dialects" (i.e. language varieties) is useful in this regard. It is also important, given the frequent comparisons between ecological and linguistic diversity, to understand what it means to consider intellectual and cultural diversity on the same level as biological diversity, as well as what are the limitations on such comparisons. Finally, since languages are part of human groups' cultural expression and ethnic heritage, we must consider whether languages are to be considered as belonging to the commonwealth of the human race or whether they are the cultural property of the people and societies who speak them.

We have seen that when languages come into conflict, there is a variety of possible outcomes. The (two) languages may peacefully coexist. One of the languages may become the target of restrictive laws in an effort by the dominant group to repress speakers of the non-dominant language. A language may become the symbol of a political movement, as in the case of many colonies. A language may take on an increased cultural significance for speakers, as for example in the case of Irish (as noted in Chapter 7). A language may be afforded special status as a national or official language. One outcome we have mentioned in passing but not touched on explicitly is that a language may cease to be viable or disappear completely, what is referred to as language endangerment and language extinction.

A language can become endangered, its existence imperiled, when the number of speakers declines to some minimum threshold number and, natu-rally, become extinct as a day-to-day spoken language when no speakers remain. Speakers shift from one language to another consciously or uncon-sciously, for social, economic, religious or political reasons (and often for a combination of these reasons). For instance, Sámi parents frequently elected to send their children to Norwegian-medium schools, not wishing to disadvantage them in the Norwegian society and economy. Some Māori parents in New Zealand welcomed the establishment of English-language schools by the British colonists for comparable reasons (described in passing in Chapter 10's additional cases). Non-Sámi Norwegian parents made a similar calculation when deciding that their children should be educated in Boksmål, the variety of Norwegian spoken in the urban centers, rather than Nynorsk, the variety spoken in outlying rural areas (as touched on briefly in Chapter 13). The number of speakers may be impacted by intermarriage, in which case the children often learn only the language of the dominant group. At the same time, government programs to assimilate the Sámi, the Māori, and other indigenous groups such as the Native Americans and the Ainu in Japan have served to socially and economically marginalize speakers of non-dominant languages; and as we have observed throughout Part III, this took place not only through education but through the active suppression of their native languages. In extreme cases, languages have become endangered or extinct through acts of genocide. Some Native American tribes were decimated through disease and genocide, and the native Tasmanians suffered the same fate at the hand of European settlers during the nineteenth century.[1] Their languages disappeared with them.

Language endangerment and death have emerged as a salient issue that has elicited more active concern in the past twenty to twenty-five years. This situation, the endangerment of minority languages, has been brought about in part by the spread of widely spoken languages such as English, Chinese, French, and other "world languages," all of which are perceived as the languages of modern, technologically advanced global economies. This dominance is starkly evident in UNESCO's reckoning that roughly 97 percent of the world's people speak 4 percent of the world's languages and some 3 percent of the people speak 96 percent of the world's languages.[2] So, a very large percentage of people speak a very small percentage of the world's living languages. Similar figures are recounted by others, who note that 90 percent of the world's population speaks the 100 most common of the estimated 6,000–7,000 languages of the world.[3] As the shift to more dominant languages and the loss of smaller languages have accelerated, many have noted the alarming rate at which languages are becoming extinct. And this has resulted in some very dire predictions. By some calculations, at least 50 percent of the thousands of languages currently spoken will have disappeared by the end of the twenty-first century,[4] while others have made the much more dramatic forecast that 90 percent of the world's languages will be lost by that time.[5]

---

[1] Matisoff (1991) speculates that some indigenous groups in Cambodia were lost during the genocide perpetrated by the Pol Pot regime from 1975 to 1978.
[2] Brenzinger et al. 2003.   [3] Nettle and Romaine 2000.
[4] Krauss 1992; Nettle and Romaine 2000.   [5] Brenzinger et al. 2003.

On the face of things, it seems clear that languages have declined and disappeared throughout history, and this is normal. While some of the world's languages have disappeared altogether, others have disappeared from daily use and are relegated to very specialized uses. Examples of the former include Hittite, Etruscan, and many others that are no longer spoken in any context, and known to us only through historical sources. Languages such as Latin and Sanskrit exemplify the latter, and still exist as liturgical languages without being used to any appreciable extent outside their religious contexts. Thus, the question arises as to whether or not language extinction is inevitable, or is simply a byproduct of the inexorable march of history. If language extinction is indeed inevitable, it might be asserted that perhaps there is little reason to be quite so concerned about it.

Even if language extinction is not inevitable, one may ask whether there is any reason to assume that it is undesirable? Many have argued that it is not. The biblical story of the Tower of Babel tells of a time when all people spoke the same language, before humankind was plunged into the confusion of multiple languages and people could not all understand one another. This allegory is often interpreted as symbolizing the desirability of all humans speaking a single language. Note that the idiomatic English expression "speak the same language" refers generally to people agreeing and getting along with one another, and is emblematic of the notion that having a common language is advantageous.[6] Historically, organized efforts on the part of some societies to assimilate minority ethnic groups have included as a key component pressuring such groups to adopt the majority language. We have observed this to be the case for indigenous groups such as the Ainu, Native Americans, and Sámi (in Chapter 10), as well as for immigrant groups such as the Roma (Chapter 12). Some proponents of assimilation have contended that everyone's "speaking the same language" would promote a more homogeneous society, one whose citizens would better understand one another (something which only the most idealistic and naïve could possibly believe, given the high level of conflict one observes in any society in which people are able to argue, contend, and rail against each other in a common tongue). From such perspectives, language extinction or loss may be viewed as desirable rather than undesirable.

Clearly, distinct perspectives underlie these different positions. But if language extinction is considered undesirable and if it need not be inevitable, what can be done to combat it? Before attempting to answer such questions, we need to dig deeper and better understand its genesis and what is at stake.

---

[6] Allan Bell (2011: 519) suggests that "Babel can be interpreted as a manifesto against the monolingual and monocultural impetus of empires ancient and contemporary. The multilingual outcome is a positive affirmation of sociocultural and linguistic diversity."

Linguistic Taxonomy: Identifying, Delimiting, and Enumerating Languages

Dire warnings have been issued about language endangerment. However, in order for a language to become extinct and in order for linguists and others to claim that 50 percent, 75 percent, or 90 percent of all languages will be lost by some particular point in time, it is necessary to be able to identify a language and enumerate how many languages are currently being spoken in the world. Where does such a number come from and what is it based on?

One hears various estimates about the number of living languages, generally somewhere between 5,000 and 7,000. An oft-cited, trusted source among linguists is *Ethnologue*, compiled by the Summer Institute of Linguistics (SIL) and published both in print and as a website.[7] SIL is a Bible translation society that trains linguists to go out into the field all over the world to study languages, in order to create dictionaries, grammars, and, of course, translations of the Christian Bible. Because of their mission, they have a natural interest in knowing how many languages there are (and how many still need Bible translations). *Ethnologue* contains a catalog of the world's languages that provides classification information, including such things as geographical distribution and genetic affiliation and, of course, the approximate number of speakers, both native speakers and those who use it as a second or additional language. As of this writing, the nineteenth edition of *Ethnologue* identifies 7,097 living languages.[8] Included among these are languages that have very few speakers (for example, ten or fewer). But these numbers are frequently based on censuses that may be a decade or more old, particularly those with a small number of speakers. *Ethnologue* also provides its own assessment regarding the vitality of a language, identifying languages that it considers "in trouble" or "dying" in addition to those that appear not to be endangered. It also identifies "extinct" languages.[9]

Although *Ethnologue* arrives at a very specific number, the authors caution that it is very difficult to determine how many unwritten languages there are in the world. And there is a variety of estimates regarding the number of languages. Why should that be? One of the reasons for variance is that it is necessary to identify what a language is and that a particular language variety is a distinct language. In the discussion of dialects and language change in Chapter 4, we noted that it can be difficult to decide precisely when you've got a dialect and when you've got a language. Linguists often use as a rule of thumb that dialects are mutually intelligible[10] (that is, speakers of two dialects can

---

[7] Lewis, Simons, and Fennig 2016.   [8] The figure on December 8, 2016.
[9] Criteria by which languages are judged to be endangered or not are discussed in Chapter 16.
[10] Of course, determining precisely what is meant by "intelligible" can itself be a bone of contention.

basically understand what the others are saying) and languages are not mutually intelligible (speakers of different languages cannot understand one another). However, that is not necessarily the way things fall out. In Chapter 4, we noted that not all regional varieties of Latin came to be identified as independent languages – (Castilian) Spanish did whereas Venetian (Italian) did not. These dichotomies and uncertainty were neatly summed up in Max Weinreich's statement, which has become a bit of an aphorism in linguistics, "A language is a dialect with an army and navy."

What underlies this saying is that what is considered a language and what is considered a dialect sometimes comes down to non-linguistic factors: social, cultural, and geopolitical. At times, what a language is may occasionally be determined by socially and culturally dominant peoples with a certain degree of political power. This sometimes results in languages that actually contain varieties none of which are mutually intelligible. We saw that play out in a number of cases in preceding chapters, for instance, the dialects of Japanese that are not mutually intelligible (Chapter 13). Among such languages are what are sometimes referred to as *macrolanguages*: "languages" that have multiple varieties that are not mutually intelligible. Most well known among them are Chinese, for which *Ethnologue* lists thirteen distinct varieties (Mandarin being identified as the standard variety), and Arabic, for which nineteen varieties are listed (Modern Standard Arabic being the standard). Chinese is deemed a language in an attempt to achieve political unity, while the dialects of Arabic are identified as Arabic largely for religious reasons. However, Egyptian Arabic is no more intelligible to a speaker of Moroccan Arabic than French is to a speaker of Portuguese. On the other hand, mutually or near-mutually intelligible varieties are sometimes identified as distinct languages. Although there are vocabulary differences, a speaker of Standard Malay can understand with little difficulty when someone is speaking Standard Indonesian. Nonetheless, for the sake of national identity, Malay is spoken in Malaysia and Indonesian in Indonesia. (Recall from Chapter 7 that the language Indonesian was a variety of Malay renamed Indonesian as a symbol of the independence movement.) Before Yugoslavia disintegrated during the Balkans war of the 1990s, a single language referred to as Serbo-Croatian was recognized. In its place today four languages are recognized, Bosnian, Croatian, Montenegrin, and Serbian, each identified with a distinct nation-state.

Some make the case that identifying each of the world's languages is an impossible and basically artificial task. For example, Jane Hill contends, "It is not possible to scientifically determine the number of languages in the world, and, of course, to even make the attempt requires an ideology that permits their enumeration."[11] In examining the state of languages in the Pacific islands,

---

[11] Hill 2002: 128.

Peter Mühlhäusler makes much the same point, arguing that the notion that languages can be counted and named is a recent idea introduced by Westerners and not one recognized by natives of that region.[12] Lionel Wee concurs wih these assessments and contends, citing Hopper, that we need to "rethink the ontological status of a language ... it is 'not a circumscribed object but a confederation of available and overlapping social experiences'."[13] Hill, Mühlhäusler, and Wee all promote the position that due to its dynamic and constantly changing nature, a discrete object that is a "language" is difficult to pin down. Rather it is an amalgam of many varieties that change and mutate based on who is speaking to whom, Hopper's "confederation of available and overlapping experiences."

To better understand the difficulty, the notion of *dialect continuum* is helpful. Embodied in this concept is the fact that as one travels across a territory or country in a straight line, the varieties of language that one encounters are apt to change only incrementally. The variety spoken in each town will be mutually intelligible with the one spoken in the next, with only slight, barely perceptible differences (provided their proximity is such that there is contact between the inhabitants of each). However, these varieties will change continuously, and so the farther one gets from the initial location, the more differences one will notice between the current variety and that spoken at the starting point. If one travels far enough, the variety spoken will eventually be unintelligible to speakers of the variety at the point of departure. But the varieties change in a relatively smooth continuum rather than there being sharp or discrete boundaries between them. This is unlike the sharp political boundaries we find between states. To take a more concrete example, the West Germanic dialect continuum includes the territory from southern Germany through the northern part of the Netherlands. Moving from southern Germany all the way through the Netherlands, the variety of language spoken changes steadily, incrementally. And it is not the case that when one crosses the German–Netherlands border, the colloquial variety spoken in that area changes dramatically. People living on either side of the border are likely to speak mutually intelligible varieties (as they are on the continuum) and are likely to have an easier time understanding one another than they will understanding someone at the other side of their own country. Yet those people living on the Netherlands side of the border will be said to speak a dialect of Dutch and those in Germany to speak a dialect of German. Thus, what is called a dialect of German is mutually intelligible with a dialect of Dutch. In this case, the criterion of mutual intelligibility does not identify what gets described as a single language. Mühlhäusler makes this argument with

---

[12] Mühlhäusler 1996.   [13] Hopper 1998: 171, cited by Wee 2011: 12.

respect to the dialect continuum in the Pacific region, where it is adjacent islands rather than towns that speak mutually intelligible varieties.

These real-world examples help explain the difficulty inherent in identifying precisely what is and what is not a language.[14] Inherent in the notion of a dialect continuum is the local nature of language varieties. Regardless of how dramatic distinctions are between different locations, the varieties are tied to specific geographical areas. Although advances in communication and travel have made this somewhat less true of large, global languages, the fact is that the majority of the world's languages have both relatively small numbers of speakers and limited geographical ranges.[15] The locality of language is underscored by the fact that, in contrast to the large state languages, linguists often refer to these smaller varieties as "local languages." The language-location nexus also surfaces in the Universal Declaration of Language Rights (Chapter 9). The Declaration distinguishes a *language community*, which refers to a linguistic society "established historically in a particular territorial space," from a *language group*, which does not have the historical tie to a location, for example, migrants. Recall that the Declaration hierarchizes the two, according greater rights to language communities than language groups. All this said, nothing we've said here negates the fact that language endangerment is a widespread phenomenon throughout the world, whether one is speaking of language varieties, autonomous "languages," the language of a community, or the language of a group.

Linguistic Ecology: Valuing Linguistic versus Ecological Diversity

The fact of language endangerment and language extinction begs comparisons with the endangerment and extinction of plant and animal species in local ecosystems, and indeed this comparison is frequently made and used to call attention to the urgency of the world's language situation. Just as flora and fauna have been lost or endangered through human activity, sometimes through hunting as in the case of the dodo bird or through the loss of habitat as in the case of grey wolves in North America, languages have also been endangered or extinguished, sometimes through genocide and other times through altering the

---

[14] Recall that the first step in creating a standard language (an important step in creating the language of a nation-state) is selection of a dialect to consider standard, usually the prestige variety spoken by the politically and economically powerful. People who speak non-prestige varieties at the borders of the nation-state may thus find themselves at a disadvantage.

[15] Even global languages such as English have local varieties associated with them. In addition to British English, American English, Canadian English, Australian English, New Zealand English, and South African English, there are local varieties in India, Jamaica, Nigeria, Pakistan, the Philippines, Singapore, and a host of other countries. Of course, the same point can be made regarding French, Spanish, and some others.

social environment required for them to thrive, as in the case of the Ainu, Sámi, and Native Americans.

The global importance of the diversity of species and of diversity within species has long been acknowledged fairly universally by the scientific community. It is argued in this regard that biodiversity better ensures the sustainability of ecosystems, the adaptability of species to some environmental changes (such as fire and flood); thus if one particular species does not survive, the existence of a rich diversity in species might ensure that another can take over its role in the ecosystem. On the other hand, widespread plant and animal extinctions can lead to vast disruption of local ecosystems, and these disruptions can in turn have far-reaching adverse environmental effects on the entire planet, as has been hypothesized regarding the destruction of the rainforests around the world. Drawing on the established importance of biodiversity, some have proposed that linguistic diversity is important in a parallel fashion: the suggestion being that the extinction of languages could have detrimental effects on human ecology, reducing the intellectual resources available to humankind, including: (i) knowledge of ecosystems that may contain unknown but potentially beneficial plants and animals; (ii) communal history and the transmission of unique methods of solving problems; and (iii) the richness and originality of language-embodied thought.

Biodiversity and linguistic diversity are connected and parallel in another very real, but perhaps surprising, way. The areas of greatest biodiversity in the world coincide with the areas of greatest linguistic diversity – both linguistic and biological variation is greatest in tropical regions as opposed to temperate and polar regions. One can find a particularly striking example in Papua New Guinea, the territory comprising the eastern half of the second largest island in the world, the island of New Guinea, which is located north of Australia. One of the most biologically diverse places in the world, Papua New Guinea is well known for the incredible richness of its plant, animal, and insect species. Over 20,000 species of plants alone are found here. At the same time, Papua New Guinea also ranks as the most linguistically diverse area in the world. There are over 800 identifiable languages spoken in this relatively small corner of the planet, or fully 12–15 percent of the world's total. These 800 languages are spoken by a population estimated at approximately 6.7 million people in an area of under 180,000 square miles, only slightly larger than the state of California.[16]

Further, the local nature of language underscores the biodiversity and linguistic diversity nexus: languages are repositories of not only cultural information but also knowledge of the ecology of the territories that encompass them. Bound up in a language are the names of native plants and animals potentially

[16] *CIA World Factbook* 2016.

unknown to outsiders as well as traditional knowledge of these species, including their potential value to humans, as in the realms of medicine and nutrition, and the means of sustaining their existence (through knowledge of how they relate to the local ecosystem). An oft-heard argument for why diverse environments should be protected is the potential use of as yet unknown species that might benefit humankind. For example, new species are discovered on a regular basis in Papua New Guinea. During the period 1998–2008, it is estimated that well over 1,000 new plant and animal species were discovered, and in 2009, scientists discovered more than 200 species during a single two-month expedition.[17] To the extent that information about these species is most easily accessible within a local language, when a language disappears, a wealth of knowledge may well be lost with it.

In recent years, climate change has dramatically highlighted the environment–language nexus. The warming of the Earth and the rising sea levels have a perceptible impact on the habitat and the culture of some groups. In Arctic regions, melting of the ice in Greenland and warm, wet winters in the Sakha Republic (Yakutia) in Russia disrupt the livelihood of the indigenous people and so their culture.[18] Rising sea levels imperil many islands in the Pacific. The president of Kiribati is considering plans to relocate the whole island nation, which he fears will be completely under water in fifty years or fewer.[19] Changing habitat and culture imperil traditional societies and the languages they speak.

Why Try to Preserve Endangered Languages?

Preserving linguistic diversity by combatting language endangerment and extinction thus gains traction from the perceived benefits to the greater good of humanity: the knowledge gained about local ecosystems can potentially impact us all, not simply the speakers of particular languages. In addition to the ecological knowledge however, languages are often viewed as repositories of cultural knowledge and reflect the manner in which humans experience and understand the world (as discussed in Chapter 7). For example, on its website, the Alliance for Linguistic Diversity asserts that when a language dies "a unique vision of the world is lost." Implicit in this is the idea that like biological information this "unique vision" is of value to all of humanity, not just the people whose vision it is. Thus, many who have been at the forefront of the endangered language movement view languages as a valuable resource, treasures from which we all may learn, and therefore must be preserved. This is explicit in the statement of the Foundation for Endangered Languages that "Once the knowledge is lost … a community and the whole of humanity is

---

[17] National Geographic Society 2011.   [18] Krouleck 2016.   [19] Worland 2015.

poorer." In this way, languages are seen as belonging not only to their speakers but to the entire world, what Jane Hill describes as an attitude of the "universal ownership" of language.[20]

Another argument promulgated for preserving languages is the scientific significance of the language for researchers who study the human mind. As made plain in Part I, the grammar of an individual language is a rule-governed system, a set of principles that capture phonological, morphological, syntactic, and semantic generalizations about that language. More generally, linguists endeavor to understand the principles governing the organization of language (in general), with the goal of discovering the ways the brain stores and communicates experience. Put differently, linguists seek to discover how languages are alike and how they differ: what is and is not found in the phonology, morphology, syntax, semantics, in all aspects of language. As affirmed by the Linguistic Society of America and the National Science Foundation (to name just two organizations), only by analyzing as many languages as possible can such a goal be achieved. And while much is known about some languages, there are thousands of others that have not been studied in detail or have not been studied at all. Each individual language contains the potential to contribute to our understanding. Therefore, whenever a language is lost, valuable data that may be able to help push the frontiers of human knowledge are lost. Such a view again embraces the notion of the universal ownership of languages.

The reasons considered thus far for combatting language endangerment focus largely on benefits for society at large and not solely (and to a degree only secondarily) for the speakers of a language. This differs dramatically from the rationale for language rights, which focuses on the individual or the speakers of languages. However, preserving a culture and the cultural and personal identities of the speakers is clearly compelling. If it is true that a unique vision of the world is lost when a language dies, it follows that descendants of those who spoke that language will be denied at least a portion of the worldview of their ancestors. In addition, the relationship between language and culture has figured prominently in advocating for languages rights (and in their suppression as well). Any argument for the right of speakers to use their language represents a strong rationale for preserving a language and combatting its demise. In fact, many endangered language advocates cite loss of cultural identity as perhaps the most convincing reason for their position. This is not to say that Native American Choctaws who do not speak the Choctaw language have lost their Choctaw identities, nor that Chinese in Singapore who speak no Chinese have lost their Chinese identities, nor that Bretons in Brittany who

---

[20] As we see, while endorsing the importance of the issue of language endangerment, Hill does not endorse this view.

speak no Breton have lost their identities as Bretons. But as Anthony Woodbury notes in the Linguistic Society of America's pamphlet on endangered languages:

Much of the cultural, spiritual, and intellectual life of a people is experienced through language. This ranges from prayers, myths, ceremonies, poetry, oratory, and technical vocabulary to everyday greetings, leavetakings, conversational styles, humor, ways of speaking to children, and terms for habits, behaviors, and emotions. When a language is lost, all of this must be refashioned in the new language – with different words, sounds, and grammar – if it is to be kept at all.[21]

Any loss of identity is clearly felt more acutely by speakers of a language than by the world at large and thus may be considered a primary reason to fight for the continued existence of a language.

Against Language Preservation?

Despite those arguments in its favor, it is not the case that linguists and anthropologists universally subscribe to the position that all languages must be maintained and language shift needs to be resisted. Many proponents of combatting language endangerment cite language rights in their advocacy. It therefore stands to reason that some of the objections to universally preserving endangered languages are the same as those leveled against language rights. As discussed in Chapter 9, some researchers assert that language is not essential to culture and that language is only a secondary trait in identity. That is, these researchers assert that one's cultural or ethnic identity is not determined by one's language,[22] and all characteristics of any culture can be translated or recreated in a newly adopted language. Thus, when speakers shift to another language the only thing that is lost is the language itself.[23] Although there is some truth to this assertion, as mentioned above (and discussed in Chapter 6), some important aspects of a culture are claimed to actually be encoded by the language, in the manner in which people greet and take leave of one another, in the rituals that are part of the culture, in poetry, and in a host of other domains. It can be argued that when cultural concepts are translated into a new language the culture shifts and to some degree a new culture is constructed.

Of course, in order to counteract language shift, speakers must see the value of using the language in question. If domains in which a language can be used are diminished, speakers may shift to a language perceived as socially and economically more beneficial, enabling them to potentially take part in the advantages of the greater society. Some researchers contend that insisting that

---

[21] Woodbury (no date).   [22] Edwards 1985.   [23] Eastman 1984.

speakers of endangered languages continue to use them so that the languages can be preserved may very well put those speakers at a disadvantage, if not restricting access to the dominant language then jeopardizing their fluency.[24] Also, the view that languages should be preserved so that linguists, psychologists, and others may study them or the whole world may benefit from them is rejected by some, such as McWhorter, who cautions, "our case for preserving the world's languages cannot be based on how fascinating their variegation appears to a few people in the world." As Peter Ladefoged observes, "It is paternalistic of linguists to assume that they know what is best for the community."[25]

This type of paternalistic attitude and the notion of "universal ownership" that undergirds it are rejected by many indigenous people. Anthropological linguist Jane Hill relates the story of a native speaker of Cupeno (a Native American language) who was impatient for her to finish some field notes to share with others, telling her, "*You* [JHH] have *our* language," driving home the point that it is the speakers themselves that own and should control the language. As Hill points out, many indigenous people believe that language rightly belongs to those who have ties to it, either through inhabiting the area where it is spoken or through kinship: "For them, it may make little sense to say that a language 'belongs' to someone who has no intention of learning it, has never heard it, and has never known any of its speakers."[26] Linguist Keren Rice reports a similar sentiment among the First Nations in Canada.[27] And Jane Simpson describes the fact that many aboriginal Australians as well as speakers of other endangered languages take their language to be "their intellectual property, passed down to them by their ancestors."[28] Many want to be consulted in advance and be given right of refusal before their language is shared with the general public. At times the local community of speakers may oppose the dissemination of linguists' findings, no matter how benign they might seem. Hill tells of the concern of the officers of the Hopi Tribe that the publication of a Hopi dictionary in 1998 would take away some of their control over the Hopi language by making it part of the public domain. The bottom line is that the perspective of speakers is liable to differ from that of outsiders, and in the end, the ones who "own" the language are those who speak (or whose elders speak) the language, not humankind writ large.

The Inevitability of Language Extinction?

All that said, isn't language extinction a natural and inevitable outcome of progress and globalization? Might the extinction of languages actually be

---

[24] Mufwene 2002; McWhorter 2009.   [25] Ladefoged 1992: 810.   [26] Hill 2002: 122.
[27] Rice 2009.   [28] Simpson 2006.

a desirable outcome? Answering these questions in the affirmative seems to make combatting language endangerment a waste of energy and resources. These are both positions taken by many advocates of making English the official language of the United States, groups such as the US English Foundation, ProEnglish, and English First. These groups argue that if language extinction is inevitable, making English the official language of the United States should not threaten minority languages and many benefits would follow. If everyone spoke the same language, they reason, communication would improve and conflicts could be avoided. It is explicitly stated on the ProEnglish website that one of the reasons for adopting English as the official language of the United States is to avoid the "conflicts that afflict societies divided by language." However, it is demonstrably untrue that a common language necessarily eases conflict. One need look no further than the United States to see this: both Northerners and Southerners spoke English, but that fact did not prevent the Civil War. Similarly, Bosnians, Croats, and Serbians spoke mutually intelligible language varieties, but that did not prevent the war in the Balkans during the 1990s, which saw the violent dissolution of Yugoslavia and the establishment of the states of Bosnia-Herzegovina, Croatia, Serbia, and Montenegro. The Hutus and the Tutsis of central Africa provide another recent example. In the Rwandan genocide of 1994, between 1 and 2 million Tutsis and moderate Hutus were slaughtered during a 100-day period. The two groups speak the same language, Kinyarwanda.[29] Many of the worst conflicts in world history have involved antagonists who spoke the same language: the Thirty Years' War, pitting German-speaking Catholics against German-speaking Protestants and leaving one out of every three Germans dead, and the thirty years of Joseph Stalin's rule over the Soviet Union, in which the political-economic campaigns of the regime resulted in some 20 million Russian speakers being killed at the hands of other Russian speakers.

These conflicts, and many others like them, are additional evidence that conflicts do not arise solely because the opposing groups speak different languages; the root causes in these cases are clearly sociocultural, economic, or religious. Thus, the desirability of everyone speaking the same language is no reason for not resisting language endangerment.

---

[29] This is a long-standing conflict. In 1972, upwards of 200,000 Hutus perished at the hands of the Tutsis in Burundi.

16 Language Revitalization and Revival

Having in the previous chapter discussed some conceptual issues surrounding the endangerment of languages, and explored some of the debates that these issues have inspired, we turn in this chapter to the practical matters of identifying and revitalizing or reviving endangered languages. The chapter will explore, in turn, the means by which one might determine that a language is endangered and evaluate the severity of its endangerment, the possible goals that one might have in attempting to preserve and revitalize it, the question of how to determine which variety of an endangered language merits rehabilitation, and the means and methods by which one might attempt to do this. The chapter will also describe and discuss two instances of such efforts, that of Welsh and that of Modern (Israeli) Hebrew.

Identifying Endangered Languages

All these considerations raise the question of how to identify endangered languages and determine their degree of endangerment. Numerous measures have been proposed to assess a language's vitality, its "strength" and its capacity for survival, yielding various types of scales. Some scales identify as few as three categories for living languages, *moribund*, *endangered*, and *safe*,[1] while others produce more fine-grained distinctions with up to thirteen categories and subcategories.[2] *Ethnologue* includes in its catalog of languages the best estimates available of the number of speakers in the entry for each language. And on the face of it, the size of the speaker population using a language would seem like an obvious predictor of the fate of a language. However, while the number of speakers often figures into assessments of the vitality of a language, it is by no means the only factor or even the principal factor taken into consideration. For instance, a language in Papua New Guinea with a few thousand speakers may be more vital, hence less endangered, than a language with hundreds of thousands of speakers. Breton, spoken in the northeast of France, with roughly 200,000 speakers is classified as "severely

---

[1] Krauss 1992.   [2] Lewis, Simons, and Fennig 2016.

endangered" in UNESCO's *Atlas of the World's Languages in Danger*, while Bumita Arapesh, a language of Papua New Guinea with fewer than 2,500 speakers, is merely classified as "vulnerable."[3] In fact, only 98 of the more than 800 languages spoken in Papua New Guinea are even included in the *Atlas*.

A more important indicator of a language's vitality is whether or not children are learning the language from their elders in their community, what is referred to as *intergenerational transmission*. So important is it that it is the basis of the name of Joshua Fishman's eight-point Graded Intergenerational Disruption Scale (GIDS), and intergenerational transmission is the critical criterion distinguishing "safe" languages from "endangered" languages.[4] In Michael Krauss's scale, *moribund* languages are those that are no longer being learned as mother tongues by children,[5] and it is the first factor in UNESCO's scale,[6] in which languages are rated as *definitely endangered* if children are no longer learning the language. In *Ethnologue*'s Expanded Graded Intergenerational Disruption Scale, an elaboration of Fishman's GIDS, *shifting* languages, those that will be lost, are those which are "not being transmitted to children."

A number of other factors included in some of these scales of endangerment are familiar from language rights issues, including:

- the attitude of the speakers: Is the language considered culturally significant enough that speakers want it promoted?
- the domains in which the language is used: Are there print and broadcast media? Is it the language of instruction in primary schools (and beyond)? Is it a topic of study in schools? Is it a language in which local business is conducted?
- the degree to which it is recognized by the government: Does the language have status as a national or official language? Can the language be used in court proceedings without prejudice? Are government services available in the language?

Of course, depending on the particular context, some factors may be irrelevant, as in isolated language communities where there may be neither print nor broadcast media, nor much interaction with a central government that does not recognize the use of the language in official domains.

Goals of Revitalization

Each particular case of an endangered language brings a unique context and a unique set of issues. Thus, while there are similarities among cases, not all language revitalization efforts will have the same goals or use the same strategies. In an ideal world, the goal of every language revitalization effort

---

[3] Moseley 2010.   [4] Fishman 1991.   [5] Krauss 1992.   [6] Brenzinger et al. 2003.

would result in a language with a fully functioning speaker community. However, this is an unrealistic goal in the overwhelming majority of cases. For many severely endangered languages, the existing native-speaker population numbers well under 100 (and often can be counted on one or both hands). Many Native American and Australian aboriginal-language revitalization programs can realistically only hope to make lists of words and expressions, and to provide these to members of the community. These, rather than being usable as resources for the restoration of the language as a language per se, are utilized in order to preserve cultural connections to the language, for use in limited environments such as greetings, leave-takings, and traditional ceremonies, and to record and preserve traditional folklore. The implementation of such realistically modest goals in such cases can be deemed successful insofar as the revitalization efforts manage to keep the community in touch with the language in some limited and practically sustainable contexts, and they are appropriate goals given the typically small populations of speakers and the limited domains of utility for the language.

Of course, many revitalization efforts aspire to do more, and some are successful in doing quite a bit more. For example, Yurok, the language of the Yurok people of Northern California, was at one point reduced to six fluent elderly speakers. Due to a dedicated cadre of tribal members who did not want to see their language die out altogether, incremental progress was made in reviving and rehabilitating the language, starting in the early 1990s, which exposed more young children to the language of the elders. As of 2013, Yurok language study is offered in five Northern California public high schools, and those identifying as conversationally fluent has risen to almost twenty, with an additional 400 more with basic to advanced language skills.[7] In another notable case, the last speaker of the Australian language Kaurna is reported to have died in the 1920s. However, Kaurna community members pairing with independent linguists unearthed a grammar, word list, and limited texts from missionaries who arrived in the area in 1838, and several community members have been using the language with one another.[8] One has spoken only Kaurna to his child from infancy, hoping to raise the first native speaker of Kaurna in almost 100 years. There are currently Kaurna language classes offered at some private language schools and the University of Adelaide.[9] Of course, the rehabilitation/revival of a language with no living native speakers, relying only on written records, raises the question of what exactly is being revived. We address this issue in the following section on "authenticity" and explore it in some further detail in the section on the revival of (Israeli) Hebrew.

---

[7] Romney 2013.   [8] Mercer 2013.   [9] Kaurna Warra Pintyanthi 2016.

Authenticity

One issue that arises in these efforts is precisely what language is being revitalized. Often learners are not acquiring the language as young children in the home, but learn it as a second language in a school setting or even an informal setting. Even supposing they can become fluent speakers, it is not exactly clear what they are becoming fluent in, and it might be claimed that they are in fact learning to speak a new language, one that is an amalgam of what is/ was known of the targeted endangered language along with influences from their first language and the language of their instructors. This language may bear some strong resemblance to, and preserve many features of, the target endangered language, but it can hardly be said to fully represent the whole of it. In the case of the Australian child learning Kaurna as her first language, she is learning a form of the language as reconstructed by her father and others. On the one hand, one could consider this a nonissue. After all, we can see through historical linguistics (and often our own experience) that language changes constantly and varieties are not static. However, this can become an issue when there is a significant group of living native speakers who reject the language spoken by schooled learners as inauthentic, as has been reported in the revitalization of Welsh.[10] And even if the language is not "rejected" as inauthentic, it nonetheless remains the case that there is a gap in its transmission, virtually ensuring that many if not most of the subtle nuances of meaning and structure will have been lost for all time.

Another issue that arises is the question of what variety of a living language (when there are still native speakers of it) is to be revitalized. Just as disputes can arise over the adoption of a particular variety or dialect in the establishment of a standard language when redressing language rights concerns, so too can the selection of the variety or dialect for a revitalization project be a contentious issue. Some revitalization efforts have been severely hampered or stymied altogether due to disagreements of this kind.

Methods and Applications

What steps can be taken to preserve endangered languages and what are the desired (and realistic) outcomes? Of course, not all situations are the same, but in each case it is necessary to identify the degree of endangerment by examination of the responsible factors. These may be the factors set out by UNESCO or by Fishman in the stages of his Graded Intergenerational Disruption Scale or in *Ethnologue*'s adaptation of the GIDS. This basically means determining who the speakers are and assessing the domains in which the language is used.

---

[10] Cosslett 2013.

Some measures intended to correct violations of language rights examined in previous chapters are, in effect, measures designed to counteract language loss. These include provisions implemented in formal education (such as using the language as the medium of instruction), corrective measures in public naming and signage (as in restoring native names for villages or erecting bilingual signs), and remediation in the courts, penal systems, and government services (as in allowing the language in court or providing government services in the language). Recognition as a national or official language can also signal a positive change in the government's attitude toward the minority language. Regardless of whether the number of speakers is small, as in the case of the Sámi, or large, as in the case of the Kurds, these measures have the effect of increasing the domains in which the threatened language can be used and thus contribute to its vitality, hence counteracting language loss.

Education is likely to be a key ingredient in any of these efforts, inasmuch as revitalization of endangered languages necessarily involves the development of new speakers. Frequently, dedicated community members collaborate with a linguist or linguistics professor at a nearby university to create materials for classroom use, as in the case of Yurok discussed above. Regardless of who contributes to the process, the impetus in revival efforts must have its roots in the speakers themselves. This is underscored by one strategy that has proved relatively effective: bringing together young children with native-speaking elders of their grandparents' generation, sometimes in pairs but more frequently in what are referred to as "language nests." Language nests are immersion nursery schools in which elders care for preschool children in a communal setting with the explicit intent of transmitting the language intergenerationally. (Recall that intergenerational transmission is the primary factor in most language vitality scales.) The Māori and Sámi first developed the practice of using language nests, and they have since been employed by Hawaiians, Native Americans in the United States and Canada, and Australian groups in their revitalization efforts. Immersion programs are available for older learners as well. For instance, Israel has a well-developed system for short-term, intensive learning of Hebrew for individual adults who are immigrating to the country or who are about to enter a multi-year degree or professional licensing program. Private and publicly funded school programs also play an important role in larger-scale national revitalization programs (such as Welsh, discussed below), as do non-intensive language classes offered in schools (such as the Yurok classes mentioned earlier) and in adult community-based programs. Education played an integral role in both the abrogation and restoration of language rights in the cases that we examined in previous chapters.

The issue of language endangerment and revitalization covers a vast array of situations worldwide and has engendered a very sizable literature, including the work of community members, academics, and the popular press. We make no pretense of providing anything more than a cursory view of the topic, our intention being to highlight its close connection to language rights. With this in mind, we turn to two of the most celebrated cases of revitalization, Welsh and Hebrew.

The Revitalization of Welsh

Welsh is frequently held up as a model for successful language revitalization (or at least modest success at combatting language decline), in both the academic[11] and popular press.[12] A Celtic language (along with Irish, Scots Gaelic, Breton, and others), Welsh is structurally quite distinct from English (known especially for its consonant clusters and the length of some of its words and names).[13] Once spoken by an estimated 1 million,[14] the number of speakers has declined to fewer than 600,000, largely owing to a systematic effort of the English to eradicate it from public life through government decrees and public education.

The English laid claim to Wales in 1284 but largely left local institutions intact for many years. This changed under Henry VIII, at which time the Act of Union (1536, 1542) declared the Welsh English citizens and set out to Anglicize the territory. The Act made English the language of government and the courts, severely restricting access to these institutions for most of the Welsh population.[15] While many continued to speak Welsh in their daily lives, a radical shift began with the Education Act of 1870, which established a network of government-subsidized English-medium schools; attendance became compulsory in 1880. By the 1891 census, only 54 percent of the population could speak Welsh, while it was reported that 69 percent could speak English. The decline continued through the twentieth century due to urban migration, the influx of English speakers, the secularization of society (churches were traditionally bastions of the language), the rise of popular media, continued active discouragement of the language in schools, and the general perception of the economic benefits and modernity attached to English and the low prestige of the Welsh language. By the 1991 census, a mere

---

[11] De Bres 2008; May 2001.   [12] Reid 2001; Cox 2015.
[13] The Welsh town *Llanfairpwllgwyngyllgogerychwyrndrobwllllantysiliogogogoch* was purportedly the longest place name in Great Britain. The name was coined as a publicity gimmick in the 1860s by concatenating the names of *Llanfairpwllgwyngyll* ('St. Mary's church in the hollow of the white hazel'), the nearby hamlet of *Llantysilio Gogogoch* ('the church of St. Tysilio of the red cave'), and the *chwyrn drobwll* ('rapid whirlpool') between them.
[14] Leach and Warnes 2015.
[15] C. H. Williams notes that the encroachment of English (and Latin and French) among the "upper classes" had begun before the Acts of Union and that the Acts "merely formalised certain forces which had been quietly at work for some years" (2009: 204).

18.7 percent of the population reported being able to speak Welsh and mono-lingual Welsh speakers had all but vanished. The fate of Welsh under the dominion of the English thus bears a strong resemblance to the fate of Ainu, Sami, Maori, and a host of other indigenous languages.

So why do many point to Welsh as a revitalization success story? Despite the precipitous decline, there were some moves in the first half of the twentieth century. The nationalist political party Plaid Cymru, formed in the 1920s, began to agitate for the Welsh language, and there were Acts related to the courts and education passed in the 1940s. However, these provisions did not place Welsh on a par with English, which remained the only official language of the courts (Welsh Courts Act of 1942). It was not until popular opinion was galvanized that there was any significant progress in the status of Welsh. There were several incidents in the 1950s and 1960s responsible for this, but none more prominent than a 1962 radio lecture delivered in Welsh by the activist Saunders Lewis entitled "Tynged yr Iaith" 'The Fate of the Language'. In it, Lewis cites the importance of the language to the Welsh identity and outlines how the English systematically went about trying to destroy the language (and culture) through the laws and decrees noted above. Lewis declared that the language would die unless revolutionary methods were used to defend it and called for direct action, "Let us set about it in seriousness and without hesitation to make it impossible for the business of local and central government to continue without using Welsh."[16]

Lewis's speech triggered the formation of Cymdeithas yr Iaith Gymraeg (the Welsh language Society) in 1962, which began a campaign of direct action during the 1960s–1980s, including demonstrations, sit-ins, painting over monolingual English street signs, painting slogans on businesses, refusing to pay tax bills presented in English, and more. These actions increased public awareness and galvanized greater, though by no means universal, public sup-port, and the increased pressure brought some accommodation by the govern-ment in London including measures such as the Welsh Language Act of 1967, the Education Reform Act (1988), a strengthened Welsh Language Act in 1993, and the creation of Welsh-language BBC radio (1977) and television (1982) stations. Simultaneously, Welsh-language print publications increased. Two of the most far-reaching developments were making eleven years of Welsh language study (either as a first or second language) compulsory and the establishment of the functionally bilingual National Assembly of Wales in 1999, which afforded the Welsh greater governmental autonomy.

Although official measures – such as bilingual signage, the limited use of indigenous languages in court, and so on – never guarantee success, in the case of Welsh, the constellation of factors has resulted in a qualified revitalization of

[16] Lewis 1962.

the Welsh language. Official census figures show a modest increase in those reporting Welsh language ability from 18.7 percent of the population in 1991 to 20.8 percent in 2001, though there was a decline in the 2011 census. At the same time the Welsh Language Use Survey put the figure at 21.7 percent in 2004, showing an increase to 23 percent in the 2013–2014 survey.[17] Regardless of discrepancies in the figures, there has been a substantial decrease in Welsh language attrition compared with what had occurred from the late nineteenth century to the late twentieth century.

Comparing the Welsh situation with the criteria included in UNESCO's language vitality assessment scale provides some insight into the near equilibrium. While intergeneration transmission is included as perhaps the most important factor in language endangerment (and figures prominently in the UNESCO scale), a key ingredient in language revitalization is "community members' attitudes toward their own language" (factor 8). Up until the Welsh Language Society's garnering public support for the language, use of Welsh was in dramatic decline. In its 1995 report *Public attitudes to the Welsh language*, NOP Social and Political reported that 71 percent of those polled favored the use of Welsh, 75 percent felt that Welsh and English should be co-equals, and 88 percent took pride in the Welsh language.[18] There are, of course, those Welsh citizens who do not consider this a positive development.

The Welsh case stacks up fairly well against some of the other UNESCO factors as well. There has been some expansion into new domains (factor 5), such as the Internet. There are materials available for education and literacy building (factor 6), owing in part to the compulsory study of Welsh in school and evening classes for adults. Government language policies are in place (factor 7), though business and many private agencies have shown resistance. Reports of the frequency of Welsh language use by speakers has been encouraging – one in eight report using the language daily.[19] There is ample evidence of a significant lessening of the rapid rate of decline in the number of citizens of Wales who claim knowledge of Welsh.

However, such success does not guarantee a continued resurgence of the Welsh language. The fact is that new speakers are by and large second language learners. And so, in addition to the issues related to authenticity discussed above, it is unclear what level of proficiency they will obtain and the role it will play in their daily lives. In fact, the percentage of speakers reporting that they speak the language fluently has declined (representing 11 percent of the Welsh population), the steepest declines being for those under the age of 29 (and those aged 45–64). Only among those aged 65 and over has the decline been minimal.[20]

[17] Deans 2015.   [18] Reported in May 2001.   [19] Welsh Government 2015.
[20] https://en.wikipedia.org/wiki/Welsh_language#/media/File:Welsh_speakers_in_the_2011_cen sus.png

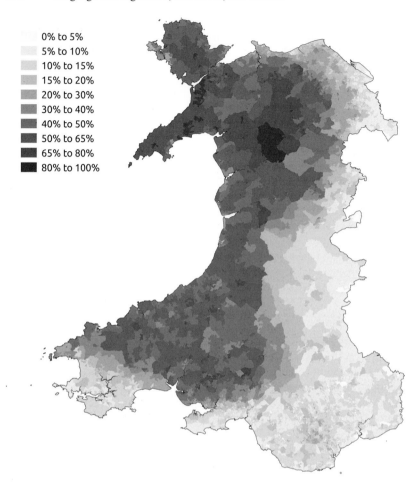

0% to 5%
5% to 10%
10% to 15%
15% to 20%
20% to 30%
30% to 40%
40% to 50%
50% to 65%
65% to 80%
80% to 100%

Figure 16.1 Welsh speakers according to the 2011 census

Significantly, the most important factor identified by linguist Joshua Fishman in his seminal language endangerment scale (and echoed in all other scales proposed since then), intergenerational transmission, is not robust. And Fishman cautions that language shift cannot be reversed in the absence of substantial numbers of adults passing the language on to children in the home.[21] So, while there has been definite success in slowing the decline of the language, the avowed plan to create a truly bilingual Wales perhaps seems in jeopardy.[22]

[21] Fishman 1991.   [22] Pawb 2003.

The Rebirth of Hebrew as a National Language

The resuscitation of Hebrew as a national language was in some ways similar to the revitalization of Welsh, but in other ways vastly different. Consider, first of all, the fact that Hebrew was not exactly revitalized, as was Welsh. This is to say that Welsh was, and is, a language which had never gone out of use. The Welsh language has been in continuous use as the language of the Welsh people for well over a millennium, and efforts in Wales to promote the language were made in order to reverse or at least to slow its decline.

Not so, for Hebrew. Through the Middle Ages and into the Renaissance, the Hebrew language was not much in daily use as a vernacular means of expression. However, this is not to say that the language was by any means "dead," as were Hittite and Ancient Egyptian. While Hebrew was not any longer a language of daily discourse, as it had been in biblical times, it was still very much in use as a classical language of study, prayer, and other intellectual pursuits. Observant Jews were minimally capable of reading Hebrew orthography and understanding the meaning of the most important and commonly used texts (i.e. the liturgy and the Hebrew Bible). More erudite members of the community would also use it for written communication in books, letters, and legal documents. And even though Jews did not use Hebrew as a first language for communication, they "were able to speak [it] on occasion, Jews from different countries are known to have conversed with each other in the Sacred Tongue, visiting scholars gave sermons in it, some spoke it on Sabbaths and festivals, while others spoke it in order not to be understood by the Gentiles." In these respects, it played a role similar to that of "Latin in medieval Catholic Europe, Byzantine Greek and Old Church Slavonic in Orthodox Christian Eastern Europe, and Classical Arabic in Moslem Southwest Asia and North Africa."[23]

During the nineteenth century, the rise of European nationalism and the use of common vernacular to convey realism in literature worked both against and in favor of the revival of Hebrew. On the negative side, Biblical Hebrew had a limited and somewhat archaic vocabulary that was seen as an anachronism for those Jews who aspired to the nationality and the national languages of the countries they lived in. It was also a poor vehicle for realistic and modern expression, in comparison with national vernaculars. At the same time, for those Jews who had Jewish national aspirations (so inspired by their European contemporaries), Hebrew stood as a linguistic emblem that could be used to express and cradle those aspirations.

This said, the selection of Hebrew as a national language for the Jews trying to reestablish their homeland was not a straightforward one. The leaders of the

---

[23] Fellman 1973: 251.

Zionist movement (i.e. movement for Jewish self-determination) were primarily from Eastern Europe, where Yiddish (i.e. the Judeo-German language written using a Hebrew alphabet) was the lingua franca for Jews. In addition, European Jews had developed, using Yiddish, a rich tradition of literature, song, and folklore – much richer than that of Hebrew (which had primarily been a vehicle for liturgical and scholastic traditions). The prevalence of Yiddish as a means of communication for European Jews thus made it a natural candidate for anointment as the language of Jewish national self-determination. However, there was also a good deal of opposition to Yiddish for this purpose. Many of those who aspired to rebuilding the Jewish homeland saw Yiddish as a language of the exile, a language of a people without a land. And in the debate between supporters of the diasporic language of convenience and supporters of the ancient language of the Kingdom of Israel, it was the latter that held sway.

One of those who imagined the restoration of Hebrew as a national language was Eliezer Ben-Yehuda, the reviver of Modern Hebrew. Ben-Yehuda (born Eliezer Yitzhak Perelman in Lithuania in 1858), in an 1879 article in a Hebrew periodical, promoting Jewish emigration to Palestine, first promoted the revival of Hebrew as the national language of the Jewish people. He wrote that "if a language is to be taken, on the European model, as a criterion of nationalism and nationhood, we have a language in which we can write everything we want to and we can speak it if we only want to. This language is Hebrew."[24]

It was Ben-Yehuda, primarily if not exclusively, who set the wheels in motion for the rebirth of Hebrew as a national language. Emigrating to Palestine in 1881, during the first period of Jewish immigration from Eastern Europe, Ben-Yehudah arrived with a plan to make Hebrew the national language of the Jewish renaissance in Palestine. His three-pronged plan was to bring the language back from its role as a language of prayer, study, disputation, law, and liturgy, and to restore it to its former role as a language of the people, of the nation. This plan, simply put, involved "Hebrew in the home," "Hebrew in the schools," and "Words, words, words." It was Ben-Yehuda's contention that, for Hebrew to once again be the language it had been, it must be learned by the children as their first language, it must be the medium of instruction in the schools, and it must have created for it words for all the modern concepts for which there are no Biblical Hebrew words.[25]

Suffice it to say that Ben-Yehuda was, at the very least, prescient. Decades before anyone had evidence to distinguish between first and second language acquisition, Ben-Yehuda was sufficiently intuitive to know that his revival plans depended on raising a generation of children for whom Hebrew would be their first language. These children would then, by being educated in

[24] Ben-Yehuda 1879.   [25] Fellman 1973.

Figure 16.2 Eliezer Ben-Yehuda, 1905

Hebrew-medium schools, become proficient in their new language. In regards to the creation of words, Ben-Yehuda was aiming to bring Biblical Hebrew up to date by submitting it to a process of "intellectualization," whereby an ancient language is modernized or a vernacular language is made into a vehicle for sophisticated thought, through the creation of new vocabulary for the purpose. Ben-Yehuda began his lexicography campaign for the "modern" Hebrew language in his own home, coining new Hebrew words for his own son, "for objects such as doll, ice-cream, jelly, omelette, handkerchief, towel, bicycle, and hundreds more."[26]

From these household beginnings, Ben-Yehuda's lexicographic project grew into a national language building enterprise, the creation and compilation of

---

[26] https://commons.wikimedia.org/wiki/File:Eliezer_Ben-Yehuda.1905.jpg

a comprehensive dictionary for the newly revived language. "Appropriately, the first word Ben-Yehuda created [for his project] was *millon* for 'dictionary,' which replaced the construction *sefer millim* ('a book of words') which had been used until then as a translation of the German *Woerterbuch*." Ultimately, his decades of dedication and labor culminated in *The Complete Dictionary of Ancient and Modern Hebrew*. This seventeen-volume work, compiled by Ben-Yehuda and others between 1908 and 1959, "stands as the largest and most comprehensive Hebrew dictionary of his era."[27]

It would not be an exaggeration to say that the success of the Hebrew revival effort stands on the shoulders of Eliezer Ben-Yehuda – and the effort was certainly successful. The Hebrew language revival program, beginning with Ben-Yehuda's arrival in Palestine in 1881, was so successful that "by the end of World War I fully 40% of the Jewish population of the country used Hebrew as their first or daily language, this including more than three-quarters of the children."[28] Cecil Roth summed up Ben-Yehuda's contribution to the Hebrew language, saying: "Before Ben-Yehuda, Jews could speak Hebrew; after him, they did."[29]

---

[27] The Academy of the Hebrew Language (no date).   [28] Fellman 1973: 255.
[29] Bensadoun 2010.

Further Reading and Resources for Part IV

Suggested Reading on Language Endangerment and Revitalization

Austin, Peter, and Julia Sallabank. 2010. *The Cambridge handbook of endangered languages*. Cambridge University Press.

Bradley, David, and Maya Bradley, eds. 2002. *Language endangerment and language maintenance*. London: Routledge.

Brenzinger, Matthias, Arienne M. Dwyer, Tjeerd de Graaf, Colette Grinevald, Michael Krauss, Osahito Miyaoka, Nicholas Ostler, Osamu Sakiyama, María E. Villalón, Akira Y. Yamamoto, and Ofelia Zepeda. 2003. Language vitality and endangerment. International Expert Meeting on UNESCO Programme Safeguarding of Endangered Languages. www.unesco.org/culture/ich/doc/src/00120-EN.pdf

Crystal, David. 2000. *Language death*. Cambridge University Press.

Fishman, Joshua A. 1991. *Reversing language shift: Theoretical and empirical foundations of assistance to threatened languages*. Clevedon: Multilingual Matters.

Flores Farfán, José Antonio, and Fernando Ramallo (eds.) 2010. *New perspectives on endangered languages*. Amsterdam: John Benjamins.

Grenoble, Lenore A. and Lindsay J. Whaley (eds.) 1998. *Endangered languages: Language loss and community response*. Cambridge University Press.

Hill, Jane. 2002. Expert rhetorics in advocacy for endangered languages: Who is listening, and what do they hear? *Journal of Linguistic Anthropology* 12:119–133.

Hinton, Leanne, and Kenneth Hale (eds.). 2001. *The green book of language revitalization in practice*. New York: Academic Press.

Lewis, M. Paul, and Gary F. Simons. (2010). Assessing endangerment: Expanding Fishman's GIDS. *Romanian Review of Linguistics 55*, 103–120.

Mihas, Elena, Bernard Perley, Gabriel Rei-Doval, and Kathleen Wheatley (eds.). (2013). *Responses to language endangerment: In honor of Mickey Noonan: New directions in language documentation and language revitalization*. Amsterdam: John Benjamins.

Moseley, Christopher (ed.). 2010. *Atlas of the world's languages in danger*, 3rd edn. Paris: UNESCO Publishing.

Nettle, Daniel, and Romaine, Suzanne. 2000. *Vanishing voices: The extinction of the world's languages*. New York: Oxford University Press.

Shaul, David Leedom. 2014. *Linguistic ideologies of Native American language revitalization: Doing the lost language ghost dance*. New York: Springer.

Thomason, Sarah G. 2015. *Endangered languages: An introduction.* Cambridge University Press.
Woodbury, Anthony. No date. What is an endangered language? Pamphlet, Linguistic Society of America. www.linguisticsociety.org/sites/default/files/Endangered_ Languages.pdf

Welsh

Cosslett, Rhiannon Lucy. 2013. Why is the Welsh language dying? Because the land of my fathers is obsessed with purity. *New Statesman*, Aug 14, 2013. www.newstates man.com/culture/2013/08/why-welsh-language-dying-because-land-my-fathers-obsessed-purity
Cox, Patrick. 2015. Welsh is considered a model for language revitalization, but its fate is still uncertain. www.pri.org/stories/2015–06-24/welsh-considered-model-language-revitalization-its-fate-uncertain
Leach, Anna, and Sophie Warnes 2015. Welsh speaking has only declined by 1% in four hundred years. *Daily Mirror.* www.mirror.co.uk/news/ampp3d/welsh-speaking-o nly-declined-1–5090082
Lewis, Saunders. 1962. Tynged yr iaith [The fate of the language]. BBC radio lecture. Translation into English by G. Aled Williams. https://morris.cymru/testun/saun ders-lewis-fate-of-the-language.html
Pawb, Iaith. 2003. *A national action plan for a bilingual Wales.* Welsh Government Publications. http://gov.wales/topics/welshlanguage/publications/iaithpawb/? lang=en

Hebrew

Academy of the Hebrew Language. No date. Ben-Yehuda. *Ha-akademia la-lashon ha-'ivrit* [The Academy of the Hebrew Language]. http://hebrew-academy.huji.ac.il/ English/BenYehuda/Pages/default.aspx
Bensadoun, Daniel. 2010. This week in history: Revival of the Hebrew language. *Jerusalem Post*, October 15, 2010. www.jpost.com/printarticle.aspx?id=191505
Ben-Yehuda, Eliezer. 1879. Sheela nikhbada [A serious question]. *Ha-Shahar.* The article is found in folio 7, pages 3–13. See Jack Fellman, *The revival of a classical tongue: Eliezer Ben Yehuda and the Modern Hebrew language* (The Hague: Mouton, 1974).
Fellman, Jack. 1973. Concerning the 'Revival' of the Hebrew Language. *Anthropological Linguistics* 15(5): 250–257.

References

Abas, Husen. 1987. *Indonesian as a unifying language of wider communication: A historical and sociolinguistic perspective*. Canberra: Department of Linguistics, Research School of Pacific Studies, Australian National University.

Abeykon, John. 1884. The progress of the Sinhalese in literature, arts, and sciences. *The Orientalist* 1: 55–56, 82–86, 163–165, 271–273.

Academy of the Hebrew Language. No date. Ben-Yehuda. *Ha-akademia la-lashon ha-'ivrit* [The Academy of the Hebrew Language]. http://hebrew-academy.huji.ac.il/English/BenYehuda/Pages/default.aspx

Adams, David Wallace. 1995. *Education for extinction*. Topeka: University of Kansas Press.

Alexander, Neville. 2001. *Language education policy, national and sub-national identities in South Africa*. Reference Study. Strasbourg: Language Policy Division DG IV – Directorate of School, Out-of-School and Higher Education, Council of Europe. www.coe.int/t/dg4/linguistic/Source/AlexanderEN.pdf

Alisbjahbana, S. T. 1974. Language policy and literacy in Indonesia and Malaysia. In Joshua Fishman (ed.), *Advances in language planning*, 391–416. The Hague: Mouton.

American Convention on Human Rights (Organization of American States 1978). www.hrcr.org/docs/American_Convention/oashr.html

American Declaration of the Rights and Duties of Man (Organization of American States 1948). www.cidh.org/basicos/english/Basic2.American%20Declaration.htm

American Declaration on the Rights of Indigenous Peoples [draft] (Organization of American States 1997). www.oas.org/en/iachr/indigenous/activities/declaration.asp

American Dialect Society. 2016. 2015 word of the year is singular 'they'. www.americandialect.org/2015-word-of-the-year-is-singular-they

Anderson, Benedict. 1983. *Imagined communities: Reflections on the origin and spread of nationalism*. London: Verso.

Andrássy, György. 2012. Freedom of language: A universal human right to be recognised. *International Journal on Minority and Group Rights* 19: 195–232.

Anthonisz, Richard Gerald. 1907. *Report on the Dutch records in the government archives at Columbo*. Colombo: H. C. Cottle.

Anwar, Kaidhir. 1980. *Indonesian: Development and use of a national language*. Yogyakarta: Gadjah Mada University Press.

Arasaratnam, Sinnappah, and Gerald Hubert Peiris. 2016. Sri Lanka. www.britannica
.com/place/Sri-Lanka/Conversion-to-Buddhism

Atkins, J. D. C. 1887. *Annual report of the Secretary of the Interior*, vol. 1. Washington, DC: Government Printing Office.

Austin, Peter K., and Julia Sallabank. 2011. Introduction. In Peter K. Austin and Julia Sallabank (eds.), *Cambridge handbook of endangered languages*. Cambridge University Press.

Aygen, Gülşat. 2007. *Kurmanjî Kurdish*. Munich: Lincom Europa.

Aygen Bartoš, Jozef, and Joseph Gagnaire. 1972. *Grammaire de la langue Slovaque*. Bratislava: Matica Slovenská.

Aytürk, İlker. 2008. Politics and language reform in Turkey: The "Academy" debate. *Wiener Zeitschrift für die Kunde des Morgenlandes* 98: 13–30.

Bailey, Guy, John Baugh, Salikoko S. Mufwene, and John R. Rickford. 1998. *African-American English: Structure, history, and use*. London: Routledge.

Bairon, Fija, Matthias Brenzinger, and Patrick Heinrich. 2009. The Ryūkyūs and the new, but endangered, languages of Japan. *Asia-Pacific Journal* 19(2). www.japanfocus .org/articles/print_article/3138. Reproduced in *OGMIOS Newsletter* 38: 6–12.

Baluja, Tamara, and James Bradshaw. 2012. Is bilingualism still relevant in Canada? *The Globe and Mail*. www.theglobeandmail.com/news/national/is-bilingualism-still-relevant-in-canada/article4365620/?page=all

Barclay, Kate. 2006. Okinawan identity. *Nations and Nationalism* 12(1): 117–137.

Batchelor, John. 1905. *An Ainu–English–Japanese dictionary (including a grammar of the Ainu language)*. Tokyo: Methodist Publishing House.

Baugh, John. 1999. *Out of the mouths of slaves: African American language and educational malpractice*. Austin: University of Texas Press
2000. *Beyond Ebonics: Linguistic pride and racial prejudice*. New York: Oxford University Press.

BBC. 2010. Try the McGurk Effect! "Is seeing believing?" *Horizon*. BBC Two. October 18.
2012. Slovaks retaliate over Hungarian citizenship law. March 12. www.bbc.com/ news/10166610
2013. Icelandic girl Blaer wins right to use given name. *BBC News Europe*. www.bbc .com/news/world-europe-21280101

Beheydt, Ludo. 1995. The linguistic situation in the new Belgium. In Sue Wright (ed.), *Languages in contact and conflict: Contrasting experiences in the Netherlands and Belgium*, 48–64. Avon: Multilingual Matters.

Behiels, M. D., and R. Hudon. 2013. Bill 101 (Charte de la langue française). *The Canadian encyclopedia*. Toronto: Historica Canada.

Beinart, William. 2001. *Twentieth-century South Africa*. Oxford University Press.

Bélanger, Claude. 2005. Treaty of Paris 1763. *L'Encyclopédie de l'histoire du Québec / The Quebec history encyclopedia*. Montreal: Marianopolis College.

Belien, Paul. 2005. *A throne in Brussels: Britain, the Saxe-Coburgs and the Belgianisation of Europe*. Exeter: Imprint Academic.

Bell, Allan. 2011. Re-constructing Babel: Discourse analysis, hermeneutics, and the Interpretive Arc. *Discourse Studies* 13(5): 519–568.

Bensadoun, Daniel. 2010. This week in history: Revival of the Hebrew language. *Jerusalem Post*, October 15. www.jpost.com/printarticle.aspx?id=191505

Ben-Yehuda, Eliezer. 1879. Sheela nikhbada [A serious question]. *Ha-Shahar* (folio 7), 3–13. See Jack Fellman, *The revival of a classical tongue: Eliezer Ben Yehuda and the Modern Hebrew language* (The Hague: Mouton, 1973).

Bideleux, Robert, and Ian Jeffries. 1998. *A history of Eastern Europe: Crisis and change.* London: Routledge.

Blenkinsop, Philip. 2010. Belgian king accepts government's resignation. Reuters. www.reuters.com/article/2010/04/26/us-belgium-government-idUSTRE63P3UE2 0100426

Bowring, Richard, and Haruko Uryu Laurie. 2004. *An introduction to Modern Japanese*, book 1: *Grammar lessons.* Cambridge University Press.

Brännlund, I., and Axelsson, P. (2011). Reindeer management during the colonization of Sami lands: A long-term perspective of vulnerability and adaptation strategies. *Global Environmental Change*, 21: 1095–1105.

Brenzinger, Matthias, Arienne M. Dwyer, Tjeerd de Graaf, Colette Grinevald, Michael Krauss, Osahito Miyaoka, Nicholas Ostler, Osamu Sakiyama, María E. Villalón, Akira Y. Yamamoto, and Ofelia Zepeda. 2003. Language vitality and endangerment. Document submitted to the International Expert Meeting on UNESCO Programme Safeguarding of Endangered Languages, Paris, March 10–12. www .unesco.org/culture/ich/doc/src/00120-EN.pdf

Bruce, Leslie P. 1988. Serialisation: From syntax to lexicon. *Studies in Language* 12: 19–49.

Bucken-Knapp, Gregg. 2003. *Elites, language and the politics of identity: The Norwegian case in comparative perspective.* Albany: State University of New York Press.

Bull, Tove. 2002. The Sámi language(s), maintenance and intellectualization. *Current Issues in Language Planning* 3(1): 28–39.

Busque, Anne-Marie. 2006. Québec language policy. *The Canadian encyclopedia.* Toronto: Historica Canada. www.thecanadianencyclopedia.ca/en/article/quebec-language-policy/

Caldwell, Robert. 1856. *A comparative grammar of the Dravidian or South-Indian family of languages.* London: Williams and Norgate.

1875. *A comparative grammar of the Dravidian or South-Indian family of languages*, 2nd edn. London: Williams and Norgate.

Carmen Rodriguez, Antonio Avalos, Hakan Yilmaz, and Ana I. Planet. 2013. *Turkey's democratization process.* London: Routledge.

Carroll, John Bissell (ed.). 1956. *Language, thought, and reality: Selected writings of Benjamin Lee Whorf.* Cambridge, MA: MIT Press.

Castillo, Mariano. 2012. Puerto Ricans favor statehood for the first time. CNN, November 8. www.cnn.com/2012/11/07/politics/election-puerto-rico/

Cemiloglu, Dicle. 2009. The dilemma of the Kurdish language in Turkey: A case study on language policy between 1924–2009. University of Pennsylvania honors thesis.

Charity, Anne Harper. 2008. African American English. In H. Neville, B. Tynes, and S. Utsey (eds.), *Handbook of African American psychology.* Thousand Oaks, CA: Sage Publications.

CBC News. 2013. Quebec language police aim at more Montreal restaurants. Feb 25. CBC/Radio Canada. www.cbc.ca/news/canada/montreal/quebec-language-police-aim-at-more-montreal-restaurants-1.1332751

Chew Jr., John J. 1976. Standard Japanese and the Hirara dialect: A case of linguistic convergence. *Journal of the Association of Teachers of Japanese* 11(2): 235–248.

CIA World Factbook. Papua New Guinea. www.cia.gov/library/publications/the-world-factbook/geos/pp.html

Cole, Douglas. 2016. Serial verb constructions in Lao and their event representations. PhD dissertation, University of Iowa.

Constitution of the Commonwealth of Puerto Rico 1952. Wikisource. https://en.wiki source.org/wiki/Constitution_of_the_Commonwealth_of_Puerto_Rico

Constitution of the State of California 1849. California Secretary of State Alex Padilla www.sos.ca.gov/archives/collections/constitutions/1849/

Constitution of the State of California 1879. Sacramento: State Office. www.sos.ca.gov/archives/collections/constitutions/1879/

Constitution of the State of California. State Constitution. www.citizensinchargefounda tion.org/files/California Constitution.pdf

Cosslett, Rhiannon Lucy. 2013. Why is the Welsh language dying? Because the land of my fathers is obsessed with purity. *New Statesman*, August 14. www.newstates man.com/culture/2013/08/why-welsh-language-dying-because-land-my-father s-obsessed-purity

Coulmas, Florian. 1988. What's a national language good for? In Florian Coulmas (ed.), *With forked* tongues: *What are national languages good for?* 1–24. Ann Arbor, MI: Karoma Publishers.

Cox, Patrick. 2015. Welsh is considered a model for language revitalization, but its fate is still uncertain. www.pri.org/stories/2015–06-24/welsh-considered-model-lan guage-revitalization-its-fate-uncertain

Curtis, Glenn E. (ed.). 1992. *Bulgaria: A country study.* Washington, DC: GPO for the Library of Congress.

Dacey-Fondelius, Elizabeth. 2007. Forbidden names, identity and the law. *The Local: Sweden's News in English.* November 26. www.thelocal.se/20071126/9212

Daftary, Farimah, and Kinga Gál. 2000. The new Slovak language law: Internal or external politics. ECMI Working Paper no. 8. Flensburg: European Centre for Minority Issues.

Daley, Suzanne. 2010. The language divide, writ small, in Belgian town. *New York Times*, July 15. www.nytimes.com/2010/07/16/world/europe/16belgium.html

Daniels, Harvey A. 1983. *Famous last words: The American language crisis recon-sidered.* Carbondale: Southern Illinois University Press.

Daniels, Peter T., and William Bright (eds.). 1996. *The world's writing systems.* Oxford University Press.

Dardjowidjojo, Soenjono. 1998. Strategies for a successful national language policy: The Indonesian case. *International Journal of the Sociology of Language* 130: 35–46.

Das Gupta, Jyotirindra. 1970. *Language conflict and national development.* Berkeley: University of California Press.

Davitt, Michael. 1902. *The Boer Fight for Freedom.* New York: Funk & Wagnalls.

Deans, David 2015. The state of the Welsh language: Number of people speaking Welsh fluently falls by 7,000 over the last decade. *Wales online.* www.walesonline.co.uk/news/wales-news/state-welsh-language-number-people-8538272

Debo, Angie. 1975. *The rise and fall of the Choctaw Nation.* Norman: University of Oklahoma Press.

De Bres, Julia. 2008. Planning for tolerability in New Zealand, Wales and Catalonia. *Current Issues in Language Planning* 9: 464–482.

DeFrancis, John. 1984. *The Chinese language: Fact and fantasy.* Honolulu: University of Hawaii Press.

de Groof, Jetje. 2002. Two hundred years of language planning in Belgium. In Andrew Linn and Nicola McLelland (eds.), *Standardization: Studies from the Germanic languages,* 117–134. Amsterdam: John Benjamins.

Deraniyagala, Siran Upendra. 1996. Pre- and protohistoric settlement in Sri Lanka. *International Union of Prehistoric and Protohistoric Sciences, Proceedings of the XIII Congress.* 5.16 (The prehistory of Asia and Oceania): 277–285. www.lankalibrary.com/geo/dera1.html

de Varennes, Fernand. 2010. Political participation and power-sharing in ethnic peace settlements. In Marc Weller and Katherine Nobbs (eds.), *Political participation of minorities: A commentary on international standards and practice,* 453–474. Oxford University Press.

DeVotta, Neil. 2003. Ethnolinguistic nationalism and ethnic conflict in Sri Lanka. In Michael E. Brown and Šumit Ganguly (eds.), *Fighting words: Language policy and ethnic relations in Asia,* 105–140. Cambridge, MA: MIT Press.

2004. *Blowback: Linguistic nationalism, institutional decay, and ethnic conflict in Sri Lanka.* Stanford University Press.

Diamond, Jared M. 1997. *Guns, germs, and steel: The fates of human societies.* W. W. Norton.

Dorian, Nancy C. 1994. Choices and values in language shift and its study. *International Journal of the Sociology of Language* 110: 113–124.

Dubinsky, Stanley, and William D. Davies. 2013. Language conflict and language rights: The Ainu, Ryūkyūans, and Koreans in Japan. *Japan Studies Review* 17: 3–27.

Dubinsky, Stanley, and Christopher Holcomb. 2011. *Understanding language through humor.* Cambridge University Press.

Duignan, Peter J. 1998. *Bilingual education: A critique.* Stanford University Hoover Institution. www.hoover.org/research/bilingual-education-critique

Eastman, Carol. 1984. Language, ethnic identity and change. In J. Edwards (ed.), *Linguistic minorities, policies and pluralism.* London: Academic Press.

Edwards, John. 1985. *Language, society, and identity.* Oxford: Blackwell.

2003. Contextualizing language rights. *Journal of Human Rights* 2: 551–571.

2009. *Language and identity: An introduction.* Cambridge University Press.

Egerö, Bertil. 1991. South Africa's Bantustans: From dumping grounds to battlefronts. Nordiska Afrikainstitutet Discussion Paper 4. Uppsala: Nordiska Afrikainstitutet.

Encyclopaedia Britannica. 1894. *The Encyclopaedia Britannica: A dictionary of arts, science, and general literature,* vol. XII. Philadelphia: Maxwell Sommerville.

English First. 2011a. The American public supports English First. www.englishfirst.org/d/americapublicsupportsenglish

2011b. The mission of English First. www.englishfirst.org

Erikson, Erik H. 1968. *Identity and youth crisis.* New York: W. W. Norton.

Errington, Joseph. 2003. Getting language rights: The rhetorics of language endangerment and loss. *American Anthropologist* 105: 723–732.

European Charter for Regional or Minority Languages (Council of Europe 1992) http://conventions.coe.int/Treaty/en/Treaties/Html/148.htm

Faingold, Eduardo D. 2004. Language rights and language justice in the constitutions of the world. *Language Problems and Language Planning* 28: 11–24.

Fasold, Ralph. 1988. What national languages are good for. In Florian Coulmas (ed.), *With forked tongues: What are national languages good for?* Ann Arbor, MI: Karoma Publishers.

Fear, Jacqueline. 1980. English versus the vernacular: the suppression of Indian languages in reservation schools at the end of the nineteenth century. *Revue française d'études américaines* 9: 13–24.

Fellman, Jack. 1973. Concerning the "revival" of the Hebrew language. *Anthropological Linguistics* 15(5): 250–257.

Fishman, Joshua A. 1978. The Indonesian language planning experience: What does it teach us? In S. Udin (ed.), *Spectrum: Essays presented to Sutan Takdir Alisjahbana on his seventieth birthday.* Jakarta: Dian Rakyat.

  1991. *Reversing language shift: Theoretical and empirical foundations of assistance to threatened languages.* Clevedon: Multilingual Matters.

Frankental, Sally, and Owen Sichone. 2005. *South Africa's diverse peoples: A reference sourcebook.* Santa Barbara: ABC-CLIO.

Franklin, Benjamin. 1751 [published 1755]. Observations concerning the increase of mankind, peopling of countries, etc. https://archive.org/stream/increasemankind00franrich/increasemankind00franrich_djvu.txt

Fraser, Angus. 1992. *The Gypsies.* Oxford: Blackwell.

Frese, Stephen J. 2005. Divided by a common language: The Babel proclamation and its influence in Iowa history. *The History Teacher* 39(1): 59–88.

Friedman, Victor. 2005. The Romani language in Macedonia in the third millennium: Progresss and problems. In Dieter W. Halwachs, Barbara Schrammel, and Gerd Ambrosch (eds.), *General and applied Romani linguistics: Proceedings from the 6th International Conference on Romani Linguistics*, 163–173. Munich: Lincom Europa.

Gallaher, Carolyn, Carl T. Dahlman, and Mary Gilmartin. 2009. *Key concepts in political geography.* Thousand Oaks, CA: Sage.

Gandhi, K. L. 1984. *The problem of official language in India.* New Delhi: Arya Book Depot.

Gandhi, M. K. 1956. *Thoughts on national language.* Ahmedabad: Navajivan Publishing.

Gates, Paul. 1971. The California Land Act of 1851. *California Historical Quarterly* 50: 395–430.

Gelb, I. J. 1952. *A study of writing.* University of Chicago Press.

Gibbons, Ann. 2014. Dwindling African tribe may have been most populous group on planet. *Science* online. www.sciencemag.org/news/2014/12/dwindling-african-tribe-may-have-been-most-populous-group-planet

Goddard, Ives. 1984. Synonymy. In David Damas (ed.), *Arctic*, vol. 5 of William C. Sturtevant (ed.), *Handbook of North American Indians*, 5–7. Washington, DC: Smithsonian Institution.

Goldwasser, Orly (2010). How the alphabet was born from hieroglyphs. *Biblical Archaeology Review* (Washington, DC: Biblical Archaeology Society) 36(1).

Gouvernement du Québec. 2016. C-11 – Charter of the French language. Légis Québec. Québec: Les Publications du Québec. http://legisquebec.gouv.qc.ca/en/ShowDoc/cs/C-11

Government of Canada. 2016. Official Languages Act (R.S.C., 1985, c. 31 (4th Supp.)). Justice Laws Website. http://laws-lois.justice.gc.ca/eng/acts/o-3.01/FullText.html

Graddol, David, Dick Leith, Joan Swann, Martin Rhys, and Julia Gillen (eds.). *Changing English*. London: Routledge.

Grenersen, Geir. 2012. What is a document institution? A case study from the South Sámi community. *Journal of Documentation* 68: 127–133.

Groff, Cynthia. 2007. Status and acquisition planning and linguistic minorities in India. *Working Papers in Educational Linguistics* 22: 15–41.

Groszkowski, Jakub, and Mariusz Bocian. 2009. The Slovak–Hungarian dispute over Slovakia's language law. *OSW Commentary* (Issue 30). Warsaw: Centre for Eastern Studies. www.isn.ethz.ch/Digital-Library/Publications/Detail/?id=110682&lng=en

Hancock, Ian. 2007a. Issues in the standardization of the Romani language: An overview and some recommendations. RADOC. www.radoc.net/radoc.php?doc=art_c_language_recommendations&lang=en&articles=true

2007b. On Romani origins and identity. RADOC. www.radoc.net/radoc.php?doc=art_b_history_origins&lang=en&articles=true

Hanihara, Kazuro. 1991. Dual structure model for the population history of the Japanese. *Japan Review* 2: 1–33

Harris, John F. 1996. US bilingual education funds ruled out for Ebonics speakers. *Washington Post*, December 25. www.washingtonpost.com/wp-srv/politics/govt/admin/stories/riley122596.htm

Harris, Roy, and Talbot Taylor. 1989. *Landmarks in linguistic thought: The Western tradition from Socrates to Saussure*. London: Routledge.

Hassanpour, Amir. 1992. *Nationalism and language in Kurdistan, 1918–1985*. San Francisco: Mellen Research University Press.

1999. Language rights in the emerging world linguistic order: The state, the market, and communication technologies. In Miklós Kontra, Robert Phillipson, Tove Skutnabb-Kangas, and Tibor Várady (eds.), *Language: A right and a resource. Approaching linguistic human rights*, 223–241. Budapest and New York: Central European University Press.

Hatori, Reiko. 2005. Policy on language education in Japan: Beyond nationalism and linguicism. *Second Language Studies* 23(2): 45–69. Manoa, HI: Department of Second Language Studies, University of Hawai'i. www.hawaii.edu/sls/wp-content/uploads/2014/09/6-Hatori-Reiko.pdf

Hattori, Shiso. 1964. *Ainugo hōgen jiten* [Ainu dialect dictionary]. Tokyo: Iwanami Shoten.

1976. Ryūkyuu hōgen to hondo hōgen. *Okinawagaku no reimei*, 7–55. Tokyo: Okinawa Bunka Kyōkai.

Heese, Hans F. A. 2011. *Cape melting pot: The role and status of the mixed population at the Cape 1652–1795*, trans. Delia A. Robertson. Johannesburg: D. A. Robertson. (First published in 1985 as *Groep sonder grense: Die rol en status van die gemengde bevolking aan die Kaap, 1652–1795*.)

Heinrich, Patrick. 2004. Language planning and language ideology in the Ryūkyū Islands. *Language Policy* 3(2): 153–179.

2005. Language loss and language revitalization in the Ryūkyū Islands. *Asia-Pacific Journal: Japan Focus* 3(11). www.japanfocus.org/-Patrick-Heinrich/1596

Hill, Jane. 2002. Expert rhetorics in advocacy for endangered languages: Who is listening, and what do they hear? *Journal of Linguistic Anthropology* 12: 119–133.

History.com Staff 2010. US immigration since 1965. www.history.com/topics/us-immigration-since-1965

Hockett, Charles F. 1960. The origins of speech. *Scientific American* 203: 88–96.

Hoffman, Michael. 2009. The long road to identity. *Japan Times*, October 11. www.japantimes.co.jp/cgi-bin/fl20091011x2.html

Holmberg, Gunnar. 2010. Japanese, Austronesian, and Altaic: A study of possible connections. Bachelor's thesis, Lund University.

Hopper, Paul. 1998. Emergent grammar. In Michael Tomasello (ed.), *The new psychology of language: Cognitive and functional approaches to language structure*. Mahwah, NJ: Lawrence Erlbaum Associates.

Hurley, Meghan. 2016. Lemonade in both languages: NCC grants kids permit for stand, with conditions. *Ottawa Citizen*. http://ottawacitizen.com/news/local-news/lemonade-in-both-official-languages-ncc-grants-permit-for-stand-to-kid-with-conditions

Huysmanns, M. Camille. 1930. The Flemish question. *Journal of the Royal Institute of International Affairs* 9(5): 680–690.

Indigenous and Tribal Peoples Convention (No. 169) (International Labour Organization 1989). www.ilo.org/global/topics/indigenous-tribal/lang–en/index.htm

Institutul Naţional de Statistică. 2011. *Rezultate definitive ale Recensământului Populaţiei şi al Locuinţelor* [The definitive results of the Population and Housing Census]. Romania.

Irish, Ann B. 2009. *Hokkaido: A history of ethnic transition and development on Japan's Northern Island*. Jefferson, NC: McFarland and Company.

Ishikida, Miki Y. 2005. *Living together: Minority people and disadvantaged groups in Japan*. Lincoln, NE: iUniverse. www.iuniverse.com/bookstore/BookDetail.aspx?BookId=SKU-000027958

Jaszi, Oscar. 1929. *The dissolution of the Habsburg Monarchy*. University of Chicago Press.

Johnstone, Paula Lightening Woman. 1998. Hair raising – a spiritual journey. Manataka American Indian Council. www.manataka.org/page1936.html

Joseph, John E. 2000. *Limiting the arbitrary: Linguistic naturalism and its opposites in Plato's Cratylus and modern theories of grammar*. Amsterdam: John Benjamins.

2002. *From Whitney to Chomsky: Essays in the history of American linguistics*. Amsterdam: John Benjamins.

2004. *Language and identity: National, ethnic, religious*. Basingstoke: Palgrave Macmillan.

Julku, Kyösti. 2002. The European origin of the Finns and their relation to the Indo-Europeans. *Mankind Quarterly* 43: 177–212.

Kamwangamalu, Nkonko M. 2009. South African Englishes. In Braj Kachru, Yamuna Kachru, and Cecil Nelson. *The handbook of world Englishes*, 158–171. Hoboken, NJ: John Wiley & Sons.

Kaplan, Lawrence. 2003. Inuit snow terms: How many and what does it mean? In François Trudel (ed.), *Building capacity in Arctic societies: Dynamics and shifting perspectives. Proceedings from the 2nd IPSSAS Seminar. Iqaluit, Nunavut, Canada: May 26 – June 6, 2003*. Montreal: CIÉRA – Faculté des sciences sociales Université Laval.

Karady, Victor. 2002. Symbolic nation-building in a multi-ethnic society: The case of surname nationalization in Hungary. In Moshe Zuckermann (ed.), *Ethnizität, Moderne und Enttraditionalisierung: Tel Aviver Jahrbuch für deutsche Geschichte* [Ethnicity, modernity and detraditionalization. Tel Aviv Yearbook of German History], 81–103. Göttingen: Wallenstein Verlag.

Kaschula, Russell H. 2015. Tower of Babel: Challenges of multilingualism in South African education. Lecture delivered at the University of South Carolina. October.

Kaurna Warra Pintyanthi. 2016. University of Adelaide. www.adelaide.edu.au/kwp/

Kenesei, Istvan, Robert M. Vago, and Anna Fenyvesi. 1998. *Hungarian*. London: Routledge.

Kindaichi, Kyōsuke. 1937. *Kokugo to Ainugo to no kankei* [Relationship between Japanese and Ainu]. Reprinted in Kindaichi. 1960. *Ainugo kenkyū. Kindaichi Kyōsuke senshū*, vol. 1. Tokyo: Sanseidō.

Kloss, Heinz. 1977. *The American bilingual tradition*. Rowley, MA: Newbury House.

Kontra, Miklós. 1995/1996. English only's cousin: Slovak only. *Acta Linguistica Hungarica* 43: 345–372.

1997. On the right to use the language of one's choice in Slovakia. *Canadian Centre for Linguistic Rights Bulletin* 4(1): 5–8.

1998. Language rights arguments in Central Europe and the USA: How similar are they? In Douglas A. Kibbee (ed.), *Language legislation and linguistic rights*, 142–178. Amsterdam and Philadelphia: John Benjamins.

1999. "Don't speak Hungarian in public!" A documentation and analysis of folk linguistic rights. In Miklós Kontra, Robert Phillipson, Tove Skutnabb-Kangas, and Tibor Várady (eds.), *Language: A right and a resource: Approaching linguistic human rights*, 81–97. Budapest and New York: Central European University Press.

2009. Szilágyi's Bill: The viability of universal language rights. privatewww.essex.ac.uk/~patrickp/lhr/KontraSzilagyisBill.pdf

Kopf, Dan. 2016. The Great Migration: The African American exodus from the South. *Priceonomics*. http://priceonomics.com/the-great-migration-the-african-american-exodus/

Krauss. Michael. 1992. The world's languages in crisis. *Language* 68: 1–42.

Kreyenbroek, Philip, and Stefan Sperl (eds.). 1992. *The Kurds: A contemporary overview*. London: Routledge.

Krouleck, Alison. 2016. How climate change threatens endangered languages and cultures. k-international. www.k-international.com/blog/climate-change-and-endangered-languages/

Kumaramangalam, S. Mohan. 1965. *India's language crisis*. Madras: New Century Book House Ltd.

Kurdish Academy of Language. *The history of the Kurdish language*. www.kurdisha cademy.org/?q=node/37

Kyuchukov, Hristo. 2009. The importance of Romani language in the cognitive development of Roma children. 17th International Steering Committee Meeting (Decade of Roma Inclusion 2005–2015). September 22–23. Spisska Nova Ves, Slovakia.

Labov, William. 1970. *The logic of nonstandard English*. Champaign, IL: National Council of Teachers of English.

Ladefoged, Peter. 1992. Another view of endangered languages. *Language* 68: 809–811.

Lamar, Lucius Q. C. 1886. *Annual report of the Secretary of the Interior*. Washington, DC: Government Printing Office.

Landes, David. 2009. Tax agency rejects Swedes' Michael Jackson naming tribute. *The Local: Sweden's News in English*. July 29. www.thelocal.se/20090929/20966

Language Files, 11th edn. 2011. The Ohio State University Press.

Leach, Anna, and Sophie Warnes 2015. Welsh speaking has only declined by 1% in four hundred years. *Daily Mirror*. www.mirror.co.uk/news/ampp3d/welsh-speaking-o nly-declined-1-5090082

Lee, Wal-sun. 1999. Zainichi chōsenjin no minzoku kyōiku. In Chonmyon Paku (ed.), *Zainichi chōsenjin: Rekishi, genjō, tenbō*, 135–173. Tokyo: Akashi Shoten.

Leibowitz, Arnold H. 1969–1970. English literacy: Legal sanction for discrimination *Notre Dame Lawyer* 45: 7–67

    1971. *Educational policy and political acceptance: The imposition of English as the language of instruction in American schools*. Washington, DC: ERIC Clearinghouse for Linguistics, Center for Applied Linguistics.

Leith, Dick, David Graddol, and Liz Jackson. 2007. Modernity and English as a national language. In David Graddol, Dick Leith, Joan Swann, Martin Rhys, and Julia Gillen (eds.), *Changing English*, 79–116. Abingdon: Routledge.

Lewis, M. Paul, Gary F. Simons, and Charles D. Fennig (eds.). 2016. *Ethnologue: Languages of the world*, 19th edn. Dallas, TX: SIL International. Online version: www.ethnologue.com

Lewis, Saunders. 1962. Tynged yr iaith [The fate of the language]. BBC radio lecture. Translation into English by G. Aled Williams. https://morris.cymru/testun/saun ders-lewis-fate-of-the-language.html

Liberman, Anatoly. 2008. *An analytic dictionary of the English Etymology*. Minneapolis: University of Minnesota Press.

Library of Congress. *Classroom resources: Immigration*. www.loc.gov/teachers/class roommaterials/presentationsandactivities/presentations/immigration/cuban3.html

Lillian Goldman Law Library. 2008. Treaty of Peace Between the United States and Spain; December 10, 1898. *The Avalon Project: Documents in law, history, and diplomacy* [Source: A Treaty of Peace Between the United States and Spain, US Congress, 55th Cong., 3d sess., Senate Doc. No. 62, Part 1 (Washington, DC: Government Printing Office, 1899), 5–11.]. New Haven: Yale University. http:// avalon.law.yale.edu/19th_century/sp1898.asp

Linguistic Society of America Statement on Language Rights. 1996. www.linguisticso
ciety.org/sites/default/files/lsa-stmt-language-rights.pdf

Linteau, Paul-André. 2006. Québec since confederation. *The Canadian encyclopedia*.
Toronto: Historica Canada. www.thecanadianencyclopedia.ca/en/article/quebec-
since-confederation/

Loomis, Charles Battell. 1917. *A book of American humorous verse*. New York:
Duffield & Company.

Lord, Nancy. 1998. Native tongues. In Virginia Clark, Paul Eschholz, and Alfred Rosa
(eds.). *Language: Readings in language and culture*, 19–25 (chapter 3). New York:
St. Martin's Press.

Louw, P. Eric. 1992. Language and national unity in a post-apartheid South Africa.
Critical Arts: A Journal of Media Studies 6(1): 52–60.

Lyon, Philip W. 2008. After empire: Ethnic Germans and minority nationalism in
interwar Yugoslavia. PhD dissertation, University of Maryland.

Macdonald, David Bruce. 2013. *Balkan holocausts? Serbian and Croatian victim-
centred propaganda and the war in Yugoslavia* (New Approaches to Conflict
Analysis). Manchester University Press.

Macías, Reynaldo F. 2001. Minority languages in the United States, with a focus on
Spanish in California. In Dürk Gorter and Guus Extra (eds.), *The other languages
of Europe*, 331–354. Clevedon: Multilingual Matters.

MacMaster, John Bach. 1921. *A history of the people of the United States from the
Revolution to the Civil War*, vol. III: *1803–1812*. New York: D. Appleton and
Company.

Magga, Ole Henrik. 1994. The Sami Language Act. In Tove Skutnabb-Kangas and
Robert Phillipson (eds.), *Linguistic human rights: Overcoming linguistic discrimination*, 219–233. Berlin: Mouton de Gruyter.

Magocsi, Paul Robert. 1993. *Historical Atlas of East Central Europe*. Seattle and
London: University of Washington Press.

Manning, Patrick. 1992. The slave trade: The formal demographics of a global system.
In Joseph E. Inikori and Stanley L. Engerman (eds.), *The Atlantic slave trade:
Effects on economies, societies, and peoples in Africa, the Americas, and Europe*,
117–144. Durham, NC: Duke University Press.

Martin, Laura. 1988. "Eskimo words for snow": A case study in the genesis and decay of
an anthropological example. *Americn Anthropologist* 88: 418–423.

Maruyama, Hiroshi. 2012. Ainu landowners' struggle for justice and the illegitimacy of
the Nibutani Dam project in Hokkaido Japan. *International Community Law
Review* 14: 63–80.

Matisoff, James A. 1991. Endangered languages of mainland Southeast Asia. In R. H.
Robins and E. M. Uhlenbeck (eds.), *Endangered languages*. Oxford: Berg.

Matras, Yaron. 2005. *The status of Romani in Europe*. Report submitted to the Council
of Europe's Language Policy Division, October. http://romani.humanities.manche
ster.ac.uk/downloads/1/statusofromani.pdf

  2015. *Romani Linguistics Website*. Manchester Romani Project. University of
Manchester. http://romani.humanities.manchester.ac.uk/index.shtml

May, Stephen. 2001. *Language and minority rights: Ethnicity, nationalism and the
politics of language*. Harlow: Longman.

2005. Language rights: Moving the debate forward. *Journal of Sociolinguistics* 9: 319–347.

2011. Language rights: The "Cinderella" human right. *Journal of Human Rights* 10: 265–289.

2012. *Language and minority rights: Ethnicity, nationalism, and the politics of language.* Abingdon: Routledge.

McRae, Kenneth Douglas. 1986. *Conflict and compromise in multilingual societies,* vol. 2: *Belgium,* 3rd edn. Waterloo, ON: Wilfrid Laurier University Press.

McWhorter, John. 2009. The cosmopolitan tongue: The universality of English. *World Affairs Journal,* Fall. www.worldaffairsjournal.org/article/cosmopolitan-tongue-universality-english

Mendizabal, Isabel, et al. 2012. Reconstructing the population history of European Romani from genome-wide data. *Current Biology* 22(24): 2342–2349.

Mercer, Phil. 2013. Lost indigenous language revived in Australia. *BBC News,* January 22. www.bbc.com/news/world-asia-20066624

Meriam, Lewis, Roy A. Brown, Henry Roe Cloud, Edward Everett Dale, Emma Duke, Herbert R. Edwards, Fayette Avery McKenzie, Mary Louise Mark, W. Carson Ryan, and William J. Spillman. 1928. *The problem of Indian administration.* Baltimore, MD: Johns Hopkins University Press.

Mesthrie, Rajend. 2002. South Africa: A sociolinguistic overview. In Rajend Mesthrie (ed.), *Language* in *South Africa,* 11–26. Cambridge University Press.

Miller, Roy Andrew. 1971. *Japanese and the other Altaic languages.* University of Chicago Press.

1974. The origins of Japanese: Review of Murayama Shichiro and Obayashi Taryo. *Nihongo no Kigen. Monumenta Nipponica* 29(1): 93–102.

Minde, Henry. (2003). Assimilation of the Sami: implementation and consequences. *Acta Borealia: A Nordic Journal of Circumpolar Societies* 20: 121–146.

Ministry of Foreign Affairs of Japan. 1999. International Convention on the Elimination of All Forms of Racial Discrimination (First and Second Report). www.mofa.go .jp/policy/human/race_rep1/]

Mnookin, Robert, and Alain Verbeke. 2009. Persistent nonviolent conflict with no reconciliation: The Flemish and Walloons in Belgium. *Law and Contemporary Problems: Group-Conflict Resolution: Sources of Resistance to Reconciliation* 72 (2): 151–186.

Morgan, Marcyliena. 2002. The African American speech community: Culture, language ideology, and social face. In *Language, discourse, and power in African American culture,* 10–29. Cambridge University Press.

Moseley, Christopher (ed.). 2010. *Atlas of the world's languages in danger,* 3rd edn. Paris: UNESCO Publishing. Online version: www.unesco.org/culture/en/endangeredlanguages/atlas

Mufwene, Saliko S. 2002. Colonization, globalization and the plight of "weak" languages. *Journal of Linguistics* 38: 530–555.

Mühlhäusler, Peter. 1996. *Linguistic ecology: Language change and linguistic imperialism in the Pacific region.* London: Routledge.

Muniz-Arguelles, Luis. 1988. *The status of languages in Puerto Rico.* University of Puerto Rico. http://muniz-arguelles.com/resources/The+status+of+languages+in+Puerto+Rico.pdf

Murazumi, Mie. 2000. Japan's laws on dual nationality in the context of a globalized world. *Pacific Rim Law and Policy Journal* 9(2): 415–443.

Myhill, John. 2006. *Language, religion and national identity in Europe and the Middle East*. Amsterdam: John Benjamins.

National Geographic Society 2011. http://news.nationalgeographic.com/news/2011/06/ pictures/110627-new-species-rare-animals-papua-new-guinea-wwf/

Nebez, Jemal. 2000. The Kurdish language from oral tradition to written language. Kurdish Academy of Language. www.kurdishacademy.org/?q=node/135

Nettle, Daniel, and Romaine, Suzanne. 2000. *Vanishing voices: The extinction of the world's languages*. New York: Oxford University Press.

New, William. 2014. Regulating Roma Language and Culture in Central Europe. *Journal of Language and Cultural Education (JoLaCE)* 2(2): 165–181. www.academia.edu/7 262547/Journal_of_Language_and_Cultural_Education_-_2014_2_a_complete_ issue_

Nishimura, Hiroko. 2001. Hōgen kinshi kara hōgen sonkei e, soshite hōgen keishō e. [From dialect prohibition to dialect esteem, and then to dialect inheritance.] *Kotoba to shakai* [Language and Society] 5: 164–184.

Niskanen, Markku. 2002. The origin of the Baltic-Finns. *Mankind Quarterly* 43: 121–153.

Official Language Act (No. 33 of 1956). Sri Lanka Consolidated Acts. Commonwealth Legal Information Institute. Australasian Legal Information Institute. www.com monlii.org/lk/legis/num_act/ola33o1956180/

O'Dwyer, Conor. 2008. *Runaway state-building: Patronage politics and democratic development*. Baltimore: Johns Hopkins University Press.

O'Neill, Michael. 2000. Belgium: Language, ethnicity and nationality. *Parliamentary Affairs* 53(1): 114–134.

O'Sullivan, John L. 1845. Annexation. *The United States Democratic Review* 17(5): 5–10.

Özkaragöz, İnci. 1986. The relational structure of Turkish syntax. PhD dissertation, University of California, San Diego.

Panico, Christopher. 1999. *Turkey: Violations of free expression in Turkey*. New York: Human Rights Watch.

Parliament of Sri Lanka. 2013. 1978 Constitution. www.parliament.lk/constitution/19 78-constitution

Park, Ju-min. 2009. Korea scripts and Indonesian tribe's survival. *Los Angeles Times*, December 27. http://articles.latimes.com/2009/dec/27/world/la-fg-korea-alpha bet27-2009dec27

Patrick, Peter. 2007. Linguistic human rights: A sociolinguistic introduction. privatewww .essex.ac.uk/~patrickp/lhr/lhrlingperspex.htm

Pawb, Iaith. 2003. *A national action plan for a bilingual Wales*. Cardiff: Welsh Government Publications. http://gov.wales/topics/welshlanguage/publications/iai thpawb/?lang=en

PBS. 2006. The Gold Rush. *American Experience*. www.pbs.org/wgbh/amex/goldrush/ peopleevents/e_goldrush.html

Peace, Hannah. 2009. Linguistic analysis of internet language as used in World of Warcraft. Honors thesis, University of South Carolina.

Perez, Cris. 1982. Ranchos. Excerpted from *Grants of land in California made by Spanish or Mexican authorities*. California State Lands Commission report. http://vm136.lib.berkeley.edu/EART/rancho.html

Pew Research Center. 2015. Hispanics of Puerto Rican origin in the United States, 2013. *Hispanic Trends*. www.pewhispanic.org/2015/09/15/hispanics-of-puerto-rican-ori gin-in-the-united-states-2013/

Phillipson, Robert, and Tove Skutnabb-Kangas. 1995. Linguistic rights and wrongs. *Applied Linguistics* 16: 438–504.

Pieris, Paulus Edward. 1918. *Ceylon and the Hollanders, 1658–1796*. Tellippalai, Ceylon: American Ceylon Mission Press.

1920. *Ceylon and the Portuguese, 1505–1658*. Tellippalai, Ceylon: American Ceylon Mission Press.

Poplack, Shana (ed.). 2000. *The English history of African American Vernacular English*. Malden, MA, and Oxford: Blackwell.

Powell, M. A. 1981. Three problems in the history of cuneiform writing: Origins, direction of script, literacy. *Visible Language* 15: 419–440.

Pratt, Richard H. 1964. *Battlefield and classroom: Four decades with the American Indian, 1867–1904*. New Haven: Yale University Press.

Presidential Secretariat of Sri Lanka. 2008. Thirteenth Amendment to the Constitution. Policy Research and Information Unit. www.priu.gov.lk/Cons/1978Constitution/ AMENDMENTS.html#Thirteenth Amendment

Preston, Dennis. 1989. *Perceptual dialectology*. Dordrecht: Foris.

Preston, Dennis, and Gregory Robinson. 2005. Dialect perception and attitudes to variation. In Martin Ball (ed.), *Clinical sociolinguistics*, 133–149. Oxford: Blackwell.

ProEnglish. 2015. https://proenglish.org

Pukui, Mary Kawena, E. W. Haertig, and Catherine A. Lee. 1972. *Nānā i ke kumu* [Look to the source], vol. 1. Honolulu: Hui Hanai.

Pullum, Geoffrey K. 1990. Constraints on intransitive quasi-serial verb constructions in Modern Colloquial English. *Ohio State Working Papers in Linguistics* 39: 218–239.

1991. *The great Eskimo vocabulary hoax and other irreverent essays on the study of language*. University of Chicago Press.

1997. The language that dare not speak its name. *Nature* 386: 321–322.

2011. Pronoun agreement out the window. *Lingua Franca: The Chronicle of Higher Education*. December 16. http://chronicle.com/blogs/linguafranca/2011/12/16/pro noun-agreement-out-the-window/

Purnell, Thomas, William Idsardi, and John Baugh. 1999. Perceptual and phonetic experiments on American English dialect identification. *Journal of Language and Social Psychology* 18: 10–30.

Quebec Community Groups Network (QCGN). 2016. http://qcgn.ca/us/

Quinn, George. 2001. *The learner's dictionary of today's Indonesian*. Crows Nest, Australia: Allen and Unwin.

Radford, Andrew, et al. 2009. *Linguistics: An introduction*. Cambridge University Press.

Reid, T. R. 2001. Reviving dying language is great Welsh success story. *Seattle Times*. http://community.seattletimes.nwsource.com/archive/?date=20010822&slug= wales22

Rice, Keren. 2009. Must there be two solitudes? Language activists and linguists working together. In Jon Reyhner and Louise Lockard (eds.), *Indigenous language revitalization: Encouragement, guidance and lessons learned*. Flagstaff, AZ: Northern Arizona University College of Education.

Robbeets, Martine I. 2005. *Is Japanese related to Korean, Tungusic, Mongolic and Turkic?* Wiesbaden: Otto Harrassowitz.

Romaine, Suzanne. 1994. From the fish's point of view. *International Journal of the Sociology of Language* 110: 177–185.

Romney, Lee. 2013. Revival of nearly extinct Yurok language is a success story. *Los Angeles Times*, February 6. http://articles.latimes.com/2013/feb/06/local/la-me-yurok-language-20130207

Ruppel, Kristin T. 2008. *Unearthing Indian land: Living with the legacies of allotment*. Tucson: University of Arizona Press.

Sajantila, A., P. Lahermo, T. Anttinen, M. Lukka, P. Sistonen, M. L. Savontaus, P. Aula, L. Beckman, L.Tranebjaerg, T. Gedde-Dahl, L. Issel-Tarver, A. DiRienzo, and S. Pääbo, 1995. Genes and languages in Europe: An analysis of mitochondrial lineages. *Genome Research* 5:42–52.

Sampson, Geoffrey. 1985. *Writing systems: A linguistic introduction*. Stanford University Press.

Samuel, Henry. 2001. France's Académie française battles to protect language from English. *The Telegraph*. www.telegraph.co.uk/news/worldnews/europe/france/8820304/Frances-Academie-francaise-battles-to-protect-language-from-English.html

Sanders, Seth L. 2004. What was the alphabet for? The rise of written vernaculars and the making of Israelite national literature. *Maarav* 11: 25–56.

Sandvik, Gudmund. 1993. Non-existent Sámi language rights in Norway 1850–1940. In Sergij Vilfan (ed.), *Comparative studies on governments and nondominant ethnic groups in Europe, 1850–1940*, vol. 3: *Ethnic groups and language rights*, 129–150. New York: NYU Press.

Sapir, Edward. 1921. *Language*. New York: Harcourt, Brace & World.

　1927. Speech as a personality trait. *American Journal of Sociology* 32: 892–905.

　1929. The status of linguistics as a science. *Language* 5(4): 207–14.

　1933. Language. *Encyclopaedia of the Social Sciences* 9: 155–169.

　1949. The psychological reality of phonemes. In David G. Mandelbaum, *Selected writings of Edward Sapir in language, culture and personality*, 46–60. Berkeley: University of California Press [originally published in French as "La réalité psychologique des phonèmes." *Journal de Psychologie Normale et Pathologique* 30 (1933): 247–265].

SB-1174. 2014. *English language education*. California State Legislative Information. http://leginfo.legislature.ca.gov/faces/billNavClient.xhtml?bill_id=201320140SB1174

Schiffman, Harold F. 1982. Review of *Language and linguistic area: Essays by Murray B. Emeneau*, selected and introduced by Anwar S. Dil (1980). *Language* 58: 185–193.

Schmandt-Besserat, Denise. 1979. Reckoning before writing. *Archaeology* 32(2): 22–31.

Schwegler, Brian A. 2008. Confronting the devil: Europe, nationalism, and municipal governance in Slovakia. PhD dissertation, University of Chicago.

Scott, Brian M., and Joshua Mittleman. 1999. *A brief introduction to medieval bynames*. www.s-gabriel.org/names/arval/bynames/

Seeley, Christopher. 1991. *A history of writing in Japan*. Boston: Brill Academic Publishers.

Seton-Watson, Hugh. 1977. *Nations and states: An enquiry into the origins of nations and the politics of nationalism*. Boulder, CO: Westview Press.

Shibatani, Masayoshi. 1990. *The languages of Japan*. Cambridge University Press.

Shoji, Shinichi. 2016. The repeated name penalty and overt pronoun penalty in Japanese. PhD dissertation, University of South Carolina.

Shousterman, Cara, Ayeska Baez, Nicole Holliday, and Renée Blake (African American English blog team). 2009. The origins of AAE. *Word: The Online Journal on African American English*. https://africanamericanenglish.com/2009/04/16/the-origins-of-aae/

Siddle, Richard. 1996. *Race, resistance and the Ainu of Japan*. London: Routledge.

Simpson, Jane. 2006. Sovereignty over languages and land. Posted on *Transient Languages and Cultures*. http://blogs.usyd.edu.au/elac/2006/11/sovereignty_over_languages_and_1.html.

Site for Language Management in Canada (SLMC). 2016a. Canada at the Time of New France. University of Ottawa. https://slmc.uottawa.ca/?q=canada_new_france

2016b. The Constitution Act of 1867 and the Language Question. University of Ottawa. https://slmc.uottawa.ca/?q=bnaa_linguistic_question

2016c. The Québec Act of 1774 and Tentative Linguistic Duality. University of Ottawa. https://slmc.uottawa.ca/?q=quebec_act_1774

2016d. The Royal Proclamation of 1763 and the Use of Languages. University of Ottawa. https://slmc.uottawa.ca/?q=canada_new_france

Sjöberg, Katarina. 1993. *The return of the Ainu: Cultural mobilization and the practice of ethnicity in Japan*. Amsterdam: Harwood Academic Publishers.

Skura, Elyse, and Joran Konek. 2016. Nunavut student allegedly punished for speaking Inuktitut, says MLA. *CBC News*, October 26. www.cbc.ca/news/canada/north/no-inuktitut-school-policy-1.3821504?cmp=abfb

Skutnabb-Kangas, Tove. 2000 [2012]. *Linguistic genocide in education – or worldwide diversity and human rights?* Mahwah, NJ: Lawrence Erlbaum [2012 edn. published by Routledge].

2012. Linguistic human rights. In Peter M. Tiersma and Lawrence M. Solan (eds.), *Language and Law*, 235–247. Oxford University Press.

Skutnabb-Kangas, Tove, and Sertar Bucak. 1994. Killing a mother tongue: How the Kurds are deprived of linguistic human rights. In Tove Skutnabb-Kangas and Robert Phillipson (eds.), *Linguistic human rights: Overcoming linguistic discrimination*, 347–370. Berlin: Mouton de Gruyter.

Skutnabb-Kangas, Tove, Miklos Kontra, and Robert Phillipson. 2006. Getting linguistic human rights right: A trio response to Wee (2005). *Applied Linguistics* 27: 318–324.

Sneddon, James. 2003. *The Indonesian language: Its history and role in modern society*. Sydney: UNSW Press.

Spike Japan. Shiraoi: Where the first arrows of the last war fell. http://spikejapan.wor dpress.com/spike-hokkaido-2/shiraoi-where-the-first-arrows-of-the-last-war-fell.

Statistics Canada. 2008. Census of 1665–1666. www.statcan.gc.ca/kits-trousses/jt2-eng.htm

Statistics Canada. 2016. Language highlight tables, 2011 Census. www12.statcan.gc.ca

Sullivan, Raymond L. 1970. *Castro* v. *State of California*, 2 Cal.3d 223. http://scocal.stanford.edu/opinion/castro-v-state-california-27547

Tanaka, Y. 2001. Kyoshu no "nihon" [The "Japan" of nostalgia]. *Edge* 12: 12–15.

Tattrie, Jon. 2014. Québec and Confederation. *The Canadian encyclopedia*. Toronto: Historica Canada. www.thecanadianencyclopedia.ca/en/article/quebec-and-confederation/

Tay, Leslie. 1971. Bilingual education in California. MA thesis, UCLA.

TESOL. 2005. Position paper on English-only legislation in the United States. www.tesol.org/docs/pdf/4162.pdf

Texas Historical Society. 2010. Census and census data. https://tshaonline.org/hand book/online/articles/ulc01

Thomas, Erik R., and Alicia Beckford Wassink. 2010. Variation and identity in African-American English. In Carmen Llamas and Dominic Watt (eds.), *Language and identities*, 157–165. Edinburgh University Press.

Thomas, Lorrin. 2015. Puerto Ricans in the United States. *Oxford Research Encyclopedia of American History*. http://americanhistory.oxfordre.com/view/10.1093/acrefore/9780199329175.001.0001/acrefore-9780199329175-e-32

Trudgill, Peter. 2016. *Dialect matters: Respecting vernacular language*. Cambridge University Press.

Tucker, James T. 2013. *The battle over bilingual ballots: Language minorities and political access*. Farnham, Surrey, and Burlington, VT: Ashgate.

Türköz, Meltem. 2007. Surname narratives and the state–society boundary: Memories of Turkey's Family Name Law of 1934. *Middle Eastern Studies* 43: 893–908.

Turner, R. 1926. The position of Romani in Indo-Aryan. *Journal of the Gypsy Lore Society* (3)4: 145–189.

Umeda, Sayuri. 2009. *The education of non-native language speaking children: Japan. Report for the Law Library of Congress*. www.loc.gov/law/help/non-native-educa tion/japan.php

Üngör, Uğur Ü. 2008. Seeing like a nation-state: Young Turk social engineering in Eastern Turkey. *Journal of Genocide Research* 10: 15–39.

UNESCO. 2005. *Children out of school: Measuring exclusion from primary school*. Montreal: UNESCO Institute for Statistics.

UN Data http://data.un.org/Data.aspx?d=SOWC&f=inID%3A74

United Nations. 1948. Universal Declaration of Human Rights. www.un.org/en/univer sal-declaration-human-rights/

  1959. United Nations Declaration of the Rights of the Child. www.un-documents.net/a14r1386.htm

  1966. UN International Covenant on Civil and Political Rights. www.ohchr.org/en/professionalinterest/pages/ccpr.aspx

1992. UN Declaration on the Rights of Persons Belonging to National or Ethnic, Religious or Linguistic Minorities. www.ohchr.org/Documents/Publications/Guid eMinoritiesDeclarationen.pdf

1996–2016. UN Human Rights. Office of the High Commissioner. www.ohchr.org/ EN/Issues/Pages/WhatareHumanRights.aspx

2007. UN Declaration on the Rights of Indigenous Peoples. http://undesadspd.org/ IndigenousPeoples.aspx

United States Census Bureau. 2015. Hispanic or Latino origin by specific origin. *American Fact Finder*. Department of Congress. https://factfinder.census.gov/faces/tableservi ces/jsf/pages/productview.xhtml?pid=ACS_15_1YR_B03001&prodType=table

United States Congress. 1917. An act to provide a civil government for Porto Rico, and for other purposes. 64th Congress, Session II, Chapter 145: 951–968. *Statutes at Large*, vol. 39 (1915–1917): 951–968. www.legisworks.org/congress/64/publaw-368.pdf

United States Congress. 1950. An Act to Provide for the Organization of a Constitutional Government by the People of Puerto Rico. 81st Congress, Session II, Chapter 446: 319–320. *Statutes at Large*, vol. 64 (1950–1951): 319–320. http:// legisworks.org/congress/81/publaw-600.pdf

2015–2016. English Language Unity Act of 2015. www.congress.gov/bill/114th-co ngress/house-bill/997/text

United States Government Publishing Office. 1965. Public Law 89–236 – October 3, 1965. www.gpo.gov/fdsys/pkg/STATUTE-79/pdf/STATUTE-79-Pg911.pdf

1986. Public Law 99–603 – November 6, 1986. www.gpo.gov/fdsys/pkg/STATUTE-100/pdf/STATUTE-100-Pg3445.pdf

United States State Department. 2008. *Country reports on human rights: Japan*. Bureau of Democracy, Human Rights, and Labor. www.state.gov/g/drl/rls/hrrpt/2008/eap/ 119041.htm.

2012. Belgium. www.state.gov/outofdate/bgn/belgium/197865.htm

Universal Declaration of Linguistic Rights. 1996. www.linguistic-declaration.org/inde x-gb.htm

Urciuoli, Bonnie. 1996. *Exposing prejudice: Puerto Rican experiences of language, race, and class*. Boulder, CO: Waveland Press.

U.S. English. 2016a. www.usenglish.org

2016b. Puerto Rico: The 51st state? www.us-english.org/view/899

Vaux, Bert, and Scott Golder. 2003. *The Harvard Dialect Survey*. Cambridge, MA: Harvard University Linguistics Department.

Velez, Mandy. 2014. 10-year-old Icelandic girl denied a passport because her name is "Harriet." *Huffington Post*. www.huffingtonpost.com/2014/06/30/icelandic-girl-denied-passport-because-her-name-harriet_n_5544326.html

Vos, Louis. 1993. Shifting nationalism: Belgians, Flemings and Walloons. In Mikulas Teich and Roy Porter (eds.), *The national question in Europe in historical context*, 128–147. Cambridge University Press.

Vygotsky, Lev. 1962. *Thought and language*. Cambridge, MA: MIT Press.

Walker, Brett L. 2001. *The conquest of Ainu lands: Ecology and culture in Japanese expansion, 1590–1800*. Berkeley: University of California Press.

Wardyn, Łukasz, and Jan Fiala. 2009. The 2009 amendment of the Slovakian state language law and its impact on minority rights. *Polish Yearbook of International Law* 29: 153–173.

Watts, Nicole F. 1999. Allies and enemies: Pro-Kurdish parties in Turkish politics, 1990–1994. *International Journal of Middle East Studies* 31: 631–656.

Wee, Lionel. 2005. Intra-language discrimination and linguistic human rights: The case of Singlish. *Applied Linguistics* 26: 48–69.

2011. *Language without rights*. New York: Oxford University Press.

Weinreich, Max. 1945. Der YIVO un di problemen fun undzer tsayt [The YIVO faces the post-war world]. *YIVO Bleter* 25: 3–18. http://download.hebrewbooks.org/do wnloadhandler.ashx?req=43629

Weldon, Tracey. 2000. Reflections on the Ebonics Controversy. *American Speech* 75: 275–277.

Welsh Government. 2015. *Welsh language use survey 2013–15*. http://gov.wales/statis tics-and-research/welsh-language-use-survey/?lang=en

WGBH Educational Foundation. 1995–2014. Hunting bin Laden. *Frontline*. www.pbs .org/wgbh/pages/frontline/shows/binladen/who/family.html

Whorf, Benjamin Lee. 1940a. Linguistics as an exact science. *Technology Review* 43: 61–63, 80–83. Reprinted in Carroll (ed.) 1956: 220–232.

1940b. Science and linguistics. *Technology Review* 42: 229–231, 247–248. Reprinted in Carroll (ed.) 1956: 207–219.

Wilkerson, Isabel. 2010. *The warmth of other suns: The epic story of America's Great Migration*. New York: Random House.

Williams, Colin H. 2009. Commentary: The primacy of renewal. *International Journal of the Sociology of Language* 195: 201–217.

Williams, Joseph M. 1975. *Origins of the English language: A social and linguistic history*. New York: Free Press.

Woodbury, Anthony. 1991. Counting Eskimo words for snow: A citizen's guide. http:// linguistlist.org/issues/5/5–1239.html

No date. What is an endangered language? (pamphlet). Linguistic Society of America. www.linguisticsociety.org/sites/default/files/Endangered_Languages .pdf

Worland, Justin. 2015. Meet the president trying to save his island nation from climate change. *Time*, October 9. http://time.com/4058851/kiribati-climate-change/

Wolfram, Walt. 1998. Language ideology and dialect: Understanding the Oakland Ebonics controversy. *Journal of English Linguistics* 26(2): 108–121.

Wolfram, Walt, and Natalie Schilling. 2015. *American English: Dialects and variation*, 3rd edn. Malden, MA, and Oxford: Wiley-Blackwell.

Wyloge, Evan. 2009. Immigration amnesty in the 1980s. *Arizona State University News21*. http://asu.news21.com/archive/2009/immigration_amnesty_in_the_1980s/

Zaken, Mordechai. 2007. *Jewish subjects and their tribal cheiftans in Kurdistan: A study in survival*. Leiden: Brill.

Zvelebil, Kamil Václav. 1990. *Dravidian linguistics: An introduction*. Pondicherry: Pondicherry Institute of Linguistics and Culture.

Index of Names

Index of Languages, Nationalities, Ethnicities, and Places

Index of General Concepts and Events